I0817583

THE CARING UNIVERSITY

REIMAGINING THE HIGHER EDUCATION WORKPLACE AFTER THE GREAT RESIGNATION

THE CARING UNIVERSITY

KEVIN R. McCLURE

JOHNS HOPKINS UNIVERSITY PRESS | *Baltimore*

Printed in the United States of America on acid-free paper
9 8 7 6 5 4 3 2 1

Johns Hopkins University Press
2715 North Charles Street
Baltimore, Maryland 21218
www.press.jhu.edu

Library of Congress Cataloging-in-Publication Data

Names: McClure, Kevin R., author.
Title: The caring university : reimagining the higher education workplace after the great resignation / Kevin R. McClure.
Description: Baltimore : Johns Hopkins University Press, 2025. | Includes bibliographical references and index.
Identifiers: LCCN 2024042557 | ISBN 9781421451947 (hardcover) | ISBN 9781421451954 (ebook)
Subjects: LCSH: College personnel management—United States. | Universities and colleges—United States—Planning. | Work environment—United States. | College environment—United States.
Classification: LCC LB2331.66 .M44 2025 | DDC 378.1/10973—dc23/eng/20241211
LC record available at https://lccn.loc.gov/2024042557

A catalog record for this book is available from the British Library.

ISBN 978-1-4214-5194-7 (hardcover)
ISBN 978-1-4214-5195-4 (ebook)

Special discounts are available for bulk purchases of this book. For more information, please contact Special Sales at specialsales@jh.edu

EU GPSR Authorized Representative
LOGOS EUROPE, 9 rue Nicolas Poussin, 17000, La Rochelle, France
E-mail: Contact@logoseurope.eu

To Nathan and Colin—being your dad is the best job I'll ever have

CONTENTS

A Note on Sources and Methods ix
Acknowledgments xi

Introduction. The Caring University 1

1. Organizational Problems of the Higher Education Workplace 31
2. Making the Employee Experience a Strategic Priority 57
3. Creating Working Cultures and Conditions for Real (Not Ideal) Workers 93
4. Committing to Professional Growth and Fair Compensation 130
5. Pursuing Cultural and Structural Change for Equity and Belonging 169
6. Empowering Employees' Rights and Voice 205
7. Cultivating and Sustaining Caring Leaders 237

Conclusion. First-Step Pathways to Change 270

Notes 281
References 301
Index 327

A NOTE ON SOURCES AND METHODS

This book does not report the findings of a single study. It was not guided by an explicit research question and accompanying methodology. Rather, data—principally from interviews—came from several interrelated projects. I started conducting interviews for my public scholarship in the early days of the pandemic and continued to do so for the next three years. Data from many of these interviews were worked into the book. In the fall of 2022, I started a research project examining employee turnover in the University of North Carolina System with several doctoral students. Some of the interviews from that project were also incorporated into the book. Finally, as I was writing the chapters, I interviewed dozens of people with applicable expertise or who had developed promising practices. In total, the book is based on insights from 116 interviews.

Although data came from several projects, I followed similar procedures for all interviews. Most interviews happened via Zoom, except in the case of site visits. Interviews were recorded, and any quotations in the book came from transcriptions of those recordings. I began each interview by explaining the purpose of the research and how the interview data would be used, then I asked participants for their consent to be recorded. I gave every participant the opportunity to use a pseudonym or to be anonymous. Every participant who is quoted in the book received a copy of the full chapter so that they could review their quotations in context. I gave them an opportunity to edit their quotations, with a promise not to publish anything they were not comfortable with. Stewarding and retelling those stories in a way that felt true and authentic for participants was my primary concern.

Identifying examples and case studies to highlight in the book was a significant challenge. There isn't a database or repository of institutional practices, nor are there widely accepted standards by which to evaluate programs or initiatives. In many cases, I relied on my network, web searches, awards announcements, and popular media articles. Consequently, it was easy for certain biases to creep in. For example, stories about larger colleges and universities were more common to encounter because they have more robust communications offices. Nevertheless, my background studying broad-access institutions helped me to counter some of this bias, and I worked hard to vary the types of institutions mentioned in the book as well as the institutional affiliations of interview participants. My hope is that you will notice a mix of institutions, individuals, and roles that reflects the diversity within higher education.

My goal was to write a narrative-driven book that, though certainly informed by data and research, put a human face on workplace issues and trends. For this reason, I tried to not simply cite scholars but also interview them to have them explain their ideas in conversational terms. It is not just the case that I wanted the tone to be accessible for readers. I also wanted the people, institutions, and stories to feel anchored in real life—for readers to nod and say, "This sounds like my experience," or "I've seen that problem so many times." Whether I accomplished this goal is another matter, and while I do not claim that these approaches rise to the level of a methodology, there was at least intentionality.

Ultimately, this book came together through a combination of heart and head, instinct and training. I followed my curiosity and opened myself to new ideas and possibilities. In the words of novelist Leif Enger, "When a flame is lit move toward it."

ACKNOWLEDGMENTS

I wrote this book in airport terminals, hotel lobbies, and campus bookstores. I wrote it from parking lots, playgrounds, practice fields, and park benches. I wrote it in seven states and three time zones. Most of all, I wrote it in community.

I am forever grateful to the interview participants who generously volunteered their time to tell me their stories and share their brilliance. The desire to accurately retell their stories and honor their contributions propelled this work. Brian Buford, Cara Crowley, and Aaron Krall went out of their way to help me during site visits, and I am grateful to have met and learned from them during this project.

This book would not be possible without the labor and ingenuity of scholars and practitioners in higher education. There are large swaths of this workforce that we would know very little about without the field of higher education and student affairs, and I am indebted to my colleagues for their research. Similarly, higher education practitioners regularly showed up to help me identify promising practices and connect with experts. I feel very fortunate to be part of this community of scholar-practitioners.

Chunks of this book were dreamed up and written during writing retreats and weekly writing sessions. A big thanks to Jorge Bumicky and Sarah Rodriguez for their unfailing support, as well as to Erica Wiborg, Catherine Hartman, and Rachel Friedensen. Writing a book means spending a lot of time in your head and forging ahead alone for long stretches. I was so fortunate to have friends along the way to keep me focused and laughing.

A few people provided extra support and encouragement at critical points in the writing process. My sincerest thanks to Josh Brown for regularly checking in and sending me arm-flex emojis. Teresa Valerio Parrot has been a steadfast advocate for this work and early reader of the book proposal. I am very thankful to have met Alisa Hicklin Fryar, my academic life coach, who has routinely given her time and advice while asking for very little in return. One day, I will return the favor!

My thanks to the rest of the crew at the Alliance for Research on Regional Colleges—Andrew Koricich, Cecilia Orphan, and Vanessa Sansone—who never once pressured me to sideline this project so that I could get back to research on regional public universities. Similarly, my colleagues at the University of North Carolina Wilmington have been constant cheerleaders for this work and have given me space to think, write, and grow. Thanks in particular to Andy Ryder, Symphony Oxendine, Sam Silberstein, Denise Henning, Nathan Crowe, Aaron King, and David Houpt for their advice and friendship.

I was too anxious to write a book without a thought partner who could be immersed in the ideas and drafts with me, chapter by chapter. Olson Pook was that thought partner, and he made this book much better than if I were left to my own devices.

I want to acknowledge that I was able to write this book thanks to a three-year endowed chair position, which provided resources and time to research and write. Linden Hillhouse was my graduate assistant throughout this project and helped me stay on track in countless ways.

Thanks to The National, Death Cab for Cutie, Frightened Rabbit, Pinegrove, Zach Bryan, and Olivia Rodrigo, who didn't read any drafts but provided the soundtrack to keep the words flowing.

And to my wife, Kati. Writing this book meant I was traveling and lost in thought and sometimes stressed. She was there through it all. Thank you, always and forever.

My name is on the cover, but so many minds, eyes, and hands brought this idea to life. Writing this book changed me, and I am incredibly humbled and grateful.

THE CARING UNIVERSITY

INTRODUCTION

The Caring University

DAWN[1] IS AN AWARD-WINNING FACULTY member at a public research university—one of exceptionally few Indigenous professors with tenure in the country.[2] She is multitalented, excelling in the classroom and publishing research in her field's most respected textbooks and journals. While some faculty steer clear of service roles, Dawn has assumed faculty leadership positions and relishes the policy committees from which many of her peers flee. Despite a growing list of accolades and glowing features in her university's promotional materials, Dawn's place in higher education has always been tenuous. On multiple occasions, she was nearly pushed out of academia—a brilliant career in higher education that almost wasn't.

Dawn was provisionally accepted to most of the academic programs that she applied to because of her standardized test scores. In one of her first jobs in higher education as a staff member in student affairs, she was unceremoniously let go as part of a reorganization right after returning from maternity leave. At the tail end of her doctoral program, Dawn landed a visiting lecturer gig with the assurance that she was a shoo-in for a permanent job, only to be passed over for a candidate with a more prestigious pedigree. Dawn had all but given up on higher education when she landed a coveted tenure-track position within commuting distance of the Indigenous community where she wanted to raise her family. The workload—compounded by anxiety about the tenure process and the prospect of losing it all—caused her blood pressure to spike, landing her in the hospital.

Although I have known Dawn for years, I asked her to sit for an interview as a trial run early in my research on the higher education workplace. She invited me to her office, where we ended up chatting for nearly two hours. I vividly remember leaning back from the small table where she normally met with students, feeling a mix of awe and dismay. By all accounts, Dawn was a highly respected teacher-scholar and an asset to her institution. And yet I rattled off all she had to overcome to attain that esteem: *Provisionally accepted. Position eliminated while caring for an infant. Passed over for a permanent job. Pressed and stressed until nearly passing out.* Finally, I asked a question that she had wrestled with multiple times: Why didn't she just quit? Dawn laughed and initially said, "Spite." But after a moment, she chalked it up to "survivance."

According to Gerald Vizenor, the Anishinaabe writer and scholar who coined the term, survivance (a portmanteau of "survival" and "resistance") describes the active presence and continuance of Indigenous people and cultures, instead of absence, tragedy, and oblivion.[3] Dawn explained that she "comes from real life," and after stints working in fast food, on horse farms, and as a nail technician, she was accustomed to hard jobs. Opportunity rarely came knocking—in most cases, she had to knock down doors and carve out a space for herself and others. For Dawn, staying is a declaration of her presence and commitment to Indigenous students and scholars—past, present, and future.

This commitment was on full display in her office. Covering one entire wall is an Indigenous-designed blanket that she received as part of an award from one of her field's associations. She told me the blanket was created by a company whose name evokes the "Seventh Generation" principle in Indigenous thought: every decision should consider how it will affect descendants seven generations in the future. Dawn told me that she is trying to use her position to make it easier for others to find their way to and through higher education.

Although her sense of purpose inspired me, Dawn's reasons for staying never once touched on the efforts of *institutions*—her employers—to actively attract, support, and retain her. It is true that Dawn had mentors, family, and friends who helped her to manage the stress and slights of academe. Some of these people were even colleagues and advisers at the colleges and universities where she worked and studied. But having a supportive supervisor is a small solace when you are confronted with a barrage of practices, policies, and processes trying to push you out. As Dawn said, "Throughout my whole journey, I learned to put my trust in people, not processes. Institutions were doing everything they could to put barriers up."

Dawn's story is uniquely hers, but I have now spent the last five years researching the higher education workplace, and I hear echoes of her experiences in the scores of interviews that I have conducted with staff and faculty across the country. Like Dawn, there are higher education employees who give generously and work tirelessly for the benefit of institutions and the students they serve—despite working cultures and conditions that undervalue their talent, exploit their labor, and compromise their mental and physical health. For every story like Dawn's, there are numerous staff and faculty who have left colleges and universities for organizations that better demonstrate *care* for employees—nurturing their growth, rewarding their contributions, and respecting their lives outside work.

Searching for greener pastures has been particularly prevalent throughout the COVID-19 pandemic, when unprecedented numbers of staff and faculty questioned their future in higher education as part of what has popularly been called the Great Resignation. Data have raised the alarm about higher turnover—or higher risk for turnover—among faculty and staff in various positions and departments, from admissions to human resources and financial aid offices. Hiring managers have reported more vacancies than in the past and greater challenges filling jobs.[4] It is a moment with no parallel in the recent history of higher education, upending decades of accepted norms and redefining how we think about work and what we consider a good job.

The Great Resignation swept through higher education like wildfire, partly because colleges and universities have a poor track record of prioritizing employee well-being. This reputation for overlooking the employee experience was dry kindling for a labor force whose pandemic experiences sparked new expectations of employers and workplaces. After being asked to pivot several times during the pandemic,[5] employees see no reason why their employers should be anchored to tradition. Workers are less willing to blame themselves for being unable to cope or rise above obstacles; instead, they feel empowered to question how institutions are supporting the success of their employees as a means of supporting students' success.

While colleges and universities may have previously been able to lean on simply replacing disaffected workers, it is getting harder to sell jobseekers and would-be applicants on the value proposition of a career in higher education.[6] Compensation and benefits lag behind competing knowledge organizations.[7] Excessive workloads and constant crises lead to exhaustion or worse.[8] Insufficient attention to career pathways produces workers who feel undervalued and stuck.[9] The result has been a range of issues across institutions: lengthy vacancies, shallow applicant pools, interim positions, failed searches, and understaffed offices.[10]

Although it is tantalizing to attribute these trends to unpredictable pandemic-induced challenges, the root problems of the higher education workplace predate the pandemic and are unlikely to disappear simply because case counts dropped. As many institutions pushed to "return to normal," the support, flexibility, and grace granted to employees during the pandemic have evaporated. Workers have been left to navigate the same old organizations, plus the cumulative effects of enduring Pandemic U. If leaders haven't yet picked up on the new human resources landscape, they should take heed now: the approaches for attracting, growing, and retaining talent that prevailed in the past do not match the moment.

The main argument of this book is that many of the problems of the higher education workplace are baked into the organizational cultures and structures of colleges and universities. They reflect workplace norms around professionalism, values about effectiveness that influence decision-making, and beliefs about people and strategies worthy of investment. Problems become codified in the structures of organizations through policies and widely accepted practices that govern everyday working conditions, such as workload, hours, compensation, promotion, and leave. If institutions are going to effectively serve students, meet contemporary and future challenges, and achieve lofty goals, they must reimagine the higher education workplace and pursue organization-level changes to cultures and structures.

Change needs champions, and institutions will need forward-thinking leaders who can handle some uncomfortable truths and are prepared to design and implement solutions that go beyond self-care or wellness days. I don't just mean people with a fancy title or power on campus. My conception of leaders includes faculty leaders and staff whose titles may not immediately indicate leadership but who are, nevertheless, leaders among their colleagues and within their institutions. This book is a research-based resource for all these employees dedicated to building organizations where the best and brightest want to work, grow, and stay.

The Caring University

It is easy for books to proclaim the need for organizational change but harder to determine the direction of such change. In this book, I explain prominent problems of the higher education workplace, excavate their roots in the cultures and structures of organizations, and then describe organization-level changes that offer colleges and universities a pathway to move beyond the causes and outcomes of the Great Resignation.

I refer to the collective, proactive, ongoing work to enact organizational changes in support of employee well-being as the Caring University. Let's break down each of the components of this definition to give a fuller picture of what it means to work toward the Caring University.

Collective. Sociologist and *New York Times* columnist Tressie McMillan Cottom has famously argued that "institutions cannot love you."

She meant that we should not lay down our lives to earn the affection of something that isn't capable of feelings, let alone love. And she's right. We cannot expect institutions to care about employees. A brick building with columns and Latin inscriptions will not wrap us in a warm embrace. But Cottom was also clear that understanding the limits of institutions shouldn't prevent people from contributing to the creation of more humane organizations. The Caring University is shorthand for collections of *people* who make up institutions coming together to do exactly that.

Proactive. The Caring University does not happen organically—it is the product of planned and intentional effort. Colleges and universities tend to be reactive when it comes to addressing workplace problems and meeting employee expectations. They will pay graduate students more only after they have gone on strike. They will hire a company to administer an engagement survey only after turnover rates spike. They will institute a well-being initiative only after concerns about mental health crescendo. Reactive responses usually mean institutions are trying to put out fires and minimize damage rather than pursuing a true talent management strategy. By contrast, leaders pursuing the Caring University proactively plan for and implement improvements *before* crises force their hand.

Ongoing. The Caring University won't materialize overnight, and it is unlikely to take root through short bursts of effort. This is partly because organizational change often entails the time-intensive work of shifting mindsets. It is also because demonstrating care is not exactly the default setting of US society. Without ongoing opportunities to consider how to better support employee well-being, many colleges and universities are hardwired to prioritize competition, status, and extractive labor practices.[11] And so, the Caring University is less about reaching a final destination or attaining an ideal state and more about turning support for employee well-being into a routine of campus life, with no end date.

Organizational Changes. Pursuing the Caring University calls for what Adrianna Kezar, perhaps the foremost expert on change management in higher education, calls deep or "second-order" change. This is change that is "so substantial that it alters the operating systems, underlying values, and culture of an organization."[12] Deep change is a process whose success often depends on a range of actors using multiple approaches across an institution. Leaders may read "process" and assume it means a linear model or following a change checklist. In reality, deep change is about learning, customizing, and revising when things don't go according to plan. The organizational changes discussed in this book should be read as a set of possibilities grounded in research to be wrestled with and adjusted, not a prepackaged plan that can be plugged into a given unit or institution.

Employee Well-Being. According to the US surgeon general, workplace well-being hinges on five essential components, each of which centers the employee's voice and equity and incorporates human needs:

- protection from harm, which includes the human need for safety and security
- connection and community, which includes the human need for social support and belonging
- work-life harmony, which includes the human need for autonomy and flexibility
- mattering at work, which includes the human need for dignity and meaning
- opportunity for growth, which includes the human need for learning and accomplishment

Why is the surgeon general giving attention to employee well-being? Because it is a "critical priority for public health" with "numerous and cascading impacts" for individuals, families, organizations, and communities.[13] Simply put, reducing stress and encouraging forms of community in the workplace is a national health concern.

How does the Caring University support employee well-being? In the following chapters, I detail a range of approaches that exemplify six overarching organizational changes designed to address both organizational cultures and structures that give rise to workplace problems fueling the Great Resignation. As Figure I.1 shows, the Caring University supports employee well-being by:

- making the employee experience a strategic priority
- creating working cultures and conditions for real workers

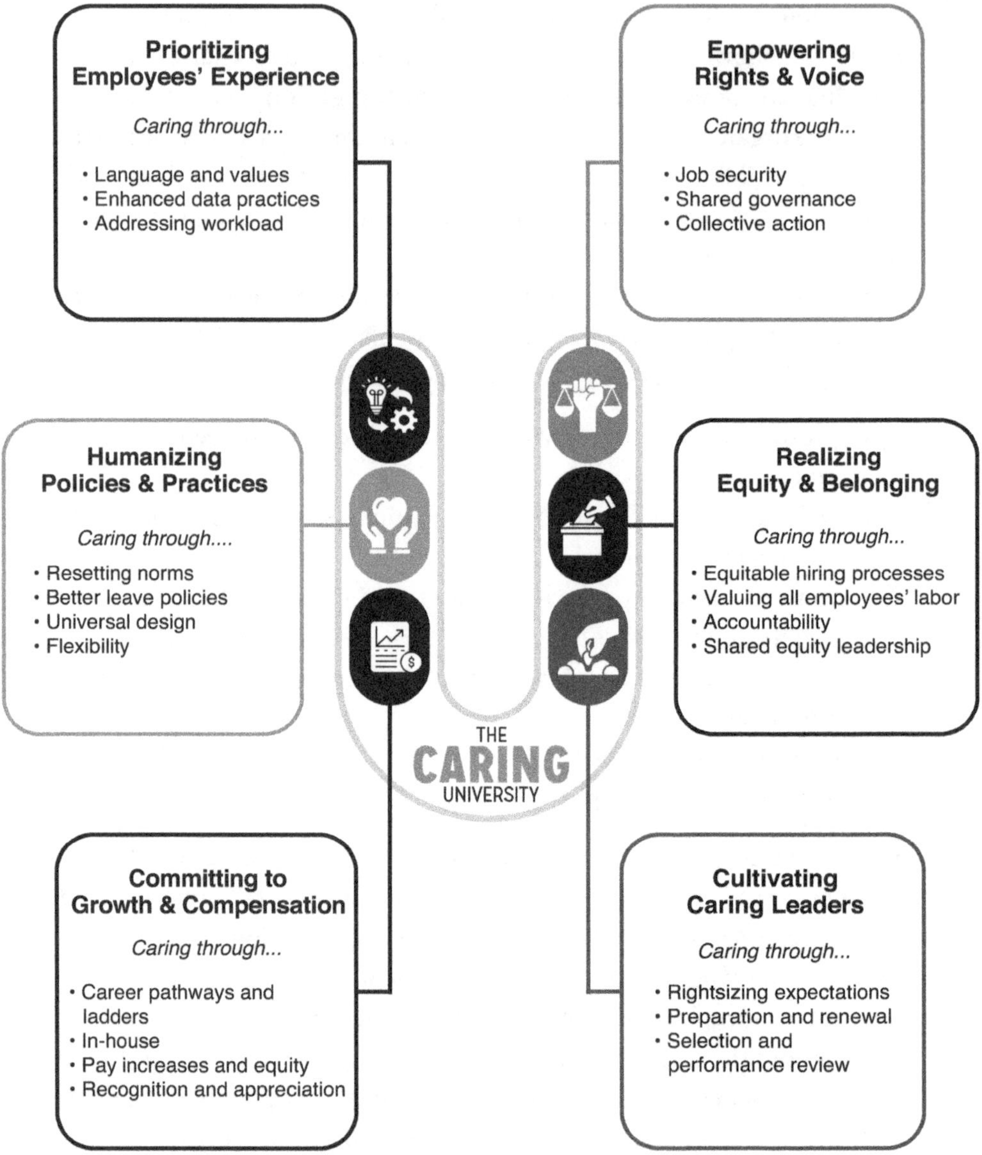

Prioritizing Employees' Experience

Caring through...

- Language and values
- Enhanced data practices
- Addressing workload

Empowering Rights & Voice

Caring through...

- Job security
- Shared governance
- Collective action

Humanizing Policies & Practices

Caring through....

- Resetting norms
- Better leave policies
- Universal design
- Flexibility

Realizing Equity & Belonging

Caring through...

- Equitable hiring processes
- Valuing all employees' labor
- Accountability
- Shared equity leadership

THE CARING UNIVERSITY

Committing to Growth & Compensation

Caring through...

- Career pathways and ladders
- In-house
- Pay increases and equity
- Recognition and appreciation

Cultivating Caring Leaders

Caring through...

- Rightsizing expectations
- Preparation and renewal
- Selection and performance review

Figure I.1. *The Caring University (Blair Dempster)*

- committing to professional growth and fair compensation
- pursuing cultural and structural change for equity and belonging
- empowering employees' rights and voice
- cultivating and sustaining caring leaders.

Although these changes do not map perfectly onto the surgeon general's framework, they share a common vision of what is required to create organizations that better attend to employee well-being.

This isn't the first book to bring attention to the shortcomings of colleges and universities as employers. Nor is it the first book to suggest that institutions need to become more caring communities.[14] My goal in this book is to honor and build on this scholarship in several ways. First, I bring a wide-angle lens to the topic by exploring workplace problems that cut across different types of institutions and employees. Second, I weave disparate strands of research into one account. Third, I extend existing analyses oriented primarily toward problems by foregrounding promising ideas to address them. Fourth, I pay attention to the *how* of organizational change (in addition to the *what*) by integrating the wisdom of organizational change theories. Lastly, I draw on my on-site visits to three institutions and over 100 interviews with staff, faculty, and administrators at these and dozens of other campuses to substantiate my arguments with real-life experiences and concrete examples.[15]

Working toward the Caring University isn't about making every employee happy, nor does it require subscribing to pop psychology or faddish management theories. It is a smart strategy based on what the data clearly show: knowledge organizations depend on capable, invested, and creative employees to prosper. For higher education to fulfill its purpose and serve students, institutions cannot afford to make employee retention an act of individual perseverance or to be blasé about good workers walking away.[16] Fortunately, colleges and universities are more often than not led by caring educators and administrators. It is just a matter of ensuring that organizational cultures and structures reflect that personal ethic of care.

This chapter lays the foundation for the rest of the book. I explain how I came to this work and the four shifts that comprise the Great Resignation in higher education. I show how the concepts we have commonly used to explain these shifts tell us much more about workplaces than individual workers. With all signs pointing to the need for organizational change, I map out the remaining chapters whose function is to help leaders take an initial step toward building stronger institutions by prioritizing the well-being of staff and faculty.

My Route to the Caring University

I count myself among those in higher education for whom the employee experience was not a priority in the years leading up to the pandemic. In February 2020, I was deep in the throes of my own issues and a demanding workload. I was still recovering from a pre-tenure period marked by leaving close friends and starting over in a new city, losing my father to chronic illness, and the birth of my two children. With a full teaching load and program coordination duties, my days were packed with course management, committee meetings, and advising appointments. My research on regional public universities filled any available crevices in my calendar, and I tried to squeeze in some public scholarship on the side. Like many of my colleagues across the country, I was running an unforgiving race and typically crawled to the finish line each semester.

I was just coming up for air post-tenure when the pandemic wave of March 2020 crashed down. We went into lockdown hoping that doing so would rein in the virus by summer. My days became a routine of ending one Zoom meeting with a silent wave and clicking the link for the next. Students' needs escalated, and I was maxing out my helping skills. My wife and I split the workdays; each morning I took the kids—usually to a nearby pond or creek to throw rocks—then each afternoon, I sequestered myself upstairs to finish a few work tasks before the little ones came knocking at the door or I heard shrieking downstairs. We soon were putting in a few hours of work every night to keep up. Time sped up and lost all meaning. What were business hours when work happened at all hours of the day? What was a weekend when the days all looked the same? I lived by the mantra: *If I can make it to graduation, I'll be able to recharge my batteries.*

I made it to early May, but I wasn't just tired. Like so many of my friends in academia, I was completely depleted. It felt like there was nothing left in my batteries to charge. My bandwidth for taking on new tasks or thinking creatively was nil. And while the shock, stress, and day-to-day realities of working and parenting through a pandemic justify above-average exhaustion, something else was at play. I had become cynical about my work for the first time in my career. I found myself asking questions: *What was the point of the manuscript I was writing? Couldn't someone else coordinate this program better than me? Are the next 30 years of my career just more of the same?*

Matters reached a tipping point as we inched toward graduation. During one of my meetings with faculty colleagues, one of them suggested that we organize a creative way to recognize our graduate students since we couldn't do our usual hooding ceremony. As program coordinator, it would fall to me to implement whatever we decided. I like to think that the pre-lockdown me would have encouraged this idea and brainstormed options. Instead of encouragement, the words that fell out of my mouth were: "Do we have to? Could we just . . . skip it?" As soon as I said those words, I knew I had entered uncharted waters, drifting with no perceptible wind.

We mustered enough energy as a team to cook up a virtual ceremony, and I made it through graduation. Because of my mantra, I thought donning my cap and gown would mark an important milestone; summer would bring some relief from my job duties and the time they required. But instead of feeling the typical levity of early summer and jumping into unfinished projects, in the days that followed, I simply collapsed.

While recovering from the hardest semester of my career, I decided I needed to reflect on my experiences. I started by downloading a meditation app, which brought some temporary calm but few actionable insights. As space opened up in my calendar and the urgency of the work diminished, I realized that I didn't want to make peace with what had happened. I wanted to understand it and see what could be done to prevent it from happening again. Granted, I also had a very practical motivation. The thought of returning to school in the fall and running the same gauntlet for nine months instead of just four truly terrified me.

So, I did what came naturally and started asking questions and gathering research. Some early articles about burnout crossed my social media feed, and it didn't take long for me to connect the dots. Exhaustion? Check. Cynicism? Check. Feelings of inadequacy? Check. When I started to think about my career stretching back to graduate school, I saw a pattern of stress, burnout, and shutting down. Rinse and repeat. And then came the self-doubt and shame of realizing that I had pushed myself to burnout . . . again. *If this wasn't the first time, why hadn't I adopted better self-care measures by now?* I started seeing a therapist who helped me unpack those feelings and recognize that there was more to the story than being a self-care dropout. I had an emerging awareness that the pandemic had brought a deeper institutional dysfunction to the fore.

When I shared my experience with friends and colleagues, it quickly became clear that I wasn't alone. Countless people told me that they, too, were drifting or dreading the thought of returning to campus in the fall. Evidence was mounting that colleges and universities were facing a dramatic spike in burnout among staff and faculty.[17] I decided to write an article featuring interviews with staff and faculty who were navigating burnout—and offering advice for leaders on how to respond.[18]

After the article was published, the response was overwhelming. I received emails for weeks after its release. Some faculty and staff were relieved that someone finally acknowledged how they felt. Some expressed their fear—for themselves or family members—and a sense of betrayal as their employers asked them to become frontline workers. A few leaders reached out to convey agreement but also uncertainty about what to do next. By far, the most common response I received was people telling me that they were warning their institutions about burnout, but leaders either dismissed their concerns or were too caught up in what they considered to be more pressing matters of pandemic response to take action. In those responses, I saw that there was work to be done.

Over the next five years, I continued asking questions, reading, and conducting interviews. And I continued chronicling what I learned about employee engagement, morale, leadership, understaffing, remote work, and other topics. The seeds of this book were planted and had begun to sprout. But tending to the garden turned out to be an entirely different task.

An Unexpected Foundation

Writing and speaking about the higher education workplace was not in my five-year plan. I am a scholar of higher education leadership, management, and finance. My research focuses on how privatization brings about changes at colleges and universities, including new forms of revenue generation, decision-making, organizational structures, and personnel configurations. As a professor, I teach courses in higher education that focus on law, policy, finance, and organizational theory. Workplace issues were not generally in my wheelhouse—or so I thought.

When I started to look more deeply at these topics, something funny happened. I discovered that I had been building a foundation for understanding working cultures and conditions in higher education. Learning about topics such as compensation, staffing, and shared governance was a standard part of my course prep process. And I was exposed to plenty of stories about the higher education workplace because my students are almost all full-time staff in higher education. Counseling students through the highs and lows of job searches and transitions in higher education is a regular feature of my job. It turns out that years spent teaching about organizational culture, institutional governance, and austerity measures have come in handy as I study the Great Resignation.

Being a professor wasn't my first job in higher education, either. I started as a graduate assistant and then became a graduate hall director in a campus-owned apartment complex. My first full-time job in higher education was as a staff member coordinating a global studies living-learning program. I periodically taught undergraduate courses in cross-cultural communication and managed a Greek house to make extra money. Before graduating with my doctorate, I worked in the provost's office, supporting several initiatives in faculty affairs, including the creation of career ladders and promotion guidelines for full-time contingent faculty (i.e., lecturers and instructors). I have worn many hats in a university setting, and I don't have to imagine what it's like sitting with cabinet-level leaders in the main administration building, responding to an on-call duty pager, or debating a proposal in a faculty senate meeting.

When I write about the higher education workplace, I try to center the experiences of staff, graduate students, postdocs, and contingent faculty (both full- and part-time). This is partly because many leaders tend to immediately think about faculty when it comes to employment policies and practices. Since a small but vocal fraction of faculty are protected by tenure, we are more likely to see their opinions published in popular media outlets. On the other hand, staff, graduate students, postdocs, and contingent faculty have fewer opportunities and less freedom to speak about their experiences. As I consider the feasibility of organizational changes, I naturally envision the institutions that I generally study—broadly accessible institutions that are not swimming in resources. Many exclusionary, wealthy colleges and universities already receive plenty of limelight. My goal is to lift up the hard work and innovation at community colleges, regional public universities, and small private colleges that often get overlooked.

No matter how varied my past professional experiences are, there is no getting around the fact that I am at the pinnacle of privilege in academia. I am a tenured professor at a financially stable public university. I am a white, cisgender, straight man without a chronic illness. My time in higher education hasn't always been sunshine and rainbows—I started my first full-time job in higher education at the height of a recession in 2009 and quickly learned the meaning of "furlough." Still, I enjoy substantial security and better-than-average working conditions. An important question is whether I am positioned to understand and comment on the state of the higher education workplace.

I have decided to be part of this conversation but in a purposeful way. My approach has been to remain vigilantly aware of how my identity and my work conditions influence my analyses. I don't pretend to set these factors aside; rather, I grapple with them routinely during research. This means rejecting my own experience as a universally reliable source of insights or as a yardstick to measure what is normal in higher education. Who I am matters to the questions I ask and the approaches I identify. But ultimately, this book is not about *me*.

Leaders need not worry that I am unfairly targeting them or creating a compendium of complaints. I have, after all, spent most of my career interviewing deans, provosts, and presidents. These conversations have helped me forge a deep understanding of—and respect for—those who serve their institutions in leadership roles. I am specifically addressing leaders in this book because, by virtue of supervising employees, managing resources, and shaping practices and policies, leaders are best positioned to bring the Caring University to fruition. Instead of calling out or shaming leaders, my goal is to invite them in. As co-constructors of the Caring University, leaders can and should be beneficiaries of it.

Reckoning with the Great Resignation

This book calls for reimagining the higher education workplace *after* the Great Resignation. One hiccup is that, as of this writing, the Great Resignation is not, in fact, over.[19] Like the pandemic, the Great Resignation is a pebble whose water strike will ripple years into the future. But the book's title represents something of an aspiration—we will eventually move beyond the pandemic, raising the question of what ought to come next for the employee experience in higher education. What can we learn from this period that will keep institutions from becoming dry kindling when the next wildfire erupts?

In their book for managers after the first year of the pandemic, leadership experts Jonathan and Melissa Nightingale wrote, "There is no way to talk about what happens next without standing in what the past year has been."[20] Some leaders have jumped headfirst into discussions about the "future of work" without really grasping the past or present. Before meaningfully pursuing the Caring University, leaders must first reckon with what the Great Resignation and its antecedents have meant for higher education workers. The point is not to dwell on problems but rather to appreciate that transformation often means acknowledging and being prepared for complexity, discomfort, and conflict.[21]

We can start by appreciating the complexity of the Great Resignation itself, which isn't just about quitting. As Derek Thompson noted in *The Atlantic*, workers in the Great Resignation have not entirely left the workforce but rather hopped to new jobs.[22] Moreover, "resignation" implies leaving a job voluntarily, when reality frequently has been far more brutal. Over a million Americans died because of COVID-19, and research suggests as many as one in five adults who contracted the virus have experienced symptoms of long COVID.[23] Some older Americans saw the disproportionate risk to people in their age group, and according to one estimate, 2.4 million more people retired between March 2020 and July 2021 than expected.[24] In the summer of 2021, 6.2 million Americans did not work because their employer closed or lost business because of the pandemic.[25] Many childcare centers closed or reduced operations, and women in particular shouldered the burden of the childcare crisis. In January 2022, there were 1.8 million fewer women in the workforce compared to the same time in 2020.[26] In other words, "resignation" is a misnomer for what were often cruel forces pushing people out of work.

Still, the phrase "Great Resignation" captures something real. After all, federal data show that more than 50 million American workers voluntarily left their jobs in 2022, breaking a record set the previous year.[27] Although the percentage of American workers who quit has declined from its peak in late 2021 and early 2022, the figure remains above historic standards.[28] More specific to higher education, a 2022 survey of 3,815 employees conducted by the College and University Professional Association for Human Resources showed that over half of respondents were at least somewhat likely to seek a new job in the next 12 months.[29] Another survey of 720 higher education employees (primarily administrators) found that 8 in 10 respondents believed their campus had more open positions compared to the previous year.[30] Turnover has been especially acute in certain units of colleges and universities. For example, one vice president for student affairs at a regional public university told me that at one point during the pandemic, his financial aid office was down

40 percent of its typical staff. Eighty percent of the 500 institutions surveyed in 2022 by the National Association of Student Financial Aid Administrators were concerned about their ability to meet federal administrative requirements, and over half were concerned about adequately serving students at current staffing levels.[31]

At this point, the Great Resignation is imprinted on the American psyche and, as such, is a useful neologism because it instantly conjures a memory and mood. Judging by the number of articles, webinars, podcast episodes, and conference sessions on the Great Resignation, it is safe to say that many people in higher education are worried about turnover and interested in figuring out ways to stem the exodus. Yet Derek Thompson is right that there's more afoot than people leaving the workforce altogether. It is better to think of the Great Resignation as an umbrella concept covering multiple shifts among workers, in response to the pandemic and other factors.

Through my research, I have identified four shifts among higher education workers, which I call the Four Rs of the Great Resignation: *reevaluation*, *reassignment*, *resistance*, and *resignation* (Box I.1). Although each of these shifts has distinguishing characteristics, they are not mutually exclusive. As artist and writer Tricia Hersey has argued, someone's reevaluation can lead them to more rest, which is an act of resistance.[32] Resistance can propel a desire for change strong enough that an employee decides to resign. These shifts are not inherently bad—in some cases, they are perfectly rational responses to the organizational cultures and structures that employees have encountered. But they can also signal the existence of problems that, if left unaddressed, produce real consequences for organizations.

A Closer Look at the Four Rs of the Great Resignation

For many higher education employees, the pandemic prompted a *reevaluation* of priorities and what they desired or expected from the workplace and employers. They have become more attuned to working cultures and conditions within and beyond academe, and they have

Box I.1

The Four Rs of the Great Resignation in Higher Education

Reevaluation: When employees examine their priorities and what they desire or expect from the workplace and employers. They may be asking more questions, emphasizing well-being for themselves and others, and dialing back on the time and energy they give to work.

Reassignment: When employees pursue new roles or duties within their current organization. They may switch jobs to find better alignment between their own priorities and workplace expectations, or they may negotiate changes to their title, duties, hours, workload, or work location.

Resistance: When employees adopt covert or overt ways of pushing against the status quo of the higher education workplace. They may organize other employees for collective action, advocate for policy changes through existing governance bodies, or refuse to participate in problematic practices they associate with the status quo.

Resignation: When employees resign their position at an institution. They may take a new job at another institution, leave higher education, or step away from the workforce to consider options.

new language to describe their on-the-job experiences. Many have become more interested in alternatives to the status quo and have developed a deeper repertoire of possibilities to support well-being for themselves and others. For some workers, reevaluation has meant giving work less headspace, preventing work from consuming their personal lives, and dialing back ambitions.

As a result of reevaluation, employees may be less willing to take work home with them or make themselves constantly available to supervisors or students, more protective of their time with family or hobbies, and more dedicated to relationship-building and activities that enrich their physical and mental health. My experience of the Great Resignation was marked by reevaluation: I thought critically about the higher education workplace, learned new concepts to describe my experience, and was more judicious about the cups into which I poured my energy. Although

I haven't left my job, I have shifted my perspective to such a degree that I am a different employee than in 2020.

For some higher education employees, the combination of reevaluation and increasing vacancies encouraged them to seek *reassignment* at their institutions. They may not have quit to take a job outside higher education or at another institution, but they have pursued a new role or responsibility at their college or university that better aligns with their priorities, desires, or expectations. Included in this group are workers who were able to work remotely at times during the pandemic and want to continue working remotely. They may have gravitated toward jobs or units at the institution that would grant them greater flexibility to fulfill caregiving responsibilities.

Reassignment doesn't necessarily entail switching positions, as some higher education employees used the upheaval of the pandemic and period of change to start a conversation with their supervisor about their title, duties, hours, workload, or work location. Given the specter of turnover and having to replace employees, supervisors may have been more receptive to experimentation and more willing to push the boundaries of what was possible. And in some cases, reassignment wasn't planned or proactively sought. Many higher education employees were asked to shift into new roles or step into interim positions as a short-term solution to resignations. Reassignment may not show up in turnover data that might only count instances when an employee leaves the organization. Nevertheless, switching jobs within an organization creates new vacancies to fill, new people to train, and new challenges for leaders to maintain the continuity of operations or services.

The way that colleges and universities responded to the pandemic forever changed how some employees saw their institutions. When faculty and staff members saw their expertise disregarded, when they were asked to make accommodations for students but saw their requests rejected, and when they saw investment in productivity-tracking systems but not mental health resources, some experienced a deep sense of betrayal. In some cases, the pandemic was the last straw in a steady erosion of trust between higher education employees and their employers. For some employees, the Great Resignation catalyzed an awareness that colleges and universities may not magically change or confront problems with sufficient urgency—if change is going to happen, it may depend on forms of *resistance.*

The Great Resignation is about movement in terms of people leaving or switching jobs, but it is also about a growing labor movement in higher education. Some workers organized to achieve collective bargaining, while others pushed against the status quo in subtler ways. They may have resisted the culture's demand for constant hustling or going "above and beyond" by choosing to meet their contractual obligations without altruistically taking on extra labor. They may have become more active in shared governance bodies like the staff senate or used a service commitment to push for changes to policies or practices that better support employees. Dawn was an overt and covert resister before and throughout the pandemic. She would go toe-to-toe with administrators over policy language and push the institution to acknowledge its relationship with the land it occupies. But she also refused to participate in the individualistic, competitive nature of academic life, focusing on appreciative practices that gave back to her community.

And that leaves the ultimate R—*resignation.* Some employees resigned from one institution only to take a job at another, perhaps for better pay or to be closer to family. A pandemic-era boom in educational technology companies meant that some higher education employees were recruited away. And some left their jobs not knowing for sure what would come next. Figuring out precisely how many people quit their jobs in higher education is not easy. Dan Bauman of *The Chronicle of Higher Education* reported that higher education shed 410,000 jobs between the start of the pandemic and December 2020—a pace of loss not seen since the 1960s. The total number of higher education employees, however, had returned to its pre-pandemic size by 2022.[33] Although this figure reflects changes in the total number of employees, it doesn't perfectly measure resignations. As previously noted, several surveys showed most respondents planned to seek new employment in the near future.[34]

Of course, planning to leave and actually leaving are two different things. When I discussed some of this data with a table of college presidents, one replied, "Everyone says they are looking at other jobs right now." The Great Resignation may have generated *openness* to new opportunities more than resignations. Even so, significant numbers of employees being open to alternatives, proactively seeking new jobs, and planning to leave aren't things to shrug off. Those workers may pay less attention to their current responsibilities because they are thinking about their next job. And in the event some of that thinking translates into resignations, it can mean losing a beloved mentor to students, losing a storehouse of institutional knowledge, or losing skills that cannot always be easily replaced. Some institutions learned the hard way how essential an employee could be *after* that person left and no one was prepared to step in and manage a critical system or process. Resignations in units can create an avalanche of work for other employees, giving them a reason to eye the exit.

In sum, the Great Resignation has led to employees leaving higher education and others asking questions about the place of work in their lives, reallocating attention and energy to protect themselves from overwork, and pushing for changes to support employee well-being. It has manifested in movement, and with all that movement has come a nontrivial amount of turbulence for institutions that lean heavily on continuity and constancy. If leaders are just looking at turnover data, they are not truly standing in the totality of the past five years (and counting) for higher education workers. And they are missing an important point about the Great Resignation: it may have less to do with workers than with *employers*.

Don't Blame the Pandemic

While I was wrapping up a virtual presentation for a university, an anonymous attendee posted a question through the Zoom chat feature: "Is the higher education workplace really so bad, or are people just tired of the pandemic?" It's a valid question. Higher education workers *are* tired of the pandemic and how it has affected their work and workplace. The pandemic forced people into work situations that made it harder for them to feel safe or effective. Balancing work and caregiving, which was challenging in the best of circumstances, became next to impossible with school closures and disruptions to health care. Leaders faced hard choices because of the pandemic, sometimes under significant external pressures and in the face of constantly evolving information. It was often up to employees down the organizational chart to implement plans, even if the plans were at odds with their values. Maybe the only change higher education really needs is to get on the other side of the pandemic.

If only it were that simple. Because of the stress, threats to safety, and values-based conflict in the higher education workplace of late, researchers like me have turned to three concepts to make sense of shifts associated with the Great Resignation: *burnout*, *disengagement*, and *demoralization* (Box I.2). Digging into the research makes clear that the pandemic alone isn't to blame for the widespread reevaluation of priorities, increased unionization, and heightened turnover. Yes, the pandemic created a unique set of challenges. Few of us in higher education were prepared to teach, house, and feed students in the presence of a deadly virus. Remember the plexiglass? But the pandemic largely dialed up *preexisting* stressors. As one staff member in student affairs put it when interviewed, the pandemic "shined a light on existing cracks in the foundation." Burnout, demoralization, and disengagement illuminate employee experiences that precipitated the Four Rs of the Great Resignation and explain why change focused on organizational cultures and structures is necessary.

Let's start with *burnout*. Although it is often measured by asking individuals how frequently they experience exhaustion, cynicism toward work, and reduced professional efficacy on the job,[35] the World Health Organization emphasizes that burnout is an *occupational* syndrome resulting from chronic *workplace* stress.[36] Researchers do not consider burnout a mental illness or medical disease, but faculty burnout expert Rebecca Pope-Ruark explained that it can lead to or co-occur with depression and anxiety as well as more physical effects of stress like pain, fatigue, insomnia, and digestive problems.[37] One of the pioneers of burnout research, Christina Maslach, attributed burnout to failures at the organizational level. These failures are evident in poor working condi-

Box I.2

Three Concepts to Make Sense of the Pandemic-Era Employee Experience

Burnout: Chronic workplace stress characterized by exhaustion, cynicism toward work, and reduced professional efficacy. Burnout is common among highly devoted workers whose ideals push them to work until they break down. My analogy: driving while drowsy with cruise control on.

Disengagement: Distancing yourself cognitively, emotionally, and even physically from work. Workers don't invest when work isn't meaningful, when they feel physically or socially unsafe, and when they are not provided enough resources. My analogy: taking your foot off the gas pedal and slowing down as an act of self-preservation.

Demoralization: Dissonance that arises when workers' morals, values, and beliefs conflict with working conditions. It is an indictment of organizations and professions that make our work and morals increasingly irreconcilable, providing a strong push for people to leave. My analogy: seeking the nearest off-ramp because you don't see a path forward.

tions, such as an overly demanding workload, insufficient rewards, inequities and unfairness, and lack of community. A 2018 Gallup survey of 7,500 workers confirmed these causes, finding that the top-five drivers of burnout were unfair treatment at work, unmanageable workloads, lack of role clarity, lack of communication and support from managers, and unreasonable time pressures.[38] Research shows that burnout isn't just about people struggling to cope with stress; it's about people struggling in workplaces where stress never subsides. According to Emily and Amelia Nagoski, although stress is a normal biological response, it is not meant to be chronically activated. As they noted, burnout happens when employees are "soaked in stress juice" day after day.[39]

In *The End of Burnout: Why Work Drains Us and How to Build Better Lives*, Jonathan Malesic points out that burnout is deeply ingrained in our culture. "To participate in the work culture of our era," he wrote, "*just is* to risk burnout. You may as well try to swim without getting wet."[40] He argues that we need a more precise understanding of burnout if we have any hope of changing this culture. To this end, he advises coupling Maslach's insights on the importance of working conditions with psychologist Herbert Freudenberger's research arguing that burnout often surfaces among highly devoted workers whose ideals compel them to "throw everything into the work, hit an obstacle, and then work even harder, right up to the point of breakdown."[41] Anne Helen Peterson, author of *Can't Even: How Millennials Became the Burnout Generation*, echoes this view, explaining to me during an interview that burnout is "when you get to a feeling of exhaustion with life. It's not just physical or psychological exhaustion; it's everything together. But instead of collapsing and saying, 'I can't do this anymore,' you hit the wall and climb over it." For this reason, I have sometimes thought of burnout as driving while drowsy with the cruise control on. Acknowledging the role of culture-based ideals pushing us to keep going and on-the-job realities producing stress is one way that Malesic brings more nuance to discussions of burnout. Rather than seeing burnout as a "one-dimensional, burnout-or-not" state, he prefers recent research framing it as a spectrum along which multiple profiles of burnout can be found.[42]

If burnout is driving while drowsy, we might think of *disengagement* as taking your foot off the gas pedal and slowing down as an act of self-preservation. Researchers define disengagement as distancing yourself cognitively, emotionally, and even physically from work.[43] One theory posits that disengagement is about whether conditions are in place for you to feel as if you can invest fully in the work. These conditions include whether the work is meaningful, whether employees feel safe and can bring their true selves to work, and whether there are sufficient resources.[44] If faculty and staff encounter workplace cultures in which they can't openly talk about aspects of their identities or policies that prevent them from growing professionally, they are less likely to invest in their work.

One way disengagement differs from burnout is that it can be healthy. As Brad Shuck, a professor of human and organizational development at the University of Louisville, told me in an interview, "Engagement isn't a boundless reservoir from which we can just draw all the time. But instead we go through these natural ebbs and flows, and those cycles are healthy because they allow us to heal and to rest and to reflect." Shuck explained that engagement at work is a product of healthy organizational cultures, including the extent to which workers feel included. The fact that some higher education employees found their productivity and satisfaction improved when they could work at home—away from offices where they may have experienced forms of exclusion or discrimination—underscores how engagement is in some measure about whether the workplace enables a sense of belonging for employees.

Like burnout, *demoralization* involves workers struggling to bridge a chasm—not between unrealistic ideals and the reality of the workplace but between their values and outside forces shaping work. Doris Santoro, a philosopher of education, has researched demoralization among elementary- and secondary-school teachers for over a decade, describing it as when "the conditions of teaching change so dramatically that moral rewards, previously available in ever-challenging work, are now inaccessible."[45] These moral rewards are activated when "educators feel they are doing what is right in terms of one's students, the teaching profession, and themselves."[46] Demoralization happens when teachers feel that policies and practices prevent them from upholding the values that brought them to the profession. Drawing on Santoro's work as well as literature on moral injury in helping professions, Erin Sugrue, a professor of social work, conceptualized moral suffering as "an experience of dissonance between an individual's moral beliefs, values, and expectations and an experience of moral transgression."[47] She emphasizes that paying attention to moral suffering is important because people in helping professions "experience real psychological and existential pain when they are involved in actions and environments that violate their moral beliefs and expectations."[48]

More specific to the higher education workplace, Kaetrena Davis Kendrick, dean of the library at Winthrop University, has found in her research on academic librarians that low morale derives from repeated, protracted workplace abuse and neglect.[49] In particular, she found low morale in libraries whose cultures tolerate incivility, toxicity, and bullying. When I interviewed higher education workers about their morale during the second year of the pandemic, they revealed a pervasive frustration that leaders did not learn lessons from the previous year and were exercising a sort of selective amnesia about the trauma it brought. Relatedly, many of the workers I interviewed felt that leaders simply weren't listening, weren't taking questions about plans in meetings, or weren't transparently answering the questions they received. Values-based conflict emerged as staff and faculty sought compassion and thoughtful answers in the face of elevated risk and instead heard, "Everything's fine! Carry on!" These frustrations were amplified by ballooning workloads, perceptions of low compensation, and inadequate staffing. Demoralization suggests an indictment of organizations and professions that make our work and morals increasingly irreconcilable. As such, it provides a strong push for people to leave their jobs. To continue the driving metaphor, demoralization results in drivers seeking the nearest off-ramp.

Burnout, demoralization, and disengagement aren't really about individuals waking up one day and feeling depleted or as if their professional values are being thwarted. They are outcomes of individuals whose beliefs and ideals intersect with organizational cultures and structures marked by unfair treatment, excessive workloads, chronic stress, inadequate resources, and threats to physical and social safety.[50] Leaders cannot address these deep-rooted organizational problems with tokens of appreciation. Few of us will say no to a free t-shirt or thank-you luncheon, but moving the dial on morale will require organizational changes that truly address organizational cultures and structures.

Overview of the Book

At the heart of the Caring University is the premise that all employees have talent, all employees should be treated as whole people, and all employees deserve to be cared for as essential contributors to organizational success. The Caring University takes a hopeful stance on the future of the higher education workplace. It seeks to build on strengths commonly found at colleges and universities, and it acknowledges the skill and passion of leaders—whether students, faculty, staff, or administrators—willing to put in the work necessary for organizational change.

According to Kezar, a good first step in any organizational change process is getting a handle on the complexity of colleges and universities as organizations. Designing a customized process means understanding the organization's particular challenges and the context in which it operates. Chapter 1 explains why colleges and universities are complex and what that means for the higher education workplace, with a review of several prominent problems in the higher education workplace. I introduce several concepts and theories that help to explain the roots of these problems in organization-level cultures and structures. What we see at the organizational level often reflects social, political, and economic forces over which colleges and universities have minimal direct control. But institutions do have some control at the organizational level, and I'll walk through several theories well suited for the deep change on which the Caring University is premised.

Chapter 2 introduces the first organizational change of the Caring University: *making the employee experience a strategic priority.* In the Caring University, institutions establish a strategy for talent management by involving employees in the creation of guiding documents, such as value statements, and collecting accurate data on who employees are and what they experience on the job. Importantly, data does not gather dust in a database but is used to inform follow-up actions. The Caring University collects data on the amount of work employee have to do, and it uses data to adjust workload inequities or excesses. This chapter, as well as those covering the other five organizational changes, incorporates stories from interview participants and institutional site visits, and each features a case study of what this change looks like in practice.

In Chapter 3, I describe another organizational change of the Caring University: *creating working cultures and conditions for real (not ideal) workers.* Instead of structuring jobs around ideal workers, the Caring University normalizes the needs of real workers: people who are parents and caring for parents, have bodies and minds whose needs cannot be shut off between business hours, and experience grief, hardship, and tragedy. The Caring University recognizes that employees are different, with unique strengths and areas for growth, and it builds flexibility and customization into workplace policies and practices to account for this diversity. An important strategy to achieve flexibility is to create additional options for remote and hybrid work. In the Caring University, leaders encourage guardrails to prevent work from consuming employees' nonwork lives. The Caring University does not exploit employees' desire to serve students through appeals to passion, mission, or vocation.

Chapter 4 focuses on *committing to professional growth and fair compensation*. The Caring University applies its considerable expertise in teaching and learning to create robust in-house professional development opportunities for employees. It does not expect employees to self-finance training that is necessary to excel at their jobs. A hallmark of the Caring University is that it is intentional about helping employees craft and follow a career pathway so that they can stay at the institution for an extended period of time. Compensation is regularly adjusted to account for living costs, and workers can expect their compensation to increase as they gain knowledge and experience. The Caring University understands that recognition is not artificially limited to a small number of "stars," and appreciation can't be conveyed through mass "thank-you" emails. Building the cultures and structures that support people's development hinges on fully investing in the concept of total rewards and showing workers how they are valued—both for what they do and who they are.

In Chapter 5, I argue that care is not compatible with the isolation, exclusion, and inequities that minoritized and marginalized staff and faculty face in the workplace. Institutions must get serious about *pursuing cultural and structural change for equity and belonging*. The Caring University understands that centering equity and belonging means more than "sprinkling diversity" across campus—it requires unsettling the systems of oppression on which academia was built. Equity-mindedness must become second nature within an organization, which means disrupting the policies and processes that have led to inequitable hiring processes and outcomes. The Caring University honors the labor and expertise of marginalized staff and faculty by listening to and trusting their experiences and rewarding their contributions. Equity leadership is distributed across the university instead of being relegated to a single office or position.

Chapter 6 centers the importance of *empowering employees' rights and voice* in the Caring University and reducing precarity through full-time positions, long-term contracts, and streamlined opportunities for part-time employees to become full-time. The Caring University demonstrates its commitment to tenure and academic freedom amid rising political attacks on higher education. Shared governance is not framed as an outdated obstacle to change but rather as a defining characteristic of an organization that values employees' voices. Given the realities of competing priorities and limited resources, the Caring University respects the right of employees to organize and collectively bargain. But it also depends on staff and faculty fulfilling their responsibilities inherent in shared governance.

In Chapter 7, I describe the final organizational change proposed in the book, which is *cultivating and sustaining caring leaders*. Simply put, the Caring University does not wait for the right leaders to simply appear but proactively nurtures caring leaders through intentional selection and preparation. Training new supervisors, managers, and department chairs is routine, resourced, and rewarded. Higher education leaders are assessed and held accountable using metrics related to the employee experience. The Caring University sees students, staff, and faculty as interconnected parts of an ecosystem, where one group's well-being depends on the well-being of the others. Leaders' well-being becomes necessary for fostering creativity and empathy everywhere, which is why leaders must have a humane workload and expectations.

Over the past four years, many leaders have expressed their support for these six organizational changes, but they acknowledge that achieving them feels like an overwhelming project. As one faculty leader confided to me, "What you're saying feels very far away from where we are." In the conclusion, I close the book with several lessons and first-step pathways for leaders to consider in collaboration with campus partners. The crucial message of the chapter is that organizational change is a journey, and as is true of all journeys, it begins with a first step.

I opened this chapter with the story of Dawn—someone who has unique talents but whose experience in higher education is hardly unique. This book asks all of us to imagine an alternative version of events in which Dawn encountered colleges and universities that demonstrated care for her well-being. I am not suggesting a counter-story in which her career was completely cleared of hardship, to be sure, but one in which she didn't have to fight so hard for her talent to be recognized, where she might have felt a little more comfortable trusting that processes would do right by her and workplace stress wouldn't put her in the hospital. Her presence would be a function of feeling included and valued rather than an act of individual perseverance.

This book is about doing better for Dawn and countless other higher education employees who have felt locked out, burned out, or pushed out. And it is about choosing right now to get started.

CHAPTER 1

Organizational Problems of the Higher Education Workplace

MILA WAS BETWEEN JOBS in 1999 when her husband began sending her openings at the regional public university where he was a police dispatcher. Since they already lived in an apartment near campus, she tossed her name into a few searches and landed a job as a receptionist in the career services office, making $19,000 a year. Over the next decade, she stayed in the same office, working her way up to a data-entry clerk, and then eventually to level IV secretary. In the latter position, she was the office's senior administrative assistant, but because of tight budgets resulting from the 2008 recession, she also continued to fulfill the responsibilities of her former role. As she put it, "I was basically the office manager, with a side of full-time employment." Two jobs for the price of one.

In 2011, a consultant recommended reducing the number of administrative support positions at the university in response to a $30 million state budget cut. Even with 12 years of experience, Mila was bumped according to the terms of the union's collective bargaining agreement. Someone with more seniority whose position was eliminated during the workforce reduction took her job in the career services office. Mila was demoted to a level III secretary position in an academic department across campus. She had eight days to prepare her office, which was losing the one person with intricate knowledge of every administrative process on which they relied. And she had eight days to prepare herself to walk away from a job she loved.

Mila was disappointed to learn that the computer in her new office was too old to continue what had become her passion: art and graphic design. In the years leading up to her move across campus, Mila had been slowly cultivating skills in web design, as well as taking courses toward her bachelor's degree in art history. A mentor had encouraged her to pursue these interests, which made a lasting impact. "It's good to have someone like that, who sees your potential," she explained, "because others just see us as 'support staff,' the person who does the crap work or clean up or whatever." Mila was grateful to soon find another person in her corner. A faculty member in her new department figured out Mila's technology skills and worked to upgrade her computer so that she could design the logo and website for a new academic program.

Mila quickly outgrew her level III secretary position and within two years was tapped to serve as the dean's assistant. She was the only dean's assistant at the university classified as a secretary instead of an executive assistant, meaning she was paid less than her colleagues in equivalent positions. She tried to have her position reclassified, filling out the forms multiple times. It wasn't just about the money—Mila was doing more complicated work in this role. She was still designing websites but also managing faculty contracts and coordinating the college's accreditation. She wanted her title to reflect her contributions and leadership, but the dean ultimately decided there wasn't money in the budget to pay her as an executive assistant. She was an executive assistant in every way—except in what she was paid.

When her request to be reclassified was denied, Mila applied for and was hired as the assistant to an associate provost overseeing institutional effectiveness. She quickly realized that the two people overseeing the institution's academic program review and assessment were overwhelmed, so Mila stepped in to coordinate travel, plan events, design publications, and create reports. I asked Mila if this expansion of her responsibilities and experience came with a pay increase. "Not exactly," she replied with a chuckle. Her office had hired a former student worker for a new administrative assistant position. While training her new colleague, Mila learned he was making more money than she was because of his bachelor's degree. After she reminded her supervisor that the minimum qualifications for her job were a bachelor's degree or equivalent experience, she finally secured a raise.

Mila ended up earning an art history degree, which qualified her for an open program coordinator job in her office. She confided that she was lukewarm about the role, which wasn't substantially different from what she was already doing. But the *title* was valuable. It would allow her to pivot out of an administrative assistant position—a pivot she described as "extremely hard to make" at the university. Despite everyone knowing she was prepared for the job, she went through a full search process and was ultimately hired. But as they were interviewing candidates for her previous job, COVID-19 hit, and the university instituted a hiring freeze. Mila covered for the vacancy created by her move while also starting her new position. Her supervisor promised the arrangement was temporary, but every time she asked to revisit hiring someone else, her supervisor said his "hands were tied."

Although the university's hiring was frozen during the pandemic, Mila was not; she went on to earn a master's degree in learning and design. Noting her additional education, her supervisor ventured that she could be making six figures somewhere else. But that vote of confidence wasn't a sign that her supervisor was working to pay her more. Despite juggling two jobs, constantly acquiring new skills, and completing a graduate degree, Mila felt she was still primarily seen as an administrative assistant. "I don't know what else I could do . . . it was so hard to shake that administrative assistant label." A friend tipped her off to a project management job in the information technology division paying significantly more, and Mila decided to give it a try. After she left, her former supervisor's hands were "suddenly" freed up—he split the job that Mila had been doing for years into two and made one an associate director position.

Mila loves her new job in information technology. "I've got my nerdy colleagues who are into Star Wars like me. They're actually utilizing my skills," she explained. She enjoys better pay, flexibility, autonomy, and professional development opportunities. Her office has discussed paying for her to get a project management certificate, and she sees new opportunities on the horizon, both internal and external to the university. After years of effectively managing people and complex processes, Mila's title now officially includes "manager." She can also work remotely, and she and her husband have talked about fulfilling a dream of moving abroad.

Mila's interview with me ended on a high note. I could almost picture a public relations article about her journey from receptionist to information technology manager—about her degrees earned and decades of distinguished service in multiple offices. And yet, I wondered how Mila felt about her journey. She put it in blunt terms: "It didn't have to take so long. I definitely have felt exploited. And it's not just me. A lot of my colleagues who were administrative assistants or who are assistants now, we all feel the same way. We do so much more than they see." It is not until they leave that leaders realize how much more labor administrative support professionals are doing than their titles, pay, or position on the organizational chart would suggest.

Mila, who is Black and Puerto Rican, attributes this invisibility in part to the fact that many of the administrative assistants are women of color. According to 2019 data from the university's union, out of 127 people with the title "administrative assistant" or "secretary," 120 were women and 75 were women of color. Research often backs up Mila's explanation, showing that gender and race can intersect for women of color in higher education, creating compounding forms of discrimination that erect rigid walls around their location and status in the organizational pecking order.[1] Her gender and race may not have been the sole factors, but there was an institutional pattern of watching Mila take on the work of multiple jobs, underpaying her, and refusing to see her as anything other than an administrative assistant. Yes, Mila is happy in her new role, but it does not change the fact that it took 23 *years* to happen.

Mila's story abounds with the kinds of problems commonly found in the higher education workplace. Some of these problems can be attributed to forces beyond the university's control, such as state funding cuts. Mila might even take partial ownership of a few of the problems; she readily admits to seeking out new projects when her routine goes stale. But I consider many of the obstacles she faced to be *organizational* problems. They reflect collective choices about where to invest resources, what type of workload is acceptable, whose skills and knowledge are valued, which issues warrant urgency, and which policies are malleable. These choices flow from and are reinforced by norms and values, or the culture of the organization and, by extension, the workplace. And they in turn become cemented into the structures of organizations through policies and taken-for-granted, widely accepted practices that shape everyday working conditions for employees—things like workload, hours, compensation, promotion, and leave time.

In this chapter, my goal is to encourage leaders to read Mila's story—and the higher education workplace more broadly—through an organizational lens. This means being able to see cultural and structural determinants of problems at the organizational level and even drawing on the wisdom of organizational theories to better bring issues into focus. I have a very down-to-earth view of organizational theories, seeing them as important *resources* in a leader's change toolkit. They are a bit like the owner's manual for a car. As leaders study and apply organizational theories, they can more effectively determine why an indicator light is flashing, what parts are necessary to improve performance, and when to seek expert help. As higher education scholar Leslie Gonzales and colleagues noted, organizational theories "provide a powerful entry point for [the] transformative work" of "re-envisioning and remaking higher education."[2]

One reason organizational change in higher education often stumbles is that leaders don't acknowledge the complexity of colleges and universities as organizations.[3] I'll explain where some of that complexity originates and how this knowledge is useful in understanding and reimagining the higher education workplace. I'll also review a few prominent problems of the higher education workplace to show how they can be linked to the cultures and structures of organizations. Then I'll explore approaches to organizational change specifically designed to address problems of this kind—approaches that explain how to go about making the Caring University a reality.

Thinking Organizationally about Workplace Problems

What makes problems organizational and not individual? For one thing, the problems persist in the organization even if you swap out a given individual. Some of Mila's problems certainly might have been less acute with a different supervisor or dean, but many of them cannot be chalked up to the presence or absence of one person. In the same vein, many of these problems are not unique to Mila—she had a stockpile of stories to tell about colleagues facing similar challenges or worse. These kinds of problems are thoroughly baked into organization-level cultures and structures—so much so that they also can't be easily changed by a single individual, even someone with deep wells of energy, resources, and political capital. Organizational problems are bigger in scope and beyond the reach of an individual or interpersonal dynamic. This does not absolve leaders of responsibility, but instead reminds us all that we can't expect a heroic figure to swoop in and solve these problems.

My attention to both structures *and* cultures within organizations is purposeful. Problems in the higher education workplace are not just a function of what's written in policy manuals or employee handbooks. They also reflect underlying systems of meaning—our language, narratives, and decision-making patterns. Higher education scholar Adrianna Kezar, who wrote the book on organizational change in higher education, explained that structural alterations alone are often insufficient in the face of problems that stem from these systems of meaning. To be clear, implementing a new policy or standing up a new office is no small accomplishment and can make a big difference for employees. But she cautioned that overlooking culture can result in "making many smaller changes that only address symptoms rather than the heart of problems."[4]

I also intentionally pair structures and cultures when thinking about organizational problems and their solutions because the line dividing the two can be a little fuzzy. Formal policies and the processes by which they are implemented reflect organizational values. For example, an institutional policy can be interpreted differently by the various units that apply it. Cultures can also normalize certain behaviors and expectations into workplace rules that, though not always written, can be just as real and rigid as a handbook. For this reason, when I refer to structural problems, I am not just talking about formal policies, legally binding contracts, or how positions and departments are arranged on the organizational chart. I am also thinking about what higher education scholar Brittany M. Williams called the "hidden curriculum," or the "vague and rarely spoken workplace rules by which a professional must abide . . . should they wish to successfully navigate their workplace."[5] The organizational changes that I propose in this book are designed to address the cultural and structural reasons higher education workers have been so prone to reevaluation, reassignment, resistance, and resignation in the wake of the pandemic.

I don't use the word "organizational" to suggest that problems are universal or uniformly experienced. Some people, by virtue of skill, luck, or privilege, can avoid or lessen the impact of these problems and therefore may not notice their prevalence. But the fact that one individual, or even a particular group of individuals, has had a relatively positive experience in the higher education workplace does not disprove the existence of problems for others. It could simply mean that they were able to navigate an organization that was tailor-made for them. While workplace problems are not universal, they are common enough to surface time and again, both in scholarly literature and in my interviews.[6] And though a given institution or department may have addressed some of these problems or may struggle with one or two of them more intensely than others, research shows that these problems appear in a range of units and institution types.

Locating problems at the organizational level doesn't mean ignoring the context in which colleges and universities operate. I agree with sociologists who contend that colleges and universities are "open systems," meaning that societal forces shape the environmental conditions to which institutions respond.[7] There is no denying the fact that institutions were born and continue to operate in the context of a racist society and capitalist economy.[8] But we also should not assume that these forces exist "out there" or only play out between individuals while organizations remain value-neutral structures. Take the example of racism. Sociologist

Victor Ray demonstrated that organizations are not race-neutral bureaucracies but rather play a role in constituting the racial social structure.[9] Social problems also manifest and can be reinforced through mechanisms at the organizational level. It is often in the workplace that we materially experience big-picture societal trends, and organizations can determine how intensely we feel the effects.

Beyond the more obvious forces shaping institutional environments, colleges and universities also pay close attention to other institutions in their orbit and conform to the rules that would grant membership in the club.[10] When deciding how to respond to environmental pressures, institutions are prone to "follow the leader," which allows them to tap into the resources that come from proximity to successful organizations and be seen as legitimate.[11] These are organizational prerogatives that can lead to creating new offices, shuffling around personnel, or striving for additional research money—with downstream effects for employees. Another result is that colleges and universities have tended to resemble one another over time.[12] They are a little like airports in this regard—whether you're in Ann Arbor or Albuquerque, you have a sense of what to expect when you step onto a college campus.

To read Mila's story and see organizational problems doesn't strip her or other employees of agency in the workplace. Rather, it is an acknowledgment that their agency is bounded. Workers can decide how to manage their to-do list or better prioritize self-care, but they can't generally rewrite the terms of their employment or easily go against the grain of widely accepted practices. For this reason, individual-level solutions to improve employee well-being, like providing access to a mental health app or incentivizing exercise, can only go so far. Encouraging workers to go for a walk doesn't help much if they come right back to a toxic workplace.

This book is about pursuing changes so that working cultures and conditions better support employee well-being, which means tackling the cultural and structural determinants of workplace problems head-on. Simply put, organizational problems require the type of solutions that come from leaders who can think organizationally. Step one is to get a solid grasp of the organization of colleges and universities in all their complexity.

A Primer on Colleges and Universities as Organizations

Organizational experts have long been intrigued by what's going on under the hood of colleges and universities. Higher education scholar Michael Bastedo pointed out that many of the modern organizational theories still widely used today were built on the study of colleges and universities.[13] It helps that organizational theorists were often faculty and could observe dynamics in their own "backyards." But it is also the case that colleges and universities are in a league of their own, organizationally speaking. They are known for being complex—and sometimes even perplexing—organizations.[14] It's not uncommon for new employees who have spent time in other industries to throw up their arms in confusion during their first few months on the job.

The organizational complexity of institutions helps explain a few of the workplace problems that I discuss throughout the book. But my main purpose in offering this primer is that bringing an organizational lens to the higher education workplace requires baseline knowledge of the nature of colleges and universities as organizations. Failing to account for important organizational features of colleges and universities can lead to change efforts that are poorly suited to the institutional context. More than one management idea and transformative change effort has been resoundingly rejected or proven ineffective for failing to appreciate what makes colleges and universities different from other organizations or workplaces.[15] Thankfully, Mila's story offers a starting point to make sense of some of these distinctive features.

For example, with her references to forms, salary grades, job qualifications, and requests to superiors, Mila's experience at the university reflects classic characteristics of bureaucracies. Like other bureaucracies, colleges and universities are hierarchical.[16] Picture the pyramidal organizational chart that many institutions are fond of scrupulously updating. Boxes represent offices or positions with distinct functions that report to a smaller number of boxes above them. Lines linking boxes represent a "chain of command" and show how information travels up or down the hierarchy. All this structure, at least in theory, helps to coordinate the tasks of many workers, establish clear communication channels, and enforce a division of labor that fosters specialization.[17] Bureaucracies are big on written rules and criteria for hiring and promotion based on competence, not charisma or connections.[18] Although they are frequently bemoaned as "red tape," establishing and enforcing rules can also protect employees by enshrining certain rights in policy or creating transparent personnel processes.

Even so, there are limits to viewing colleges and universities as bureaucratic in traditional terms. For one thing, universities serve as the prototype for "organized anarchies" because goals are ambiguous, decisions are decentralized, and the organizational chart does not necessarily reflect where power resides.[19] Decision-making in such organizations has been conceptualized as a "garbage can process," where participants, problems, and proposed solutions come together in a chaotic, nonlinear swirl whose endpoint is difficult to predict.[20] According to this line of thought, sometimes institutions buy into solutions—or even short-lived fads—before really knowing what problems they fix or if there's evidence of their effectiveness.[21] Particularly loud participants can sway which problems receive attention and which solutions carry weight. Most colleges and universities are not truly this chaotic, but there is enough truth to the "organized anarchy" model to cast doubt on institutions as pure bureaucracies.

Scholars have explained that colleges and universities are a little unruly because they are *professional* bureaucracies, making them distinct from both businesses and government.[22] As professional bureaucracies, institutions provide professionals, such as faculty and some staff, considerable autonomy because of their specialized training. This training also means professionals are subject to lighter accountability—in some cases being permitted to self-police or engage in peer review of performance. The result of this deference to professionals is a dual structure of authority. In simple terms, there is an administrative/bureaucratic structure overseeing facilities and budgeting and an academic structure where faculty are granted limited authority over curriculum and personnel matters.[23] What allows this dual power structure to work is the tradition of shared governance, or the acknowledgment that, as professionals with expertise, faculty and some staff have a right to participate in important decisions like strategic planning or who the next president should be.

The upside to this arrangement is that it can promote collegiality and deliberative decision-making processes.[24] Sometimes shared governance means encouraging or tolerating a healthy amount of conflict between faculty and administrators—the equivalent of organizational checks and balances. But the fact that institutions are organized as professional bureaucracies also introduces issues. You might have noticed that I said *some* staff can participate in shared governance. Not everyone at colleges and universities enjoys autonomy or is invited to the decision-making table. Some staff members that I interviewed had years of experience and received specialized training like Mila, but they did not believe their expertise was recognized. As one staff member at a community college explained:

> I don't like to think about it this way, but it's a class system. I don't have academic freedom. I don't have protections. I have to reapply for my job every few years. The lack of protection has become more apparent with the pandemic in terms of who is "essential" and has to be on campus. Where I work, staff have been told they have to have a presence on campus since summer of 2020, while only a handful of faculty show up.

Whether you are treated as a bureaucratic functionary or autonomous professional may in practice depend less on actual expertise or training and more on rigidly enforced perceptions of differences between position types. Case in point: Mila understood that switching jobs and achieving a particular title was perhaps the only way to be perceived as something other than an administrative assistant.

Even among faculty, the existence of a hierarchy undermines the notion of collegiality based on mutual respect and shared power. Contingent faculty are often excluded from shared governance and subjected to what Kezar and colleagues called "academic deprofessionalization," which can include being hired on a short-term contract and having reemployment determined by customer ratings.[25] Institutions have increasingly turned to outsourcing certain jobs, meaning workers in areas like housing, dining, facilities, security, and information technology are employed by private companies. Outsourcing frees institutions of responsibility over questions like wages, workload, and equity.[26] Higher education scholar Shaun Harper observed that during the pandemic, some of these outsourced employees were the first to see their jobs and hours cut.[27] It wasn't lost on Mila that people of color were clustered in positions where job security is limited and advancement was restricted. At many colleges and universities, the workplace is racially stratified, getting whiter as you move up the ranks.

The other challenge with the professional bureaucracy model is that it promotes a simultaneous orientation toward centralization on the bureaucratic side of the house and decentralization on the academic side.[28] Demands for carefully managed budgets, strategic plans, regulatory compliance, and a manicured external image are used to justify centralized coordination. At the same time, deference to professionals has led to the emergence of increasingly atomized subunits and the delegation of decision-making to the local level, where experts are believed to be best positioned to understand issues and render judgments. The result has been the emergence of what some view as "silos" that prevent collaboration and permit redundancy. Connections between the silos can be infrequent or weak, giving rise to a "loosely coupled system" in which what happens in one subunit has little bearing on another or the system as a whole.[29] When Mila moved from career services to an academic department, it was like moving to another country that shared certain words or customs but nevertheless required a cultural transition.

For higher education scholar and former college president Robert Birnbaum, the idea of governance itself helps us grasp the complexity of colleges and universities and differentiate them from other organizations. He defines governance as "the structures and processes through which institutional participants interact with and influence each other and communicate with the larger environment."[30] More simply, governance is an institution's answer to the question: Who is in charge here, and how are decisions made? Legally speaking, governing boards—or boards of trustees—are in charge but delegate much of the day-to-day management to administrators and faculty.[31] All of these groups must make decisions in a way that is responsive to external stakeholders like policymakers, foundations, federal agencies, employers, and accrediting bodies. Some scholars describe institutions as being the bull's-eye within concentric circles of regulative pressures or as nodes in a vast, interdependent network.[32] So while each college or university is distinct and has some freedom to maneuver as it sees fit, it is also tied to every other institution and an array of external stakeholders in a "spider web of oversight."[33]

There is one final feature of colleges and universities as organizations that makes them unique, at least as an employer: they tend to enjoy deep attachment or affiliation from employees. In my work with regional public universities and other broad-access institutions, it was common for employees to have grown up nearby. They received degrees from the university, sent their children to summer camps there, and attended athletic events with extended family. In other words, for some employees, colleges and universities aren't just where they work—they are sites of deep personal meaning and identity. These employees can be incredibly forgiving of institutions but can also be seriously hurt when leaders don't live up to expectations or deviate from tradition.

As Box 1.1 sums up, colleges and universities are, organizationally speaking, quite messy, but that doesn't mean they are completely illegible. When I describe problems in the higher education workplace, leaders should not underestimate the challenges posed by organizational complexity itself. Organizational change to reimagine the higher education workplace has a much better chance of sticking and being effective if leaders begin by considering key organizational features of colleges and universities.

That's (Not) a Personal Problem

In 2022, I wrote an article about the lack of career pathways for many higher education workers.[34] A four-time college chancellor (another term

Box 1.1

Features Contributing to Organizational Complexity

- Being bureaucratic, but also organized anarchies
- Granting deference to professionals, but not treating all employees as professionals
- Pursuing administrative centralization, but also enabling academic decentralization and specialization
- Sharing power and espousing egalitarian values, but also maintaining hierarchy and creating inequality
- Exercising organizational autonomy, but also being highly aware of other institutions and responsive to an array of external stakeholders

for "president") penned a letter to the editor in response to the article, noting that he worked his way up from lecturer to leadership roles over the course of a five-decade career in higher education. "When I needed advice, I sought it," he declared. "If I aspired for a new role, I prepared for it. No one was responsible for my career but me." He concluded by advising me and others to "take charge of your life, take charge of your career, and keep your whining to yourself."[35] After reading this letter, I was tempted to concede that my read of the higher education workplace was too narrowly focused on problems. Perhaps there really were no challenges so immense or entrenched that they couldn't be overcome with the right mix of preparation, pluck, and perseverance.

But then I returned to my conversation with Mila, who wasn't lacking in resilience and didn't have time—or a platform—for complaints. I thought about recurring themes in my interviews with other faculty, staff, and administrators. And I read the research, which rather unambiguously highlights a set of common problems in the higher education workplace. I realized the president's advice was the same old individualized solution in a not-so-new bottle. Responses like "stop your whining" are not only a refusal to demonstrate care—they are a refusal to see workplace problems as organizational in nature.

In what follows, I explore three examples of the kinds of problems in the higher education workplace overlooked in responses like that of the chancellor. To be sure, these problems are not unique to higher education. But their existence in other sectors doesn't make them less of a problem for those of us who have dedicated our careers to academia. These problems will look familiar because they are, not coincidentally, what researchers have identified as major drivers of burnout, disengagement, and demoralization. I'll return to these and other issues in subsequent chapters, but touching on them now highlights the cultural and structural roots of workplace problems driving the Great Resignation and show the limits of individual-level thinking.

Neglecting the Employee Experience

One problem of this nature is how the employee experience has been a low priority in institutional values statements, strategic priorities, and data collection. To the extent that college and university strategic plans mention faculty and staff, they usually only speak of recruiting "talent"—a term often reserved for faculty—or equipping faculty and staff to better contribute to outcomes of interest like retention or grants. The truth is that many institutions simply do not know very much about their employees or their perceptions of the workplace. My interviews with industry experts in human resources and information technology show that data collection is often episodic and limited to employee engagement surveys. Furthermore, many colleges and universities have a bad habit of not taking any action based on the data they collect, which makes matters worse.[36]

Support for faculty and staff has often been eclipsed by concern for the student experience and a push for student success. Over two decades ago, higher education scholars Sheila Slaughter and Gary Rhoades documented the shift toward catering to the consumer preferences of college students, often to the detriment of staff and faculty.[37] In developing their theory of academic capitalism, Slaughter and Rhoades documented how colleges and universities calibrate their goals and actions to the resources on which they depend. When state governments became an unreliable partner in funding higher education, public colleges and universities resorted to intense competition for students and trying to become masters of their own budgetary destiny by diversifying revenue sources and cost-cutting. This meant doubling down on efforts to attract and retain tuition-paying students.

Institutions invested in moneymaking departments, encouraged entrepreneurial ventures, extended the authority of certain administrative positions, and embraced corporate-like forms of management.[38] One result of this shift toward academic capitalism is that it widened the gulf between the administrative/bureaucratic side of the house and the academic side, as the prerogative to secure new revenues has eroded the shared governance on which this dual power structure depends. Academic capitalism has shaped workplace cultures by justifying more top-down forms of decision-making and communication as well as beliefs that emphasize the economic purposes of higher education. Working conditions have been affected, too, as academic capitalism fueled deprofessionalization in the form of increased part-time positions and less autonomy for faculty, greater reliance on outsourced jobs, and expanded services for students without regard for labor.

Concern for the student experience and the desire to see more students graduate is not directly to blame for problems of the higher education workplace. But academic capitalism argues that many colleges and universities responded to changes to their funding streams in ways that had clear implications for working cultures and conditions. The net effect of these implications is that employee well-being plays second fiddle to meeting student needs. When the Great Resignation hit higher education, many institutions could provide detailed data about their students because they had poured money into analytics to track recruitment and student success.[39] One survey from 2021 showed that 72 percent of respondents spent more on student success technologies in the last 12 months. But employees were lucky if they saw a periodic engagement survey.

Overworked Employees and Understaffed Offices

Research suggests that if institutions kept better track of employee perceptions, they would frequently hear about excessive workloads—

another organizational problem of the higher education workplace. Decades of research substantiate the toll of rising job responsibilities and performance expectations for tenured and tenure-track faculty, contributing to stress and burnout.[40] These costs are at least partially offset by perks like autonomy and job security, which isn't the case for contingent faculty, research faculty, and postdoctoral and graduate student employees. Studies show these workers often take on labor beyond the scope of their contract because their roles are ill-defined or they fear saying no will jeopardize their chances of securing stable employment.[41] In a survey of student affairs professionals who left the field, only half of respondents reported that they had enough time to complete work tasks, and 70 percent reported weekend and evening work commitments.[42]

Workloads for some employees have increased because there simply aren't enough of them to complete all the work. In his ethnography of campus custodians, higher education scholar Peter Magolda demonstrated how two universities sought to minimize labor costs through consolidated shifts, outsourcing, and layoffs, which are "politically and administratively easier" among custodians compared to other personnel.[43] A 2017 report by the National Education Association similarly showed widespread declines in the number of support professionals in higher education since the 2008 recession, leading to increased workloads. As Mila's story revealed, administrative support staff have been ground zero for layoffs and reorganizations in pursuit of efficiencies. The pandemic exacerbated many of these issues, as there were new and unforeseen job demands, mixed with budget cuts and turnover, that saddled remaining employees with more work.

Sociologists Laura T. Hamilton and Kelly Nielsen explained how excessive workloads and understaffing have become a feature of public colleges and universities that have been subjected to decades of fiscal austerity.[44] They linked policies that result in reduced public spending on higher education to neoliberalism, which they defined as "a moral and economic ideology, a set of policies and practices, and a broader social imaginary that supports the deflation of public spending on social welfare and the intensification of private market competition."[45] Their analysis showed that neoliberal-driven austerity has forced real financial pressures that leaders must contend with, but also that decision-making reflects "cultural logics of austerity."[46] Hamilton and Nielsen defined logics as "the cultural values, beliefs, and normative expectations that people within organizations use to organize their activities in time and space."[47] Regardless of what the numbers in the annual budget show, leaders who rose the ranks under austerity are more likely to buy into the idea that resources are always scarce, operations are always too costly, and the most prudent course of action is to wean institutions off of state support.

Hamilton and Nielsen refer to this way of thinking as "austerity administration," which has led to practices like making enrollment growth a strategic priority and cutting labor costs. Both of these practices, in turn, influence the beliefs about institutional mission and norms related to investments. And they cropped up in institutional policy that governed workload. Hamilton and Nielsen detailed one university's official policy of "tolerable suboptimization," which was an effort to address the excessive workloads of employees by reducing services to a tolerably low level rather than hiring more people. As a result, "even highly skilled and well-intentioned staff members faltered under the weight of high caseloads and insufficient resources."[48] Although this was official policy at one institution, Hamilton and Nielsen pointed out that "it was hardly alone in the use of austerity practices as a means of organizational survival."[49] In fact, across my interviews, a recurring theme was that employees felt they were expected to do more even while staffing levels were flat or falling. Organizational cultures and structures that developed under austerity help to explain the origins of these mounting demands.

Discrimination and Oppression of Marginalized Employees

A final example of the kind of problem that workers are experiencing manifests in patterns of discrimination and oppression of marginalized employees that lead to inequitable workplace experiences and outcomes. Despite being critiqued for advancing a diversity, equity, and inclusion (DEI) "agenda" or "bureaucracy,"[50] the reality is that many colleges and universities have made slow progress toward ensuring that the composition of their staff, faculty, and leaders reflect the diversity of US society.[51] For most of its centuries-long existence, higher education was the exclusive domain of wealthy white men.[52] Efforts to address this history of exclusion have often centered on increasing access for minoritized student populations. Consequently, more people of color are pursuing higher education than ever before, while the diversity of staff and faculty lags.[53] Take your pick of positions at most colleges and universities with the greatest status, authority, and earning potential, and chances are they are dominated by white men.[54]

Beyond issues of compositional diversity, many colleges and universities are simply not welcoming spaces for workers of marginalized identities. Higher education scholar Sonja Ardoin has demonstrated that "workplaces, including the academy, are classed spaces, which typically expect all employees to abide by middle- or upper-class ways of being."[55] Scholars have also shown that racism is an everyday experience for faculty and staff of color, which can lead to "racial battle fatigue" or the "emotional, psychological, and physiological stress responses from racism."[56] Pursuing a career in higher education can require moving away from families and supportive communities and forcing employees to live where there are few (if any) people who look like them or can understand their experience.

Campus climate for lesbian, gay, bisexual, and trans* faculty and staff is often hostile, with trans* employees reporting higher rates of harassment than cisgender employees.[57] Higher education scholars Jonathan T. Pryor and Garrett D. Hoffman found that LGBTQ+ student affairs staff confronted the conditions of what they call traditionally heterogendered institutions, such as isolation and tokenization, leaders lacking preparation and cultural competency, and dissonance between professional obligations and the activism they felt was necessary in their roles.[58] Although many institutions are paying attention to creating a sense of belonging among students, they are not putting the same energy into helping marginalized workers who might feel excluded from campus communities.

Researchers have tended to focus on discrimination and inequality at the societal and individual levels, viewing organizations as relatively race-, class-, and gender-neutral. But sociologist Joan Acker argued that "much of the social and economic inequality in the United States and other industrialized countries is created in organizations, in the daily activities of working and organizing work."[59] Workplaces contain "inequality regimes," which are "interrelated practices, processes, actions, and meanings that result in and maintain class, gender, and racial inequalities within particular organizations."[60] Inequality regimes are possible even in organizations with explicit DEI goals, taking shape in the form of systematic disparities over workplace decisions, opportunities for promotion, security in employment, compensation, and respect. Identifying and analyzing the impact of inequality regimes means recognizing that there are compounding forms of oppression at the intersection of marginalized identities.

In the same vein, sociologist Victor Ray theorized that organizations are racialized, meaning they "limit the personal agency and collective efficacy of subordinate racial groups while magnifying the agency of the dominant racial group."[61] Racialized organizations legitimate the unequal distribution of resources based on race; at one time, they even used overt methods like segregation. Whiteness is a credential in racialized organizations, providing access to resources and granting certain employees easier claims to "merit" and latitude for making errors. Lastly, racialized organizations do not couple their often public commitment to DEI with the enactment of policies and practices that could upend racial hierarchies. This decoupling allows organizations to present themselves as progressive even while doing little to advance racial equity. It didn't take long for scholars to map the characteristics of racialized organizations onto higher education as a way of explaining various issues, such as resource disparities between and within institutions and color-blind hiring practices.[62]

These are but a smattering of the problems that higher education employees encounter, and I'll revisit them and others with more nuance in subsequent chapters. But they reveal how the burnout, disengagement, and demoralization driving the Great Resignation in higher education can be traced back to structural and cultural features of colleges and universities. In short, if (as the four-time chancellor suggested) we should "take charge" of something, I propose we stop "whining" that employees today are coddled, entitled, or lacking resilience and instead focus on the organization-level structures and cultures that are undermining employee well-being.

Applying Organizational Thinking to Change Management

According to higher education scholars Peter Eckel and Adrianna Kezar, deep change alters the culture of the institution and its behaviors, pervades the organization, and is intentional.[63] This type of change is often long term and can't be achieved by following a simple recipe or relying on a heroic figure, no matter how admirable their vision might be.[64] If leaders really want to make lasting change, then applying organizational thinking can help them manage deep change processes.

Too often, books about reimagining higher education fail to consider the thorny question of *how* to bring about change, especially change premised on shifting mindsets and fostering the ongoing commitment of multiple stakeholders. The six organizational changes that comprise the Caring University integrate insights from theorists of organizational change that can guide leaders through ethical, successful change processes specifically designed to improve working conditions and cultures in higher education (Box 1.2).

Organizational change often necessitates helping individuals make sense of and, in some cases, challenge their mental models. The goal is to shift mindsets, which leads to changed priorities and behaviors. Kezar has identified approaches to organizational change that are particularly well suited for addressing such deep changes: social cognition theories and cultural theories.[65] The first is *sensemaking*, which is premised on the idea that workers understand organizations in disparate ways, and effective change hinges on helping employees "craft, understand, and accept new conceptualizations of the organization" before they participate in a change process. In practice, this looks like creating ways for employees to explore "what change initiatives mean for their roles and responsibilities, their identity within an organization, and their

Box 1.2

Key Insights from Organizational Change Theorists for Leaders Engaging in Deep Change

- Appreciate the complexity of colleges and universities as organizations.
- Acknowledge that employees have different understandings of the organization and their place within it.
- Create opportunities for employees to understand and shift their mindsets through ongoing campus conversations, cross-departmental working groups, and strategic and consistent language.
- Facilitate workers' learning by implementing an enhanced data infrastructure, offering professional development, and fostering collaborative teams.
- Recognize the expertise of employees and build on their existing knowledge.
- Create conditions for employees to ask questions, share concerns, cast doubt, and for leaders to listen, provide full explanations, and admit mistakes.
- Encourage an ethical process in which leaders step inside the shoes of employees, broadly share information, promote participation—even among those likely to disagree—and provide a realistic valuation of the change.
- Account for institutional culture and history by aligning with healthy values and incorporating important rituals, symbols, and language.

overall perspective of the organization."[66] It also takes shape in opportunities to rethink the meaning of existing concepts, like "merit" and what it means to be a "good worker," and by facilitating the development of new language to describe organizations, such as being a "caring campus." Scaling new mindsets from individuals to the organization requires repeated effort—and time. Leaders can encourage sensemaking through ongoing campus conversations, cross-departmental working groups, strategic and consistent language, and professional development to help employees wrestle with their former and new understanding of an issue.

Another approach to facilitating deep change is through *organizational learning*, which is premised on the idea that individuals can sometimes be stubborn in adhering to mental models of the past but also want to fix problems and errors once they understand them. The key, then, is to help employees learn—and learn in a positive direction—through the creation of enhanced data infrastructure, training, and collaborative teams. Change becomes much more successful when it recognizes the expertise that workers already have and builds on knowledge within the organization. In order for learning to occur, employees must be able to convey doubt and be skeptical, and leaders need some latitude to make mistakes and change direction. Kezar notes that organizational learning is easier said than done, and even an organization whose business is learning isn't inherently a learning organization. But both sensemaking and organizational learning, especially when paired together, can help to address resistance and "organizational defense routines" like cynicism, politics, and ego by creating conditions for people to ask questions, challenge their mental models, and grow—often in teams and small groups.

Sometimes staff, faculty, and students are suspicious of change efforts because of previous change processes they perceived to be unethical. Some of the most common ethical problems in organizational change include top-down change that serves management's interests, overselling the value of change, hiding or concealing data, and excluding individuals likely to raise challenges. The best way for leaders to bring about organizational change is through an ethical process characterized by broad information-sharing and stakeholder participation, acknowledgment of differing values and interests, and following procedures and pursuing outcomes that are seen as fair. Employees are more likely to "get on board" with an organizational change process when they are treated well during the process. This includes treating workers with respect, listening to concerns, and providing full explanations for decisions. This latter point should be underlined because it is often the case that organizational hierarchy and decentralization get in the way of information traveling to all parts of the institution. According to Kezar, these are central tenets of approaching change through the lens of *organizational justice*. This approach pushes leaders to demonstrate care for employees by stepping into their shoes before making choices.

All three of these approaches in different ways get at the heart of entrenched structural problems and organizational complexity because they are responsive to culture. Culture has been mentioned numerous times in this chapter, and that's because culture is a key part of the change process and outcome that I am advocating. Higher education scholar William Tierney defined organizational culture as the "shared assumptions of individuals participating in the organization":

> Often taken for granted by the actors themselves, these assumptions can be identified through stories, special language, norms, institutional ideology, and attitudes that emerge from individual and organizational behavior.[67]

Tierney cautioned that many leaders only pay attention to organizational culture once its assumptions have been transgressed and the resulting conflict leads to crisis. Although leaders face tough decisions, they often have more than one choice at their disposal. Leaders can select from several viable options, and having a grasp of organizational culture helps them decide which has the best chance of succeeding.

Research shows that organizational change is more successful when leaders consider institutional culture and history. This means that effective change agents must be able to step outside the culture enough to see it through the eyes of a researcher, learning the history of the organization and identifying what values (real and aspirational) guide behaviors. Cultural theories of change direct leaders to consider and modify shared meanings along multiple levels, from the mission statement to campus rituals, and to use existing symbols or events in novel ways that affirm healthy norms and values. Importantly, many colleges and universities are large enough organizations that there are subcultures, and it's possible for two units or departments at the same institution to have different workplace cultures.

If some of this sounds a little nebulous, Tierney provided a useful list of questions to parse the culture of an organization. Here are a few:

- What is the mission? How is it articulated? Is it the basis for decisions here?
- How are new members socialized? What is needed to survive/excel here?
- What constitutes information? Who has it? How is it disseminated?

- How are decisions arrived at? Who makes decisions? What is the penalty for bad decisions?
- Who are considered leaders? What does the organization expect of leaders?

If leaders wanted to take an anthropological approach to studying their organizations, answering these questions is a good starting point.

From Awareness to Action

We do so much more than they see. Mila's powerful words about the exploitation of administrative support professionals stuck with me. They remind me of one of my favorite quotes, which comes from David Foster Wallace's commencement speech at Kenyon College in 2005: "There are these two young fish swimming along and they happen to meet an older fish swimming the other way, who nods at them and says, 'Morning, boys. How's the water?' And the two young fish swim on for a bit, and then eventually one of them looks over at the other and goes, 'What the hell is water?'"[68]

The structures and cultures within organizations—which shape everyday workplace policies, practices, and norms—are the water in which higher education employees swim. They are forces "hidden in plain sight all around us, all the time," making them easy to escape our notice in the day-to-day bustle of our working lives. But once we become aware of the water we are swimming in—the type of awareness that comes with thinking organizationally—we can see that Mila's experience reflects the experiences of many. We see that Mila and her colleagues' overlooked labor is not just a part of a pattern or even a recurring theme; rather, it is a defining characteristic of colleges and universities. If we really adopt an organizational lens, before long we are able to look around our institutions and—to borrow from David Foster Wallace again—see what's been right in front of our eyes the whole time: "This is water. This is water."

I promised in the introductory chapter that this book would not be a compendium of complaints—that we didn't have to dwell on problems.

But I also cautioned leaders that they can't rush into the "future of work" or skip ahead to the solutions without truly understanding the organizational cultures and structures in higher education that caused the Great Resignation.

Awareness is not the end but only the beginning of deep organizational change. Equipped with a better sense of our institutions as organizations and workplaces, we can begin to craft a new conceptualization—the Caring University—and take action.

CHAPTER 2

Making the Employee Experience a Strategic Priority

ON A SUNNY MORNING IN LATE MAY, I boarded a plane for Amarillo, Texas. My destination was Amarillo College (AC), a community college with five campuses in the Texas Panhandle that has earned a national reputation for "going the extra mile" to support the success of low-income students through its "Culture of Caring."[1] Just a few weeks shy of my visit, Amarillo won the 2023 Aspen Prize for Community College Excellence, which former President Barack Obama once called "the Oscars for great community colleges."[2] But it was the Culture of Caring more than the "Oscar buzz" that brought me to the college.

I have been following Amarillo since 2018, when I read a case study that praised the college for "undertaking an intentional cultural shift to focus on students' basic needs, committing to ongoing staff education on the challenges facing impoverished students, and striving to fully incorporate lessons learned into institutional programs and policies."[3] What I have more recently learned is that Amarillo's "cultural shift" didn't happen all at once—it was an organizational change a decade in the making.

Back in 2010, AC joined local schools, businesses, and nonprofits in a data collection effort to understand the city's rising poverty and declining educational attainment rates. The college used the assessment as an excuse to mine its data to answer a related set of questions: *Who are our students? What are their educational goals? What stands in their way?* A handbook that Amarillo later developed didn't mince words about the outcome of this self-reflection: "Our data did not paint a pretty picture of student success."[4] Of the roughly 11,000 students enrolled at the college, less than 40 percent returned to their studies the following fall, and the rate of students finishing a two-year course of study within three years barely hit double digits. Although 80 percent declared a transfer major, only 10 percent transferred to a university that grants bachelor's degrees.

Soon thereafter, the college hosted a data summit for all staff and faculty to process the findings of its analysis and collectively consider what it meant for Amarillo's future. The summit was just the start of what became a campus routine of systematically reviewing data. Amarillo supplemented its existing data with surveys, focus groups, and "secret shoppers"—students tasked with using campus services and then sharing their experiences. All this data collection was aimed at better understanding what prevented students from attaining a degree and how the college could change its practices to meet their needs.

The college's leaders were surprised to learn that the main roadblocks students identified were not things that happened inside the classroom; rather, they were challenges related to childcare, food security, affordable housing, mental health care, and transportation. Amarillo College's answer to this revelation—what it calls its theory of change—was to take responsibility for the "whole student" and tackle the challenges they face because of poverty. As the handbook explains, "If Amarillo College removes poverty barriers for our students in an accelerated learning environment while providing a deep culture of caring, students will be successful and complete their educational goal."[5] The college boiled this statement down to its core purpose: "We love our students to success."

I immediately perked up when I read the Culture of Caring handbook and revisited the case study that first introduced me to Amarillo. My highlighter hardly left the page as I traced *data summit, campus routine, systematically reviewing data, intentional culture shift, ongoing staff edu-*

cation, and *incorporating lessons into programs and policies*. It sounded like an example of a college dedicated to organizational learning as an approach to making deep change—and a change specifically premised on care. Saying I was energized to learn more would be putting it mildly.

But most of what I read talked about caring for *students* and supporting their success. I wondered if the Culture of Caring for which Amarillo has earned accolades applied to employees and the extent to which it had been integrated into the institution's mission, values, and strategic priorities. I decided to see things for myself and lined up a full schedule of interviews with staff, faculty, and Amarillo's president at the time, Russell Lowery-Hart. Then I prepped my interview questions, packed my bags, and headed for the "Yellow Rose of Texas."

A Culture of Caring

I was on the last flight into Amarillo and deplaned in a late-night stupor. Although I wasn't in the mood for small talk, my affable ride-share driver asked if I was in town for business. After telling him I was there to visit AC, he immediately replied: "Best community college in the country." I've had some ride-share drivers tell me what they studied in college or offer their opinions about student loan debt. But I can't recall any expressing effusive praise for their local community college. "I know the president there," my driver added. "Met him at a volunteer thing. Nice guy." *That* was definitely a first.

It was one of several moments in which I found myself thinking *this place is different*. I had that thought after the director of the academic support services told me that university policy allowed employees to bring their children to the office, after which she handed me an Amarillo College coloring book to take home to my children. I thought about it a few minutes later when the director of retention introduced me to her daughter, who also worked at the college and was feeding breakfast to her infant son—three generations in one office. I thought about it when I met the dean of the science, technology, engineering, and mathematics (STEM) department and her eyes welled up as she described nearing retirement and leaving an institution that meant so much to the community. And I thought about it once more when the director of the bookstore launched into an impromptu discussion of his efforts to help adult learners make friends through board game nights.

By the time I met with Russell Lowery-Hart for a long lunch later that day, I didn't need much convincing that the Culture of Caring was alive among the workers I interviewed. I could hear it in the no-hesitation responses to my questions and see it exemplified in the way they warmly greeted students and interacted with each other. Even among faculty, a notoriously hard group to win over, I heard expressions of pride in what the institution stood for and their desire to continue advancing its mission. In my short time on campus, I could feel that caring was more than a slogan—it was the lifeblood of the college. What surprised me, however, was that this culture took shape during one of Amarillo's most painful periods.

Early in his tenure as president, Lowery-Hart received notice that a relatively small budget shortfall at the college was about to get worse. In 2015, the state cut instructional funding for community colleges, and Amarillo was suddenly over $3 million in the hole. To save money, the college offered an early retirement package to eligible employees, which helped fill the hole but wasn't enough to keep jobs from being eliminated.[6] Although Lowery-Hart bombarded employees with information about Amarillo's enrollment and costs during town hall meetings, state law placed heavy restrictions on how much he could publicly talk about employment actions. Immediately after the meetings, he retreated to his office or car to avoid questions.

"I made a lot of mistakes," Lowery-Hart recalled. "People were scared and wanted to know if their jobs were safe, and I didn't have the courage to look at them and say I didn't know or couldn't say." Rumors quickly filled the void, fueled by the local newspaper for which the budget cut was big news. Many people I interviewed at the college described this as a low point for employee morale. And Lowery-Hart couldn't deny that it weighed heavily on him, too. "I didn't approach it with a 'crisis is a terrible thing to waste' mindset. But I did want to honor the crisis. I wanted to honor the people who retired early and make sure this never happens again."

The college had no choice but to change, and Lowery-Hart turned to students to help. He engaged a small group of Amarillo's students to share what the perfect college looked and felt like to them. He asked these students to name companies known for relationships and excellent customer service, then they looked up the values for each of those companies. Students narrowed down 53 values to five that really spoke to them. Lowery-Hart saw in these five values direction for *how* Amarillo and its employees could take responsibility for the whole student.

By the fall of 2016, Amarillo's budget was back in the black, and Lowery-Hart was feeling triumphant. The worst period in his career seemed to be in the rearview mirror. He chose the general assembly with staff and faculty to share the students' vision of the perfect college and propose Amarillo's new values:

- Caring through WOW:
  Every student and colleague will say "Wow, you were so helpful, supporting, and open" after an interaction with us.
- Caring through FUN:
  We will find ways to have fun with each other and celebrate each other.
  We will find ways to make our work fun and effective.
- Caring through INNOVATION:
  We will see ourselves as a "roadblock remover," for students and for each other.
  We will always look for ways to help others and improve our processes.
- Caring through FAMILY:
  We will find ways to show we care about our students and each other.
  We will readily and effectively share information with each other.
  We will approach our interactions with each other with trust and openness.
  We will put the needs of others before our own.

- Caring through YES:
  We will think "yes" first and find solutions rather than finding "no." We will be passionate about our jobs and helping each other.

When he looked at the staff and faculty in attendance at the general assembly, their response was not exactly celebratory. Some faculty thought that the values were silly. A few long-time employees had not recovered from the pain of losing colleagues and had lost faith in the college. Lowery-Hart realized that introducing new values was just the start of a long road to rebuilding Amarillo's culture.

His first step was to create more avenues for employees to share their opinions with him. Whether through one-on-one meetings or regular anonymous surveys, Lowery-Hart had to face the hard questions he had avoided and listen as employees poured out their frustrations and fears. He had to acknowledge what the cuts and silence had meant for the college's employees.

Some of Amarillo's budget problems came from siloed departments that were not sharing information. To foster collaboration and build college-wide affinity to the new values, Lowery-Hart launched an annual innovation challenge, where upwards of 70 teams of employees from different parts of the college proposed new ideas to bring one of the college's values to fruition. Not all the ideas have been successful, but Lowery-Hart says that's not the point. The objective is to build cross-departmental teams and brainstorm about how Amarillo's values can fit into their practice. In the same vein, Lowery-Hart asked groups representing different types of employees to generate guidelines for hiring and evaluating employees based on the college's values. The goal is to ensure that the values aren't just lip service but are built on what employees already expect from one another.

Leaders at Amarillo turned the next seven years into an extended exercise in organizational learning. They introduced new data to inform decision-making and strategic priorities, as well as new language and symbols to conceptualize what it means to support students. And they infused jobs with opportunities to learn and grow in a positive direction. Lowery-Hart sent various leaders of the college to tour the online shoe company Zappos and learn about the importance of organizational culture. He also developed his own leadership institute, which brings together employees up and down the organizational chart to advance their leadership skills and work through management case studies with seasoned community college leaders.

In 2022, Lowery-Hart took around 70 leaders on a "Love × Learning" retreat, where they had time to relax and have fun while also dreaming up "moonshot" ideas to improve campus systems. As Lowery-Hart explained in the invitation to the retreat: "The last five years were about ensuring our processes were responsive and our systems aligned. . . . Now, we must build beyond these processes and reimagine these systems to ensure our students multiply our love for them into new, deeper, and applied experiences of learning."[7]

The sense I got in talking with staff and faculty was that Amarillo was not a place where employees were expected to simply absorb the values written on banners they walk by on campus. There were intentional efforts to help employees understand what the college is all about, how it wants to operate when it is at its best, and what that means for individual workers. The skeptic in me asked Lowery-Hart if bringing about this organizational change was easier because Amarillo has benefited from financial gifts that go beyond what's typical for a community college. In 2021, the college received a $15 million donation from billionaire MacKenzie Scott. But Lowery-Hart explained that the gift came *after* most elements of the change process were underway. In other words, the financial resources and awards flowed from the organizational change, not the other way around.

The Culture of Caring isn't a panacea, nor is Amarillo a perfect organization. Lowery-Hart told me that caring is not a substitute for sufficient compensation. Although the college has increased pay in recent years, the reality is that some employees are just barely making ends meet. Faculty members shared with me that they don't love every change, and sometimes they would like more opportunities to be part of the decision-making process. Amarillo still has turnover, and staff and faculty struggled during the pandemic—enough that the college used federal pandemic relief funds to hire a nonsectarian corporate chaplain to attend to the mental health of staff and faculty. But now that relief funds have expired, the college has fewer resources to support students and employees.

Still, it is hard to deny that Amarillo has developed something of a "winning formula" by making care a strategic priority. The college has won just about every award imaginable, from marketing to board relations and innovation. Between 2013 and 2018, the college saw a 75 percent increase in the number of first-generation students completing a degree or certificate and a 64 percent increase in the number of Pell-eligible students completing their studies. Individual course pass rates increased 110 percent for Hispanic students, 112 percent for African American students, and 108 percent for students overall. The numbers don't lie, yet I haven't seen many colleges and universities attempting to replicate Amarillo's success. Lowery-Hart conceded that, especially among colleges and universities that offer bachelor's degrees, there was a reluctance to harness the potential of caring as a path to organizational success.

In this chapter, I explore why institutions are reluctant to connect the employee experience with goals that underpin organizational performance, such as student success. I show how many institutions don't include employees in their mission, vision, and value statements. The employee experience is also a low priority in the strategic plans of many colleges and universities, and many institutions have limited knowledge of their employees, including information about who employees are, how they perceive the workplace, and how much they are working. In the second half of the chapter, I explain three organization-level approaches that take inspiration from the concept of talent management and are designed to make the employee experience a strategic priority.

In short, this chapter encourages leaders to explicitly involve employees in creating the formative texts that guide their institution, including its purpose, future plans, resources, and operations. Leaders must better understand who their employees are and what they experience on the job. And they need to monitor employee workload and commit to actions that relieve staff and faculty who are stretched to the limits.

Why Are Employees Absent from Institutional Guiding Documents?

People are working at colleges and universities at all hours, practically every day. Although most staff generally work during regular business hours, student affairs professionals manage programs on evenings and weekends and respond to emergencies late into the night. Similarly, someone from campus police or security sees the sun rise with landscapers trying to get a jump on summer heat or custodians de-icing sidewalks before students trek to class. Of course, faculty will tell you they work nonstop. That's not entirely true, but it is the case that courses increasingly run from morning until night, with some scheduled on weekends. As someone who teaches working professionals, I have taught classes until almost 10 p.m. and on Saturdays. And all our inboxes seem to be working overtime, with messages arriving 24/7.

Despite the round-the-clock work to make higher education happen, locating employees in an institution's guiding documents (i.e., its mission, vision, and values statements) or in its strategic priorities is not easy. The absence of any mention of employees in the campus mission, vision setting, and strategic planning is one sign of a larger workplace problem as outlined in Chapter 1: neglecting the employee experience. With the help of a graduate student, I reviewed a random sample of values statements and strategic plans at 50 institutions of various types and interviewed numerous experts. This effort led me to conclude that many colleges and universities primarily see higher education in terms of institutional inputs and outputs: Which students enroll, which faculty are hired, and how do they fare on outcomes of interest? The *labor* that people perform while teaching, programming, advising, and creating is left out of the equation. Among the many strategic goals that colleges and universities often establish, few indicate a sense of responsibility for employee well-being. In fact, only seven of the 50 institutions whose statements and plans we reviewed explicitly mentioned staff and faculty well-being. Only two stated that fostering a culture of care was a priority.

A college or university's mission and vision are usually too short and broad for employees to receive more than a passing mention. After all, these statements are supposed to briefly convey why the institution exists and where it would like to be in five or ten years.[8] In fact, mission statements are often criticized for being so generic they don't say anything useful about the institution's identity or direction.[9] By contrast, values statements are supposed to be a little different. They should articulate the principles that guide the institution, form part of its culture, and reflect the way goals are pursued.[10] In many ways, values statements are supposed to capture *how* an institution will operate. It is jarring, then, that values statements in higher education so infrequently reference the labor on which the whole enterprise depends. Instead, they tend to be little more than a collection of all-purpose words or phrases, such as "collaboration," "free inquiry," and "respect for all people."

I considered the possibility that organizations outside higher education tend to foreground what they create or aim to accomplish in their values statements. Russell Lowery-Hart and AC students learned a thing or two by exploring companies known for relationships and customer service. When I read the values statements of major companies, I picked up on another theme: they often speak about current employees when they communicate their values to prospective employees. For example, Apple profiles 12 employees on its website that exemplify its shared values, the first of which is the company's respect for well-being.[11] The supermarket chain Wegmans notes on its website that while its goal is "to be the very best at serving the needs of our customers," the company believes it "can achieve our goal only if we fulfill the needs of our people."[12] Starbucks emphasizes its culture of inclusion on its website and how "your entire experience—starting with your application—is designed to be the beginning of an inspirational journey, where you are treated warmly and with transparency, dignity, and respect."[13]

My point is not that colleges and universities should necessarily co-opt the guiding documents of major companies. Rather, it is simply to observe that there is no law prohibiting institutions from bringing employees into their values. And doing so can pay dividends. After conducting dozens of studies on the effects of corporate values, business professors Paul Ingram and Yoonjin Choi discovered: "When you align your organization's values with both your strategy and the values of your employees—

creating what we call *values alignment*—you reap all sorts of benefits: higher job satisfaction, lower turnover, better teamwork, more effective communication, bigger contributions to the organization, more productive negotiations, and, perhaps surprisingly, more diversity, equity, and inclusion."[14] In other words, values serve a powerful purpose and shouldn't just be a bunch of nice-sounding keywords.

Employees are more visible in an institution's strategic priorities and associated goals than its mission, vision, and values statements. But even in strategic plans, the emphasis is often on what employees are expected to do in service of students or organizational performance targets. And some employees are more present than others. A 2011 analysis of strategic plans for the top 200 universities according to the *Times Higher Education* rankings showed that the most common themes (in order of prevalence) were research (primarily as a marker of status), students (primarily in terms of recruitment), faculty (primarily in reference to hiring top scholars and building research facilities), academics (primarily focused on challenging curricula and preparing students for the future), and internationalization.[15] I saw these themes on display in my own review of plans. They often emphasized academic excellence, with specific goals related to enrollment, student success, and faculty impact measured through publications, sponsored research, and awards. Any mention of staff was astonishingly rare, and it was not unusual to see colleges and universities giving more attention to construction projects in their strategic plans than employee well-being.

Employees are sometimes included in strategic priorities related to becoming a "magnet for talent," a "destination college town," or an "inclusive environment." But when I dug into the details of these priorities, I learned that "talent" often refers to recruiting faculty instead of staff, becoming a "destination" college town is more about enticing prospective students and being their "first-choice" against competitors, and "inclusive" often means institution-wide student and faculty diversity more than the extent to which employees and students feel a sense of belonging. In each of these cases, one or two goals connected to strategic priorities may focus on employees, while the other ten focus on students. A tiny fraction of the strategic priorities and related goals that I reviewed explicitly mentioned well-being on campus. Yet even among these select few, the objectives tied to well-being centered on student access to mental health support, engagement with the community, and campus recreation. Many well-being goals implicated staff and faculty labor but did not attend to their well-being.

Of course, the absence of some activity among an institution's strategic priorities does not mean it isn't happening or isn't important. Nevertheless, strategic priorities are designed to give organizations focus and make decisions about where to invest often scarce resources.[16] As Michael Moss, executive director of the Society for College and University Planning, explained to me in an interview, strategic priorities enshrine a set of goals in writing and establish implementation plans designed to keep an organization moving forward. But when it comes to creating organizational cultures and structures so that employees can do their best work, colleges and universities are frequently building without a blueprint.

You Can't Know What You Don't Ask

One of the challenges of crafting strategic priorities is that they ideally should be tied to goals that can be quantitatively or qualitatively assessed to show improvement over time. Many strategic plans that I reviewed gravitate toward goals for which numerical data are readily available, such as student success or institutional finances. By contrast, many colleges and universities have limited data about their employees, especially data related to employee well-being. The trend of using data analytics to support enrollment management and student success has not been widely applied to support human resource management in higher education.[17]

To be sure, colleges and universities do not have a problem providing "directory information" on staff and faculty—how many people are employed in various job categories, how much they are paid, and where they live. But answering questions beyond this information is tricky for many colleges and universities. For example, when it comes to tracking the race and gender identity of employees, institutional practices can be inconsistent and outdated. In some cases, colleges and universities adhere to reporting conventions imposed by the federal government, which means they use a limited number of categories for race and may not have options for people who identify as biracial or multiracial. Similarly, many institutions still conflate gender and sex or use the gender binary, meaning institutions misgender their employees and report inaccurate data, sometimes even resorting to making an educated guess and assigning the employee a gender for reporting purposes.

Kiernan Mathews, who developed two faculty surveys as the principal investigator of the Collaborative on Academic Careers in Higher Education (COACHE) and is now executive director of the Ivy+ Faculty Advancement Network, told me that part of the challenge of cross-institutional collaboration is to develop a "lingua franca" around faculty diversity: "There's the simple question of, 'Can we please use the same gender categories when we collect data across institutions?' Well, some are struggling to do even that *within* their institutions." This is because colleges and universities often have multiple systems for collecting and using employee data—one might be for payroll, for instance, while another is for performance management. These systems do not always "speak" to each other and can use different categories for identities. As an experiment, Mathews once asked several institutions whether they could generate a list of where faculty received their terminal degrees. "You'd think this was a simple question," he explained, "but, sure enough, one institution said they could have a report in 15 minutes, and another jokingly said they'd have to count the colors on robes at commencement."

When collected correctly, "directory information" can be useful for answering questions about pay or providing a portrait of the racial composition of staff and faculty, but it doesn't capture the employee experience. To get at that, colleges and universities commonly rely on engagement or climate surveys. Although they are sometimes used interchangeably, these two types of surveys have distinct functions. According to the Society for Human Resource Management (SHRM), engagement surveys "measure employees' commitment, motivation, and sense of purpose and passion for their work and organization."[18] Climate surveys measure the opinions and perceptions that employees have of the organization and workplace environment, and many of these surveys in higher education focus on the climate for diversity, equity, and inclusion. I think of engagement surveys as focused on how employees feel about their *work*, while climate surveys target how they feel about the *workplace*.

One thing that engagement and climate surveys have in common is that they are deployed episodically. Some institutions administer them annually; others may only collect data every three or five years. The challenge is that a lot can happen in the span of three or five years (like a global pandemic). Todd Benson, the executive director of COACHE, told me that in some cases, spacing out surveys is purposeful. It gives institutions a chance to promote robust participation and time to act before the next survey is launched. Still, engagement surveys reflect a particular moment in institutional life. Liz Gross, who is the CEO of Campus Sonar, a company that analyzes social media to gain insights about how stakeholders view institutions, put it to me this way in an interview: "If you give the climate survey and nothing 'bad' has happened in the last four months, you might get a very different result than if you gave it the week after something was blowing up on campus."

Engagement surveys can be a great tool for measuring *engagement*, but that is just one way of conceptualizing the employee experience. Brad Shuck, an expert on employee engagement, explained in our interview that "stress and engagement can live in the same space," meaning workers can be dialed into a particular project while also experiencing constant stress that leads to burnout. He clarified that engagement isn't the same as whether an employee feels included or thinks the workplace is equitable. Getting a fuller picture of the employee experience often requires dialogue. Mary Opperman, the former chief human resource officer for Cornell University, noted:

> We did learn some good lessons during COVID. One of them is you really have to talk to people, and then you have to give them a chance to tell you what they're thinking. Engagement surveys . . . are very one way. You'll get some people who will take the time to give you comments, but nothing is quite like . . . [the] opportunity for people to engage and talk through in a deep way what's happening for them and what they really need.[19]

Another tool that colleges and universities use to understand the employee experience is exit surveys or interviews—basically asking employees about their experience as they leave to take another job. In my interviews with staff and faculty who have left higher education, some had no knowledge of being able to officially share their reasons for leaving, while others felt that the onus was on them to initiate an exit interview. No one felt confident that institutions would use the data, reducing their inclination to go out of their way to participate. The obvious problem, then, is that information from exit interviews is collected too late to improve the experience of the person who is leaving. Kiernan Mathews, who studied the use of exit surveys in higher education when COACHE developed its Faculty Retention and Exit Survey, confirmed this point: "There was very little being done with exit surveys or interviews. . . . In fact, institutional actors admitted that there was very little being done with them." He shared the story of an associate dean who kept handwritten notes from his exit interviews in a manila folder. Any insights from those interviews were quite literally locked away in a file cabinet.

Ultimately, information on employees collected from surveys and interviews is of little value without sufficient staff and resources to analyze it and translate new knowledge into actions. Some colleges and universities have considerable information on their employees collecting dust on the shelf (or in a database) because there isn't the institutional capacity to do more than collect and store it. According to Jackie Bichsel, the director of research at the College and University Professional Association for Human Resources (CUPA-HR), both institutional research and human resource departments are too bogged down with compulsory reporting to engage in meaningful data collection and analysis. "They are entirely consumed with anything but institutional research," she explained in an interview with me. "All they're doing is filling out these forms for not just the government but every little survey that's out there." The fact that these professionals can't contribute to initiatives in which they have specific training and expertise signals the low value attached to employee data on many campuses.

Both Bichsel and Mathews agree that the siloed nature of colleges and universities presents additional obstacles. As Bichsel put it: "Yes, you need more data analysts. But you also need more of a cross-department, collaborative effort to address these questions. Individuals don't feel empowered to share data across departments. There's still so much siloing—the 'we need to keep this data to ourselves' sort of thing." Keeping a tight lid on data occurs partly out of privacy concerns and a need to comply with regulations that make sharing a burdensome process involving multiple rounds of review and approval. When leaders decide to collect data beyond what is required for compulsory reporting, they sometimes restrict access to that data as a power move or use it selectively to advance particular policies or priorities. And forget about data-sharing between institutions. According to Bichsel, "When it comes right down to it, it's every institution for itself when it comes to using data. You see very few partnerships."

Recognizing the limited capacity of their institutions, some leaders may turn to data collected by the government or professional associations. But this information has significant limitations. One of the main federal data sources in higher education is the Integrated Postsecondary Education Data System, which provides institution-level data and includes several human resource–related variables. These data are aggregated at the institution level, however, and do not say anything about the employee experience. The federal government once collected additional data on faculty and instructional staff, but it stopped running the survey 20 years ago, and the website says that "there are no plans to repeat the study."[20] Some human resource departments are so thinly staffed and overwhelmed with responsibilities that they subscribe to fee-based data analysis services. For example, CUPA-HR offers extensive data and benchmarking on salaries and turnover, provided institutions can pay for the membership. As Bichsel, who leads CUPA-HR's data collection and analysis efforts, reminded me, the membership fee accounts for the fact that it takes significant time and personnel to collect, clean, and present data that institutions may currently lack.

Measuring progress on strategic goals would be difficult for many colleges and universities because of the limited data they collect on the people they employ. Collecting accurate data on the identities and on-the-job experiences of employees and their reasons for leaving is a low bar for organizations to demonstrate care about their workers and a commitment to learning more about them. Yet many colleges and universities fail to reach it. And when the Great Resignation hit higher education, many institutions discovered that they were clueless about the challenges and needs of their employees.

Accepting Employee Workloads as an Institutional Enigma

Strategic priorities can evoke mixed feelings among the higher education workers who will be asked to fulfill those goals. Colleges and universities are known for being more capable of adding services and initiatives than they are at subtracting them, meaning strategic planning can amount to a cycle of piling on new programs that repeats every five to ten years. Many of the staff and faculty that I interviewed described feeling as if job demands continued to accumulate while resources remained the same or declined. My interview data frequently pointed to higher education employees feeling as if their employers didn't comprehend the labor implications for their decisions and didn't act with urgency when workers communicated the toll of an excessive workload.

One engineering professor I interviewed said that as an undergraduate, he learned an important lesson: "You can't run a machine at 100 percent capacity, and you definitely can't run people at 100 percent capacity. You lose efficiency. I really have felt that we aren't properly evaluating how much work it takes to do some of these initiatives. . . . We're just not accurately appreciating what it means for faculty and staff." Colleges and universities have struggled to track how much their employees are working and don't have a good barometer for determining what staffing levels are sufficient to accomplish strategic priorities. Sometimes they launch new initiatives on the backs of existing workers in the hopes of generating resources to then hire enough people to sustain the effort. In these cases, institutions consciously choose to stretch employees to their limits.

Colleges and universities are most attuned to faculty workload, partly because some state legislatures have become focused on maximizing how much time faculty spend teaching to keep institutions accountable to taxpayers. Yet the methods they deploy confuse how much faculty work and the products of their labor. For many policymakers and institutions, faculty workload consists of how many courses faculty teach or how many credit hours their courses produce. Although adjusting this number up or down can have significant workload implications, higher education researchers Barbara Townsend and Vicki Rosser cautioned that products and workload are not the same. They suggest using weekly hours worked as a better measure of workload.[21] In 2014, anthropologist John Ziker asked 30 tenure-track and tenured faculty to complete time diaries, recording minute-by-minute all their activities over a week. Based on these time diaries, faculty in the study worked an average of 61 hours per week.[22]

Getting all faculty to complete time diaries would be an impossible task for colleges and universities, but many of them ask faculty to complete annual activity reports through which they document publications, presentations, grants, committees, and other contributions. If an institution uses a faculty productivity software system, these reports are completed online, and leaders are usually able to pull reports showing averages for publications or service commitments. The upside to these systems is that faculty can update them throughout the year, and they are typically vetted by department chairs and others. The downside is that they still primarily reflect work products versus workload. Nevertheless, higher education researchers KerryAnn O'Meara and colleagues suggest that activity reports can be a useful way to understand what faculty are doing and how much time they are spending on service commitments.[23]

Researchers have tried to measure faculty workload through surveys, asking them to estimate how much time they allocate to various work-related activities.[24] Although these survey findings are less detailed than time diaries, they demonstrate a few clear trends. In particular, faculty workload is increasing, and many faculty are dissatisfied as a result. Women and faculty of color report spending more time on teaching, mentoring, and service, which can slow their advancement and increase stress. Faculty of color are enlisted into what education scholar and higher education leader Bryan Brayboy called "hidden service agendas," such as mentoring students of color, serving on diversity initiatives, and providing representation on committees.[25] Although this labor (at least in principle) could be counted, a key reason that these inequities persist is that departments lack information to promote transparency and hold faculty accountable for doing their fair share of work.[26]

Although colleges and universities do not closely monitor faculty workload, they periodically launch committees and initiatives to review teaching expectations and class sizes. But institutions generally pay far less attention to the workload of contingent faculty, research faculty, and postdoctoral and graduate student employees. According to the American Association of University Professors, many contingent faculty in "part-time" positions teach the equivalent of a full course load.[27] Frequently, they receive payment for each course they teach, but they are also expected to take on administrative tasks or service commitments. These responsibilities are rarely compensated, yet contingent faculty feel they have little choice in the matter because they want to maintain employment and meet their professional ethics. Ill-defined roles or ambiguity in job assignments for these employees lead to them taking on extra labor.[28]

The workload of hourly staff positions is, of course, tracked for compensation purposes. The Fair Standards Labor Act requires institutions to pay hourly staff workers overtime for any work in excess of 40 hours per week. Salaried staff are paid as if they are working 40 hours per week, no matter how much they actually work. One study of attrition from student affairs jobs found that 51 percent of participants reported working excessive hours.[29] The persistence of heavy workloads in student affairs jobs is often justified through appeals to professionalism, an employee's passion for supporting students, and the idea that some jobs are a "lifestyle."[30] But in one survey of 954 student affairs professionals, 54 percent of participants selected unhappiness with working long days and weekends as a top reason professionals leave the field.[31] There is clearly a disconnect between expectations and reality.

Things worsened in 2020 when higher education employees saw their workloads swell during the pandemic. As one faculty member who left higher education in 2022 told me in an interview: "The pandemic exacerbated my feelings of unrest. . . . I found that teaching was more overwhelming because students needed so much and we all had so little to give." The pandemic also intensified workload inequities. Staff of color endured the additional labor and stress of being "essential workers" and supporting marginalized students and communities disproportionately harmed by the virus.[32] Higher education scholars Katherine Cho and Lauren Brassfield found that staff of color at one university felt their job demands increased, not only because of the pivot to online services and the need for additional programming but also because they were frequently tasked with contributing to anti-racism initiatives (particularly following the murder of George Floyd) and navigating everyday experiences with racism.[33]

The bottom line is that the employee experience in higher education has not been a strategic priority for colleges and universities. This is evident in the omission of workers in values statements, the limited data that institutions gather on the employee experience, and the lack of attention to how much employees work or how decisions affect workload. These are not signs of an organization proactively working to support the well-being of employees. What would the alternative look like?

Talent Management as a Strategy for Organizational Success

Many companies have turned to talent management to ensure they have the workforce they need to achieve strategic priorities. Taking a talent management perspective means seeing employees as vital assets whose value to the organization justifies the investment of thought and resources. *Managing* talent refers to the processes that organizations develop to attract, motivate, develop, and retain skilled employees. According to Edward E. Lawler, author of *Reinventing Talent Management*, "An organization's talent is not just employees who are expected to do a job. Talent comprises individuals who differ in what they can do and can learn, and what they want to do. To be effective, organizations need to manage talent in ways that make it a major contributor to their success."[34]

As Box 2.1 explains, organizations with a talent management strategy have integrated talent planning, acquisition, onboarding, performance, learning, and succession into an interconnected system that aligns with strategic priorities. Talent planning refers to organizations having a sense of the workers they have and the workers they need—and creating a plan to bridge any gap between the two through strategic hiring and training. A talent management strategy means identifying—through data—who the high-performing employees are and what is necessary to support and retain them, as well as the offices within the organization where there are staffing shortages or high potential for turnover. Succession planning asks whether the "bench strength" is sufficient for the organization and who the replacement candidates are for current incumbents.[35]

According to the *Talent Management Handbook*, having a talent management strategy includes creating a "widely publicized set of core principles, values, and mutual expectations that guide the behavior of an institution and its people. These stated doctrines depict the type of culture an organization strives to create to achieve its unique portrait of success."[36] Publicized values can be part of an employer's "brand," signaling to workers that this is somewhere they want to work and build a career. This is one way in which talent management increasingly calls on organizations to take the employee experience seriously to retain and grow talent.[37]

Box 2.1

What Is a Talent Management Strategy?

A **talent** perspective means seeing employees as a vital asset whose value to the organization justifies investment of thought and resources.

Talent management is the process of attracting, motivating, developing, and retaining skilled employees to optimize organizational performance.

A **talent management strategy** integrates talent planning, acquisition, onboarding, performance, learning, and succession into strategic planning.

Gallup defined the employee experience as "the journey an employee takes with your organization. It includes every interaction that happens along the employee lifecycle, plus the experiences that involve an employee's role, workspace, manager and well-being."[38] The University of California (UC) developed an integrated talent management model that specifically references the employee experience (Figure 2.1). According to the model: "Human resources and managers work together to guide the employee experience, through every phase of employment—from hire to retirement or transition. The manager delivers guidance through frequent feedback, professional and career development and engagement activities, all of which are aligned with the organization's short- and long-term goals."[39]

UC's model is designed to "provide the tools and structure . . . necessary to hire, deploy, develop and retain the best people in their respective fields," with potential benefits stemming from programming, including higher performance aligned with organizational goals, better retention of top performers, and greater job satisfaction. Figure 2.1 shows UC's model as a continuum that is supported at every stage with talent management analytics.

Though I have just scratched the surface of a concept from which colleges and universities can learn a great deal, I'll be revisiting the parts of talent management strategy related to integration, rewards, professional development, and succession planning in later chapters. But the basic idea is that talent management points to a different way of operating for colleges and universities—one that views making the employee experience a no-brainer for organizational effectiveness. Given that this book is a response to organizational cultures and structures that give rise to workplace problems fueling the Great Resignation, I want to propose three organization-level approaches that use a talent management strategy to prioritize employee well-being. I start with how institutions can better use language, symbols, and values—all of which are central to organizational culture—to demonstrate care.

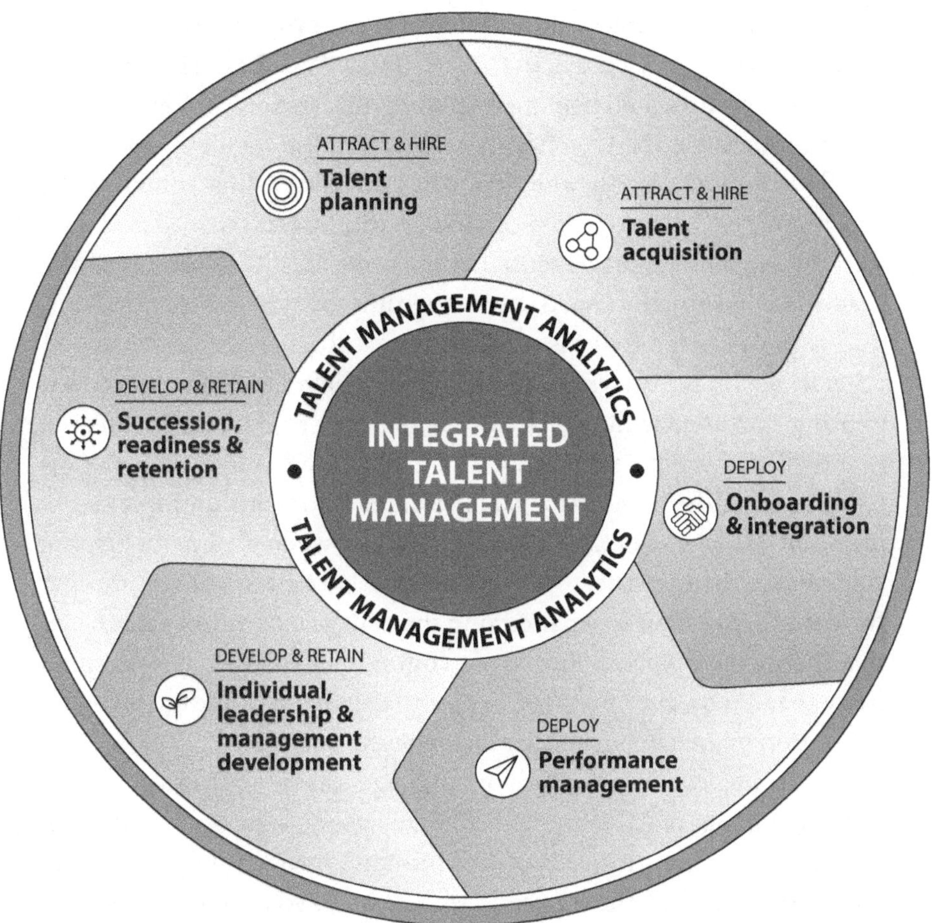

Figure 2.1. *University of California's integrated talent management model (Regents of the University of California)*

Approach 1: Caring Through Language, Symbols, and Values

Language matters in organizational life because, as organizational theorist Karl Weick and colleagues explained, "Organizations . . . are talked into existence."[40] The hectic pace of higher education leadership means that organizations may give short shrift to how writing, discussing, and editing language in the form of meeting agendas, policies, and even emails are "the media through which the invisible hand of institutions shapes conduct."[41] Sensemaking—one of the approaches for deep organizational change discussed in Chapter 1 that informs the Caring University—is premised on helping employees understand and rethink the meaning they ascribe to concepts and facilitating the development of *new language* to describe the organization. By assisting employees in articulating and making sense of their existing mental models and then introducing new language, sensemaking serves as a "way station on the road to a consensually constructed, coordinated system of action."[42]

The power of language is something that Russell Lowery-Hart and other leaders at AC understood well. The first data summit was designed to bring staff and faculty together to better understand and rethink the nature of student success at Amarillo. One of the faculty members I interviewed recalled that many people walked into that summit with the idea that AC was knocking it out of the park when it came to helping students finish or transfer. But then they had to come to terms with what the data clearly showed, challenging the college community's mindset that AC was one of the nation's best community colleges. It is no small irony that it took altering that mindset to help AC become the excellent institution many employees already believed it to be.

The strategic, consistent use of language was designed to conjure a particular image of AC in the minds of employees—one of an institution that served the holistic needs of students and, through the provision of those services, loved them to success. Although you can encounter the word "caring" in many places on campus, the language was deliberately chosen to spur a "consensually constructed, coordinated system of action." For example, every employee goes through anti-poverty certification training as part of new employee orientation. "It has given us a common language to understand the difference between generational poverty and situational poverty," Lowery-Hart explained in a presentation to the American Community College Trustees.[43] On our car ride back from lunch, he noted how some institutions have sent teams to study AC and walked away thinking they could slap the word "love" on brochures, start a food pantry, and call it a transformation. But he shared that it was never just about the language. Talking about caring was a way station on the road to organizational change.

Amarillo also developed a new symbol to galvanize the college's anti-poverty and student success efforts: Maria. Maria is a composite of what the data showed was AC's typical student: a 27-year-old first-generation Latina, working an average of two part-time jobs and raising an average of 1.2 children. Maria is smart and tenacious but faces serious financial and personal hurdles to completing a degree. The college wanted staff and faculty to see Maria when they pictured the students they educated. Consistent with the college's core purpose, AC encouraged employees to "love the students we have, not the students we wish we had." As Lowery-Hart elaborated in the presentation to community college trustees, "Instead of us spending our time and investing our money to get her to change to where we are, we have to spend our time understanding who she is and how we can reimagine ourselves for her and her success." One AC faculty member shared with me in an interview that the symbol of Maria has helped him visualize the college's work—and his contribution to that work within the college and in the wider community—in a different way than words or bar charts ever would.

Amarillo's values differ markedly from the stuffy language typical of guiding documents in higher education. I don't just mean that they use terms that might ruffle the feathers of very serious academics and administrators for whom the life of the mind has little room for "love" and "wow." But the other way that Amarillo's values are unique is that employees are unmistakably present. The college's values speak of "every student *and colleague*," declaring that "we celebrate *each other*" and "*our* work." Additionally, the college's values are not just a collection of keywords or a rewording of institutional goals—they are a declaration of how employees are expected to interact with and show up for one another. Values are about *how* colleges and universities want to operate and achieve strategic priorities and therefore should be inextricably linked to the people behind the work. From a talent management perspective, values should give employees a sense of Amarillo's brand as an employer. Many of the people I interviewed told me that the Culture of Caring made AC attractive to them as an applicant and continues to be a reason they stay.

Leaders may read this approach to organizational change and feel inclined to soften the tone of their emails and show more empathy in their formal and informal communication. These steps are laudable but are the equivalent of slapping the word "love" on a brochure. What this approach calls for is thinking about how language, symbols, and values can be used to change employees' mindsets, which is a stepping stone to organizational change. Leaders need to talk the Caring University into existence, and it will be much more effective if staff and faculty see themselves and their labor included in these words and images.

Approach 2: Caring Through Enhanced Employee Data Practices

Colleges and universities need to clean up the hot mess of employee data practices that prevail on many campuses. A good first step is to develop processes, policies, and goals for managing institutional data.[44] Having a data governance plan allows institutions to decide in advance who has responsibility over which data and ensures that cross-departmental conversations are happening about important data-related discussions. A data governance plan also informs the campus community about how to access data (which might otherwise get lost in a shared folder in the cloud) and how data will be used, which increases transparency and the likelihood that staff and faculty will be comfortable participating in data collection efforts.

According to Betsy Reinitz, director of the CIO and Senior Technology Leaders Program at EDUCAUSE, one benefit of a data governance plan is that it can push colleges and universities to inventory their data systems. This process includes figuring out where there are discrepancies in their data, deciding which data system is going to be used for official purposes, and working out any definitional inconsistencies or problems. Inventorying data systems could unearth some of the problems of "directory information" that lead to differing counts of employees by race or gender. And it could help institutions establish consistent, inclusive, and up-to-date ways of collecting information on employees' identities across the university. In some instances, it might even promote the adoption of best practices in inclusive data collection. For example, higher education scholar Jason C. Garvey recommended in response to questions I emailed him that institutions "embrace the messiness of gender and sexuality and develop infrastructures that enable flexibility." He thinks schools should expansively collect data that can later be used to meet federal government reporting requirements. Survey techniques can also encourage fluidity by using options like "check all that apply" and "another social identity, please describe: [fill in the blank]." Cognitive/affective interviewing in survey development would help colleges and universities learn how questions land with potential respondents. Although institutions may have little choice about how they report information to external agencies, there is nothing forcing them to continue using outdated methods and categories for internal purposes.

As an alternative to episodic engagement surveys, some companies have shifted toward methods of "continuous listening." While it may sound slightly Orwellian, continuous listening simply refers to collecting feedback at different stages of the employee life cycle by repeatedly asking for input about how the organization can improve the employee experience from the point of application through onboarding and beyond. Many companies have moved toward more frequent and shorter "pulse" surveys so that feedback is less of an annual event or something that only happens during an exit interview. Leaders might be surprised to learn how effective a dedicated process for listening can be to retaining talent. On more than one occasion, staff and faculty broke into tears during the interviews as they described their experiences, telling me the relief they felt simply being able to share their story and feel heard.

Some employees might understandably be hesitant to share this information with their employer, but the data could be collected anonymously for many purposes. And a data governance plan that spells out the rationale behind data collection and how the data will be used to answer questions that benefit employees could increase their trust and willingness to participate. Leaders can also grease the feedback gears by communicating regularly about actions they have taken in response to data. Some organizations have even developed a brand identity for their survey tools and the people responsible for them to clearly convey the purpose of data collection and ensure that it isn't confused with other surveys on campus. But Benjamin Granger, chief workplace psychologist at Qualtrics, cautioned in an interview that adding in opportunities for feedback should be gradual. "We get a lot of interest from people saying, 'Hey, we've been doing this annual survey for a long time. We're hearing about passive listening and collecting data, scraping Slack and Glass Door, and pulling that in.' It's like, well, let's hold on a second. Do you know how to *consume* that information?" Granger suggested that organizations that have only conducted an annual survey might start by adding open-ended questions and build from there to look at feedback on onboarding processes.

It's not just employees who need to prepare themselves for more regular feedback. Leaders, too, need to consider the extent to which they are ready to hear what employees have to say. It's quite possible that leaders might either get defensive in the face of criticism or mistake "pulse" data with long-term trends. According to Sydney Heimbrock, chief industry adviser for government at Qualtrics, the biggest obstacle she runs into when explaining how organizations can better collect and use employee data is leaders who say they don't have time: "When a manager says, 'I don't have time,' what I actually hear is, 'I don't know how to do this, and I don't think my job is actually managing people.' So that is a major problem because that's the job. If they think they don't have time, then they're actually saying that they're not willing to do the job they're paid to do."

This means that colleges and universities need to hire leaders based on their people management skills and offer regular opportunities to develop this skill set by learning from data. "Even for those for whom it does seem to come naturally, there are still tools and skills," Heimbrock added. "These things don't just happen by themselves. You have to learn them."

Being ready for data also means having sufficient staff to make sure data can be translated into actionable insights. Many institutions already employ staff and faculty who are well versed in human resources and data analytics and whose expertise could be better valued and leveraged. But colleges and universities may need to invest in additional training for employees and hiring people with specific skills in analyzing and visualizing data.[45] Some companies have successfully established human resource or talent analytics teams whose entire purpose is collecting, cleaning, storing, analyzing, and sharing information to determine organizational strengths and pain points. Consistent with a talent management perspective, human resource analytics can help identify factors driving turnover or where employee workload burdens are undermining organizational performance.

Empowering new and emerging experts may require viewing data on the employee experience less as a secret to be carefully guarded and more as an institution-wide resource to guide organizational effectiveness. A data governance plan can foster collaboration and help break down the silos that Bischel of CUPA-HR noted prevent data from being shared across departments. Hosting a data summit similar to the annual event at AC could help lay the foundation for a culture of sharing and openly discussing data. And institutions may need to provide ongoing professional development to increase the data literacy of staff and faculty—all the way up to the president's office.[46]

Enhancing employee data practices is partly about correcting indifference to the employee experience and partly about informing organizational change. A better understanding of who employees are and how they perceive their work and workplace can guide leaders in pinpointing where to focus their time and resources. At this juncture, most colleges and universities have bought into the idea that collecting data is essential in recruiting and retaining students. The same is true of harnessing talent to drive organizational performance. But it is crucial that data be paired with action. Nothing will torpedo a data collection effort like employees believing nothing will come of it.

Approach 3: Caring Through Assessing and Addressing Workload

Institutions need to develop systems for tracking employee workload and addressing inequities and other threats to organizational effectiveness. Before looking at the workloads of staff and faculty in particular units, leaders can engage in a higher-level assessment to audit the number of new strategic priorities, programs, and initiatives launched in a three- to five-year period. They can ask a set of related questions, including whether any programs or initiatives were scaled back to account for these additions or whether (and how) staff and faculty labor factored into the decision-making process. For each new initiative, they should ask how many new responsibilities were added to the plate of an existing employee? How many people were hired to support the new project? This assessment may show that multiple new strategic priorities came online without a plan for accomplishing the work.

Collecting better data to understand staff and faculty workload is essential for retaining talent. A consistent theme in my data is that workers have left or considered leaving higher education jobs because of workload—or because of the lack of awareness or urgency on the part of leaders in addressing workload issues. When I have asked leaders about the extent to which they have data on employee workload, the typical response is along the lines of, "Of course, we ask a question about workload. It's on the biannual engagement survey!" *One question. Asked every other year.* But few leaders would say that asking students about their satisfaction or sense of belonging every two years is enough to inform their programming.

Institutions need to elevate their game when it comes to understanding employee workload. This is a place where pulse surveys or other means of giving workers more frequent opportunities to provide feedback can come in handy. For example, for most employees, workload ebbs and flows. Suppose the data show that there are clear times when offices experience excessive job demands. In that case, leaders can explore cross-training employees from other units and having them ready to provide backup support. From a talent management perspective, this would help ensure offices with key personnel have a plan B in the event a worker resigns, retires, or takes leave.

Similarly, if the data show workload issues in a unit consistently over two years, then there is an opportunity to take a closer look at what those employees are being asked to do, what additional tasks they may have acquired as the institution pursued strategic goals, and whether there are supervisory, training, or other issues. Colleges and universities need to take to heart what the engineering professor told me: running people at 100 percent capacity all the time will eventually cause quality to suffer or system failure. That might sound like an exaggeration, but in my interviews, I talked with multiple staff and leaders who described important offices as overburdened during the pandemic and saw a critical mass of employees leave. That's a system failure, plain and simple. Preventing the turnover of high-performing staff and faculty is critically important, and a talent management strategy would guide institutions toward proactively providing these employees with reasons to stay.

Tracking employee workload doesn't have to hang on surveys. Amarillo College relied on regular all-college meetings, focus groups, and secret shoppers to help determine where systems were effective and where they were not. Not every employee will feel comfortable sharing their experience during a large town hall meeting, but they may open up during small-group discussions. These conversations may not identify a definitive problem or a solution but may help leaders gauge how employees are feeling and give them a sense of where to focus follow-up efforts. In this way, workload becomes part of a regular conversation on campus, ideally allowing leaders to make changes before concerns become crises.

Institutions can also get more systematic with their collection and analysis of workload data. (Box 2.2 presents an example.) KerryAnn O'Meara and colleagues recommend using faculty work activity dashboards to increase workload transparency and address departmental inequities.[47] They define a faculty work activity dashboard as an "easy-to-read display of faculty work areas across different work activities (service, teaching, and sometimes research)."[48] Examples of activities that could be counted and displayed in a dashboard include the number of advisees, student projects supervised, and committee service at the department, college, and university levels. O'Meara and colleagues suggest that dashboards allow workers to compare their performance, make important labor visible, credit faculty for different levels of effort, and provide a sense of the department's total workload. After interviewing faculty whose departments developed dashboards to help address inequities, the researchers noted benefits such as increased accountability, transparency, and understanding of what was expected for everyone to pull their weight fairly.

Box 2.2

Correcting a Culture of More

The Case of Harvey Mudd College

Harvey Mudd College is a highly selective private liberal arts college focused on science, technology, engineering, and math (STEM). The college's roughly 900 students major in one of 11 STEM fields and are accustomed to excelling academically. Similarly, faculty come from well-known graduate programs and want to pair teaching at a liberal arts college with a research program common at a large research university. Staff are highly trained and leaders in their fields, often writing articles and presenting on their practice.

It is a place where there are high expectations. Laura Palucki Blake, Harvey Mudd's assistant vice president for institutional research and effectiveness, explained to me in an interview: "We have just the right ingredients for a culture that's oriented towards more and more. The mindset is there's always something else we could be doing." Most of the time, all these high-achieving people working together produce amazing results. But it is also a bit of a mutually reinforcing pressure cooker. "We realized all these work culture questions were linked for us," Palucki Blake noted. "The student-faculty-staff culture of overwork feeds on itself."

In the report that Harvey Mudd prepared to reaffirm its accreditation, the college acknowledged that back in 2009, its accreditor had pushed leaders to continue "examining issues of workload to promote balance in personal and professional life." Since then, the college has collected "considerable data from students and faculty that indicates that in their pursuit of excellence, students and faculty are often overextended and find it difficult to fully appreciate their successes." For this reason, Harvey Mudd themed its reaffirmation efforts "Healthy Excellence: Putting Success in Perspective." The college explained in the report that it feared its workload problems "might ultimately serve as an obstacle to our aspirations for student learning and holistic development and impede the broad flourishing we wished for faculty and staff."

Given that the college was a campus community of scientists, Harvey Mudd knew that changing its working culture needed to be, in Palucki Blake's words, "quantitatively inclined." Data on faculty workload pointed to two pain points: summer pay and tenure clarity. Some faculty were paid for working the summer months through grants, but others—including many new faculty—were not. The problem is that most of the unpaid faculty members were working during this time because it is a cultural expectation that faculty mentor students in research experiences over the summer. The college realized that it could not tell faculty to do less because it was clearly a job expectation and valued by the institution. Instead, it created a fund to compensate all faculty for summer

Box 2.2 (continued)

mentoring, which it intends to make permanent through the strategic planning process. Marshaling resources for this effort was easier because campus leaders could tell the trustees, "If we don't bring our best selves, the students and curriculum suffer."

Harvey Mudd also spent a year and a half cleaning up its faculty handbook to clarify tenure expectations and processes. Informed by focus groups, the faculty set a goal to reduce anxiety and the amount of time faculty members spent trying to figure out what work counted toward promotion. The college also created a process where marginalized faculty could be exempt from service because of the time they spent supporting marginalized students on campus, and the exemption would be noted in their promotion materials. Focus groups also revealed how much time faculty members spent on advising students. Palucki Blake explained, "We're a high-touch school, and we knew advising was important. But we didn't realize how big it had gotten." The college is now exploring ways to improve the incentives for advising students and streamlining the process for receiving compensation for those efforts.

For staff, Harvey Mudd ran a survey in both English and Spanish focused on workload satisfaction and well-being. Some staff reported that their workload increased, that they were having difficulty disconnecting from work while at home, and that they lacked time for reflection and big-picture thinking. The heads of each of the college's divisions were charged with using this data to make adjustments to expectations, communication, and time off. According to Palucki Blake, the college also plans to tweak the survey and administer it again "to ensure we're getting the breadth of people's experience."

For Palucki Blake, Harvey Mudd's efforts to address workload has been a lesson in taking small steps toward a larger goal. "This was sort of groundbreaking for us, but we realized smaller measures could be undertaken along the way. As we were progressing towards this bigger goal of having a workplace culture that supported everyone, we needed to make small shifts and let them grow." As it moves forward, the college keeps a list of actions it has taken to address workload as a reminder of progress.

Harvey Mudd has also made a point of including faculty, staff, and students in the change process, so all the ideas are not coming from central administration. As Palucki Blake explained, "Faculty and staff have to believe change is possible. They have to understand that they're a part of it. It's something we're creating together. . . . That way, people say, 'Okay, I'm showing up to that meeting. And I'm going to help.'" Luckily, the scientists in the room are accustomed to ideas not succeeding the first time and revise ideas when results do not initially pan out. People are noticing the change, but they are also speaking up about what needs to happen next.

"It's not by any means done," Palucki Blake acknowledged. "But putting workload front and center in activities that are public and accountable is how the big and small changes get done."

Getting a handle on excessive workloads may require colleges and universities to figure out standards for adequate staffing. This is easier to accomplish in some jobs and offices than others. For example, it is not uncommon for academic advisers to have a stated "caseload" or expected number of advisees at any given time. Although most work in higher education—including advising—can't be easily captured in a single metric, each unit could be tasked with collaboratively discussing and articulating its standards for staffing adequacy. These standards could consider the number of hours worked per week, as reported by each employee; agreed-on measures of performance; and how the unit operates when it is fully staffed and workers are doing their best work. It could be helpful for offices to start by describing the inverse—what the office looks like when it doesn't have enough people. Leaders could then establish a process whereby they evaluate each unit's standards for staffing adequacy against the actual staffing levels and allow managers to submit requests for additional personnel or resources.

Ultimately, institutions need to be prepared to pare back strategic priorities in light of their staffing or hire more people. Otherwise, they risk spreading their people so thin that it becomes an institutional liability. Risks can multiply as offices with important legal or financial responsibilities are too overworked or understaffed to deliver services and prevent mistakes. As was the case with enhanced employee data practices, workload data will be useful only if leaders are ready to listen and act. Not every solution to workload problems requires a substantial investment of resources, but the reality is that most colleges and universities have lofty aspirations. Eventually, the ability to succeed in those goals—to do more or do better—will come down to managing and strategically investing in people.

Conclusion

I once gave a virtual presentation to a group of French higher education leaders on supporting faculty well-being. At the end of the discussion, one of the leaders who had been quietly listening chimed in: "What you're talking about is partly about the Great Resignation, but also about what kind of employer the university is, and here in France, it is bad." This chapter asks leaders in the United States a related question. What kind of employer is an organization that fails to include employees in guiding documents, has little knowledge of its employees because of a lack of data collection, and shows little regard for rising workloads? Not a great one.

For a long time, being a mediocre employer in higher education was enough. As long as there were applicants for job vacancies, students

Box 2.3

Chapter 2 Action Steps

- Organize a retreat or extended discussion of talent management and the extent to which your institution, college, department, or unit has a talent management strategy.
- Analyze guiding documents and whether language, symbols, and values (1) are inclusive of employees, (2) communicate the value proposition of working at your institution, and (3) strategically prioritize talent as a means of organizational performance.
- Develop a data governance plan to inventory existing data systems and promote data transparency, access, cross-departmental collaboration, and definitional consistency.
- Create a team of staff and faculty from across the institution to assess employee data practices and whether existing practices honor the identities of employees. Ask the group to develop recommendations for collecting data on the employee experience, then share the recommendations and a publicly available action plan to implement the recommendations.
- Conduct an audit of new strategic priorities, programs, and initiatives in the last three to five years and ask direct reports to consider the labor implications of each new initiative. Consider what, if anything, was removed from the institution's portfolio as new initiatives were added.
- Establish methods for tracking employee workload, such as the use of faculty activity dashboards.
- Encourage units or a subgroup of individuals in units to develop standards for adequate staffing. Create a process whereby leaders evaluate each unit's standards for staffing adequacy against the actual staffing levels and allow managers to submit requests for additional personnel or resources.
- Evaluate where staffing levels are too thin and represent an institutional liability. Be prepared to pare back strategic priorities or to hire more personnel as part of a talent management strategy.

paying enrollment deposits, and policymakers leaving institutions to their own devices, colleges and universities could get by neglecting the employee experience. But times have changed. Workers are less likely to tolerate mediocrity, resorting to forms of resistance or leaving for organizations that seem to take the employee experience more seriously. Many students trying to build a future in the wake of the pandemic will look right past institutions hell-bent on exclusion and competition and look directly at caring communities that will nurture their growth. And policymakers will continue to expect high quality and measures of organizational effectiveness from institutions.

The Caring University consists of people collectively and proactively working toward organizational changes that make the employee experience a strategic priority. Supporting employee well-being and building a successful organization that is well positioned to achieve big things are not parallel tracks that diverge as soon as resources get tight. The only route to the latter is through the former. This chapter introduced three approaches to organizational change that take inspiration from the concept of talent management. These approaches attend to both organizational culture and structure, and they reflect key insights from organizational change theorists. Box 2.3 summarizes several action steps connected to these approaches.

I would guess that many higher education leaders would understand that the route to remarkable outcomes is directly through the people they employ. They might even repeat the popular adage, "Our people are our greatest asset." If leaders subscribe to this adage, they need to put their money where their mouth is. And AC shows us that they may be happy with the results.

CHAPTER 3

Creating Working Cultures and Conditions for Real (Not Ideal) Workers

"I FELT INCREDIBLY FORTUNATE," Lane recalled after learning she was offered a job in interpersonal violence response at a growing rural-serving university. Although she pursued a master's degree to work in higher education, Lane took a detour after her first job and spent 15 years doing sexuality education and health promotion at small nonprofits. She was ready to spread her wings and get back to higher education, and after a short time job-searching, she saw a position at a university that was right up her alley.

Her new role at the university was as a "case manager," providing intensive, holistic support to students who were facing issues ranging from domestic violence to mental health crises. A marriage between social work and student affairs, case managers arrange and coordinate services for distressed students and employees while also monitoring and evaluating high-risk situations.[1]

Although Lane was prepared for the work, she was also glad to have a strong supervisor: "I got to move into this space with the knowledge and experience I had, but with someone who could help me navigate all the new systems. To have that level of institutional knowledge, I felt so grateful." Lane's boss had previously been the university's case manager for interpersonal violence, and she helped Lane learn the ropes: "The stuff that's written down," as Lane put it. "And *all* the stuff that's not written down." Lane also felt her supervisor sought out her opinions and trusted her decision-making—she was open to ideas, and Lane offered them. All in all, it was an auspicious start to the next chapter of her career, and Lane was optimistic: "This was a place I wanted to stay for a while."

But five months later, the pandemic began. Suddenly, the number of students in distress took off, and Lane's caseload skyrocketed. New cases materialized faster than Lane and her colleagues could clear existing ones. Her inner monologue became a running list of students in need:

Relocate a student to quarantine housing. . . .
Check on a student who wasn't responding to messages. . . .
Find support for a student who skipped classes due to visible bruises. . . .
Connect with the Title IX coordinator about a student who reported a stalker. . . .

Lane's office soon took on a whole new set of tasks, distributing over a $1 million in emergency aid to students facing hardships, such as losing family members to the virus, being in the hospital for lengthy stays, or being laid off from jobs on which they depended. Lane was doing everything in her power to stay afloat—after all, when your boat is taking on water, your only option is to keep bailing.

Making matters worse, Lane's office was experiencing the type of turnover and transitions all too common during the Great Resignation. "I've had maybe three months in my almost four years that we've been fully staffed. And so the expectation is to operate at over-full caseloads," she said. Then Lane's supervisor moved up in the organizational chart to fill a vacancy. Lane and her coworkers felt their supervisor's absence immediately since the supervisor had been taking on cases and working late into the night to shield her staff from the deluge of demands. The university had its hands full with current students, yet recruiting more students was a high priority. What Lane couldn't compute was why the university didn't hire more staff or recalibrate expectations. "Instead of having some sort of a realistic standard of what human beings can handle, it just kept coming," she said.

Not one to stay quiet, Lane repeatedly expressed to her superiors that she was struggling. "I said to my former supervisor that I can't take on anymore," she shared. "But it was like no matter what we said, the folks above her just kept pushing more on case management." Lane tried again with her new supervisor, who asked her about setting boundaries and practicing self-care, and then with a leader further up the chain, who encouraged Lane to stay strong and keep fighting. "There was no response or respect for being at my limit," Lane said. "At some point it's like, you don't care about me. I felt like they were willing to sacrifice all of us." And the question about boundaries and self-care? Lane groaned and said that she's been in helping roles for a long time: "I have a therapist. I'm doing my part." She wanted the institution to do its part to set guardrails around workload and keep her and her colleagues from falling apart.

While she was working intensively to support students, the fabric of Lane's personal life was fraying. She had been attracted to the university because the town where it was located had a reputation for being queer-friendly. She had knitted together a community of friends and found queer-friendly doctors, but then her landlord decided to sell her rental. The only thing growing faster than the university's enrollment were local housing prices. After finally finding an affordable apartment—albeit in a town down the highway—Lane's long workdays now included a one-hour commute each way, leaving her exhausted: "I'm spending a lot of my time out of work recovering to go back to work." Although the commute was taxing, losing her community *really* hurt. As Lane explained, "I'm living in a town that I don't want to live in, in a place where I don't feel especially safe, where there's very little queerness, and I'm away from my support system."

Working from home a few days each week during the height of the pandemic gave Lane back the hours she lost to the car, which helped to reduce her stress. But when the university announced it would "return to normal" and end its work-from-home flexibility, Lane worried about lax masking policies. Although she did not discuss her health with coworkers, Lane had asthma and was immunocompromised. She worked with the disability resource office on campus to continue working from home one day per week. But then came comments from superiors questioning why they weren't seeing her around or expressing concern that she wasn't getting to know new colleagues. She felt guilty for protecting her health.

Lane didn't love being so far from campus, but the office wasn't always a welcoming space, either. As a self-identified fat person, she was often caught in office conversations about dieting, body-shaming, and fitness. Lane formally asked if she could work from home two days a week, but her request was denied because she worked in a "student-facing" office. While Lane agrees that she works closely with students, she estimates that 80 percent of the time, she sees their faces through Zoom. Ultimately, Lane felt the decision came down to a lack of trust: "They don't trust me enough to work from home, but they don't pay me enough to live [nearby]."

Lane's optimism had obviously waned, and she wasn't holding her breath when it came to the university waking up to the needs of overwhelmed workers. "People above me talk like they care, but nobody's doing anything," she said. "I could be here for another five years, and I don't know that anything would change. So that's why I ultimately decided to start searching." After 15 years of supporting teen parents, counseling people with HIV, and educating others on relationship violence, Lane has had her share of tough days on the job. But it was working at a university that broke her spirit.

What Lane described was a situation where work was so intense for so long that it was dehumanizing. It was dehumanizing because the university piled on cases of students in crisis even after Lane said she was at her limit. It was dehumanizing because exhaustion from work made it nearly impossible to build a life outside work. It was dehumanizing because the conditions of her job pulled her away from the community she needed to feel loved and supported. It was dehumanizing because the institution enforced rigid workplace policies, treating thousands of employees the same. And it was dehumanizing because when Lane reached out for help, she only heard the organizational equivalent of crickets.

Lane felt that staying in her job required her to be superhuman—someone who wasn't bound by the limits of a body, immune to the emotional toll of working with students in crisis, and willing to sacrifice her well-being and put in extra hours for the good of the cause. In other words, someone who could work in a constant state of emergency and not be slowed down by obligations to family, friends, or community. To be successful—and, really, to survive—Lane needed to embody the "ideal worker," or someone who, in the words of sociologist Joan Acker, "exists only for the work" and does not have "other imperatives of existence that impinge upon the job."[2]

Lane is not alone in feeling her job expectations did not match the realities of being a living, breathing human. In this chapter, I trace the origins of the ideal worker norms that shaped Lane's experience and are common in the higher education workplace. I show how they developed in tandem with the gendered separation of work and home, especially in the postwar professional workplace, and how their persistence is attributable to notions of professionalism that guide how we prepare—or socialize—future staff and faculty. Ideal worker norms shape policies and practices in higher education that negatively affect all employees, but I show how they are particularly pernicious for people who are caregivers, disabled, and navigating loss. The result is that these workers experience a workplace that fails to treat them as whole people, contributing to the burnout, disengagement, and demoralization that propelled the Great Resignation.

The second half of the chapter sketches what it looks like to create working cultures and conditions for real (not ideal) workers. Taking cues from Frederic Laloux's model of evolutionary organizations, I explore four organization-level approaches that recognize the need for employees to express their authentic selves while prioritizing safety, wholeness, dignity, and flexibility.[3] These approaches include resetting professional norms, improving supports for caregivers, expanding options for hybrid and remote work, and creating guardrails to prevent work from consuming employees' nonwork lives. Along the way, we'll look at examples from institutions supporting employee well-being through humanizing practices and policies.

If Lane encountered a culture that prioritized human expectations and safety—with an accommodations experience that was free of stigma and guilt, a flexible work arrangement so she could better manage her well-being, and guardrails to curb work's insatiable appetite—she would not have been looking for a new job. This chapter is about why institutions have struggled to create humane working cultures and conditions and how organizational change toward the Caring University can help them better support and retain talented workers.

The Gendered Separation of Work and Home

Over the course of my interviews, I frequently heard both staff and faculty talk about their "lack of work-life balance" or "desire for more work-life balance." In most cases, they weren't seeking a perfect equilibrium between work and life. Instead, they wanted a job that didn't eat up so much of their time and headspace, making it possible to live a fuller life. Nevertheless, talk about work-life balance was ubiquitous throughout the pandemic. Media outlets, management consultants, and university lecture series were all considering what work-life balance would look like in a post-COVID world.[4]

References to *work-life balance* were so common in my research that I decided to investigate the term's origins. It turns out that the pursuit of work-life balance has a long history that goes hand-in-hand with the rise of *ideal worker norms* (Box 3.1). In fact, labor historians contend that work-life balance and ideal worker norms sprang from the same source: the gendered separation of work and home.[5]

Long before the first utterance of the words "work-life balance," labor movements fought to reclaim a greater slice of workers' time from their bosses. The idea of an eight-hour workday was popularized in the early nineteenth century by Robert Owen, a Welsh social reformer who coined the phrase "Eight hours' labor, Eight hours' recreation, Eight hours' rest."[6] In 1886, the Federation of Organized Trades and Labor Unions called for a national strike in the United States, demanding an eight-hour workday in lieu of the long-standing agricultural practice of working from sunup to sundown.[7] According to historians Andrea Rees Davies and Brenda Frink, it was during the market revolution of the nineteenth century that new income-earning jobs outside the home emerged.[8] These jobs were performed by men who became a visible class of permanent wage-earners.

Box 3.1

How Scholars Define the Ideal Worker

- Existing only for work, without other imperatives of existence impinging on the job
- Being constantly available and unfailingly loyal to the organization, without any "personal burdens" like children, emotions, or disability
- Being white, married, middle class, and a man (typically) whose personal needs and caregiving responsibilities are fulfilled by someone else, such as a spouse
- Committing to productivity, promotions, and particular forms of dress associated with professionalism
- Being able to compartmentalize time and roles to create a full, uninterrupted workday
- Working a minimum of 40 hours a week with no career interruptions (such as time off for giving birth or caring for other family members)
- Doing what is necessary for career advancement, such as putting in extra hours, financing one's own professional development, and traveling or relocating

At the same time, caring for the home and children were stripped of their status as work, soon "viewed as effortless expressions of [a] mother's love for her family."[9] The American middle class began to see work and home as separate, gendered spheres—men left for work while women stayed home.

The number of wage-earners increased with the growth of large factories, which demarcated "working hours" through shifts, whistles, and time cards. Scientific management was all the rage, and managers were tasked with measuring and timing the worker's every movement to create a machinelike routine that maximized efficiency.[10] As office-based jobs proliferated in the early twentieth century, employers adopted factorylike practices, such as tracking hours with time sheets, specifying hours of a workday, and employing efficiency-minded managers. But they devised a different tool to measure and manage workers: *professionalism*.[11]

Professionalism encompassed a set of workplace values that emphasized productivity, promotions up the ladder, and particular forms of appearance (e.g., the white-collar dress shirt). Since management positions were scarce, promotions were awarded to workers who competed to demonstrate devotion to the organization. According to Joan Acker, white middle-class men came closest to the archetypal professional, which scholars have come to term the ideal worker.[12]

The ability of white men to embody the ideal worker was a direct result of racial segregation that prevented people of color from entering many professional workplaces and the existence of someone at home (usually wives) who supported men's careers in a multitude of ways, from cleaning suits to typing memos.[13] When women worked outside the home, they were funneled into clerical positions where they were still expected, in the words of historian Angel Kwolek-Folland, "to subsume self into work" and show devotion to their boss (at least until the woman was married, at which point she would leave the workforce).[14] As Davies and Frink put it, "Men climbed the corporate ladder while women, relegated to low-paying and non-promoting clerical work, held the ladder firm from below."[15] The division of jobs and status was so strict that some offices had separate entrances, stairs, and hallways for men and women.

Suburbanization intensified the gendered separation of work and home. Between the hours of 9 a.m. and 5 p.m., men were physically distant from families, and their time belonged to their organizations or companies. According to Davies and Frink, the ability to "compartmentalize the day, setting aside uninterrupted work time," became another characteristic of the ideal worker.[16] Law professor Joan Williams notes that uninterrupted work time also involves avoiding time off for illness, childbirth, or childcare, indicating that the ideal worker is "disembodied" and not limited by their (or someone else's) physical or emotional needs.[17] Advancing in the office often hinged on sacrifice, such as putting in extra hours, traveling long distances for business, self-financing additional training or credentials, and relocating far from extended family. Workers were supposed to do all this *happily* because a career was both a calling and a community and therefore an extension of one's identity. Being professional meant showing up to work cheerful, energetic, and compliant.

The phrase "work-life balance" is a product of the 1980s, when an increasing number of women were entering the professional workforce and raising concerns about their ability to succeed in the office and carry out their multiplying responsibilities at home.[18] Employers responded to these concerns with a limited number of concessions, such as instituting paid maternity leave, allowing minor schedule adjustments, and expanding employee assistance programs initially designed to help workers with substance use disorders. Often referred to as "work-life" or "family-friendly" policies, these concessions were primarily directed at women, and "family" was narrowly construed as caring for children. The purpose of work-life policies was to protect uninterrupted work time by asking workers to take time off to attend to personal matters so that they could return as their most undistracted selves. Employees were expected to skillfully manage their allotted leave to ensure that they didn't inconvenience employers or impede productivity.

Davies and Frink stress that the ideal worker and the family structure that enabled this worker "did not match reality for most American families, based on race, class, or other factors."[19] They point to the multiple ways women resisted the gendered separation of work and home. Women were always working—working in the home without pay, doing piecemeal work for income from home, and working outside the home—only to return home to do more work. Some men also chafed at the pressures of ideal worker norms and what they saw as the sublimation of individuality and fatherhood demanded by the professional workplace. But they were swimming against a cultural rip current, as books, magazines, movies, and television shows turned the ideal worker and his family into an American cultural icon.

The Perpetuation of Ideal Worker Norms in Higher Education

Thankfully, much has changed about office culture since the era of *Mad Men*, but the ideal worker has persisted through the decades, including in higher education. There is a simple explanation for this: research shows that we teach future staff and faculty notions of professionalism and success that perpetuate ideal worker norms.[20] We even see these norms appear in position descriptions seeking "energetic" and "enthusiastic" workers, followed by lists of required qualifications and responsibilities so numerous that they could easily describe multiple jobs instead of one.

Scholars have used the concept of *socialization* to understand how newcomers to a group or community (such as graduate students) learn norms, values, and standards of conduct.[21] Socialization happens through formal training programs, like master's and doctoral programs, but also by observing the actions of and interacting with faculty and peers with more experience in the group or community. Professions represent their own kind of community, and higher education scholar Rosemary J. Perez explained that *professional* socialization "is designed to foster values acquisition, commitment to the field, organizational loyalty, the development of a professional identity, and the expansion of skills for the workplace."[22] In short, professional socialization is how we mold students into stewards of the profession who will, in due course, train future newcomers and reproduce the same norms and values.

Perez studied the professional socialization of student affairs staff through master's programs, which she calls "the primary means of socializing newcomers to student affairs practice" at colleges and universities.[23] It is customary for these programs to combine coursework with applied experiences in the field. In both cases, students are exposed to messages about professionalism and the nature of "good practice" in higher education. Right off the bat, the graduate preparation programs assume students can study full-time and work long hours in applied experiences, making it difficult for those who are parents, have a disability, or need to work full-time while completing program requirements. Although these programs espouse commitments to social justice, marginalized students report feeling that this commitment primarily manifests as educating white students and catering to their comfort in the classroom and campus community, especially at predominately white institutions.

Graduate students also receive messages about professionalism from supervisors and professors as part of their training for staff jobs. These messages prescribe values around how students should dress, communicate, and pursue professional development to meet program expectations and be competitive after graduation. As Perez observed, these values are rooted in ideal worker norms and often teach "unhealthy and unsustainable ways of engaging in work," including the idea that being a good student affairs professional requires self-sacrificing to serve students.[24] Messages about professionalism push dedication to continuous learning and loyalty to the profession and institution that may result in overcommitting to service and uncompensated labor. When students stray from standards of dress, speech, or attitude, they are reminded that the field is small and "if they do not conform to the norms of the field and constructions of the ideal worker, their reputation and employability will be damaged."[25] Higher education scholar Brittany M. Williams demonstrated how Black women professionals in particular experience "workplace policing" or "the physical, metaphorical, and/or emotional manipulation of Black women's actions to better align with white supremacist notions of professionalism."[26]

Socialization of future faculty is harder to pin down because it varies considerably by discipline and institutional context. Higher education scholar Susan K. Gardner has published numerous studies on the socialization of doctoral students, including those preparing for faculty roles. In one study, she notes that attrition from doctoral study is higher among women and graduate students of color, motivating her to study how these students are socialized.[27] Gardner found that students' identities, discipline, and institutional context shaped their experiences, yet one common theme across her interviews was that minoritized doctoral students were made to feel that they did not fit a "mold" of academic success—a mold, she argues, that was structured around white men who could study full-time, spend considerable time outside the classroom with peers, and did not have caregiving responsibilities.

If position descriptions in higher education are any indication, graduate students preparing for staff and faculty jobs have good reason to worry about measuring up to standards. One analysis of position descriptions in higher education found that they tend to require education and in-sector experience that does not match up with the level and pay of the job, such as expecting multiple years of experience for entry-level jobs.[28] Position descriptions are also longer on average than those in other sectors, detailing extensive responsibilities and, in some cases, requiring "turnkey" applicants who can hit the ground running with minimal on-the-job training.[29] When graduate students enter the job market, they see position descriptions that confirm a core message that they received during socialization processes: they need to embody perfectly polished super-professionals.

Casualties of the Professional Mask

In *Reinventing Organizations: A Guide to Creating Organizations Inspired by the Next Stage of Human Consciousness*, management expert Frederic Laloux argued that most employees are "increasingly disillusioned with organizational life" because they encounter workplaces where they "often feel they have to shut out part of who they are when they dress for work in the morning. They put on a professional mask, conforming to expectations of the workplace."[30] For some employees, donning a professional mask day-in and day-out—forcing a separation of the "professional" and "personal"—can be particularly complicated and costly.

In this section, I focus on how ideal worker norms are especially burdensome for employees who are caregivers, disabled, and grieving.[31] My goal is not to exhaustively review the studies examining the workplace experiences of employees in these groups, which could easily fill its own book. Rather, I want to illustrate how ideal worker norms shape perceptions, practices, and policies in the higher education workplace, resulting in cultural and structural problems that can break the spirit of employees like Lane and give them reason to consider employment elsewhere.

Employees Who Are Caregivers

According to a 2013 Gallup poll, nine in ten adults in the United States said they have children, plan to have children, or wish they had children.[32] Yet in many American workplaces, being pregnant, receiving fertility treatment, and caring for children are still treated as outside the norm, which leads to a host of personal and professional consequences, primarily for women. Research specific to higher education indicates that working mothers navigate negative perceptions of motherhood, confront policies and practices that underestimate childbirth realities, and penalize caregivers.[33]

For working women in higher education, problems with ideal worker norms intensify when they are pregnant. Sociologist Marjukka Ollilainen argued that the traditional academic setting presupposes that a "legitimate" academic is "married, heterosexual, fully committed to intellectual work, and has unlimited time and energy because their spouse tends to all private matters."[34] In this setting, an academic mother's pregnant body is perceived as "a deviant body—far from the (masculine) ideal—that disrupts the expectations of the rational, controlled embodiment of a professor."[35] According to Ollilainen, this deviation from the embodiment of the ideal worker fuels stereotypes that mothers are less competent and less committed to work. As a result, academic mothers are advised to put off having children and to be strategic about how and when they disclose their pregnancies to colleagues.

Negative perceptions of academic mothers can find their way into performance evaluations. Research indicates that working mothers frequently encounter a "maternal wall" in the workplace that manifests in fewer job offers, lower salaries, and less opportunity for advancement.[36] Higher performance and punctuality expectations are sometimes tied to the belief that working mothers should put in extra hours to prove their worth to organizations and account for the "deficiency" of taking time off for doctors' appointments, childbirth, adoption, and infant care. Studies suggest that there is a "pregnancy penalty" specific to higher education when it comes to how students evaluate teaching. Engineering scholar Ronke M. Olabisi found teaching effectiveness ratings went down when the participants she surveyed were pregnant, and averages dropped more for participants who had severe symptoms or gained more than 15 pounds. The decrease was most pronounced in the science, technology, engineering, and math fields and for women of color.[37]

In *Academic Motherhood*, higher education scholars Kelly Ward and Lisa Wolf-Wendel noted that "the culture of tenure has created an environment of competition that appears to reward dedication to the position . . . above all else," leading them to conclude that "the tenure system favors ideal workers."[38] One way it does this is by expecting faculty to show an uninterrupted pattern of research productivity. Academic mothers are sometimes criticized in tenure decisions for "gaps" in their publication record, and sometimes they are even pushed into service duties where they become "departmental mothers," despite these tasks being viewed as "non-promotable" during tenure review.[39]

Things do not get easier for new mothers after giving birth or adopting a child, and not just because of the long hours spent caring for a new arrival. After feeling pressure to return to work just three weeks after giving birth, Claire B. Guth collected parental leave policies for faculty, staff, and graduate students at 142 research universities.[40] She found that 43 percent of the institutions in her sample did not provide paid parental leave for staff, and 60 percent provided four weeks or less. One-third of the institutions provided no leave for graduate students. Many policies required employees to exhaust paid time off before becoming eligible for the Family and Medical Leave Act (FMLA).[41] Some policies that Guth reviewed only provided a few weeks of paid leave, even though dependable and affordable childcare is often in short supply (a fact only exacerbated by the pandemic).[42]

Once caregivers return to work, they report challenges caused by inflexible work schedules that do not neatly align with typical school days or nine-month school calendars. As a consequence, parents must either locate and pay for after-school programs, summer camps, and babysitters or use their limited allotment of paid time off to care for children when schools are closed for holidays, teacher workdays, and weather events.

Employees with Disabilities

In an article and series of portraits in the *New York Times*, artist Sarah J. Winston has argued that "each and every one of us exists on a spectrum of illness, often dipping in and out of it."[43] The disembodied nature of ideal worker norms leads to workplace policies and practices that don't attend to the reality that our minds and bodies, as Winston puts it, "require tremendous care and attention to function."[44] The result is that many workplaces, including colleges and universities, are deeply ableist—despite the fact that according to the US Centers for Disease Control and Prevention, one in four adults has some type of disability.[45]

Participants in a study of disabled academics conducted by Australian political economist Elizabeth Humphreys and colleagues were advised to hide or carefully manage their disability so that it does not undermine their performance or put their chances of promotion at risk. High performance expectations led participants to believe that they had to justify their ability to perform and overcompensate by working more, saying "yes" to extra projects, and pushing through pain and illness. Many felt they had "little choice if they were to prove themselves as fit for work and to model the ideal worker norm."[46] When participants sought accommodations, they encountered perceptions that equated their need for assistance as personal incapacity, laziness, or an unwillingness to work hard.

Writing in *The Chronicle of Higher Education*, English professor Alicia Andrzejewski noted that "academe's demands to work every spare moment of the day, miss meals, and sacrifice sleep and exercise" exacerbated her mental illness. She dedicated substantial effort every day to "mask[ing her] struggles, to seem like everyone else, to keep up."[47] Other academics she interviewed noted the difficulty with academia's sense of urgency and unexpected deadlines, making it difficult to establish a routine. Similarly, ideal worker norms that prioritize constant availability and an uninterrupted workday introduce problems for some employees with disabilities. According to higher education scholar Nancy J. Evans and colleagues, "functional limitations may arise in unpredictable ways and for unpredictable durations" for employees with disabilities, "playing havoc with norms about time lines and timeliness."[48] Unpredictability creates challenges when workers are required to be physically present in an office or classroom at set hours of day. Working from home may be necessary for workers to access medicine, work comfortably, and attend to unexpected physical and mental needs.

In some cases, these employees encounter workspaces designed for nondisabled workers. Psychologist Rhoda Olkin, who studied women academic leaders with disabilities, noted that "you might think . . . years after the passage of the Americans with Disabilities Act, that all campuses would be physically accessible. But accessibility is a relative term."[49] She rattles off the range of issues that she has personally encountered: hilly campuses, lack of parking near buildings, lack of automatic door openers, classrooms crowded with desks and other furniture, lack of bathroom access, and so on. Before meetings or events, she often spends time and energy scouting the location to be sure it is accessible. Olkin recounts that in her first year as a faculty member, there was a retreat at the chancellor's house that she could not attend because there was no entrance ramp. Olkin concluded that issues with the physical structure of workspaces alone can create extra labor and barriers to leadership for individuals with disabilities.

The challenges those with disabilities face don't end at the office, either. Ideal worker norms result in the expectation that higher education workers travel to participate in professional development or scholarly associations. According to Evans and colleagues, work-related travel can be particularly challenging and expensive for university employees with disabilities.[50] Some higher education employees choose to mask their disability, not only to avoid stigma but also because ideal worker norms encourage them to place few demands on their employer and keep the "personal" from encroaching on the "professional." D-L Stewart and Kathy Collins, higher education scholars who conducted a study of graduate students and new professionals in student affairs, found that those with less visible disabilities, such as obsessive-compulsive disorder, anxiety, and dyslexia, opted to not disclose their disability to classmates or to only tell close friends.[51]

Employees Navigating Grief

Sociologist Charlotte Bloch argues that higher education is home to strong emotions—they are, in fact, what often drives staff and faculty to dedicate their lives to developing students and advancing knowledge. At the same time, academia has an "organizational self-understanding" premised on "rationality, methodological principles, objectivity and logical argument."[52] This leads to a "culture of emotions," as Bloch terms it, where certain "emotions appear to be alien, irrelevant or disruptive."[53] Grief is one of them. Higher education scholar Terah J. Stewart wrote about starting his doctoral program two weeks after burying his mom and the challenges he faced processing his grief. "Academia is about order and decorum," he wrote, "and while there may be an acknowledgment of grief, prolonged grieving seemed to be especially egregious."[54]

Bereavement leave policies in higher education reflect this narrow tolerance of emotion. Education scholars Stephanie Anne Shelton and Nicole Sieben received support from their colleagues and mentors following the death of their fathers. But they differentiate the "people within institutions" who supported them from "the institutional structure itself," which they argue "does not seem to allow for space to mourn."[55] They point out that many advice columns encourage employees to take advantage of employee assistance programs and similar resources. But they find grief-related resources vary considerably across institutions and are often geared toward students.

Brooke Wilson, a former student affairs professional who became a certified coach for a grief and loss start-up, learned that many organizations do not educate employees on bereavement leave policies and delegate decisions on accommodations to supervisors. Forcing employees to work out bereavement leave with managers allows bias to creep in, as not every employee's grief receives equal empathy. In the same year that her mom passed away, Wilson lost a beloved pet, a close neighbor, and a long-term relationship. These experiences reinforced for her that grief is "a big bucket," and organizations often overlook exceptionally common forms of loss, such as miscarriage or divorce. Wilson figured out quickly that higher education, like many sectors, creates few affordances for employees who are grieving, despite research showing that nearly everyone in the workforce will experience grief at least once during their career.[56]

Although some colleges and universities have bereavement leave policies, they are typically short and restrict eligibility to immediate family. In fact, US workers get only three days of bereavement leave, on average, with slightly more time for the death of a spouse or child but often zero days for the death of a friend or colleague.[57] Yet three days of leave is barely enough time for many employees to attend a funeral, let alone work through family and legal responsibilities while processing their own feelings. The short length of bereavement leave is especially problematic for higher education workers who had to move far away from family and emotional support systems. Not being able to take time off from work to attend a funeral can result in prolonged or stifled feelings of grief, which can lead to anxiety, depression, sleep issues, and pain.[58] As Brooke Wilson explained to me, "When we aren't given the space or tools to process grief in the moment, that's when these things get stuck in our bodies. When we have to push them down and compartmentalize, it's having an impact, whether or not people want to recognize it."

In short, ideal worker norms thrust employees into positions where they are expected to hide their emotions, continue working without time or space to process loss, exude positivity for colleagues and students, and always maintain a professional veneer. When the pandemic hit, employees of all types experienced a staggering amount of loss, but colleges and universities were often too focused on returning students to residence halls to realize that they have a responsibility to support employees while they grieve and heal.

It should be said that not all people want or feel the need to show up to work as their full selves. Life gets messy, and some employees are perfectly happy to keep work and home separate. My point, though, is that not all employees have a choice. Their gender, bodies, minds, hearts, and responsibilities to family and community cannot be checked at the office door. And so the workplace becomes a site of constant navigation and negotiation. Each instance in which these employees go to extremes to determine if a policy or practice was really designed for them begs the question: Is this a place that cares about me?

Reclaiming the Soul of Organizations

When Frederic Laloux analyzed developmental psychology and the history of organizations, he saw a startling pattern. Every time humans made a cognitive leap, new organizational forms emerged to match how people thought and felt. For example, what Laloux termed "machine organizations" were the result of a cognitive shift that made effectiveness, achievement, and getting ahead the main goals of life. Dispassionate rationality was highly valued in machine organizations, where "identity is no longer fused with our rank and title; instead it is fused with our need to be seen as competent and successful, ready for the next promotion."[59] Anyone working in higher education will recognize the common aims of machine organizations, such as beating the competition and staying ahead through close management of objectives, as well as engineering jargon like "pulling the lever," "moving the needle," and "scaling solutions."

For Laloux, the proliferation of machine organizations in the form of corporations, schools, and hospitals led to "soulless" workplaces that expect employees to "show a masculine resolve, display determination and strength, and hide doubts and vulnerability."[60] Other aspects of the self—the parts that encourage caring and questioning—are dismissed, and the "emotional, intuitive, and spiritual parts of ourselves feel unwelcome, out of place."[61] Fear is a big reason why there is so much emotional regulation in workplaces. Organizations fear that people bringing their feelings into the workplace will breed chaos and distraction, while employees fear they will be ridiculed, ostracized, or worse if they show up as their authentic selves. But many employees aren't putting up with the antics of machine organizations any longer. In a prescient reference to what was to come during the Great Resignation, Laloux concluded we are on the cusp of another cognitive leap, one causing employees to "yearn . . . for radically better ways to be in organizations."[62]

This new developmental stage is characterized by a shift from living in a place of fear and scarcity to a place of trust and abundance. In this new way of thinking, life is understood as a journey of discovery where the goal is to "become the truest expression of ourselves, to live in authentic selfhood, to honor our birthright gifts and callings, and be of service to humanity and our world."[63] As part of this journey, we learn from setbacks and mistakes and move from seeing limitations and deficits in ourselves and others to seeing and building on strengths. Laloux uses the term *evolutionary organizations* to describe the organizational form that responded to this stage of human development. A cornerstone of evolutionary organizations is that humans desire wholeness—within the self, in relation to others, and with nature. As a result, employees want to toss aside the professional mask and stop hiding their authentic selves. The desire for wholeness will pull employees to organizations that have a clear purpose beyond profit or growth—organizations that are not governed by competition, stoicism, and toxic norms.

I have spent my whole career in machine organizations, where I heard plenty of engineering jargon and very few references to "wholeness." After spending so many years in a workplace defined by scarcity, fear, and the never-ending quest for greater productivity, it took me a minute to wrap my head around Laloux's ideas. But then I compared his description of evolutionary organizations against the US surgeon general's essential components of workplace well-being—components that informed my thinking about what it takes to create the Caring University. And the similarities were unmistakable. Safety over fear. Flexibility over rigidity. Wholeness over separation. Dignity over deficits.

Using Laloux's evolutionary organizations as a springboard, I propose four approaches that are an answer to workers' desire for workplaces that take their well-being seriously—approaches that also embrace key elements of organizational change discussed in Chapter 1, such as sensemaking, organizational learning, and organizational justice.

Approach 1: Caring Through Resetting Professional Norms

Many problems in the higher education workplace can be traced back to norms of professionalism designed by and for the ideal worker—norms that have seeped into the practices and policies of organizations. How do you go about changing norms that, as we have learned, are a century or more in the making? You start by naming them and asking questions about whether they are truly serving the organization's goals. Like the workplace culture to which they contribute, the norms of an organization are deeply ingrained, becoming routine and unquestioned. In fact, most ideal worker norms aren't explicitly written down as a set of organizational rules. Yet they become part of the "hidden curriculum" of the professional workplace.[64] An important first step in resetting notions of professionalism is exposing workplace norms and how they affect employees.

As an example of what this exposure can look like, Rosemary J. Perez recommends that faculty members and supervisors in student affairs "regularly engage in the kind of reflection they ask graduate students to do in service of becoming more reflexive practitioners."[65] She offers discussion questions to facilitate reflection, such as "How do I currently define professionalism and how did I come to this definition?" and "How would I characterize the ideal worker in student affairs? What has influenced my view?"[66] A motivating goal for this exercise is that faculty, supervisors, and students "make their underlying assumptions and beliefs more explicit" and, in the process, "trouble the concept professionalism."[67] In many cases, these reflections about assumptions lead to an examination of *practices* related to hiring, time off, performance evaluation, and awards. In the same vein, Laloux found that evolutionary organizations often raised awareness of practices undermining employees and their ability to show up authentically by creating space for collective moments of self-reflection. Whether in the form of a workshop or regular staff meeting, higher education is brimming with opportunities for employees to meet. It is just a matter of focusing some of that time on surfacing expectations of professionalism, how they are applied, and whose interests they advance or obstruct.

Suggesting that members of the organization meet to talk about ideal worker norms seems a little like navel-gazing. But research is clear that organizations *need* honest, candid discussions to innovate, create value, and avoid costly mistakes. Management professor Jim Detert finds that "organizational silence," or feeling like you can't speak up or share ideas in the workplace, is a direct driver of employee disengagement.[68] Sensemaking—that all-important means of encouraging organizational change—depends on groups of employees openly sharing their mental models and collectively crafting new conceptualizations. But here is the hitch: workers must feel safe in order to fully participate in these conversations.

The term *psychological safety* is used by scholars to describe the conditions in which people feel safe speaking up during difficult workplace conversations and not having to hide or hold back parts of themselves.[69] Leadership scholar Amy Edmondson has studied psychological safety in numerous workplaces since the 1990s. She explains that psychological safety means employees "feel comfortable sharing concerns and mistakes without fear of retribution. They are confident that they can speak up and won't be humiliated, ignored, or blamed. They know they can ask questions when they are unsure about something. They tend to trust and respect their colleagues."[70]

When these conditions are in place, organizations exhibit significantly more "learning behavior"—they confront problems, learn from mistakes, take more calculated risks, and improve the quality of services. Importantly, psychological safety doesn't mean throwing out standards, accountability, or consequences. Both Laloux and Edmondson stress the importance of leaders modeling humility and vulnerability, establishing norms to handle failure, inviting and listening to feedback, and sanctioning clear violations of organizational values. Employees can still fail and receive feedback when their performance falls short, but it is in a context that emphasizes learning from mistakes versus punishment or embarrassment.

Approach 2: Caring Through Better Leave Policies

While researching this book, I visited the human resources (HR) websites for countless colleges and universities. I saw firsthand how policies intended to support employees vary widely from institution to institution. When I clicked the link for "employee well-being" on one university's website, it took me to a list of webinars offered by insurance companies. By contrast, the University of Washington's WorkLife website lists an impressive array of resources for childcare and caregiving, eldercare and adult caregiving, and housing, as well as resources to help managers create a supportive work environment. On top of these resources, the University of Washington launched the Whole U in 2014, which offers ongoing programs for employees to foster connection and holistic well-being. These efforts matter because for many employees, the question of whether their employer cares about them boils down to features of the organizational structure, such as leave policies and benefits.

The patchwork of parental leave policies in the United States and the lack of policies at many colleges and universities undermine the health and well-being of working parents in higher education. The United States is just one of six countries that does not have a federal paid parental leave policy. FMLA ensures that workers receive three months of job-secure, unpaid leave, but many employees cannot afford to go long without pay. And by one estimate, only 44 percent of US workers are eligible for FMLA leave because they are part-time, work for a small employer, or haven't worked long enough at their organization. Workers of color are also less likely to be eligible for FMLA-supported leave.[71] In 2021, the College and University Professional Association for Human Resources found that under 40 percent of institutions offer paid parental leave.[72] The lack of parental leave sends a message that having a family isn't supported. But it is also bad for business. UNICEF points out that paid parental leave contributes to lower staff turnover rates and lower recruitment and training costs.[73]

Supporting employees should not stop at parental leave. For one thing, every working parent needs access to childcare if they are going to be able to show up to work. According to Jessica Cole, who directs WorkLife at the University of Washington, the university offers employees six on-site childcare centers, serving over 450 children and bucking a national trend of declining on-campus childcare options. The Institute for Women's Policy Research found that the number of on-campus childcare centers has declined over the past decade, with only 45 percent of public institutions offering on-campus services in 2019.[74]

When employees visit the WorkLife website, they see that support for families isn't limited to children. There are resources for adult caregiving and eldercare, which is a growing need for employees having to care for children, grandchildren, and aging parents. There is even a section of the website devoted to pets. According to Cole, few vendors provide backup care for children and adults, and it can get expensive for institutions, yet she notes that these offerings have been heavily utilized by employees. Some of these resources have been available for years, but Cole made them more prominent on the HR website: "It shows that we are thinking about those different family systems whenever we curate our websites and our marketing and our media to make sure that people know about those resources."

Much like paid parental leave, there is no US policy mandating paid bereavement leave. At a minimum, bereavement leave policies must recognize the reality that many employees need to travel to attend the funeral of a loved one. And they must be expanded to include extended and chosen family, as well as pregnancy loss. Option B is an organization founded by Sheryl Sandberg, the former Meta chief operating officer, to provide compassionate, everyday advice for people navigating loss. Option B notes that best-in-class companies offer 20 days of paid leave. It also says employees should be able to take days off nonconsecutively because "grief is not one and done."[75] Beyond bereavement leave, the organization advocates compassionate leave, a "catch-all category for life-altering and emergency losses and hardships." According to Option B, research shows these practices increase employee morale and retention.[76]

Employee assistance programs (EAPs), or "voluntary, work-based programs that provide confidential assessments, short-term counseling, referrals, and follow-up services for employees," have often been used to support employees through particularly challenging personal situations like the loss of a loved one.[77] In recent years, many organizations have expanded their EAPs to include services for employees who are navigating divorce, career changes, and personal finance. Even so, research indicates that EAPs are often underutilized because they are perceived as a crisis-response tool, there is a stigma around reaching out for help, and the quality and availability of service providers is poor.[78] It is also the case that many employees simply don't know about these resources because HR offices don't typically have staff focused on communications.

Kimberly Mishra, who helped launch the Whole U at the University of Washington (UW) and now serves as the chief of staff for human resources, explained to me that they put a lot of effort into how they communicate with employees: "We really try to talk to employees as people." In fact, the Whole U operates from a separate website from HR as a way of underscoring its mantra that the programs are for UW employees, by UW employees. And the programs are not focused solely on fitness and nutrition to boost productivity or lower health care costs. It's about helping employees connect with one another and navigate life's milestones, often leveraging the events and expertise already present on campus. The upgraded communications can sometimes convey that WorkLife and the Whole U are well-resourced. Although they would love to have more financial support and staff, Mishra and her colleagues have managed these initiatives with a small team and modest budget.

Higher education is frequently categorized as a "human service." Yet leave policies do a poor job of recognizing the humanity of employees—often failing to capture what it means for one human to bring another human into this world or to recover when a loved one passes from this world. We may see federal policies in the future guarantee some level of paid parental or bereavement leave. But what does it say about colleges and universities if they only adopt policies to support their employees *after* it is federally mandated?

Approach 3: Caring Through Universal Design

Historian and higher education professional David Perry poignantly asked why employers only create leave policies for specific events or needs? Why not make leave policies that benefit all workers? As the parent of a child with Down's syndrome, Perry has become intimately familiar with both the upsides and limits of leave policies. And as an advocate for disability rights, he is well-versed in principles of universal design, or creating "an environment so that it can be accessed, understood and used to the greatest extent possible by all people regardless of their age, size, ability or disability."[79] Universal design calls for treating employees fairly, recognizing their diverse ways of being, and eliminating barriers and risks of humiliation—all of which contribute to what psychologist Donna Hicks has termed a "dignity-centered organization."[80] Drawing on this experience and expertise, Perry has advocated for "universal design for work-life balance."[81]

As Perry puts it, rather than designing work environments around a small number of needs that are deemed "virtuous and valid," universal design favors policies that are equitable, flexible, and easy to access.[82] This means leave policies that allow for a set period of paid leave that is available to *all* employees, regardless of the reason. In Perry's thinking, the diversity of employees at colleges and universities requires a policy solution that speaks to a full range of needs: what middle-aged workers caring for parents need may differ from what new employees struggling with their mental health need. But everyone benefits from the option of time off with few questions or red tape. Policies structured around universal design for work-life balance are based on trust, giving employees power and agency to determine the conditions under which they do their best work.

Universal design can also improve workplace practices and policies. As an example, performance evaluation processes in higher education tend to treat workers from a one-size-fits-all perspective. The timelines, documentation, and criteria are the same for all employees. As a result, there may not be policies to ensure disabilities are explicitly considered as part of reviews, potentially making it harder for employees with disabilities to attain high performance ratings and be eligible for merit-based pay raises or other rewards. Antonia DeMichiel, a disability specialist at the University of San Francisco, explained to me in an interview, "Disability is a protected status. So, technically, the law and the institution's policies say you can't discriminate or evaluate performance based on their disability. But that's not always what's happening in practice."

DeMichiel cited her own experience as an example of what can happen in practice. For many years, she was informally accommodated in her job, meaning she had not officially disclosed her disabilities. Then DeMichiel contracted COVID-19 in 2022, and her doctors told her it was critical to seek formal workplace accommodations. "I was very ambivalent about it," said DeMichiel. "I feared retaliation. I feared discrimination." In the end, she decided to disclose her disabilities, a process she described as "completely dehumanizing." According to DeMichiel, requests for accommodations were treated in the same way as medical leaves, and she was required to provide extensive documentation from doctors to prove her disability. Finally, DeMichiel was granted an additional day to work at home each week on a temporary basis. Although her cerebral palsy isn't going anywhere, DeMichiel will have to go through the whole process again when her temporary accommodation ends.

The process reflected what DeMichiel called the "medical model" of disability, which emphasizes helping individuals overcome impairments and deficits. By contrast, DeMichiel and many disability services professionals advocate a "social model" of disability that views disability as a social construct and calls attention to the social, environmental, and attitudinal barriers that prevent people with disabilities from fully participating in society.[83] Now that she has disclosed her disability, DeMichiel isn't sure it was the right move. She has noticed a change in how her performance is evaluated after her university adopted a standard performance review cycle and template.

Based on her experience as a disability services professional who is also disabled, DeMichiel recommends that colleges and universities get clear on the model of disability from which they are operating. Universal design favors training supervisors and managers, regardless of whether they work with faculty and staff with disabilities. At some point, leaders are likely to encounter an employee who needs accommodations, and being prepared would cut down on stigma, confusion, and exclusionary practices, such as hosting team-building activities at inaccessible locations. With more training, supervisors might better anticipate the "tax" employees with disabilities face while working in ableist institutions. Additional training might help supervisors and managers see that providing accommodations and meeting legal obligations under the Americans with Disabilities Act (ADA) is really the "floor," or bare minimum, when it comes to providing services. It takes intentional effort to create conditions where employees with disabilities feel safe showing up as their full selves.

If institutions continue to use the medical model of disability, higher education scholars Nancy J. Evans and colleagues have noted that they should at least ensure that all policy documents are easy to access and employees are instructed on how to seek accommodations and provide proper documentation.[84] Although some colleges and universities employ staff whose job is to help communicate employment policies and processes, it is far likelier that workers are left to navigate byzantine HR websites hosting outdated PDFs. As DeMichiel explained, "If you go to the student-facing side at any institution, we have to be clear about our policies. Otherwise, the Office of Civil Rights is going to come knocking tomorrow. That's not happening on the employee side of the house." One idea is to include a discussion of disabilities and accommodations as part of new employee orientation, with regular follow-up instructions.

But if institutions are ready to move toward the social model of disability, they might consider moving requests for accommodations out of human resources and into a disability resource office, which is better prepared to help employees navigate disclosure, documentation, and accommodations. Additionally, Evans and colleagues suggest creating a council or advisory board consisting of workers with disabilities to review policies and processes, share their experiences with leaders, shape the availability and provision of services, and counter forms of ableism in academia. Over time, these changes to practices and policies may lead to more people with disabilities working in higher education.

The "universal" part of universal design captures an essential idea: designing a workplace according to these principles benefits all workers. A universally designed workplace is simply a workplace that is prepared to harness the full spectrum of human capabilities.

Approach 4: Caring Through Flexibility

The ideal worker norm is premised on creating and perpetuating a rigid, narrowly construed standard against which we are judged—and are often found lacking. Many workplace practices and policies in higher education reflect a bureaucratic perspective that equates fairness with sameness. That is, the best route to prevent favoritism or nepotism is to have a single set of workplace rules that apply to everyone. But the result is processes that don't reflect the multitude of unique talents and needs that workers bring to the workplace. For employees who are caregivers, have a disability, or are navigating grief, the lack of flexibility does not lead to fair workplace processes or outcomes. For these and other workers, standardization, sameness, and rigidity create a set of blinders where employers can't see the wholeness of employees.

My interviews with faculty and staff indicate that flexibility is most urgently needed in determining where and when higher education employees work. For many leaders in the private sector, a key concern about hybrid or remote work arrangements is how they will affect productivity. Much of the research shows that these concerns are unfounded because productivity has either been unchanged or increased among hybrid and remote workers.[85] In higher education, the biggest worry is that giving employees flexibility around when and where they work will undermine student services or diminish the residential campus experience. But the research suggests otherwise.

For example, the University of Iowa undertook a "Future of Work" project that focused on understanding the long-term potential of "flexible work," including hybrid and remote work arrangements and flexible schedules. The final report for the project is jam-packed with evidence that flexible work can be good for employees, in terms of increasing satisfaction and lowering stress, and good for the institution, in terms of service delivery and retention.[86] The consensus was that it is not just staff who have appreciated flexible work. Today's students want virtual options for many services, and they aren't phased in the least by the idea of people working remotely or hybrid. Thomas Dickson, who served as assistant vice provost for undergraduate education at the University of California, Riverside, explained it to me this way: "In the aggregate, I don't feel that remote or flexible work arrangements compromise the residential or commuter student experience at all. In most cases, flexible hours and remote options only serve to expand access for many student services areas."

Rutgers University in New Brunswick, New Jersey, formalized flexible work options in a pilot program, then continued these options for an additional year after the pilot's success. Formalizing flexible work meant creating university-wide definitions for flexible work arrangements, including compressed workweeks, flexible work schedules, and hybrid work environments.[87] Department heads and their staff completed a needs assessment and team agreement, after which employees could apply for a flexible work arrangement through an online system.

To "empower local decisions," department heads at Rutgers are responsible for reviewing and approving applications. Pushing much of the decision-making around hybrid and remote work arrangements to the local level is common in higher education and can create a few problems. Frequent turnover and organizational restructuring mean supervisors are often changing, and two supervisors may have differing views on flexible work. Leaving decisions up to supervisors also introduces opportunities for bias and discrimination. Rutgers tempers some of these issues by having a clear policy, published guidelines and FAQs, and resources for both supervisors and employees to help navigate the process and create effective multimodal teams. The university doesn't just say, "It's up to you and your supervisor to work it out." Instead, it has built out a detailed website under the brand Flex@RU to provide an institution-wide set of parameters and a framework to guide supervisors in their decision-making and conversations with employees.

To get a sense of what it looks like to operate an office under Flex@RU, I interviewed Wil Jones, Jr., executive director of the Office for Career Exploration and Success. Jones's office was experimenting with hybrid work arrangements and compressed workweeks even before the pandemic. The compressed workweeks allowed the office to be open earlier and later in the day, meeting the needs of students in different time zones and students who needed advising outside business hours. Students have positive things to say: "They've had more access to resources in the hybrid environment. So whether they want to come in person or do virtual advising appointments or workshops, the accessibility piece for many of our students has increased by having these hybrid options. And so our data is showing it. Our foot traffic is showing that we can do both."

Although there was a service-delivery rationale for Jones to pursue flexible work options in his office, there was also an employee retention rationale. Many of Jones's staff interact regularly with employers and recruiters from other industries. They are aware of the flexible work arrangements that other organizations offer employees, and Jones is pressured to be creative to keep talented staff. "It's one thing when we know that within higher ed, you know, our salaries are not in line with what similar types of roles can make within corporate. We have to identify other ways to be competitive in order to retain top talent," he said. When Jones lists an open position in his office, he markets the flexible work arrangements because candidates are telling him that is what attracted them.

It has taken work from everyone in the office to make sure that they intentionally build community and foster a sense of belonging, especially among new employees. There is a requirement that all employees are in the office on Wednesdays for staff meetings and events, and Jones tries to avoid having an employee alone in the office, which can be tricky because they occupy multiple spaces. "But, you know, we were able to figure all that out, meet the challenges that were presented to us," said Jones. "And I think, overall, it's been really helpful."

It is not the case that flexible work arrangements are the answer to every "future of work" question. There's no doubt that the work of certain jobs in higher education will require more time in-person to build teams and serve students. But we have a unique opportunity in higher ed not to chain ourselves to tradition. As organizational psychologist Scott Sonenshein told Brené Brown on an episode of her "Dare to Lead" podcast: "If you think that you're going to be leading the same workforce that you were in February 2020 with the same mindset, the same mentality, the same desires and the same priorities, you're nuts. You either have to change or get out of the way."[88]

Approach 5: Caring Through "Guardrails"

To pull off flexible work arrangements, Jones and his staff needed to rethink not just when and where work happens but also *how* it happens. Many employees working a compressed workweek didn't work on Fridays, which had implications for important events the office facilitated, such as on-campus interviews. Jones and his team reviewed data and found that employers who were recruiting students rarely came to campus for interviews on Fridays, so to make the compressed workweek possible, they decided to limit on-campus interviews to Monday through Thursday. Additionally, the office implemented #FocusFridays, where there is a rule that no internal meetings are scheduled on Fridays. That way people can focus on their work if they come in to work on Fridays or can be sure they aren't missing meetings if they are off.

Curtailing programs and meetings on Fridays to prioritize flexible work arrangements are an example of what Anne Helen Petersen and Charlie Warzel call "guardrails" in the workplace.[89] Setting boundaries became a common response to higher education workers who were overwhelmed with work. But Petersen and Warzel point out that boundaries have real shortcomings. For one thing, they put the onus on individual workers to figure out how to keep work from pushing "into the corners of what used to be your nonwork life."[90] And what if workers fail to establish or keep boundaries? That's their fault, not the fault of the working cultures or conditions. Second, it is often privileged workers who are able to set and keep boundaries. According to Petersen and Warzel, "[Boundaries are] simply not a sustainable option for the vast majority of workers, especially those who aren't in senior positions, who are women, who are people of color, or who are disabled. For those groups, attempting to maintain them can lead to an office reputation as difficult, aloof, irresponsible, or the dreaded 'such a millennial' or 'not a team player.' "[91] Third, the amorphous, unclear notion of boundaries means that some workers are trying to place limits on work, while others are striving to adhere to ideal worker norms. You can guess which is more likely to get promoted.

By contrast, guardrails are structural. They are, in the words of Petersen and Warzel, "designed with the understanding that we need protection."[92] Guardrails look like clear rules, implemented fairly, to create and maintain trust in an organization's culture. (Box 3.2 presents an example of such guardrails in higher education in the form of a 32-hour workweek.) On a more practical level, guardrails respect employees' time, both in and out of the office. Examples include thinking critically about the utility of a meeting and even establishing organization-wide parameters about what conversations merit a meeting versus an email or conversation. Some organizations have encouraged a set of practices around how to make the most out of meetings by, for example, having an agenda and ending with action items.

Box 3.2

The 32-Hour Workweek

The Case of D'Youville University

D'Youville is an urban campus on the west side of Buffalo, New York. The university got an early jump on "future of work" discussions. Back in 2018, it explored how to model better work environments and experiences for students. Initially, the focus was on improving how employees delivered services, enhancing technology and digitizing paperwork to make business processes run more smoothly, and renovating physical workspaces to encourage collaboration and bring more light into offices. These changes laid the groundwork for D'Youville's more substantial transformation: implementing a 32-hour workweek for all full-time staff.

The pandemic created an opportunity for D'Youville University to experiment. When the campus shut down during the first wave of COVID-19, the university took advantage of a shared work program in New York designed to help organizations that relied on seasonal labor. The program called for reducing some employees to a 30-hour workweek while still being paid their normal salary through a supplement from the state. D'Youville's president, Lorrie Clemo, noticed positive outcomes from what was initially a short-term response to closing the campus: "What I saw immediately was that there was more space for people to think and problem-solve. People were more relaxed and came forward with ideas that were really creative."

Clemo and her team started to consider how to continue harnessing these benefits without the shared work program. Around the same time, they took note of legislation in California proposing a 32-hour workweek. Although the law wasn't passed, Clemo wondered if the idea could work at D'Youville. In some ways, the university was already primed for this type of change. Over 80 percent of students are in health professions programs, where nontraditional schedules are common. Because the university has a focus on health professions and is located in what Clemo describes as a high-poverty area with limited health care options, D'Youville had already been pursuing a strategy to become a hub of health and well-being.

The university's leadership consulted emerging research showing the benefits of a four-day workweek, then launched a survey to gauge what employees thought of the idea. Clemo asked the managers of each of the university's main units to talk with their staff and come up with a plan to accommodate a four-day workweek. She set clear parameters that offices needed to be open five days a week, and weeks that contain a holiday would not be further shortened. Certain weeks would be all-hands-on-deck, especially when students are moving in. Still, managers and their staff were excited to

Box 3.2 (continued)

work on an initiative solely focused on employees. "I have to tell you, the enthusiasm around that was like nothing I have ever seen in higher education," Clemo said. "Because in higher education, we typically use the stick. If you don't do this, here's what will happen. This was totally the carrot approach. If we are going to try this, how can you change to help us make it happen?"

It took six months of planning before D'Youville University launched the pilot. A big question was figuring out how to reduce workloads or improve workflows so that employees weren't simply trying to squeeze 40 hours of work into 32 hours. Technology investments and reducing the number of meetings have both helped. The university also needed to figure out how offices with only one person could provide service continuity throughout the week. D'Youville has introduced cross-training of employees, moved to storing essential files on shared drives, and set up shared office phones and email inboxes. Clemo tries to model being selective about calling meetings and who needs to be present. And all units must participate in project management training and create workflow ticketing systems. The underlying idea is that you can't just switch to a 32-hour week without making changes to how work gets done.

As D'Youville's dean of students, Danielle Nesselbush oversees all student-facing units. For the offices she manages, staff were able to select their day off based on seniority, with the caveat that everyone had to be in the office on Tuesdays. They reevaluate the schedule annually as new staff are hired. Managing so many schedules hasn't posed a problem so far. According to Nesselbush, "People have grown to respect that day off. When we're scheduling, we just say, 'That's my day,' so we pick a different one." The change is part of the university's culture now, and she has seen nothing but upside. "We found that it's more effective. We are more motivated to get the work done in the days that we're here." But the change comes with new responsibility. It is important that everyone communicate and help their colleagues understand what they are working on, so that when you are able to leave work at the office, others can pick up where you left off.

For Nesselbush, the effect of the 32-hour week on retention is personal—it is much harder for her to imagine leaving and returning to a 40-hour week. Nesselbush and others are asked constantly to share with colleagues at other universities how they implemented the change. And D'Youville has put itself on the map as the first US university to adopt a 32-hour workweek—and show that it works.

Respecting employees' time and their desire to build lives outside the workplace means creating conditions for them to take time off and go on vacation without returning to an avalanche of unread emails and work tasks. Petersen and Warzel describe one company that uses software to allow employees to effectively turn off their inboxes. Emails get diverted to others in the company so that responding to messages becomes a collective responsibility. One downstream effect of an organization establishing even light guardrails is that it elevates everyone's consciousness around how work happens. People might become more intentional about when they schedule a meeting and how they prepare for it, and employees think twice before emailing a colleague who is on vacation.

Guardrails are an organization-level rebuke of the ideal worker norm of conditioning employees to exist only for work. They are an effort to manage work in better ways that give workers more time outside of the job to invest in themselves and others. In many ways, guardrails ensure what boundaries promise but often fail to deliver: the time and space to complete our work and then walk away from it.

Conclusion

In her 2022 presidential address to the Association for the Study of Higher Education, Joy Gaston Gayles declared: "The Great Resignation, I believe, is in response to the machine culture that has always been present in higher education—a culture that prioritizes productivity over humanity."[93]

Lane, the case manager introduced at the start of this chapter, was a cog in this machinery, trying to keep up with a volume and intensity of work that left her feeling less than human. She existed only for work—but not by choice. What Lane desired was to do meaningful work *and* build a full life outside the office. She wanted to feel comfortable being herself in the workplace and have her concerns about a reasonable caseload valued. When she needed help or pursued accommodations, Lane wanted to feel supported and not guilty.

To borrow from Laloux, what Lane yearned for was a radically different way of being in higher education. But if Laloux is right, what Lane seeks from her employer is not extraordinary. Rather, it is reflective of a massive shift in how humans think and feel that emphasizes authentic selfhood. Higher education workers are increasingly unwilling to take part in the "machine culture" and sacrifice their well-being in the name of competitiveness and productivity. As Gaston Gayles noted, "People are intentionally unplugging from the academic machine and choosing to plug into work that aligns with their values."[94] It is time for institutions to get with the times.

The Caring University isn't just a blueprint to attract and retain employees. It's an effort to help leaders cast off the vestiges of machine organizations and evolve into the future of work. As Box 3.3 describes,

Box 3.3

Chapter 3 Action Steps

- Set aside time for individual and collective reflection and discussion on the meanings and effects of professionalism and ideal worker norms.
- Conduct a psychological safety assessment to determine if employees feel comfortable being their authentic selves in the workplace and can speak up about important issues without fear of humiliation, rejection, or retaliation.
- Analyze the state of leave policies for employees and how they reflect the realities of human bodies and caring for loved ones. Critically examine how "family" and "care" are interpreted and who these interpretations benefit.
- Invest in mechanisms and personnel to ensure employees are aware of employee resources and understand the process for using them.
- Apply principles of universal design to all employee policies and processes to maximize access and harness the full talents of workers.
- Consider what the institution's "model" of disability is and how to reduce stigma around disabilities. Provide enhanced training and clearer policies, and relocate employee accommodations to a disability resource office.
- Implement flexible work arrangements that meet employees' needs without undermining the provision of services or student experience.
- Establish guardrails that allow employees to have a fuller nonwork life. Set organization-wide policies or parameters related to emails, meetings, vacations, and schedules.

this means disrupting problematic norms of professionalism by instilling the conditions that promote psychological safety, allowing employees to be themselves and speak up in the workplace. It means creating more realistic and humane leave policies so that employees have time to care for themselves and loved ones during moments of immense change. It means *designing* workspaces and processes for access and not accommodation. And it means taking organizational responsibility to prevent work from consuming the nonwork lives of employees.

CHAPTER 4

Committing to Professional Growth and Fair Compensation

ON A BALMY, OVERCAST DAY in late July, I found myself deep in thought on the steps of the main administration building at the University of Louisville (UofL). It was an apt place to think. The building was modeled after the Rotunda at the University of Virginia, designed by Thomas Jefferson. A few feet away from me was the first large-scale bronze cast of French sculptor Auguste Rodin's *The Thinker.* After a long day of interviews, I was in good company to work through a problem while I waited for a ride back to my hotel after a long day of interviews.

I traveled to UofL to learn about the creative and caring work of the Employee Success Center. Under the leadership of Brian Buford, who serves as executive director of University Culture and Employee Success, the center has transformed how the university onboards, recognizes, and develops employees. Everything I read about the Employee Success Center suggested it could be a model for supporting professional growth. But right before my arrival, Buford emailed me with a heads-up: UofL had just released the results of a three-year "total compensation and rewards study" for staff. "I had been bracing for this," Buford explained in his email, "because I know that expectations were high and that most people would be disappointed."

When I showed up at the Employee Success Center, the results of the study were the talk of campus. One part of the study was to create a new job classification structure, and staff had just learned how their jobs had been classified and where they fell on associated salary ranges. Only 20 percent of staff saw their pay increase, and some felt their new job classification represented an unwanted change in title—or even a demotion. I later read on the UofL human resources website that the goals of the study were to create a competitive compensation and benefits package and provide opportunities for career advancement.[1] But during my visit, it wasn't clear to staff how the classification structure would facilitate career progression because the details around how you move up newly created career ladders had not been worked out. So, on the very day I came to UofL, eager to learn all about employee success, it became clear that many staff were—in a word—pissed.

Even before my arrival, I knew UofL was going to be a complicated case. This was a place with some history. Between 2008 and 2015, the university had not one, not two, not three, but seven financial scandals involving misuse of funds—all of them under the leadership of President James Ramsey. Needless to say, things got worse before they got better. In 2015, the university learned an employee of the basketball program paid strippers to help recruit players, resulting in the team vacating the 2013 national championship. Just a few months after news of the recruitment scandal broke, Ramsey and his staff appeared in a photo wearing racist Halloween costumes. In 2016, Kentucky's then governor Matt Bevin fired the entire UofL board of trustees. Ramsey agreed to tender his resignation to the new board after it came to light that he had authorized excessive spending of the endowment on speculative ventures, gifts, and loans.[2]

Neeli Bendapudi was hired as Ramsey's successor in 2018, with a clear mandate from the board to rebuild the scandal-ridden university. Everyone I interviewed at the university lauded Bendapudi's accessibility and positivity. As Buford explained to me, "Neeli made each person she interacts with feel as though they are her highest priority." Bendapudi oversaw the creation of a new strategic plan, with one of the three pillars focused on making UofL a "great place to work" by "inspiring a culture of care," "providing all faculty and staff fair and equitable compensation," and being "dedicated to personal growth and professional development." The plan introduced the "Cardinal Principles" designed to shape the university community and the actions of its employees.[3] Making UofL better for employees would be a prominent part of the university's future, and both the Employee Success Center and the compensation study owe their existence to this strategic plan.

Yet there was something prescient about the strategic plan: it only established goals for the next three years, covering the period from 2019 to 2022. The idea was that the university would evaluate its progress, then create another three-year plan. Overseeing the second strategic plan, it turned out, would fall to another president. In December 2021, UofL learned that Bendapudi, after just three years on the job, had applied for and been selected as the next president of Penn State. Many employees who felt they had a personal connection with Bedapudi were hurt when they learned about her departure from a news story. "The same day everyone learned she was leaving," Buford explained, "she did her first press conference at Penn State. She was wearing Penn State colors and said that her name means 'blue,' which she said was a sign that she was born to be part of the Penn State family. People here watched the press conference live and were absolutely devastated." In the words of Kari Donahue, vice chair of the UofL Staff Senate, Bendapudi left the university a "half-finished renovation project."

By the time the compensation study results were released, employee confidence in leadership was not exactly sky-high. The string of scandals precipitated budget cuts and greased a revolving door in senior management positions. Many staff had gone years without a meaningful pay raise, and funds for professional development were scarce. Employees at the university were desperate for good news; instead, the compensation study poured salt on old wounds. On a Reddit thread devoted to the study, one post summed up the reactions of employees this way: "I would be more outraged if my expectations weren't already so low to begin with."[4]

A staff member I interviewed said she saw the results of the compensation study coming from a mile away: "There had been this trajectory of morale, with decisions that had been made without staff input or recognition of how it would affect people's jobs." Although she understood that there can't be shared governance or transparency with every decision, she felt leaders struggled to grasp that trust in leadership is low. "The administration keeps changing," she said. "People don't feel connected to the administration, and they don't know how or why decisions get made." Some errors with the compensation study—including how it was rolled out and communicated—might have been avoided with more staff input. "Totally reasonable questions are being asked," she told me. "They aren't answering those questions, they weren't prepared to answer those questions, but they could have predicted those questions. Had there been more involvement from staff, someone could have alerted them."

These were the sentiments that I was processing on the steps of the main administration building. On the one hand, there were undeniably good things happening at UofL. The strategic plan prioritized supporting the growth and development of employees in a way I had rarely seen in my research. It recognized the need to address compensation and called for the creation of an Employee Success Center. Yet the champion of that plan had left, leaving questions about whether fair pay and professional development would continue to be priorities. Although there was hope the new president, Kim Schatzel, would continue to invest in these efforts, she was early in her tenure, and the jury was still out. At that moment, I was preparing for the possibility that I had traveled a long way to hear about another university where workers were demoralized.

Later that night, I had something of an epiphany. Perhaps I was too fixated on top-level leadership and one particularly challenging moment in a change process. At a big, decentralized university like UofL—a university coming off nearly a decade of scandal—organizational change is going to look different. It is going to be a long road, with plenty of uphill climbs and more than a few slips on the way.

Organizational change might not always come from flashy initiatives out of the president's office. Instead, it may radiate from the sustained efforts of respected, longtime employees, caring for one another and transforming a place they love from within. And that meant I needed to talk more with Brian Buford.

The Employee Success Center

During my visit, Buford took me on a short tour of Louisville. "I would walk to that park as a grad student for free Shakespeare performances," Buford said wistfully, pointing to my right. He drove me by houses in the historic part of the city where colleagues lived. Naturally, we paid a visit to Churchill Downs—home of the Kentucky Derby—which sits a stone's throw from the UofL campus. It was clear that Buford loves Louisville. As we walked the university's tree-canopied sidewalks, I can tell he knows every nook and cranny of this place.

Buford came to the university for his master's degree in counseling in 1988 and ended up staying. After working with a professor on a drug and alcohol prevention grant as a graduate student, Buford started working full-time for human resources. In 2007, he helped create the university's LGBT center, the first of its kind in Kentucky. The LGBT center blossomed under Buford's stewardship, consistently earning the university a five-star rating on the Campus Pride Index—an indicator of institutional commitment to LGBTQ-inclusive policy, programs, and practice.[5]

Thirty-five years later, Buford is something of an institution within the institution. "Everyone loves Brian," people told me in interview after interview. Although he racked up awards for his work on campus and in the Louisville community, he did not mention these accolades in our conversations. He talked about the staff and students of the center who were working to make life better—and safer—for members of Louisville's LGBTQ community.

As the new strategic plan was taking shape in 2019, Buford was tapped to serve as the director of employee development and success. When the idea for the Employee Success Center started to emerge, Buford teamed up with his longtime friend and colleague Diane Whitlock to sketch out possibilities. Whitlock is a Louisville native who has worked at the university for over 40 years, mostly in diversity, equity, and inclusion. Buford and Whitlock envisioned a center that would serve all employees and had some degree of separation from human resources. The Employee Success Center launched in 2020 with a direct reporting line to the president. Buford and two other longtime UofL employees, Laura McDaniels and Meagan West, were the center's first employees, and they added two more full-time staff over the next three years.

I met with the whole staff of the center during my visit, and over the course of nearly two hours, they walked me through the flurry of programs and initiatives they have created or revamped in just a few years of existence. One of the first things the center tackled was new employee orientation. With a push from the strategic plan, Buford and his team wanted to move from a brief one-off orientation to a more robust employee onboarding process. The orientation they inherited was short and showed new employees a graphic active-shooter training video within the first 30 minutes. Using insights from interviews with employees about their orientation experiences, the team dreamed up an onboarding process that spanned an employee's first year at the university.

The new onboarding process starts with a warm welcome: the center distributes welcome gifts to all new employees, which include some swag and a message from the president. There is still an initial meeting, but it is now a full-day, in-person program for new employees to learn about the university's culture, the Cardinal Principles, and information about benefits, payroll, and parking. While the response to the new and improved orientation has been positive, the center learned that a breakdown in the onboarding process happened when new employees showed up at their offices or job sites. Although some offices hired new staff regularly, smaller offices may not have welcomed a new colleague in years. New employees were showing up to offices that were not prepared for them to start.

Consistent with the idea of onboarding as a process, the center developed a guide to walk supervisors through a new employee's first year. The guide includes a checklist and provides email templates for welcoming new employees and introducing them to the department. There is even a welcome sign template where supervisors can type the new employee's name and hit "Print." If a department's supervisor is swamped, the center encourages the department to name an onboarding navigator—someone who would join a new employee for lunch during orientation and greet them at the office. The goal is to help new employees get situated, with someone pointing out where supplies are kept and the nearest bathroom can be found.

The new onboarding process also builds in a six-month check-in for new employees. The two-hour group session allows new employees to share what has gone well—or not—and to ask any lingering questions. If any attendees indicate that they are experiencing significant challenges or issues, Buford and his team offer to meet one-on-one to consider resources or solutions. At the end of the year, new employees receive another note from the president, along with a gift to mark the occasion. In the past, the first-time staff would be officially recognized was after ten years of service. The one-year gift is a small gesture in the grand scheme of things, and it is not meant to be the sole form of recognition employees encounter. It is instead supposed to convey a simple message: *We see you, and we're glad you're part of this organization.*

The one-year anniversary gift is just part of a growing recognition ecosystem the center has cultivated. The center started holding receptions for staff service twice per year so that there wasn't a long wait based on someone's hire date. To make the event more celebratory and incorporate employees' voices, someone from each level of service being recognized was selected to speak and share stories about their time at the university. For employees who reached 40 years of service, the center created massive banners that were prominently displayed on campus. After learning not all departments honored retiring staff and faculty, the center organized a campus-wide event to make that milestone meaningful, too. Given the small number of awards to recognize staff for outstanding performance, the center helped create eight new awards aligned with the Cardinal Principles. Additionally, they lobbied to establish a staff equivalent of the highest honor awarded to faculty.

The center also realized that not every recognition needs to be a big event or award. Sometimes, all employees need are small affirmations or the chance to celebrate one another. The center developed both online and printed "CARDgrams" that say "Thank You," "I Appreciate You," and "Happy Birthday," with space for a personal message. Laura McDaniels, the center's engagement specialist, created a Thanksgiving CARDgram that said, "I'm Thankful for You." Even though the campus was only open for a few days that week, employees sent each other over 400 CARD-grams. "I thought that was amazing because there probably weren't even that many people on campus," McDaniels said.

As much as I loved learning about the center's approach to onboarding and recognition, the strategic plan was unequivocal about what would make UofL a "great place to work": committing to employees' personal growth and professional development. Here, too, the center had been cooking up a slew of initiatives. Coaching circles were formed so faculty and staff could come together around a common topic of interest—for example, supervision or social media—and then collaboratively decide where to take the discussion. The center also organizes a formal *Mentoring for Success* program that intentionally pairs mentors and mentees based on an application that each completes. Although the mentoring program is flexible, the center provides workshops and networking events throughout the duration of the program.

And for employees who cannot commit to a formal program, the center created the Employee Success Podcast, which typically features a UofL staff or faculty member talking about their areas of expertise, such as dealing with microaggressions in the workplace or going back to school as a working professional. Episodes of the podcast have explored the Cardinal Principles and what they look like in practice, as well as shared advice on onboarding, recognition, and mentoring. It is a way to showcase the university's in-house knowledge, share resources, and package professional development for easy consumption.

Buford and his team have received glowing feedback on the revamped staff recognition events and the Cardinal Leadership Institute. New employees now start at the university with a stronger, warmer foundation. More and more departments are identifying onboarding navigators and borrowing ideas from the center for their own recognition events. And leaders are reaching out to the center and asking for help navigating thorny issues with their staff. The center is forging new partnerships all the time, and it has big plans. But Buford admits that they need to do more formal assessments to figure out what's working and how.

Still, there is little doubt that the center is a pocket of change at UofL—a small spark that has shifted the trajectory of the university ever so slightly by introducing new traditions, routines, and expectations of what it looks like to support employee success. "What we have propelling us," Buford shared, "is a high level of trust. People know us, they trust us, and they know we're not doing any harm to them. We're here to help." When the university gets around to figuring out how employees can move up new career ladders, Buford and his team are ready to step up with coaching. And when new leaders step into their roles, they will benefit from the center's established efforts to finish the renovation project—to make UofL a great place to work.

There are not many employee success centers in higher education. In that regard, UofL stands out. Other colleges and universities do, however, struggle to facilitate professional growth and offer fair compensation to their workers. In this chapter, I explain how many higher education jobs are dead ends, with few options for staff and faculty to advance in the organization and access professional development. In the face of unclear career pathways and limited professional growth opportunities, many workers feel compelled to switch jobs. In some cases, they are encouraged to do so as the only means to secure a raise. I take a closer look at this issue and other layers of higher education's poor compensation practices, showing how pay is too low, lags living expenses, and is inequitable.

Then I switch over to organization-level approaches that can help institutions demonstrate a commitment to professional growth and fair compensation. Borrowing ideas from Robert Kegan and Lisa Laskow Lahey's deliberatively developmental organizations and research on recognition and appreciation, I show what it looks like for colleges and universities to weave professional growth into their regular operations through clear career pathways and ladders, career coaching and intentional conversations, and in-house professional development. I unpack what fair compensation means and describe promising practices to recognize and appreciate employees, including but not limited to raises.

Higher Ed Is a Land of Dead-End Jobs

My first full-time job in higher education was coordinating a global studies living-learning program, and I loved it. That love fueled me to pour my time and energy into the program, putting in hours on nights and weekends. I was the third coordinator in five years, and my onboarding for the job consisted of a binder that my predecessor left me. As the only full-time employee in an office on the outskirts of the organizational chart, I reported to an associate director who had no plans of leaving and whose experience and education placed them several pay grades above me.

It was early in 2009, and I was happy to have a job amid recession-era budget cuts and furloughs. But I could not be expected to stand in the doorway of my career forever. At some point, I would want to grow and maybe even be considered for a promotion or raise. Yet my supervisor never mentioned professional development or cultivating skills that could lead to new opportunities. I soon got the sense that if I excelled at my job, I would advance exactly to where I already was. In fact, the first person to explicitly discuss my future at the university was a dean who, in a surprise meeting, informed me of the institution's intent to close the program. I don't regret the time and energy I devoted to the program, but it didn't change a fundamental fact: it was a dead-end job.

A dead-end job in higher education is one in which the culture or structure of the workplace stifles career progression and professional growth. For example, it might be a job lacking a clear career ladder, where an employee can move into positions of increasing responsibility and compensation based on experience and performance. In my interviews, jobs lacking a career ladder tended to be in specialized units or in particularly flat offices, where there is a single supervisor overseeing a large "bullpen" of staff in the same position. Some jobs in higher education have a career ladder, but they can be heavily gated, such that getting your foot in the door or switching from one ladder to another is incredibly difficult. A good example of this is a tenure-track faculty position, which has a career ladder, but the jobs are scarce, barriers to being hired are high, and movement up the ladder depends on demanding—and sometimes nebulous—promotion criteria.[6] As usual, it is worse for contingent faculty, many of whom do not have a career ladder at all.[7]

The career ladder for faculty can also be limited to a single pathway focused largely on traditional faculty responsibilities: teaching, service, and research. I interviewed Samantha Streamer Veneruso, a former community college professor and administrator who wrote her dissertation on faculty leadership development. "[The] career path for faculty . . . is within teaching," she told me. "That's it." Faculty ascend from assistant professor to associate professor to professor, so over a 30 -year career, they might be promoted *twice*. That is more of a step stool than a ladder. Some mid-career faculty move into administrative or service roles in an effort to take on a new challenge or secure a pay increase. "But those who expand out and go into administration are viewed with suspicion," Veneruso shared. This can dissuade some faculty from seeing administration as a legitimate, rewarding career pathway. "And ad hoc service roles aren't really a career path per se," she explained. "[Faculty] want to do something more, but the experiences don't necessarily come together cohesively or draw on strengths." And so many mid-career academics feel stuck or directionless, struggling to see or feel supported in pursuing career pathways when they have outgrown traditional faculty responsibilities.

Staff sometimes have more job options available to them than faculty, whether it is a lateral move across the organization or an upward move through promotion. But like faculty, they can encounter structural impediments to career progression, including strict rules around promoting internal candidates. As discussed in Chapter 1, colleges and universities are hierarchical, but they are relatively bottom-heavy pyramids. For every provost, director, or dean, there are multiple coordinators, assistants, and lecturers. This can lead to fierce competition among a large number of employees early in their career for scarce middle-management positions. For example, I interviewed an academic adviser whose community college made advising a cornerstone of its quality-enhancement plan, leading to the creation of new middle-management positions in her office. All the full-time advisers in the office applied for the few management positions that were open. When none of them were selected, the interviewee said, "it just started really feeling like . . . you have to move outside of the institution to find any type of upper movement in advising."

Many workers assume they will eventually need to leave their role or institutions to advance, and so they constantly keep an eye out for opportunities. This can result in workers making multiple costly moves over the course of their careers and spending time they could otherwise devote to serving the organization job-searching. And structuring advancement around leaving an institution creates problems for employees who, for a variety of good reasons, cannot or do not want to move. They might be connected to their community, have spouses or children with their own plans and desires, or need access to particular doctors or family support. For these employees, putting down roots and investing in a place can barricade them in a career cul-de-sac.

Culturally, some colleges and universities don't make it a priority to have regular career conversations with employees, which can further stifle career progression. By career conversations, I mean intentional discussions where supervisors or managers ask their staff about where they see their career going and how they can support their growth. I interviewed Carrie Hawes, who coauthored with Samara Reynolds an article on "radical retention" in higher education during the height of the Great Resignation.[8] Hawes worked at four institutions before leaving for a job at a professional services firm. While working in higher education, she often felt that talking about her future was "very secretive." She experienced a different approach when she moved to her corporate job: "When someone asks, 'What do you want to do next?' I'm like, 'Am I allowed to talk about what I want?'" She has come to believe "the whole model of 'we want you to grow, we want you to be fulfilled in your career' is so foreign to higher education."

Julie M. Forster, a leadership coach and senior consultant at the University of Arizona, told me in an interview that across higher education, to the extent that career conversations are happening at all, they tend to be backward-looking performance reviews. By contrast, her office has developed a career conversations program that is forward-looking. "So for us, the career conversation is an opportunity to step away from that retrospective look and to plan out your goals for the upcoming year. Are there certain projects you want to tackle? Are there certain skills you want to learn?" Forster said. "Do you want to move into a different role? If so, how can you prepare to do that?" Forster's office created a comprehensive annual program with videos, guides, resources, and FAQs just to help supervisors have open, honest discussions with employees about their professional growth and aspirations.

Outsourcing Professional Development

It is not the case that every employee wants to ascend the ranks of management. Jaime Hunt organized a workplace culture survey when she served as the chief marketing officer at Miami University in Ohio. According to the survey findings, "people saw as a barrier to being satisfied with their job that they felt stuck," and some were particularly frustrated that "the only way they could advance is if they took on supervisory roles." Although not everyone wanted to be supervisors, "they still wanted to have their skills and expertise recognized," Hunt said. Despite evolving over centuries and dedicating resources to perfect the art and science of human development, colleges and universities tend to give short shrift to promoting and rewarding the growth and learning of their employees, frequently outsourcing professional development to other organizations.

Many of the functional areas of the higher education workplace, from financial aid to faculty development, have professional associations that run conferences and workshops and sometimes even offer certificates or other credentials. These associations can foster community among people working in similar areas, facilitate the exchange of promising ideas, and generally improve professional practice. But they are also not free—association membership dues, conference registration fees, and travel expenses can add up. Some institutions cover some or all these costs, but consistently across my interviews with staff, I heard about anemic professional development budgets. One interviewee received $400 a year, which was barely enough to cover airfare to a conference. Another could apply for a small number of competitive grants in their department. Sometimes policies around applying for funds were unclear, and practices could vary widely within a given institution. For many employees, especially graduate students and contingent faculty, taking on out-of-pocket expenses for professional development isn't feasible. Yet they have no less desire to grow and learn than other employees.

Tenure-track faculty have generally enjoyed access to more resources for professional development. Because presenting research and remaining active in your discipline are often criteria for promotion, institutions provide faculty with money for travel. Unfortunately, this money doesn't always grow as travel expenses increase, and budgets for professional development are often trimmed when budget cuts arise. Presenting research at a conference also isn't always viewed as professional development because it may not help a faculty member become a better teacher, mentor, or project manager. For this reason, some institutions have created centers for faculty development or teaching excellence, which provide programming and one-on-one support to help faculty develop their knowledge and skills, particularly related to instruction. Some of this programming is heavily oriented toward new faculty and how they can achieve the type of instructional success that results in tenure.[9] Professional development for mid-career and contingent faculty is harder to come by. These centers also need investment, which is not always available despite the importance of teaching on most campuses.[10]

Martha Kalnin Diede spent 12 years as a professor before she started working in faculty development, first at a regional public university and then at a private research university. At the regional public university, she rose to director of an office overseeing faculty research support, faculty teaching support, and the learning management system. When the university needed the learning management system to produce a new report, she had to fight tooth and nail to get an additional staff person, literally clocking everyone's work in 15-minute increments to show that no time existed to take on an additional project. "Everybody's running lean and leaner," she said. One such moment came in 2018, by which point Diede had been hired to establish a teaching center for a private research university. Initially, she was an office of one, serving a university with 22,000 students. She was able to make the case for two additional staff. "So then we were an office of three: me, a program assistant, and a faculty developer. And then there's a pandemic. They're like, 'Oh, we've got to move everybody online.' And I'm like, not to put too fine a point on it, but we have *two* faculty developers." According to Diede, they were able to make it through the crisis, but not without stretching themselves to their limit. After clocking 18-hour days and reaching burnout, Diede left for a job at an information technology company. "You can't grow a unit that's going to support your faculty on a starvation diet," she explained.

In an effort to overcome barriers to career mobility, some higher education employees have pursued additional degrees or credentials. Some colleges and universities pay the tuition (and sometimes other fees) for workers who wish to take credit-bearing courses at the institution where they are employed. This is not an insignificant benefit, and many employees have earned subsidized or low-cost degrees while working in higher education. Nevertheless, taking advantage of this benefit often depends on having a particular academic program at the institution and gaining admission. Some programs aren't set up for working professionals, meaning employees would need permission from their supervisors to attend class during working hours. And it is not universally the case that earning degrees leads to new opportunities or higher pay—some people still end up having to leave their college or university for their additional skills or knowledge to pay off.

Peeling Away the Many Problems with Pay

Compensation is a big, multilayered problem in higher education. The first layer of the problem is that, fundamentally, too many workers are not paid enough. Data from the 2019 Collaborative on Academic Careers in Higher Education shows that 44 percent of all faculty who completed the survey are either dissatisfied or very dissatisfied with their compensation.[11] In a 2021 survey of 957 professionals in higher education, 88 percent of respondents indicated that individuals who leave the field do so because salaries and compensation packages are not competitive for the experience and education required.[12] The National Education Association found in 2023 that education support professionals—people working in administrative support, custodial services, food services, and skilled trades—earn less than a living wage in all 50 states and Washington, DC.[13] Concerns about the low salaries of both postdoctoral researchers and graduate student employees have persisted for decades, and these workers have been some of the most active and successful in recent unionization efforts aimed at improving compensation through collective bargaining.[14]

Most institutions classify jobs based on their responsibilities, then assign them a salary range of 80 percent to 120 percent of a midpoint target.[15] Typically, averages and ranges are determined by analyzing the labor market to see how similar positions are compensated. This can be tricky in higher education because there are sometimes very specialized roles, and data on pay may not be readily available. There is also the question of how to construct the "market." Some institutions build a group of peer institutions for salary comparison, while others may look at similar roles in the region.[16] Employees who are new to a position or early in their career may be paid at the lower end of the range, with the idea that they can move up over time. But too often, there is no clear system in place for progression through a salary range or reclassification of jobs when an employee's responsibilities expand. Salary ranges also need to be regularly updated. Failure to do so means institutions are using outdated data or wait so long to update the range that salaries sink below market, which one HR professional I interviewed referred to as the "deferred maintenance of human resources." It is not uncommon for institutions to set a goal to bring all employees up to 80 percent of the market rate—a tacit admission that they have fallen behind and are simply trying to reduce the amount they underpay employees.

For Glen Colby, who manages the annual faculty compensation survey at the American Association of University Professors (AAUP), "the greatest concern we have now is this growth of contingent faculty appointments." Non-tenure-track faculty appointments now account for 70 percent of all instructional staff appointments in higher education.[17] Faculty in these positions are often on short-term contracts and cannot plan around their employment—or compensation—from one semester to the next. A 2020 survey by the American Federation of Teachers showed that one-third of the 3,076 contingent faculty who responded earned under $25,000 annually, placing them under the federal poverty threshold for a family of four, and only 15 percent reported being able to comfortably cover basic monthly expenses.[18] Full-time, non-tenure-track faculty enjoy salaries and benefits closer to tenure-track faculty, and they are often able to tap into professional development funds and receive salary adjustments.[19] Part-time faculty are usually ineligible for benefits, however. One study found that 57 percent of contingent faculty (and nearly all the adjuncts at community colleges) do not receive medical benefits.[20] Part-time faculty also "have little recourse to substantially grow their salary or earn rewards for good performance. Even years of positive student evaluations can do little to help their case."[21]

Another layer of the problem is that pay has lagged growth in living expenses. The College and University Professional Association for Human Resources (CUPA-HR) has released data showing that all higher education employees were paid less in 2023–2024 than they were before the pandemic, adjusting for inflation.[22] Higher education scholar Martin J. Finkelstein and colleagues showed that, after accounting for inflation, "the hard reality is that faculty salaries have remained virtually stagnant for a four-decade period."[23] The 2021–2022 report from the AAUP on the economic status of the profession found that average salaries for full-time faculty increased 2 percent between 2020–2021 and 2021–2022, continuing a trend of flat wage growth since the 2008 recession (in fact, after factoring in inflation, average salaries actually decreased).[24] A 2020 survey of 550 faculty and instructors at four community colleges and one university found that 38 percent of respondents experienced some form of basic needs insecurity, affecting educators of color, LGBTQ educators, and contingent faculty disproportionately.[25] Graduate Assistants United at the University of Florida surveyed research and teaching assistants at the university in 2021, and 72 percent of over 1,000 respondents said they could not cover all their living expenses (groceries, rent, transportation, utilities, university fees, etc.) on their stipend. Half of respondents indicated that they have been unable to afford (or had to delay) medical care because of a lack of money.[26]

I interviewed a faculty member in biology who left her position at a public liberal arts university for a better-resourced private university. Pay was a big factor in her decision. When she first started at her former institution, she quickly discerned that "there was a lot of frustration among colleagues, and it seemed like a good portion of that frustration came from lack of meaningful, reasonable compensation," she said. When she tried to purchase a home, she found that the stock of available houses was low; furthermore, the entry price for a house in town (which was also a popular tourist destination) wasn't that different from a home in the major city where she had been a postdoctoral researcher. "They don't have condos. They don't have, you know, smaller units for sale. It's mostly standalone houses. Trying to buy a $400,000 home on a one-person salary is like, mathematically, not really possible," she said. The colleagues who appeared to be able to make it work financially and purchase a home could rely on a spouse's income, or else they were from well-off families. When she spoke with her dean about her salary being too low, he informed her that the only way to secure a raise was to get an outside job offer. "And so, you know, I started applying," she explained.

This introduces a third layer of the problem connected to pay in higher education—namely, there are few opportunities to get a raise. Unless they are forced to do so as part of a collective bargaining agreement, many colleges and universities have stopped the practice of regular cost-of-living adjustments, as evidenced by the stagnant salaries and wages for faculty and staff. Some institutions require an outside offer for someone to negotiate a raise. Higher education scholar KerryAnn O'Meara studied the effects of this type of policy and found that it made it harder to retain faculty, partly because it forced institutions into salary competitions that they could not win, but also because it "sent a message to faculty that in order to be recognized and valued (at least salary-wise), they had to prove their worth."[27]

Aware of the limited prospects for a raise, new hires are becoming savvier in negotiating their starting salary. Many institutions now struggle with salary compression or inversion, where new hires earn nearly the same or more than peers who have been at the institution for years. Some institutions moved from regular cost-of-living adjustments to pay based on "merit" or "performance." But employees have raised concerns over how merit is determined and who is (or is not) deemed meritorious.

One study showed that merit pay increases were too small to motivate faculty, and institutions used performance criteria that were difficult to measure.[28]

Of course, compensation is not bad for *all* higher education employees. Growing pay disparities between different higher education jobs—especially between senior administrators and rank-and-file faculty and staff—is a fourth layer of the problem. According to CUPA-HR data from 2020, provosts on average earned $205,000 a year, business school deans earned $204,000, and chief financial officers earned $190,000. Compare that to the average salary of the highest-ranked tenure-track faculty, who on average earned $95,000 a year. Academic advisers brought home just $46,000 a year on average, and it was lower still for admissions counselors ($42,000) and administrative assistants ($37,000).[29] Examining the salaries for faculty and senior administrators between 2007 and 2015, Finkelstein and colleagues saw evidence of "the general trend in higher education and the economy as a whole of increasing distance between senior executives and production workers."[30] It is not necessarily the case that administrators are universally overpaid—many are at an advanced stage in their careers, have developed considerable expertise, and make significant contributions to their campuses. Instead, the problem is that everyone else isn't getting paid enough, they don't have the same earning possibilities, and they aren't seeing their compensation grow.

There can also be major pay differences based on scholarly discipline. Finkelstein and colleagues explained how, until the 1970s, differences in pay between academic disciplines were small and stable. Then, as it became more difficult to recruit experts into high-demand fields like computer science and engineering, institutions started paying faculty in these disciplines salaries closer to market rates, meaning they quickly outearned colleagues in education, humanities, and social sciences. Evidence suggests these pay disparities have only increased in the intervening decades.[31] Because of how resources are allocated and where philanthropic money tends to flow, certain academic colleges are richer than others. The result is that, despite their public allegiance to bureaucratic sameness, many institutions permit more affluent academic colleges to pay staff more than people doing the same work at academic colleges with fewer resources. A business officer in the education college of an institution could anticipate a raise simply by taking a job with the same responsibilities at the engineering college one building over. This problem can be particularly pronounced at decentralized institutions, where different colleges can be financially independent from one another and develop their own compensation customs.

Higher education also isn't immune to well-established salary disparities by gender and race. A 2017 report from CUPA-HR showed that, although administrator salaries for men and women increased steadily between 2001 and 2016, the gender pay gap remained at $20,000 over the 15-year period.[32] In 2002, female administrators were paid $0.90 for every $1.00 their male counterparts were paid. As of 2022, the number only marginally improved to $0.93 per $1.00.[33] According to the AAUP, women receiving a full professor's salary earn approximately 85.1 percent of what men earn. Among associate professors and assistant professors, women earn approximately 92.7 percent and 90.7 percent, respectively, of what men earn.[34] In 2020–2021, faculty at historically Black colleges and universities (HBCUs) were paid, on average, $24,000 less per year than faculty at other institutions. In Missouri and Ohio, HBCU faculty earn half as much as those teaching in non-HBCU land-grant universities.[35] In a study of faculty at 40 public universities, economists Diyi Li and Corey Koedel showed that Black and Hispanic faculty earned, on average, $10,000 and $15,000 less than white faculty.[36] Black employees are also underrepresented in administrative positions, and those who are in administrative positions are, on average, paid less than white colleagues.[37]

The final layer of the problem is less about pay than other forms of compensation and recognition. Finkelstein and colleagues explained that cutting benefits packages, especially retirement benefits, has become a preferred strategy when states face budget shortfalls. Faculty and staff have reported higher monthly contributions for health and other insurance.[38] For many years, colleges and universities were able to fall back on good benefits packages to offset bad pay. But as Kezar and colleagues noted: "Benefit packages are . . . being pared back, with employee healthcare premiums rising as employers offload more of these costs. Further, the range of medical benefits has narrowed, tuition benefits are being withdrawn, and available vacation and sick days are decreasing as well. Workers' compensation and disability benefits are disappearing as part of a growing trend."[39]

Uniting the growing number of contingent, temporary, and part-time employees is their ineligibility for benefits, retirement funds, and vacation time.[40] Along with furloughs and layoffs, some colleges and universities suspended contributions to employee retirement accounts as a strategy to save money in the early months of the pandemic. Dan Bauman of *The Chronicle of Higher Education* reported that between 2019 and 2020, contributions made by private institutions to retirement accounts cumulatively fell by $728 million.[41]

Although pay is critically important, it is not the only way that employees gauge whether their labor is valued. Colleges and universities can be stingy when it comes to nonmonetary recognitions. At many institutions, the approach to employee recognition reflects common pitfalls identified in research: it is mainly awarded for length of service, based on past performance, doled out in a top-down fashion, and scarce.[42] Many institutions send out mass "thank you" emails and focus on the achievements of a small number of employees. On campuses, you might see banners publicizing the grants or inventions of star faculty. Similarly, institutional publications might highlight a small number of faculty conducting cutting-edge research or publishing award-winning books. But that leaves hordes of hardworking staff and faculty who for years go unrecognized for what they do or remain unappreciated for who they are. And the costs for institutions are becoming clear—a 2023 CUPA-HR analysis found that out of 16 aspects of job satisfaction, the three with the strongest association with staff retention were being recognized for contributions, being valued by others at work, and having a sense of belonging.[43]

Many higher education workers have watched their institutions grow and pursue new aspirations year after year. They have seen the careers of senior leaders take off, allowing them to learn new skills, move up the ladder, and earn more. And they ask why wanting the same for themselves is treated like such a foreign concept. My sense is that these employees are not seeking to accumulate titles or wealth. They want their growth to be seen and validated. They want to know their work matters.

Becoming Deliberately Developmental Employers

"Adults, not just children, can and need to keep growing," write psychologist Robert Kegan and organizational change expert Lisa Laskow Lahey. "This principle," they continue, "can be stated in ten simple words, but it represents a discontinuous departure from the fundamental operation of nearly all organizations in every sector we've explored (including, ironically, education)."[44] And yet the workplace often calls on us to be learning all the time; the pace of change in many jobs has created new, more frequent demands for workers to be mentally agile and flexible. Although there are plenty of organizations focused on growth in terms of size, revenues, and impact, only a few are "great and relentless at people development."[45] Kegan and Lahey set out to learn more about the practices of what they called *deliberately developmental organizations* (DDOs), believing them to be models of successful organizations that are able to engage and retain employees.

What are some of the practices that define DDOs? For one thing, DDOs do not let employees sit in jobs they have already mastered for too long. They spend a lot of time figuring out the right fit between employees and the roles they occupy, which usually leads to pushing people into stretch assignments or time-limited, manageable experiments where they are supported through the moments of discomfort, vulnerability, and mistakes that accompany trying something new and challenging. DDOs also don't sit long on gaps in the organization—gaps between what an organization says it does and actually does; gaps between what gets said in a meeting and gossip in the hallway; and gaps between someone's performance and providing constructive feedback on it. Rather than let those gaps lengthen and multiply, Kegan and Lahey found that DDOs prioritize continuous feedback through "interpersonal and cognitive immediacy": people talk about core issues and work through problems right when they pop up so they don't fester. DDOs don't see a trade-off between developing their employees and achieving productivity goals or organizational outcomes: "A DDO looks at the way bold institutional aspirations, on the one hand . . . and further-developed human capabilities, on the other, are part of a single whole. Each depends on the other."[46]

Tony Schwartz wrote about implementing some of these practices in his business after finding that "the same forces rocking businesses are also overwhelming employees, driving up their fear, and compromising their capacity."[47] Where many business leaders have stumbled is in trying to build cultures that are focused performance, which often creates a zero-sum game where people are winners or losers. "The irony, we've found," said Schwartz, "is that building a culture focused on performance may not be the best, healthiest, or most sustainable way to fuel results. Instead, it may be more effective to focus on creating a culture of growth."[48]

To pull off a culture of growth where it is possible to have hard conversations about operations, there needs to be a community where people feel valued as human beings. The conventional wisdom is that organizations show workers they are valued through compensation and other tangible rewards. After all, fair pay is critically important. In fact, looking back to Chapter 2, compensation represents an integral part of a talent management strategy. Writing in the *Talent Management Handbook*, Juan Pablo Gonzalez argued that many organizations overlook the importance of compensation when they are pursuing organizational change. Employees notice when expectations change but rewards don't.[49] From a talent management perspective, higher education's constant pursuit of competitiveness and better outcomes while allowing salaries to stagnate amounts to a comically inept strategy.

But pay is not the only way that organizations show employees they are valued. The concept of total rewards has become a popular way for organizations to strategically think about everything they offer in exchange for an employee's contributions and the extent to which rewards align with organizational values and priorities. Total rewards include base salary, short- and long-term incentives, as well as health care and retirement benefits. It also includes career pathways, opportunities for professional learning, and forms of recognition. Although many colleges and universities have embraced the concept of total rewards (recall UofL's "total compensation and rewards study"), they struggle to truly invest in all the rewards. It is a little like knowing all the ingredients for a great dish but only buying a few of them or only using the cheapest ones.

Take the example of recognition. Research increasingly shows that, beyond fair compensation and monetary bonuses, employees want to feel appreciated.[50] Appreciation is, in the words of leadership expert Mike Robbins, about "acknowledging a person's inherent value. The point isn't their accomplishments. It's their worth as a colleague and human being."[51] Appreciation doesn't just have to come from leaders, either. Employees are able to demonstrate appreciation for one another and for reasons unrelated to their professional accomplishments. Appreciation in the workplace is a main contributor to employee engagement, but the key is that appreciation must be authentic and personalized, which is why mass "thank you" emails fall flat. Authentic and personalized appreciation means listening to and routinely checking in with employees.[52] That's not unlike the efforts at the UofL Employee Success Center. The center strives to make milestones meaningful and, in small ways, help employees to feel like they matter to the university. Only a few of the center's initiatives are focused on productivity or performance. They are often employees telling fellow employees that they are valued.

The realist in me doesn't predict too many colleges and universities will become DDOs. Nevertheless, I see an opportunity for institutions to become *more* developmental in their purposes and practices. While it is true that colleges and universities exist to teach students and advance knowledge, they only fulfill these purposes through the ingenuity and labor of people. And so, if institutions want to fulfill their core purposes, they also have to attend to their responsibilities as *employers*.

Colleges and universities need to embrace this responsibility and commit to developing the capabilities of the people they employ. An important lesson from DDOs is that assuming this responsibility does not compromise other purposes: they are two sides of the same coin. Building the cultures and structures that support people development hinges on fully investing in the concept of total rewards and showing workers how they are valued—both for what they do and who they are. Here are three approaches to do exactly that.

Approach 1: Caring Through Clear Career Pathways and Ladders

What does it look like to structure a job to facilitate career progression instead of leading to a dead end? Establishing and clearly communicating career pathways and ladders is an important first step. *Career pathways* are a collection of positions mapped out to show how they can connect to one another through developmental opportunities. *Career ladders* are steps within a given job category, allowing someone to move into roles of increasing responsibility and compensation based on experience and performance—without having to move to another unit or institution.

To get started, institutions need to examine their organizational structures to identify where employees get stuck or have difficulty seeing career growth options. This is precisely what Miami University's communications and marketing department did as part of its workplace culture survey, which showed that people did not see a path to advancement and felt they needed to leave to get a raise. The department created a Career Pathways Committee to analyze the survey data, and the committee proposed the creation of two new career pathways: one for managers who wanted to supervise and one for non-managers. Each pathway has a career ladder with defined responsibilities and qualifications. Part of the goal was to create a way for staff to move up and earn more to prevent salary compression and turnover. The new career pathways and associated ladders do not guarantee anyone a promotion or give away new titles. But those who gained experience and took on new challenges could move up the ladder with a new title and raise, without needing to go through an open search.

Career ladders do not need to have a dozen rungs or sidestep fair search rules to be effective. For Miami's communications and marketing department, the ladders eventually lead to director-level positions where there must be an open search. But before they reach that point, employees can progress in their careers and be rewarded for their contributions and expertise if they stick with the organization. According to Jessica

Rivinius, Miami University's current chief marketing officer and an architect of the career pathways proposal, the clarity of the process is an overriding principle: "We want to be able to share with our team that this is how you progress. These are the types of projects you need to master and take on. These are the types of skills you may need to advance. So it's not a question of why one person gets promoted and another doesn't. It's very transparent, and people know that there can be a future."

Pulling off the new career ladders has meant working closely with human resources to comply with state and institutional policies and being prepared for any challenges that might come from implementing a new system where titles and pay are involved. I asked Rivinius if she was worried about the additional cost to the department of the pathways and ladders. She pointed out that the department had 13 vacancies when she was hired—they desperately needed to try something new. But Rivinius said she wasn't worried about resources: "Maybe in the short-term things will be a little tight. But we will be okay because this is the right thing to do. And I'm a firm believer that when you do the right thing, the results follow." And they have already seen positive results. "Our culture has never been better," said Rivinius. "We still have challenges, but people really like that we're doing this."

Once career ladders are in place, institutions need to make sure that they are clearly communicated to help employees understand how they can advance. UofL's compensation study may have had the right idea when it established a new job classification structure. But UofL released it before facilitating a sensemaking process among employees so they could understand the change and what it meant for them. Employees need clarity around eligibility criteria, performance expectations, and the application process to be promoted. The University Advising Center at the University of South Carolina offers a good example of how to communicate a career ladder clearly to workers. Its website has a dedicated section explaining what career ladders are and why they are beneficial. It also explains how a tier I academic adviser can move to tier II and tier III of the ladder, with clearly delineated instructions for applying and sample application materials. The website also has a sidebar congratulating advisers who have moved up in tiers, conveying to employees that the unit *wants* them to advance and is trying to simplify the process and minimize confusion.

In some cases, employees need more than a clear pathway and a map for climbing up career ladders. They need someone to help them see opportunities, prepare for the next stage of their career, and provide tailored advice. University of Virginia President James Ryan commissioned a Pipelines and Pathways Working Group to explore how to enable community members from underrepresented groups to access careers at the university and increase internal mobility for existing staff. Joseph Arton, who at the time was a senior talent mobility consultant at the university, was part of a group tasked with addressing the challenge. As Arton explained, "There was a systemic problem that had been identified, and it was that there was just a lack of career pathways for individuals to grow." Arton and his colleagues ran a survey, focus groups, and one-on-one interviews to better understand the "technical and nontechnical barriers to internal career mobility" at the university.

Arton—originally from the United Kingdom—used the London Underground to explain some of the barriers:

> Let's say you're at a certain train station, and you wanted to get somewhere else. And imagine all the different train stations have different lines, and each of these lines represents a different career track, like an executive career track or an individual contributor career track. There was no current way to identify how to get from point A to point B and what skills you needed to get to make that journey. And there didn't seem to be anything within our human resources management system that could really help facilitate that. Even just searching for jobs and identifying jobs was a challenge.

When Arton and his colleagues looked at the data, they learned supervisors were often enthusiastic about helping supervisees grow but didn't always know how. Data showed that internal candidates had a pretty good chance of being hired if they were among the finalists, but internal candidates struggled to break into the top three. They found that it wasn't common to use stretch assignments or special positions to help employees gain new skills or try something new.

Based on this data, Arton and his colleagues proposed creating what became the Career Navigation Center. The center employs coaches who work one-on-one and confidentially with internal candidates to develop their application materials and strategize around their career plans. Many of the people who come to the center are early in their tenure at the university, and according to the data, their top reason for seeking out coaching isn't the desire for more pay—most are looking for progression and growth opportunities. Sometimes coaches help identify positions across the university that match a client's skills; sometimes they help clients design a stretch assignment; and, in some cases, they help clients leave the university if they have truly hit a ceiling. Although most clients want to stay at the university, the willingness to help employees pursue outside opportunities demonstrates that the center is here for them and not for the institution.

Part of what the center is trying to accomplish is a cultural shift at the university. As Arton noted: "We're a public institution. We have to abide by the law and a fair search. A lot of heads of departments say, 'Well, I want to get the best in the world. I want to get the best candidate.' And we're trying to get them to see the people who are around them in a different light." So far, the response to the center from employees has been incredibly positive, summed up by one employee's feedback: "You gave me hope. . . . And then you gave me skills to develop in my career." When I suggested that establishing a center and hiring coaches wasn't cheap, Arton noted that the center paid for itself through the retention of employees: "My back-of-the-envelope estimation for this was for every dollar that we're spending on coaches, we're saving the organization $40,000 in turnover costs. . . . The return on investment is kind of extraordinary."

Approach 2: Caring Through Robust In-House Professional Development

Coaching is an example of the type of in-house professional development in which institutions need to invest—and not just for the sake of helping staff progress. Maria LaMonaca Wisdom directs mentoring and coaching programs for doctoral students and faculty at Duke University's Office for Faculty Advancement, which uses an approach similar to the Career Navigation Center. Wisdom sees value in coaching and intentional conversations to help faculty see through and around career cul-de-sacs. Wisdom views coaching as a good supplement to mentoring. "Coaching is not directive," she explained. "It supports people in thinking through problems, then empowering them to make their own decisions about how to move forward."

When she first arrived at Duke, coaching was practiced in the medical school but not in other parts of campus. As Wisdom told me in an interview, "It was almost on the down-low. And often for what was considered remedial. If I heard colleagues of mine and senior leadership mention coaching, it was because someone was having trouble, so they were talking to a coach. Or a professor might go and use an external coaching service." Wisdom took her idea of expanding coaching to senior leaders in the Office of the Provost, and they provided significant support to get it started. Wisdom was able to gain additional training in coaching before piloting a group coaching program for as many as 50 doctoral students and 10 groups per semester. These students found it incredibly helpful to talk through issues in a "safe space outside their department" with the help of peers from multiple disciplines and a trained coach. As a result, they reported improved relationships with their advisers, more confidence in their work, and progress toward milestones such as finishing their dissertation.

Based on these results, Wisdom piloted a group coaching program for new faculty at a slightly larger scale than the doctoral student program. Each program requires participants to attend four to five sessions per semester. As she explained, coaching is ideal for people going through transitions, particularly faculty going through career transitions, some of whom haven't been well prepared for managing change. She said, "I'll sometimes have someone show up to my office who in the past year has accepted a new job, moved across the country, gotten married, bought a house. And . . . they're completely falling apart. They're coming in and saying, 'Well, I need to work on my time management skills.' And it's like, okay, but let's talk about all the changes you've been through." Some people might argue that faculty do not need career coaching because they have mentors and department chairs. But Wisdom challenges this assumption: "There are many problems, I think, with expecting faculty just to get career advice from mentors within their department. I mean, first of all, there are power dynamics. And there are so many things faculty are afraid to share with senior faculty for good reason. Because, you know, those senior faculty are going to vote on their tenure."

Wisdom has also started doing one-on-one coaching, during which she explores her clients' career questions and helps them figure out how their strengths align with their institution's goals, how they can talk with their department chair or other leaders about new ways to contribute, and how they can get comfortable explicitly asking for things and preparing to hear "no." Coaching still happens in an institutional setting where someone may only have limited options on the table. "So much of coaching," Wisdom explained, "is helping them find a tiny point of light." Often, Wisdom sees coaching as improvisational and draws on her knowledge of the organization to remind faculty of choices they may not see. And sometimes, issues are big enough that the best thing a coach can do is refer someone to therapy. Wisdom is just one person, and she feels her work is still very much in a pilot phase. But even with a small footprint, she sees value in "changing the culture here at the university. You know, this high-performing culture of anxious achievers where it's shameful to get help. We're pushing against the idea that people should intuitively just know how to succeed."

Faculty professional development and one-on-one consultations have typically been the province of centers for faculty development or teaching excellence. Yet according to one estimate, only about one-quarter of colleges and universities have such a center.[53] If they are going to be tasked with doing more than instruction-focused programming, these centers will need additional resources and staffing. According to a report jointly produced by the Professional and Organizational Development (POD) Network in Higher Education and the American Council on Education, exemplary resources and infrastructure for centers for faculty development or teaching excellence include a predictable budget that does not rely on external sources (e.g., donations and grants). Exemplary staffing is "substantial" and includes a full-time director, associate or assistant director, program coordinator, instructional technology consultant, faculty associate, and student staff.[54] Yet a 2016 survey of POD Network members showed that over 60 percent of respondents saw their funding decrease or stay the same over the past three years, and 44 percent expected it to decrease in the next three years.[55] In her 2020 study of centers for teaching and learning, Mary C. Wright found that centers are being asked to take on more functions without an increase in personnel.[56]

If centers for faculty development or teaching excellence want to remain focused on the worthwhile mission of serving the instructional needs of faculty, institutions should explore additional investments in professional development for faculty and other employees. UofL's Employee Success Center offers an example of what's possible with even a small investment in in-house professional development. In addition to the onboarding, coaching circles, and mentoring programs that I described earlier in the chapter, the center has created two particularly innovative professional development opportunities. The first is a staff fellowship program, which places staff in a setting where they can learn new skills and explore other careers at the university. The center matches selected participants with a university department or program, then cocreates a plan that includes specific activities to be completed and identifies an adviser in the host department to guide and support the experience. The staff fellowship program echoes the stretch experiences common in DDOs.

Perhaps my favorite professional development opportunity the center devised is the Cardinal Leadership Institute, which is a partnership between the center and the Department of Organizational Leadership and Learning (OLL) at UofL's College of Education and Human Development. Participants use their tuition benefits at the university to enroll in the credit-bearing experience, which is co-taught by faculty in the OLL department. It's not a small time commitment—participants meet weekly for a three-hour class session throughout the spring semester and even have some homework to complete. Rather than making leadership development an add-on to already full schedules, the intensity of the program ensures that participants carve out time and have the blessing of their supervisors. When all is said and done, participants complete nine credit hours of instruction in supporting organizational change, leadership and management, and talent and development that they can apply to a degree program or use in their work.

Colleges and universities cannot reasonably meet every employee's professional development needs through in-house coaching, employee success centers, or similar programs. There will still be reasons for staff and faculty to participate in professional associations, attend conferences, and participate in specific training experiences offered outside the institution. Investment in professional development requires ensuring that all employees have access to sufficient funds to take advantage of these opportunities. Institutions should consider professional development funds a routine part of an employee's total compensation package. Whenever possible, these funds should be a guaranteed amount each year and adjusted regularly to account for increases in travel and related costs. If institutions elect to create centralized professional development funds and allow employees to apply for them, the process needs to be clearly explained and equitable. Administrative assistants should be able to pursue professional development just as easily as managers and faculty.

Approach 3: Caring Through Salary Increases and Pay Equity

Career ladders and coaching are not just for career progression and professional growth—they can also help with compensation issues. For this to work, institutions must ensure that the salaries they are paying for positions across the organization are truly fair and competitive. This means regularly conducting market analyses, using multiple comparison groups for benchmarking (e.g., institutional size, mission, and location), and updating the data on which salary ranges are determined. When institutions defer maintenance of their compensation structure, they can quickly find themselves underwater. Before long, employees aren't just being paid below 80 percent of the market rate, they are being paid below 80 percent of the market rate *from five years ago.* As institutional goals have multiplied, employees have noticed that their salaries have not kept up with performance expectations. When colleges and universities update their compensation structure, as in the case of UofL's compensation study, workers have high expectations.

Another way that institutions can reduce the pressure that builds up around salaries is to commit to annual cost-of-living adjustments (Box 4.1 gives an example). Juan Pablo Gonzalez noted that organizations typically increase the base salary of their employees by 3 to 4 percent annually.[57] He must not have been thinking about colleges and universities because, in my 15 years of working in public higher education, I have never seen a commitment to adjust my salary by 3 percent annually to account for living expenses, and the evidence suggests my experience is not unique. In my research, I have encountered a small number of colleges and universities that guarantee a 3 to 4 percent cost-of-living adjustment, and many of them have done so as part of a collective bargaining process. It is time for institutions to stop treating annual cost-of-living adjustments like a luxury or a hard-fought concession of collective bargaining and instead treat them like a nonnegotiable cost of operating. To continue asking more of employees without increasing pay in step with living expenses is an exploitative labor practice. This message about the importance of annual cost-of-living adjustments is not just for campus leaders: it's also for policymakers, philanthropic organizations, and trustees who continually ask for better outcomes but want them on the cheap.

Raising base salaries by even a single percentage point requires substantial financial resources for most colleges and universities. But as Joseph Arton pointed out, turnover also has direct and indirect costs. Gallup estimates that the cost of replacing an employee conservatively ranges between one-half and two times the employee's annual salary. Based on the 2017 overall turnover rate of 26 percent as reported by the Bureau of Labor Statistics, Gallup calculated that a 100-person organization paying an average salary of $50,000 could have turnover costs of approximately $660,000 to $2.6 million per year.[58]

Identifying resources for annual cost-of-living adjustments may require institutions to look at compensation practices across the organization and, in particular, compensation for senior administrators. The number of administrators and how much they earn are favorite punch-

Box 4.1

Budgeting for Annual Raises

The Case of Trinity Washington University

"Things got so bad," Patricia McGuire said with a laugh, "they let *me* be president." That was back in 1989, when Trinity Washington University in Washington, DC, faced an enrollment and financial crisis. McGuire was teaching law and working in external affairs at Georgetown Law Center, and as an accomplished alumna of Trinity, she sat on the board of trustees. The university had cycled through six presidents in eight years and was trying to fill the position once again. "I kept running my mouth about what the university needed, until the chair finally looked at me and said, 'Why don't you do it?'"

At the age of 36, with a mandate from the board to "fix it or close it," McGuire became president and made faculty compensation one of her first priorities. "The faculty were demoralized. Salaries had been frozen and were very, very low," McGuire explained. "So I said to the board, 'Look, if we are going to be able to rebuild this institution . . . we have to take care of the faculty. We have to take care of salaries.'" After raising salaries that first year, Trinity made it an annual practice. "Faculty salaries are the first item we set in the budget every year, no matter what other belt-tightening we need to do."

Orchestrating an annual raise process was made more complicated by the fact that when McGuire started as president there was no human resources office. A single person oversaw payroll, and salaries were not set systematically. McGuire drafted a salary scale and shared it with faculty for input. "And that has happened every year. Faculty get the whole scale every year so that everybody can see how it works. It's very transparent," she said. The salary scale is revised annually to achieve "external parity" and ensure that the average salary in every rank meets or exceeds the average for a cohort of similar institutions. Usually, the university exceeds its goal and hits 100 percent of its cohort comparison. It is also adjusted each year to account for cost-of-living increases. These adjustments for external parity are combined with an automatic step up annually for all faculty.

At the same time that it is reviewing the scale for external parity, Trinity also prioritizes internal equity. If there is salary compression or other inequities, the president can move faculty up steps. Faculty can also apply to move up more than one step in a given year based on the quantity and quality of their contributions to various criteria, such as teaching innovation, curriculum development, program development, and uncompensated accumulated service. Faculty whose workload exceeds the norms established in the faculty handbook can also receive stipends, and in the interest of equity, the university publishes a list of activities that carry stipends and the amount distributed each year.

Box 4.1 (continued)

Trinity Washington University is not a wealthy institution. It is a small, private, Catholic university and the only one of its kind in Washington, DC that is designated as both a predominantly Black institution and Hispanic-serving institution. Where does it get resources for annual salary increases? McGuire says even in its leanest years, they can identify pockets of money. Sometimes it is just a matter of being creative. There are not huge salary differences based on disciplines or departments—faculty are all paid according to the same scale. And the university also keeps an eye on the salaries of senior administrators. According to McGuire:

> We don't take the upper end of pay. I'm not saying that to be a saint or something, but I do believe that the president's salary, the executive salaries, should have some rational relationship to everybody else's salary. And I've actually done that analysis from time to time for our board. You see these colleges where the president's salary is, like, six to eight to ten times the average faculty salary. Well, that's preposterous. Executive compensation can really blow the budget very quickly, and we've even had years where we freeze it.

McGuire believes that paying people fairly makes good business sense. "Especially for the small private colleges in trouble, you absolutely gain not one penny if the faculty is demoralized. You do well by doing good." Beyond the business case for raises, the social justice mission of a Catholic institution also guides McGuire. "I believe that the people should be taken care of before anything else. I think it's a question of institutional values. I really do. You know, if you're raising tuition, the very first beneficiary of the tuition raise should be the talent that is delivering the product that the customer is buying."

ing bags for disgruntled faculty, but here's the deal: it is not uncommon for college presidents to be paid five times what full professors are paid. My point is not that administrators have it easy or that we ought to start eliminating administrator positions, but there is a legitimate question about whether being a college president is five times harder than being a faculty member. The justification for paying senior administrators so much is that it is necessary to recruit and retain talented leaders. Yet that logic is rarely applied down the organizational chart. It is possible that some of the money needed to better pay all employees can be found in reducing the yawning gap between the rich and poor of the higher education workforce.

The reality is that institutions will likely need to prepare for raises beyond annual cost-of-living adjustments to attract and retain employees. Research suggests that merit pay may not truly improve performance, but when it is transparent and collaborative in design and implementation, merit pay can improve morale, clarify what matters to the institution, reward exemplary performance, and reduce salary compression.[59] For faculty who often have fewer rungs on their career ladder and are less likely to negotiate starting salaries after changing jobs, increasing salary raises at each promotion point may be necessary so that newly hired professors are not outearning more senior colleagues. Institutions may still have reason to set aside dedicated funds to retain employees, but they should not establish a policy that requires securing an outside offer before someone is offered a raise. And retention funds should be available for all employees—not just faculty.

The continuation of pay inequities by race and gender in higher education is inexcusable and eminently fixable. Colleges and universities can evaluate pay equity internally based on gender, race, and the intersection of the two. Dedicated funds for equity-based pay increases are another strategy to help correct salary inequities. In 2007, the University of Massachusetts Amherst established a system of equity raises. Under its system, departmental committees could recommend pay increases for someone whose current salary is below the starting salary of a new hire, below the median for that rank after three years, or less than the salary of peers with comparable service or accomplishments. As a result, women faculty at the same rank and college as men do not experience a pay gap. In 2019, the system was replaced with a section of the collective bargaining agreement whereby a university-wide committee determines the existence of salary inequities and makes recommendations for addressing them through a dedicated fund in the provost's office.

Rochester Institute of Technology (RIT) also addressed salary inequities as part of a National Science Foundation ADVANCE Institutional Transformation grant. The grant convened a committee of administrators and faculty to develop a process for conducting annual salary equity studies for faculty and disseminating findings to the campus. The committee jointly developed a request for proposals from outside firms to conduct a salary analysis, drawing on campus-based experts in faculty hiring, institutional data, equity, and statistics. After conducting the study, the committee developed an interactive workshop for full-time RIT faculty titled "Let's Talk Money: Understanding RIT Pay Practices." This workshop aimed to improve faculty understanding of the university's compensation philosophy and salary practices. The collaboration between faculty and administration has continued with annual salary studies and a faculty governance compensation committee that makes recommendations to the president, provost, and board of trustees on issues such as salary benchmarking and faculty promotion raises.

Conclusion

When higher education workers hit a professional dead end or want a raise, institutions have tended to let them leave. According to this model, employees can simply be replaced thanks to the throngs of people who want to work at colleges and universities. But that model is starting to show cracks as vacancies and turnover costs snowball, with data suggesting that supervisors and hiring managers are having a harder time filling positions. And unless colleges and universities rethink their organizational cultures and structures, what reason do they have to believe the number of job applicants will suddenly rebound? Steve Cadigan, former chief human resources officer for LinkedIn, made this prediction: "If you want to compete, you're going to have to be a place that grows talent. The supply of qualified talent isn't going to increase. You won't find qualified candidates at scale any longer. . . . You have to become a talent-development business."[60]

UofL started to walk the path of becoming what Cadigan describes—something akin to a deliberately developmental organization. It had the right idea when it said that it wanted to create a "culture of care, trust, accountability, and equity" and "[provide] all faculty and staff fair and equitable compensation." It has stumbled a few times in pursuit of these goals, losing momentum because of the instability of leadership. But there are pockets of change, and the Employee Success Center is still forging ahead with efforts to translate the words of the plan into action. And though the center wants to see outcomes such as more engaged employees and higher retention rates, I get the sense that Brian Buford and his staff are motivated by something else: they deeply care about the people who, like them, get up every day to make the university a better place. Helping employees grow and feel valued comes easy for the staff at the center because it' is the right thing to do.

That idea is what animated the interviews and approaches in this chapter (see Box 4.2 for a summary of approaches), whether at Miami

Box 4.2

Chapter 4 Action Steps

- Examine organizational structures to identify where employees get stuck or have difficulty seeing career growth options. Use this analysis to establish and clearly communicate career pathways and ladders for all employees.
- Hire one-on-one career navigators or coaches to help employees overcome obstacles to career progression, and craft a career strategy at the institution.
- Appropriately resource existing faculty development and teaching excellence centers or establish new centers focused on the professional growth of employees.
- Ensure all employees have equitable and transparent access to sufficient funds for external professional development opportunities.
- Treat annual cost-of-living adjustments to base salaries as a necessary, nonnegotiable cost of operating.
- Examine the compensation of senior administrators and the rate of pay increases for these positions relative to faculty and staff pay and raises. Address the rising gaps in pay between employees who are doing similar work.
- Set aside dedicated funds for equity-based salary adjustments and staff and faculty retention that is not pegged to an outside job offer.
- Develop a recognition and appreciation ecosystem that is not premised on scarcity, competition, and performance.
- Replace short orientations with more robust onboarding. Make career milestones meaningful and seek opportunities for authentic, personalized appreciation.

University or Trinity Washington University. *Take care of your people. When you do the right thing, the results will follow. The return on investment is extraordinary.*

The Caring University and its focus on professional growth and fair compensation is not a story about costs, perks, handouts, or distractions from the core purpose of higher education. It is a story about the stuff of effective organizations defined by world-class professional growth and rewards that convince people to stay and build something great.

CHAPTER 5

Pursuing Cultural and Structural Change for Equity and Belonging

ROBERT W. FERNANDEZ learned about college application deadlines when his friends at school started receiving their acceptance letters. Realizing that it was too late to apply to many colleges and universities, Robert thought his chances of attending college had slipped away. But then a representative from the local community college came to his high school and said they were still enrolling students. Looking over the application, Robert saw a question that gave him pause, so he asked his mom about it. "Ma, cuál es mi social? [Ma, what is my Social Security number?]" She replied simply: "Tú no tienes, hijo. [You don't have one, son.]"

Robert knew this had to do with his immigration status. Born in Lima, Peru, Robert came to the United States with his parents when he was four. Robert knew that his family's immigration status was something he had no control over—and something to keep secret. It wasn't until he was filling out the application for community college that the full weight of being undocumented began to sink in. Robert decided not to fill in a Social Security number on the application and sent it in. He did not know it at the time, but the community college was one of the few institutions that accepted undocumented students and where Robert could afford the in-state tuition.

Robert excelled at community college, earning a 3.9 grade point average, participating in an honors society, and majoring in business administration. During his final year at community college, Robert had to decide between taking an elective course in astronomy or biology. He went with biology, and the combination of a particularly engaging professor and an independent study on evolution sparked a deep interest in the subject. He decided he wanted to continue studying biology and started looking into bachelor's degree programs. At a college fair that the community college hosted, Robert visited the tables for nearby bachelor's-granting institutions: "I went to every single college representative, and I told them, 'Look, I'm interested in biology. This is my GPA; these are my extracurricular activities. Can I go to your college?' But the moment I told them I was undocumented, every single one of them said no, or they were going to charge me out-of-state tuition, even though I've been in New Jersey for over a decade."

This was before the Deferred Action for Childhood Arrivals (DACA) policy was signed by President Barack Obama in 2012. DACA provided eligible young adults with temporary relief from deportation, renewable two-year work permits, and a Social Security number that allowed them to apply for certain forms of financial aid.[1] For Robert, pursuing a bachelor's degree before DACA meant there was not much information about which institutions accepted undocumented students. "I would find out from newspaper clippings," he said, "and I remember reading Brown and Columbia accepted undocumented students." So he applied to Brown and Columbia and was rejected. Finally, a classmate at his community college who was also undocumented told him the City University of New York (CUNY) accepted undocumented students.

With $400 in his pocket for the first month's rent, Robert moved to nearby Flushing to attend Queens College and study biology. As an out-of-state student, tuition was expensive, and Robert could only afford to take a few courses at a time. He started working full-time at a deli in Manhattan to help pay the bills. After living for a year in New York, Robert qualified for in-state tuition and started to consider his options. In search of smaller class sizes and mentors, Robert transferred to York College (which was also in the CUNY system and accepted undocumented students). At York, everything changed. Robert's professor for a biology course, Dr. Anne Simon, asked him if he had thought about doing more research. Robert ended up spending two years in Dr. Simon's lab studying fruit fly behavior. Her investment in him created what Robert described as a domino effect, where other professors in the biology department also took an interest in his success. As he remarked, "I found a community of mentors, even though I was undocumented. They taught me how to be a scientist and made me believe that I could be one."

Robert's mentors helped him gain additional research experience. He presented at a fruit fly meeting, did a summer program at Princeton, and participated in a quantitative biology workshop at MIT. The biotechnology program director personally invited Robert to attend a diversity preview weekend at Brown. "I think it was all these mentors advocating for me or telling me about these resources that helped my professional development," he explained. "It would have been very difficult otherwise, like I had no idea what summer programs were or that they were paid. But my undergraduate principal investigator (PI) encouraged me to apply for them."

Through these experiences, Robert gained enough research experience to apply for PhD programs. Here again his mentors came through. "They taught me what a PhD was, how to prepare for one, and how to be accepted," he explained. Robert applied to a biochemistry and biophysics program at Yale on a whim and attended the recruitment weekend, presuming it wouldn't be a good fit. "I met one of the faculty directors hosting the recruitment weekend who took an interest in me, and I could tell that, even though I didn't understand any of the graphs in the poster sessions, this could be a supportive environment," Robert said. An undocumented immigrant whose journey in biology started with a community college elective was going to be a doctoral student at Yale.

But any illusion of having finally arrived popped during Robert's first semester. He showed up to Yale feeling stressed because he only received his green card a month before the start of classes, and he wasn't sure if his parents would get theirs. Robert quickly surmised that he was the only Latino in his PhD class (and one of only two in the department), and he felt socially isolated. "Outside of coursework, it was very difficult to connect with my peers just because a lot of them talk about having lake houses or summer houses, and that's not what my summer vacations were like," he said. Whereas many of his classmates did not have an issue with the $33,000 PhD stipend because their parents were financially supporting them, Robert sometimes struggled to afford food. "I noticed the others weren't going through the things that I was going through."

On top of the social isolation, Robert struggled with the pivot from biotechnology to what he called a "hard-core biochemistry" program. "At the time, I didn't really want to ask for help just because I didn't want any negative perceptions like, 'Oh, of course he's asking for help. He's Latino.' " As a result, he failed one course and got Cs in the others. Talking with the director of graduate studies helped Robert articulate some of his challenges, and he slowly became more comfortable asking for help from teaching assistants and peers. "From that point on, I realized that a PhD is not really something you do by yourself. It's something you do as a community."

Feeling more confident academically, Robert wanted to continue building out his community. By his third year, he attended a meeting for minoritized students in biology,[2] but it was more of a lecture series than a chance to interact with others. He befriended a Black woman in microbiology, and together they planned "a very informal student-led town hall to hear about . . . the problems that exist within our respective departments, and how can we help each other out, or learn from each other." Robert started to meet more students of color and students from working-class backgrounds. But he increasingly felt "it wasn't enough that I felt a sense of belonging. I needed to make sure others like me belong here, too."

Robert launched a mentoring program within his department. He and a few peers would pair first-year students with a third- or fourth-year student to help them tackle that all-important first semester of graduate school. He started working for a program called STARS, which "is designed to support women, minority, economically underprivileged, and other historically underrepresented students in science, technology, engineer, and mathematics (STEM)."[3] In this role, Robert hosted professional development workshops and helped students with applications to postbaccalaureate programs, especially those who wanted to go to graduate school. By this point, Robert had become close with other minoritized students who cared about diversity, equity, and inclusion (DEI) issues at Yale.

Building on his experience in the STARS program, Robert started playing around with an idea to make the workshops and guidance he had developed more broadly available. "I'm only here because of mentors who have guided me," Robert explained. "I want to give other people the same guidance I received and help inspire future generations of underrepresented scientists." Along with Olivia Goldman, Robert launched Científico Latino with the idea of compiling and sharing resources on undergraduate fellowships, summer research programs, and postbaccalaureate programs. Their logic was that "even if a student isn't lucky enough to have a mentor, it would be great if they had all the resources they needed to succeed." Soon, Científico Latino added more team members and developed the Graduate Student Mentoring Initiative to pair minoritized prospective graduate students with STEM professionals in their respective disciplines. In addition to mentoring, students receive help with application fees, feedback on application materials, and access to webinars and mock interviews.

Between 2019 and 2021, Científico Latino helped 443 students enter graduate school, and after taking 2022 off, they received funding in 2023 from the Simons Foundation to continue their work. Robert has since finished his PhD and become a US citizen before starting as a postdoctoral fellow at Columbia University, studying how the nervous system develops. As he looks at jobs in higher education, he is considering "the landscape at those universities, and what type of support they have for underrepresented students, or for [principal investigators] who want to build DEI initiatives." He wants wherever he lands to support his work mentoring minoritized scientists—and it has become clear to him that some institutions are much more amenable than others.

Robert's story is compelling on many levels. A community college changed the trajectory of Robert's life by giving him a chance when options were scarce. He gravitated to biology after an elective course with a gifted community college professor sparked his interest. Robert's relationship with faculty demonstrates the incredible power of good mentorship. And yet I couldn't help noticing the heaviness of Robert's words as he described being turned away from institutions simply because he spent the first few years of his life in another country. When I interviewed him, I could hear in his voice the toll financial precarity and loneliness had taken while navigating academic spaces where so few people looked like him and understood his experience. Robert shouldered the responsibility of developing both mentoring and DEI programming when the institutions he attended—several with abundant resources—failed to do so.

Robert is part of a long tradition of minoritized and marginalized staff and faculty who carry the dual burden of trying to access (and then survive) higher education while also frequently being expected to transform institutions to make them more equitable and inclusive. There are people like Robert spanning higher education—people of color, people who were not born in the United States, people who did not grow up speaking English, people from working-class families, people who are the first in their families to attend college—who have researched, documented, and voiced their experiences with systems of oppression while working in higher education. They have done so not out of a burning desire to tell these stories and relive these experiences but rather to change the higher education workplace. The premise of this chapter is quite simple. You can't have a Caring University without cultural and structural change to promote equity and belonging for minoritized and marginalized staff and faculty. Institutions need to step up and do the work of organization-level change so that it is not up to individuals like Robert to devise solutions to problems they didn't create.

In this chapter, I explain what marginalization means and how it takes shape for staff and faculty in the higher education workplace, drawing on collections of first-person accounts that scholars and practitioners have offered to share their experiences.[4] I then bring attention to scholarship arguing that promoting diversity alone has been an inadequate institutional strategy for creating a fair, just, and welcoming workplace;

instead, I emphasize the need for approaches aligned with a model of equity-minded organizations developed by Román Liera and Steve Desir. I then share four organization-level approaches designed to create environments where all staff and faculty have resources and opportunities to thrive and belong: equitable hiring processes, valuing the labor of marginalized employees, commitment to institutional accountability, and shared equity leadership.[5]

College and university leaders are fond of referencing the "university community" or "our [insert mascot] family." In reality, many institutions fail to demonstrate the type of care that we expect in a healthy, functioning community or family. The Caring University isn't about creating a big, happy family—it's about creating cultures and structures for organizational excellence by ensuring equity and belonging.

Marginalization in the Higher Education Workplace

It was only recently that some institutions—at least in words if not in actions—begrudgingly came around to the idea that it was important to ensure that the composition of employees resembles the communities they serve; that policies and practices are fair and just so that all employees have resources and opportunities to thrive; and that institutions have a role to play in making the workplace an environment where workers feel they belong. Consequently, there has been a long stretch of time during which certain groups of employees have been denied the chance to work in higher education or, once they are hired, experience isolation, discrimination, and inequities.[6] In fact, literature in which marginalized staff and faculty document their workplace experiences is abundant. The question is how much time college leaders—the majority of them white men at historically white colleges and universities—have spent with these narratives.[7]

In this section, I invite leaders to pause and process excerpts from first-person narratives authored by staff and faculty who have been marginalized within the higher education workplace. This section is organized into four patterns that I repeatedly saw in research. It isn't meant to be accusatory—I am not shining the bright lamp of an interrogation room.

Rather, my point is that if leaders want to better demonstrate care for the well-being of marginalized employees, listening to what they have *already* been telling us for several decades is a good place to start. My aim is to encourage leaders to sit with their words, trust that their experiences are real, and realize that they cannot easily be shrugged off as anecdotes—that their marginalization was not the product of a "bad actor" or one-off experience; rather, it is baked into organizational cultures and structures. For one thing, the narratives are manifold—there are simply too many of them in print alone to be discounted as a product of a few ugly moments at otherwise "good" organizations. Second, the experiences that authors share are too similar to be discounted as isolated occurrences—they repeat and syncopate like an anxious heartbeat.

I am using "marginalized employees" as an umbrella concept in this chapter because so many groups have experienced some manner of marginalization that listing them each time they occur would get tedious. Whiteness, racism, patriarchy, heterosexism, sexism, ableism, classism, and colonialism are *systems of oppression* intertwined with the history of the United States as a nation.[8] Oppression differs from individual-level discrimination in that it draws on the power of institutions to intentionally disadvantage certain groups and elevate others based on their identity.[9] Oppression shows up in our economic, political, and cultural systems, resulting in a series of everyday practices, policies, and norms that in this country render anyone who isn't a white, heterosexual, non-disabled, middle- or upper-class, Christian, cisgender man as less deserving of rights, health, and prosperity.[10] By using an umbrella concept, there is admittedly a risk of lumping together groups who have had very different histories and experiences with these systems of oppression. I have tried, wherever possible, to counter this by incorporating many voices, using specific examples, and retaining how authors and other experts self-identify in their writing.

Another other choice I have made is to refrain from talking about marginalized staff and faculty in terms of the percentages of groups serving in particular roles. To be clear, I believe in the importance of increasing the diversity of employees by hiring and retaining people who have been excluded from higher education. The problem with leaning on statistics that measure representation is that identities are multifaceted and fluid, defying easy quantification. Plus, statistics do not always effectively account for people who hold multiple marginalized identities. And in a similar vein, it is not the case that a single system of oppression is switched on at a given moment—they are all in play all the time, teaming up and building on one another. *Intersectionality* is a framework that explains how systems of oppression overlap and result in unique experiences and outcomes.[11] One of the first-person accounts I read—from Katherine H. Betts—provides a concrete illustration of the importance of intersectionality: "While there may be a limited population of Black women administrators with shared experiences working in higher education that can provide support, guidance, and mentorship, throughout most of my career there have been no examples of Black disabled women to learn from."[12] Although numbers can convey useful information, other research has already documented various measures of underrepresentation. I am coming at the problem from a different angle, foregrounding stories in this chapter and the book as a whole.

Finally, I acknowledge that my approach in this section pulls a few narratives out of their institutional contexts. The reality is that different institutions have different historical and contemporary relationships to systems of oppression. An institution built by enslaved people that didn't admit people of color for 200 years and remains overwhelmingly white is a very different workplace than a Hispanic-serving community college established in the 1960s. That said, no institution type has a complete monopoly on oppression, and no institution can plausibly claim to operate completely outside these systems. In fact, while reading narratives, I was struck by the variety of types of institutions in which staff and faculty have been oppressed.

Tokenization, Hypervisibility, and Invisibility

One pattern that emerges in staff and faculty narratives is that marginalization stems from being one of very few people of a particular identity—or sometimes the only one—at the institution, college, or department (Box 5.1). In some cases, authors described forms of "cultural

Box 5.1

Narratives of Tokenization, Hypervisibility, and Invisibility

"While I was stunned about the realization that the university was actively making sure racial diversity among faculty did not grow beyond the representational (in opposition to the narrative of diversity and inclusion it professed), my colleagues were clear that having only 'one of us' was indeed the modus operandi of the institution. Looking around the table, we were, as one of my friends put it, 'a United Colors of Benetton ad,' each of us exemplifying a different racialized ethnic minority."

—Lorgia García Peña in *Community as Rebellion: A Syllabus for Surviving Academe as a Woman of Color*, 15

"The concept and feeling of tokenization hold a lot of tension for me. I hold the feeling of repeatedly being 'the only one' alongside the additional layer of emotional and intellectual labor that comes from being asked to share with non-disabled colleagues. Intellectually, I know a decent amount about other disabilities, which helps me do my job as a disability specialist and guide students through the accommodation process. But this cognitive knowledge can only go so far. I experience a deep feeling of exhaustion and mental burnout when faculty or campus partners who knowingly or unknowingly view 'disability' as homogenous ask me to educate them."

—Antonia DeMichiel in *Disabled Faculty and Staff*, 64

"The feeling of invisibility with my name, coupled with my research agenda, makes me a place of inquiry in academia: a probe into my identity, body, and worth. My identity as a Lao American woman is considered statistically insignificant in research. My body in the classroom, as I do not speak very often, makes me wonder if my classmates question my admittance into the program or if I am just the 'quiet Asian girl.' At the same time, the feeling that I am 'the only one' to ask, 'are you including Asian American in this' or 'what about the underrepresented Asian American subgroups like the Southeast Asians?' Lastly, my worth, because I have to constantly explain why focusing on [Southeast Asian American] students is relevant within the field of higher education, despite being a small population. I feel that my worth in higher education is based on the marketability of a broader research agenda, not the impact it can have on my community."

—Latana Jennifer Thaviseth in *The Power of Names in Identity and Oppression: Narratives for Equity in Higher Education and Student Affairs*, 146 taxation"—or the additional, uncompensated, and often non-promotable labor they were asked to assume, such as serving as institutional diversity experts, educating colleagues, and being called on to represent a particular community.[13] Others felt that being the "only one" confirmed their status as a token, someone whose presence was primarily to check the "diversity" box. Authors wrote about feeling hypervisible as a result and having their appearance, speech, customs, and decisions scrutinized. At the same time, being one of so few made it easy for their experiences to be overlooked, ignored, forgotten, and rendered invisible as norms and practices catered to the institution's dominant group.

Discrimination, Abuse, and Inequitable Access

Another pattern in the various first-person accounts that I read is repeated, nonambiguous experiences with discrimination, bullying, harassment, stereotypes, abuse, and inequitable access to resources and rewards (Box 5.2). Whereas some individuals described being on the receiving end of overtly racist comments or questions, others experienced microaggressions and silencing, such as having ideas dismissed, contributions undervalued or credited to someone else, or participation in meetings and hallway conversations thwarted. Many recounted examples of how promotions, awards, fellowships, grants, and coveted positions noncoincidentally flowed to "those for whom the walls of the academy were built," as sociologist Victoria Reyes put it.[14] Her book *Academic Outsider: Stories of Exclusion and Hope* elaborated on many of the patterns in this chapter. She explained: "The active exclusion of racialized and gendered outsiders . . . [structures] all aspects of academic life, from our interactions with others, to the courses we take (for students), the materials we teach, and the system of rewards that punctuate careers. This form of active exclusion means that marginalized outsiders are denied academic citizenship, that is, the legal rights and responsibilities of, as well as full acceptance and inclusion into, academic life."[15] For marginalized staff and faculty, talent and competence were not presumed—they had to regularly fight to prove they should be in higher education.

Box 5.2

Narratives of Discrimination, Abuse, and Inequitable Access

"Being an Indigenous mother and faculty member in higher education requires me to navigate multiple structures of oppression, including white supremacy, patriarchy, and ideologies of individualism and capitalism. Because of the common acceptance of media stereotypes, Indian mascots, and cultural appropriation, all Indigenous students, staff, and faculty navigate legitimized racism. Throughout my twenty-two years working as a well-educated executive in prestigious organizations and attending graduate programs at three public universities, I tolerated and coped with racist language and inequitable treatment as an Indigenous woman and mother."

—Dwanna L. McKay in *Indigenous Motherhood in the Academy*, 88

"Being Black in the academy placed us on full display for our students and colleagues. Because Black women were not commonplace at either of our institutions, our baby bumps were extra noticeable. Nonetheless, as mothers, especially new mothers, we believed that the changes to our bodies should be celebrated, not masked, hidden, or otherwise concealed. Often, however, we were subject to comments and actions that made us feel embarrassed or ashamed, while simultaneously being encouraged to maintain our physical and emotional composure as we came to work each day. We understood that, as Black women, our tenure and promotion was automatically more political and personal than academic—that we would be held to a higher standard and presumed incompetent and unworthy."

—Jemimah Li Young and Dorothy E. Hines in *Presumed Incompetent II: Race, Class, Power, and Resistance of Women in Academia*, 78

"It has now been six months since I told people at my community college that I identify as agender, and it feels as if I never stop having to come out, which seems to be a common situation among openly LGBTQIA+ people. Compared to what some trans individuals face when they come out, I cannot say that I have had a terrible experience, but it has also not been easy. Even though my coworkers are aware of my identity, many still misgender me on a regular basis by not using the appropriate pronouns. I correct them, so that they are cognizant of what they are saying, which leads some to become visibly frustrated with me. I do not like having other people upset with me, but I know that if I do not raise the issue, they will continue to misgender me, which I find even more hurtful. I take it a step at a time and use my position as the only out trans employee at the college (at least that I and others are aware of) to educate other staff members and try to bring about change on a personal level on my campus."

—Kei Graves in *Trans People in Higher Education*, 72

Isolation, Alienation, and Hypervigilance

The combination of being one of few people of a particular identity and regularly encountering discrimination and silencing results in a pattern of marginalized staff and faculty being physically and emotionally isolated on campuses (Box 5.3). Narratives point to struggles with developing and sustaining relationships, finding culturally affirming support systems outside work, and talking openly about their lives and families with colleagues. Many picked up on how promoting a sense of belonging was a priority when it came to students but not staff and faculty. Some authors discussed feeling unable to trust how sharing about themselves or their experiences would be received in the workplace and needing to keep their guard up during social interactions. As Reyes explained, "To be an outsider, a racialized outsider, is to be uncomfortable. It means never letting your guard down, especially with people whom you do not completely trust. And it's hard to know whom to trust."[16]

Stress, Mental Health, and Physical Consequences

The first-person accounts that I consulted conveyed sadness and exhaustion mixed with triumph and hope, similar to Robert's story. Many authors described how they have survived, overcome barriers, built careers, and pushed for change at their institutions. Some were propelled by a desire to serve, mentor, and even protect students facing similar hardships. But doing so was often costly, both professionally and personally, and could be incredibly painful (Box 5.4). Reyes described feeling "bitter and resentful" for the "lack of accountability" for those who "perpetuate or enable" discrimination.[17] Marginalized staff and faculty often noted the stress they carried after having to constantly battle with oppression. They felt the cumulative effects of that stress, contributing to mental and physical illness. This often drained them of the capacity necessary to complete intellectually demanding work—giving employees a reason to leave a position or higher education altogether for the sake of their well-being. As Reyes put it, "I cannot stay in a place that harms me, physically, emotionally, and intellectually. A place whose harms are

Box 5.3

Narratives of Isolation, Alienation, and Hypervigilance

"My experiences in higher education have involved both belonging and not belonging—existing in a dialectical and fluid relationship. My extended career track (gaining my PhD at age 41) happened in large part because of my hesitancy to believe that academia could ever be a home for someone without a family pedigree of academic achievement. Now I find that my father's legacy of being part of a union is crucial to my own academic labor being valued in a way that provides any degree of security for me and my family. I was wrong when, as a young child, I believed that social class determined profession. Perhaps what I was noticing then was the presence of hierarchical structures and their capacity to reproduce themselves across professions and exploit those positioned on the lower rungs of the institution, whether that individual is sorting the mail, shelving books, or teaching courses in philosophical ethics."

—Loren Cannon in *Straddling Class in the Academy*, 117

"My first two days actually on campus and in the office, I didn't see anyone Black for two days. Two days. Imagine being on a campus and you don't see anyone like you. No professional staff, no workers, no students, nothing. For two days. So I was like, 'Did I make a good decision, did they pick the right person, did they just see my name and assume I was white?' There were a lot of things going through my mind, trying to justify why I was here. It was really scary because I'm in a place where nobody else is around who can identify with me. I had no one to talk to, had no one who looks like me to give me encouragement and say, 'Hey, we can get through this together.'"

—Timothy Johnson in "A Personal Exploration of Involvement"

"When I found myself at a large campus in a rural location, I was fortunate to have the chance to participate in a support group for junior women of color faculty. Since we came from different disciplines, our focus was not on reading or critiquing each other's work, a practice I had engaged in at other institutions. We just gathered over delicious meals (you are compelled to learn how to make your favorite ethnic foods in these locations) and shared stories about overcoming isolation. We shared advice on campus policies, networking opportunities, and the promotion process. It was one of the few opportunities I have had to participate in a sustained effort to bring junior African American, Asian American, Latina, and Native American faculty together. There were only a handful of us on campus, and although we came from different backgrounds and fields, this was one of the few spaces where we felt like we belonged."

—Linda Trinh Võ in *Presumed Incompetent: The Intersections of Race and Class for Women in Academia*, 98–99

Box 5.4

Narratives of Stress, Mental Health, and Physical Consequences

"The harassment became so insidious that the day my director came into my office and tossed the termination and demotion papers on my desk, three days after I had been publicly commended in a division meeting by the vice president (who also signed those papers), I had a severe panic attack and was rolled out to an ambulance in a gurney in a semiconscious state. I blacked in and out en route to the hospital, and when I awoke in the ER, the doctor told me I not only had a panic attack but also a small TIA (ministroke) and needed to remain in the hospital for testing. That was the first week of the pandemic, and knowing I was immunocompromised (lupus and rheumatoid arthritis), I refused to stay in the hospital and signed myself out against doctor's orders."

—Maria Pena in *Disabled Faculty and Staff*, 15

"As an Asian American Woman of Color, an associate professor from a working-class background in a predominantly White university that ostensibly champions a commitment to diversity, it is challenging to expose the injuries of institutional violence and the persistence of racial harm. By institutional violence, I refer to both structural and cultural practices of White privilege that marginalize Faculty of Color, but are legitimized and 'normalized' as objective, color-blind operations that deem any detriment to the Faculty of Color to be caused by their own doing or explained by extraneous circumstances for which the institution is not at fault. Racial harm, then, is the outcome experienced by Faculty of Color who have endured some form of institutional violence with no recourse, expected institutional accountability, or hope for amelioration."

—Lynn Fujiwara in *Presumed Incompetent II: Race, Class, Power, and Resistance of Women in Academia*, 107

"During the last few years of feeling great emotional anguish and physical pain over the things I've both witnessed and experienced at the hands of my institution and so-called colleagues, I have also read about the effects of chronic stress and lifelong trauma. It turns out that medical research shows that when we experience, swallow, and suppress all of these affronts over a lifetime, we often end up sick, or dead. . . . This is, unfortunately, not hyperbole."

—Susie E. Nam in *Presumed Incompetent II: Race, Class, Power, and Resistance of Women in Academia*, 170 manifesting in the kinds of physical pain that keeps me from being able to walk. I feel pushed out, forced to choose between my well-being and employment in a disciplinary department."[18]

Part of the anger and hurt that comes through in the stories written by marginalized staff and faculty is the sense that it doesn't have to be this way. It is true that institutions often reflect and reproduce the societies that gave rise to them, but they aren't naturally occurring that way. That is, colleges and universities are not preordained to perpetuate systems of oppression. They are human creations that have been built up over time, and they can be rebuilt.

Making Equity Institutional "Second Nature"

Colleges and universities have DEI targets, initiatives, and offices—at least in states where it is still legal to do so. They have hired professional staff with the purview of advancing DEI across the institution. And they have invoked the value of diversity on their websites and in campus publications. Through such diversity work, institutions have tried to convey a willingness to address their ties to systems of oppression. According to Sara Ahmed, a writer and scholar of race and gender studies, many DEI practitioners understand their charge as institutionalizing DEI or making it part of the "tendencies and habitual forms of action that are not named or made explicit."[19] Institutionalizing DEI would mean that it becomes "second nature"—an instinctual set of actions.

But that is not really what has happened—at least not yet. If DEI were institutionalized, colleges and universities wouldn't need all those targets, initiatives, and offices—it would already (in the words of Ahmed) be in the "organizational flow of things."[20] The problem is that many of the people hired to do diversity work feel like the lofty diversity goals and statements issued by institutions are not followed by action. Diversity professionals report feeling like they are battling institutions that are, ultimately, resistant to change. The DEI professionals Ahmed interviewed regularly referred to their work as being akin to banging their head against a brick wall. Ahmed asked how we should make sense of "the paradox between, on the one hand, the routine uses of the language of diversity by institutions and, on the other, the experience of many practitioners of an institutional resistance to diversity becoming routine? . . . Or more simply: how does will become wall?"[21]

Part of the answer, for Ahmed, lies in institutions' embrace of the word "diversity" itself—how it has become "polite speech" and viewed as the "right way to speak," allowing institutions to cling onto something perceived as positive and "feel-good" without changing policies and practices.[22] Education philosopher Ariana González Stokas argued that many institutions have attempted to "evade the need for historical remedy of the chronic exclusion of certain groups in favor of the sprinkling of different identities."[23] In this way, diversity becomes detached from equity, "serving as a self-congratulatory mechanism for the appearance of difference" and "[facilitating] the drift away from practices needed for redress of society's inequitable structures."[24] In the words of González Stokas, building "cabinets of diversity" does not necessarily upend systems of oppression.

Narrowly focusing on diversity can be an institutional sleight of hand, drawing attention to the careful dribbling in of difference while systems of oppression like whiteness go untouched. *Whiteness*, in particular, merits attention because it comes up frequently in accounts written by marginalized staff and faculty. According to higher education scholars Zak Foste and Tenisha L. Tevis, whiteness "functions ideologically, structurally, institutionally, and epistemically to produce inequitable outcomes across the education landscape."[25] As an ideology, whiteness normalizes white supremacy, which higher education scholars Moira L. Ozias and Penny Pasque defined as "a system of white racial domination that normalizes violence, discrimination, and unequal power relations that privilege white people and harm People of Color."[26] The result is that white employees like me rarely feel isolated, excluded, or unsafe in the higher education workplace because of our racial identity. White workers at many institutions do not have to worry about how their hair, speech, dress, or weekend plans will be perceived. Whiteness becomes a credential, making it easier for white people to navigate and find success in admissions, hiring, and promotion processes.[27] Whiteness is the voice in the back of my head telling me to downplay or not talk about whiteness because it will make some readers uncomfortable.

Research shows that whiteness profoundly shapes the workplace experiences of many staff and faculty in higher education.[28] In 2022, ACPA-College Student Educators International convened a taskforce on twenty-first century employment in higher education. Their report argued that "higher education has long benefited from caste systems based in racism, institutionalized racial language and meaning, produced knowledge legitimizing white supremacy, and perpetuated a divisive system based on race."[29] Using Tema Okun's framework on white supremacy culture, the report identified seven domains of the higher education workplace that illustrate the maintenance of white supremacy: fear, perfectionism, paternalism, quantity over quality, denial, right to comfort, and urgency. In practice, these domains show up as fear that drives conformity to particular racialized or gendered presentations, as well as striving to be perfect or minimize your identity so as to not "rock the boat."

As I reflect on the narratives of marginalized staff and faculty, I sense that they too have run into "institutional defense routines" and resistance to change. I don't think that what these employees seek is a "sprinkling of different identities" or to be one of the select few who is let in and gets to be "included" within organizations that otherwise remain the same. They want organization-level change that is aimed at the practices, policies, and norms that sustain systems of oppression. For this reason, in thinking about change toward the Caring University, I have emphasized equity that leads to environments where all staff and faculty have resources and opportunities to thrive and belong.

Creating Equity-Minded Organizations

It was institutional resistance to change that led higher education scholars Román Liera and Steve Desir to explore organization-level transformation specifically focused on equity. Liera and Desir contend that relying too heavily on individualized efforts, like mandatory DEI trainings, often fail to bring about organizational change if they are not paired with cultural and structural transformation. Building on sociologist Victor Ray's theory of racialized organizations (which I described in Chapter 1), Liera and Desir developed a framework for *equity-minded organizations* that "[create] opportunities for university leaders, stakeholders, and researchers to move beyond the prose of campus DEI efforts to the design of programs, policies, and practices that can lead to more lasting structural changes."[30]

What does it mean to be an equity-minded organization? At the individual level, it means "having the knowledge to be conscious of race; being aware that racialized patterns are embedded in university policies, practices, and norms; using data disaggregated by race and ethnicity to identify racial equity gaps in their practice; and taking responsibility for changing policies, practices, and norms that sustain racial inequity."[31] At the organizational level, equity-mindedness means

- enhancing the agency of racially minoritized groups and racially conscious staff,
- redistributing resources with the intention of disrupting inequitable outcomes,
- delegitimizing whiteness as a credential, and
- being attuned to the structural disadvantages experienced by members of minoritized groups.[32]

I interviewed Liera and Desir to learn more about their framework, and Desir conceded that they are not aware of an institution that has all four attributes of an equity-minded organization. "But we wanted to create something to help institutions move closer to their equity goals and objectives. . . . How can we help them think about ways that they could be doing something different?"

Liera and Desir think of equity-mindedness as a type of "organizational cognitive frame" that can be applied to any number of problems. They see it as grounded in practitioner inquiry that strategically brings people together to collaborate around problems of practice: "We're a university, right?" Liera asked. "We're about research. We're about evidence. We're about growing. Practitioner inquiry allows us to leverage the mission of higher education institutions to say, 'We're all part of this community, and it's our responsibility to engage in this type of work.'" In this way, Liera and Desir see the pursuit of equity-mindedness as connected to organizational learning. In our conversation, Liera and Desir stressed that it is not just a matter of institutions committing to equity—it has to be operationalized. "Accountability is critical for this work to happen," Desir explained. "For me, I think it's recognizing that institutional leaders, unit leaders need to hold people accountable . . . or they're going to continue to do what they have been doing."

In practice, equity-mindedness takes shape in colleges and universities hiring and developing a critical mass of minoritized and marginalized people in positions with the authority and resources to shape practices and policies at the institution. Liera and Desir pointed to research showing how racially conscious Hispanic-serving institutions delegitimize whiteness as a credential through faculty search processes that prioritized candidates who understand and value the experiences of Latinx students and the university's broad-access mission. In a nod to the type of change processes that inform the Caring University, Liera emphasized (in a separate article) that equity at the organizational level requires collaborative change across multiple organizational units. As an example, he cites a long-term professional development series with broad participation from campus stakeholders.[33] The series includes defining key terms, presenting data disaggregated by race and ethnicity, providing tools to assess prevailing practices that perpetuate inequities, and then strategizing how to develop and implement new approaches.

I want to highlight four practices of equity-minded organizations that scholars and practitioners have proposed to disrupt the patterns I observed in various employee stories. These practices show how cultural and structural change can advance equity and improve the workplace experiences of marginalized staff and faculty. Rather than repeat—or, worse, co-opt—these approaches, my goal is to keep them tethered to the scholars who have researched and championed them.

Approach 1: Caring Through Equitable Hiring Processes and Outcomes

Marginalized staff and faculty would like not to be the "only one" in their departments or institutions, and they would like to avoid the associated isolation, tokenization, and uncompensated labor. Being able to see people who look like them and understand their experience across the organization is not typically rooted in a desire for perfectly proportionate representation or populating more colorful campus imagery. Rather, they want policies, practices, and norms that recognize talent in all its forms and build organizations where a worker doesn't feel that their presence is an anomaly, glitch, or publicity stunt. In short, they want to feel like they belong, which means taking on the very organizationally located problem of hiring.

I put the question of what hiring policies and processes have to do with equity to Kimberly Griffin, who is dean of the College of Education at the University of Maryland and an expert on equity in faculty hiring. "I do think that institutions sometimes place too much emphasis on it," she said, "like their diversity strategy *is* hiring." She adds that focusing on the "pipeline" or hiring more people appeals to institutions because it feels more contained and manageable. "Institutions say, 'We can make these tweaks and bring in folks, then our work is done.' It sometimes doesn't require the comprehensive reform that retaining people does." Griffin noted that while hiring may be just one element in a portfolio of institutional endeavors toward equity, it is still important in any effort to achieve organization-level change.

Griffin and colleagues at the Association of Public and Land Grant Universities developed the Institutional Model of Faculty Diversity. The model focuses on where barriers to equitable hiring arise and where institutions need targeted interventions to "create a more equitable environment and increase faculty diversity."[34] Emphasizing that what happens before a search is just as important as what happens during the search, the model stresses the importance of outreach—the ways in which institutions create opportunities for marginalized scholars to visit and become familiar with campus. The transition period between when an offer is extended and the formal start of a job can also be a critical time. Institutions need to think about their practices for welcoming new faculty and incorporating them into campus communities. Hiring must be combined with retention efforts. "I have seen institutions say, 'We're going to hire colleagues based on their commitments to equity and diversity and their investments in students and mentorship,' Griffin shared. "But they haven't revisited or thought about their promotion and merit pay criteria. So what they hired them for and the unique skills and gifts that they brought them to campus to use aren't recognized and rewarded."

Griffin has seen promising results at her institution from several approaches, including slowing searches down and educating search committee members to make sure a fair and just search process is a group responsibility. When a search committee receives their charge to initiate the search, it is part of a workshop, during which members of the committee review research on effective practices for recruiting a diverse pool and crafting inclusive position descriptions. Slowing down the search process ensures that the search committee has articulated the most important criteria they will use to evaluate candidates, compares those criteria to organizational values, and develops rubrics and other evaluative tools. In many ways, what Griffin is described is creating the infrastructure needed for running a professional and fair search process. "The way that we approach this work is not so much about short-term diversity goals," she said, "but rather how we construct good processes that allow you to identify an excellent candidate who's aligned with our strengths, our mission, our vision as a college."

Institutions may need to be prepared to build more accountability into search processes to arrive at equitable outcomes.[35] Román Liera, who codeveloped the equity-minded organization framework, teamed up with Theresa E. Hernandez to study how search committee members can still routinely disadvantage marginalized scholars even at institutions that have enacted policies to center equity in faculty hiring.[36] Liera and Hernandez found that criteria were selectively applied, with marginalized candidates often having to clear a higher bar. Search committee members who had undergone special "equity advocate" training had their recommendations overlooked and their input on committee deliberations sidelined. Based on this research, Liera and Hernandez recommended that institutions shouldn't rely on a small number of faculty on search committees to serve as "equity advocates"—rather, all faculty should participate in experiential learning to develop equity-minded competencies. They also recommended "equity checkpoints," where someone in a position of authority reviews evaluation criteria, decision-making processes, and the composition of candidates at each stage. Checkpoints could also involve all members of the committee signing off on the process and the result at each stage so that someone with more seniority does not overrule other voices.

When I interviewed Liera and Desir about equity-minded organizations, they suggested that leaders might need to step outside the box of conventional searches. They pointed to the potential of cluster hires—hiring a group of people into one or more departments based on shared interests and skills—to redistribute resources with the intention of disrupting inequitable outcomes. Many search processes start from a "tactical" perspective, with a narrow list of what the department or unit needs, often using the individual who held the position previously as a mental model. This process can sometimes result in replicating the type of people who have fulfilled those responsibilities in the past. By contrast, cluster hiring can be more strategic, pushing departments to take a strengths-based approach and hire multiple talented candidates based on what they offer the institution as a whole.

And there is another benefit to cluster hires: community. Higher education scholar Candace Hall explained how the approach foregrounds "the creation of an intentional community to support Black faculty toward thriving and experiencing joy at the institution."[37] When done with intentionality and clear objectives, cluster hires can signal not just a desire to recruit marginalized staff and faculty but also to retain them by fostering community and belonging.

Approach 2: Caring Through Valuing the Expertise and Labor of Marginalized Employees

Marginalized staff and faculty wrote about having their voices silenced, their intellectual contributions undervalued or disregarded, and their ways of being at work questioned or judged. Higher education scholar Wilson Okello sees this silencing as the same "quieting and smothering" at play when it comes to academic research, where "Western constructions of epistemology function to control and surveil the production of knowledge, research, and value in academic spaces."[38] Okello terms this process "epistemic asphyxiation" and explained what it looks like in practice through the examples of two Black scholars who were denied tenure at their institutions, despite having outstanding teaching, research, and service records.

In both cases, academic publishing was their undoing. Okello noted how academic publishing reflects and maintains whiteness by setting boundaries around what research gets selected and disseminated. It demands conformity to certain scholarly forms and language, establishing norms around what is considered "readable" and has an "audience" willing to engage ideas and reciprocate. When an audience refuses or fails to reciprocate, they silence Black scholars by positioning them as unqualified knowers. Black scholars, in turn, feel compelled to silence themselves by "[truncating] their testimony to ensure that the linguistic act is intelligible for the audience."[39] As a result, their ways of knowing and being are overlooked and constrained. Black scholars then must work harder to have their contributions seen, used, and judged as meritorious, while research that does not adhere to white standards of academic publishing is rejected or doesn't count for promotion purposes.

Writing about epistemic asphyxiation isn't just an academic exercise for Okello—it is personal. "This notion of legibility," he told me in an interview, raises the question of "what does it mean for me to write not toward a particular sense of clarity, but in ways that are perhaps accessible, translatable for those who are not as familiar with Black critical theories or Black ways of knowing and being." Part of the "extra work" and "psychological gymnastics" of being a Black scholar is fitting his ideas and voice into "narrow conceptions of how research is supposed to look, how it's supposed to sound, how it's supposed to flow." Okello learned early on that the feedback he would receive from editors, reviewers, or grant-makers wasn't really about clarity or the accuracy of ideas. It was about conforming to the preferences of those in power.

Okello reiterated that when he talks about "ways of knowing and being," he is not just talking about how a peer reviewer assesses his writing: "This is how individuals come to the university. This is how individuals show up in the classroom. When that is not regarded, or when that's not taken seriously . . . it pushes those ideas out. There's something that's not being added to an organization. Because folks are making deliberate decisions to hold it back and or to keep it to themselves."

As higher education scholar Leslie Gonzales pointed out to me, the failure of colleges and universities to create breathing room for the creativity of marginalized staff and faculty has significant implications. Although Gonzales wants to see greater demographic diversity in higher education, that goal alone has felt increasingly "shallow" to her. "Demographic diversity has to go hand-in-hand with epistemic questions. How are we prepared as scholars, search committee members, deans, and chairs to allow faculty to come in here and ask different kinds of questions? To unsettle the field where they are entering?" That unsettling, Gonzales notes, is how we advance knowledge and better serve students who are themselves asking questions and seeking creative solutions. In this way, epistemic asphyxiation doesn't just silence scholars—it constrains the excellence of knowledge-creating organizations and does a disservice to students.

Gonzales acknowledged that departments and units willing to hire someone who challenges them is one thing. Supporting and retaining them once they are in the department and pushing against the status quo is another. "In diversifying the academy, it's not only about what the scholar is bringing in, it's about what we as scholars have to do to receive that work, to interpret that work, to support it, to make sense of it," she said. Higher education scholars KerryAnn O'Meara and Lindsey Templeton have developed a set of resources to help institutions build systems to evaluate faculty work more equitably.[40] They articulated eight equity-minded principles that institutions can use to audit institutional policies around faculty evaluation:

- Transparency: Is salient information related to faculty evaluation intentionally shared, accessible, and accurate? If salient information is intentionally left out, is there a good reason?
- Clarity: Is information provided in a way that is easily understood? Is there ambiguity that could invite bias, guessing, and misinterpretation?
- Accountability: Are there responsible actors and steps identified if faculty evaluation policies and practices are not followed? Are there common enough deviations that might be foreseen and a process for addressing them laid out in the policy?
- Consistency: Are essential parts of the faculty evaluation process standardized and applied consistently so that when the same kind of activity is evaluated, faculty can expect similar treatment? If units are allowed to differ, are there disciplinary/field reasons?
- Context: Do the policies and practices provide ways to bring relevant contexts into view for the evaluation of faculty work? Does the evaluation invite comparisons that do not fit the circumstances?
- Credit: Do faculty evaluation policies recognize mission-critical work (e.g., mentoring, institutional service, DEI)? Do policies provide a way to differentiate between levels of effort when it is important to do so?
- Flexibility: Are faculty evaluation policies flexible enough to adapt to the new, different, and changing set of contexts shaping faculty careers and work?
- Agency and representation: Do policies provide ways for candidates to represent themselves in ways that are advantageous to their tenure case? Can faculty expect that they will be evaluated by colleagues who understand the relevant contexts of their work (e.g., appointment type, field, methods, and epistemologies as relevant)?

These principles are not exhaustive, and O'Meara and Templeton do not suggest that this audit approach will produce "perfect" evaluation practices and policies. Instead, they see it as an "iterative process . . . meant to aid an institution as it continuously learns how policies might be more equitable and inclusive."[41]

In a follow-up report focused on helping institutions translate equity-minded principles into action, O'Meara and colleagues devote specific attention to recognizing DEI work in faculty evaluation policies and practices.[42] They note that the labor of institutional DEI goals has often fallen to women and Black, Latinx, and Indigenous faculty. "Yet in national surveys, interviews, exit studies, and tenure denials," they write, "faculty consistently report that when it comes to faculty evaluation, they are not sure whether and how DEI work counted in decision-making."[43] As a result, these contributions are either invisible, in the sense that they are unacknowledged and uncompensated, or non-promotable visible labor, which may be captured in evaluation systems but viewed as less valuable. The report recommends that institutions have clear policies that invite and instruct faculty in the documentation of this labor as well as the expectation that committees show faculty how their labor in these areas is seen and valued (Box 5.5 presents an example).

Approach 3: Caring Through Accountability and Developing a "Theoretical Practice"

Sometimes writing about DEI can be laden with concepts and abstractions, and leaders who are uncomfortable with the terminology or worry about saying the wrong thing can fall back on euphemisms and coded language. The result is that it is possible to talk about diversity in a way that is divorced from the fact that we are talking about real people, real lives, and real bodies. But that is not the case for Wilson Okello, whose scholarship frequently considers the physicality of racism. Okello coauthored an article that talks about racism as an "ordinary, everyday occurrence for Black people"—one whose effects accumulate over time and are viscerally felt, leading to exhaustion, stress, depression, trauma, and physical illness.[44] Coping with these effects is sometimes referred to as "racial battle fatigue," and the student affairs professionals Okello and his colleagues interviewed described feeling hyperalert, heavy, and angry as they expended energy navigating racism and managing the fragility, feelings, and ignorance of their white colleagues.

The literature on burnout is replete with examples of physical manifestations of stress; indeed, as I wrote this chapter, the interim president of Temple University, JoAnne Epps, a Black woman, collapsed on stage at an event and passed away. The event continued after she was carried off the stage, which for many Black women symbolized the willingness of institutions to, quite literally, work them to death. Writing in the aftermath of this tragedy, higher education scholar Brittany M. Williams noted that Black women tend to carry a higher stress load compared to all other races of women, putting them at higher risk for heart disease and cancer.[45] To explain these outcomes, Williams pointed to the concept of weathering, or "Black people's earlier and disproportionate health deterioration" due to the "systemic stress from cumulative political, social, and socioeconomic disadvantage."[46] What Williams is driving at is that racism—including racism in the workplace—can have dire health consequences for Black people, especially Black women.

In *Reparative Universities*, Ariana González Stokas argues that diversity may produce a number of benefits for colleges and universities, but taking responsibility for this kind of harm isn't one of them. Instead, as the title of her book attests, González Stokas advocates for reparations—something she concedes sparks strong reactions: "Far too often even uttering the word elicits ridicule or disbelief that the inequalities of our present life have any connection or responsibility for past harm."[47] As someone unfamiliar with reparations, I am guilty of thinking of reparations purely in terms of "financial recompense and redistribution as a way to redress harm."[48] But what González Stokas has in mind is reparations as a "complex set of values, beliefs, and practices that a society recognizes as an essential part of healthy and just governments and institutions."[49]

González Stokas draws attention to a United Nations resolution that outlines basic principles of reparation. The principles go beyond restitution and compensation to include rehabilitation for psychological harm, truth-seeking efforts, and guarantees of non-repetition. "Describing reparations as a peace treaty offers a means to grapple with its character," González Stokas writes. "Reparative knowing and action must be able to perceive where the violence and injury persist in order to undo and unsettle them. To establish peace necessitates an undoing, an unraveling of where and how oppression persists."[50] Much like Liera and Desir's emphasis on accountability in equity-minded organizations, González Stokas argues that reparations include acts of institutional "responsibility-taking." These acts include promoting the self-determination of oppressed groups, refraining from attempting to manage equity and justice activities, and enabling counter-spaces for marginalized staff and faculty who "refuse to use the institution as it has been prescribed."[51]

González Stokas is hesitant to suggest a checklist of recommendations because her conceptualization of reparations is about "the practice of directing energy toward what needs undoing" and "a method for creating new modes of existence."[52] The push to translate ideas to practice sometimes places the onus on marginalized staff and faculty to be sensitive to the needs or shortcomings of dominant groups who say, "Tell me what to do with this." Instead, she calls on leaders to "participate, don't manage, offer resources, don't call university police and fundamentally listen, learn, and change."[53] Okello arrived at a similar stance, offering that those of us in higher education need to develop our "theoretical practice": "If we're going to be serious about moving toward ideas like care and equity and justice, we need to process and practice these conceptual ideas before we ever talk about caring as an organizational practice."

During a conversation with higher education scholar Ángel Gonzalez, I was reminded of the importance of not overly managing equity and belonging and of enabling counter-spaces. Gonzalez wrote about improving hiring practices for LGBTQ+ professionals at community colleges. As a queer-non-binary scholar of color, Gonzalez said, "We might not always understand what care for ourselves looks like. That in itself is an ongoing journey of exploration because for so long we've been not cared for." This is where supporting employee resource groups or similar collectives can be beneficial because marginalized staff and faculty can "begin to realize and create those futures for ourselves around caring." For these groups to be effective, they need access to financial support and physical spaces for people to safely meet. But then, according to Gonzalez, "there needs to be enough autonomy within the resource groups for them to create what makes sense for them." Sometimes, the best thing leaders can do is provide resources and encouragement, then get out of the way.

Approach 4: Caring Through Shared Equity Leadership

Higher education scholar Adrianna Kezar, whose work on organizational change informs the approaches proposed in this book, noted that many state legislatures have targeted campus-based DEI efforts. They have been effective in cutting or undermining these efforts because "DEI has not been made part of campus culture or normalized practice."[54] It is easy to cut DEI when it is largely siloed to a single position or office. According to González Stokas, for some institutions, simply creating the position of a chief diversity officer (CDO) is all that matters and as far as they intend to go.

In addition to making it easier to target DEI efforts, the tendency to foist all diversity hopes and dreams on a single person or office also hasn't been effective. "Higher education remains profoundly inequitable," Kezar and colleagues write, "and institutions have not made the transformational changes necessary to create truly inclusive environments and equitable outcomes."[55] Building on research that shows the importance of equity-minded leadership, Kezar and colleagues developed a model of shared equity leadership through a multiple case study of eight different institutions. The goal of shared equity leadership is to scale DEI work and create culture change, partly by developing a "critical mass of individuals across faculty, staff, and administrators who are all committed to the work, capable of leading the work, and supported through institutional processes, policies, and structures to do the work."[56]

According to Kezar and colleagues, there are three main elements of shared equity leadership. The first step in shared equity leadership is leaders who have done the work of developing their own "theoretical practice" with the goal of "cementing their commitment to equity."[57] Values that center equity and are shared across members of the leadership team represent the second element. These values, which include love, courage, humility, vulnerability, and experimentation, are "not typically associated with traditional forms of leadership"—an idea that I return to in Chapter 7. The final element is a set of practices that leaders continually enact to create more just and equitable conditions on their campuses, including building trust, diminishing hierarchy, using language intentionally, and making decisions through a structural or systemic lens.

Shared equity leadership does not just happen—institutions have to build capacity for it in the form of "ongoing investment at multiple levels that is meant to support and develop a repertoire of knowledge, skills, and dispositions to collectively lead equity-minded change efforts."[58] The researchers identified several collective strategies, including professional learning communities and communities of practice, or formalized, cross-departmental groups of staff, faculty, and leadership who come together to learn and improve their practice. Part of the idea is to move away from the assumption that learning has to happen individually or in preexisting institutional silos. Another strategy the authors highlight is affinity groups and healing circles, which are less about professional learning and more about creating opportunities for people who share social identities to build a sense of belonging and process their experiences with oppression.

To understand what shared equity leadership looks like in practice, I interviewed Amy Fulton, the director of the New Leadership Academy at the University of Utah. In an article that she wrote for *Inside Higher Ed*, Fulton describes the University of Utah as one of the first public institutions in the nation to adopt shared equity leadership.[59] "We've moved from this 'hub and spoke model' toward a 'woven model,' where equity is everyone's work," Fulton explained to me in an interview. In the "hub and spoke model," DEI activities are led by a CDO whose office serves as the hub and is connected to various "spokes" around campus. By contrast, the "woven model" integrates equity into everyone's work, "weaving it into the fabric of the institution as part of institutional strategic plans and goals and into individuals' roles."[60] Part of this shift was an effort to move beyond what Fulton and her colleagues called "random acts of diversity" and an approach where the CDO and its office was simply the "clean up crew" for a haphazard institutional strategy toward equity. Fulton told me that shared equity leadership isn't about "changing everyone's hearts and minds." Rather, it is "about taking a look at our policies and our practices and our everyday behaviors, and starting to make sure that those have equity embedded within them."

The University of Utah has piloted a shared equity leadership curriculum, developed a self-study guide for staff and faculty, and implemented shared equity leadership learning circles. Another part of the University of Utah's approach was the creation of a strategy and accompanying council that "brings together people from across the institution to become the change agents who center equity at the university."[61] The council has four pillars, each with a working group: belonging, community engagement, health equity, and campus climate. At a big university like the University of Utah, it is hard to get every part of the organization moving in the same direction, and there are some colleges more "on board" than others. But having a strategy gives the institution's various departments and units a set of goals with which they can align their efforts, because—as Fulton pointed out—the "[CDO] and our team can't be in all places at once."

It is worth noting that the University of Utah has pursued shared equity leadership in a state where policymakers are scrutinizing DEI initiatives and, in some cases, seeking to ban or defund them. When responsibility for equity is distributed across the organization, it becomes much harder to target particular offices and positions. This doesn't mean the work of shared equity leadership is easy in Utah. Leaders still have to be very careful about what they say in public when it comes to DEI. But it also doesn't mean that institutions need to preemptively end their initiatives to advance equity. Instead, shared equity leadership can make equity efforts more resilient in the face of political headwinds by moving steadily to a model where equity-mindedness is woven into the fabric of the institution so that it becomes an organizational habit.

Box 5.5

Rewarding DEI in Promotion and Tenure Policies

The Case of Indiana University-Purdue University Indianapolis

As far back as 2008, Indiana University-Purdue University Indianapolis (IUPUI)'s promotion and tenure guidelines stipulated that "faculty work that contributes to the diversity of learners and scholars at IUPUI and that enhances [the] environment of equity and inclusion is highly valued and should be acknowledged and rewarded in the review process." However, the guidelines stopped short of articulating clear criteria for evaluation. This was a problem because one of the goals of IUPUI's strategic plan was "developing and maintaining an unapologetically equitable and inclusive campus culture," and it employed faculty working toward this goal. Yet among employees, their "most impactful work is not currently recognized or rewarded within the traditional [promotion and tenure] system."

According to Gina Sanchez Gibau, IUPUI's associate vice chancellor for faculty diversity and inclusion, the university undertook work to "better align the university's values to what we actually want faculty to do and that is a measurement of excellence for them." Gibau had seen other institutions integrate contributions to DEI in their promotion and tenure criteria, and she first tried to change IUPUI's policies in 2017, with no success. But after the murder of George Floyd in the summer of 2020, there was more institutional willingness to explore these changes. The main priority in the 2020–21 academic year was to ensure that the "mechanisms by which we recognize and reward faculty . . . in areas that enhance equity and inclusion" align with campus values. In short, IUPUI wanted to look at how contributions to diversity, equity, and inclusion were recognized in its policies for promotion and tenure.

Faculty across higher education are typically evaluated based on their teaching, research, and service to their programs, departments, colleges, institutions, and disciplines. IUPUI already had a somewhat unconventional promotion and tenure policy because faculty could be promoted based on excellence in one of these areas or what they call a "balanced case." In the former case, faculty would need to demonstrate excellence in one area and satisfactory performance in the others. In a balanced case, a "faculty member's career and accomplishments may be more or less integrated across teaching, research, and service." Faculty may be able to show highly satisfactory contributions in all areas according to a specific philosophy or theme, such as community engagement.

Box 5.5 (continued)

To better recognize and reward faculty contributions to DEI, Gibau and her colleagues made use of existing policy structures and proposed two changes. First, they developed a special DEI designation that faculty can add to their curricula vitae (similar to markings they already use to indicate work co-authored with students), with the opportunity to elaborate on their DEI-focused work in the statement they submit as part of their promotion and tenure materials. Second, they created a balanced case that shows integrative contributions to DEI through teaching, research, and service. Part of the logic is that "for many faculty, particularly those that engage in diversity, equity, and inclusion work, the work is all of a piece rather than dividing neatly into categories," said Gibau.

Folding these changes into existing policy was strategic because there was concern that making contributions to DEI a separate category would marginalize the work. Some of the committee members tasked with proposing revised policy language struggled to see what a balanced DEI case would look like. "My mantra to them," said Gibau, "was that this is still faculty work. It's still research. It's still teaching. It's not this weird thing that you can't wrap your head around." Nor was it viewed as a mandatory pathway that all faculty must follow for promotion and tenure. As Gibau explained, "The purpose behind this is to say we recognize these scholars, the ones who are really involved in this work, and their identity as scholars. . . . Previously they would have to focus on one of the three other areas and really suppress all of the integration that they typically do." As part of these changes, they developed a document with definitions and examples of work that could be considered minimum standards or equate to excellence. Gibau's office has also developed a community of practice for people who are considering pursuing the DEI balanced case pathway.

Although these changes required considerable effort, IUPUI also recognizes there is more work to be done. For example, they note that there is a need for more flexibility and less bias in assessing the quality of outlets that disseminate scholarship. Some of the most prestigious journal articles and book publishers, for example, have favored certain authors, institutions, and topics. Moreover, being published in a prestigious journal does not guarantee the scholarship will have an impact, since some articles in top journals are never used or cited. In this way, IUPUI is working to disrupt some of the traditional ways that contributions have been assessed.

Summing up their work so far in terms of caring about all faculty and valuing their work, Gibau said, "At the heart of this, people want to feel that they are valued. And not just, 'I care about you because you are diverse so let me put you on my search committee.' We want to create environments where folks are successful, where they're not just seen and utilized for their diversity."

Conclusion

The default setting of most colleges and universities runs on code as old as the United States (if not older). That code reflects a scientifically debunked logic that a human being's competence, rights, and value can be hierarchically categorized based largely on how they look or present. Some institutions were founded to specifically uphold this logic, and many operated for centuries before they were legally mandated to add new users or features. But the code itself is still there, giving structure to colleges and universities in countless ways. Even though the people studying and working at institutions have changed considerably since the code was written, the operating system of colleges and universities feels locked in time.

Box 5.6

Chapter 5 Action Steps

- Use the Institutional Model of Faculty Diversity to determine where barriers to equitable hiring arise and where your institution needs targeted interventions. Review efforts in each area of the model, including outreach, hiring, transition, and institutional commitment.
- Allow enough time to conduct search processes so that all search committee members can participate in experiential learning to develop equity-minded competencies. Ensure they understand how to run a professional, fair search while allowing enough time for the inclusion of "equity checkpoints."
- Consider moving from short-term tactical searches to strategic searches (i.e., cluster hires) that advance the institution's goals and mission for the long term.
- Use equity-minded principles to evaluate recognition and reward systems for transparency, consistency, and flexibility. Ensure there is accountability when processes and policies are not followed or the system continues to elevate or disadvantage particular groups.
- Read, cite, and use the work of marginalized staff and faculty. Begin developing a "theoretical practice" that focuses on personally practicing care, justice, and equity.
- Do not relegate all DEI initiatives to a single person or office without sufficient resources. Distribute equity work across the institution and weave equity-minded expectations and competencies into all job descriptions.

The result is that many people have been systematically denied the chance to share their brilliance. They were never afforded the opportunity to apply for positions at higher education institutions, or their talents were overlooked in inequitable hiring practices. Maybe they were one of a few who were let in, only to find it was a hostile place—one that would silence them, devalue their contributions, and overload them with stress in ways that snuffed out their light. To care is to be deeply uncomfortable with the patterns of marginalization that persist for certain higher education workers. A Caring University must be organizationally unsettled to such an extent that it is compelled—in the name of fairness, justice, and decency—to rewrite the code. This is a prerequisite for reimagining the higher education workplace.

Box 5.6 summarizes the steps that leaders can take to initiate this type of unsettling. Pursuing cultural and structural change for equity and belonging is difficult for sure, but it is also an upgrade for excellence. It makes space for more people to do their best work, especially those who ask big questions, take risks, and apply their creativity to dreaming up new and better ways to understand and improve our lives. Isn't that what higher education is all about?

CHAPTER 6

Empowering Employees' Rights and Voice

THE EISENHOWER EXPRESSWAY runs adjacent to the University of Illinois Chicago (UIC) campus. This part of "the Ike" (as it is known locally) is cut deep into the land, almost as if they made a road in the remnants of a dried-up riverbed. In reality, the expressway paved over large swaths of Chicago's Near West End neighborhood. Both the expressway and university were part of a vision in the 1960s to "revitalize" the area, resulting in the displacement of Black- and immigrant-owned homes and businesses in Little Italy and Greek Town.[1]

Looming above one side of the expressway is University Hall, which at 28 stories is the tallest building on Chicago's west side.[2] UIC's administration occupies the top floor of the brutalist-style concrete building, and the corner office belongs to Michael Ginsburg, interim vice chancellor for budget, HR, and financial administration. I met with Ginsburg in his office, complete with sweeping views of the city, to get his perspective on labor unions and collective bargaining in higher education. Ginsburg has worked at the university for over 40 years and represented it in numerous contract negotiations with unions.

On the other side of the expressway is a nondescript red brick building where UIC United Faculty and the UIC Graduate Employees Organization

(GEO) have their offices. There—and at the coffeeshop down the block—I met with the leaders of GEO, which represents graduate workers, and UIC United Faculty, which represents tenure-track and non-tenure-track faculty. I couldn't help but observe that the offices representing labor and management at UIC were separated by what appeared to be a wide chasm. But there was a footbridge stretching across the expressway, suggesting that the two sides were not entirely cut off from one another.

My reason for meeting with both sides of the negotiating table was the same: I wanted to learn more about unions and how they negotiate contracts for their members—also known as *collective bargaining*.[3] I did so with considerable humility. My knowledge of unions was limited to news stories about strikes and distant memories of my mom's time in a teachers' union. I had a nagging sense that many stories simplified contract negotiations to the latest battle in an eternal conflict between bitter enemies. I wanted to get to know the people behind the picket lines and challenge the prevailing caricatures of unions and administrators.

Selecting UIC as a site to study admittedly came down to luck more than the university meeting particular criteria. I already had a long-planned trip to Chicago in the works when a story about the end of UIC United Faculty's strike popped up in my search results. I knew that the city had a rich labor history and was unsurprised to learn UIC is no stranger to working with unions. As Ginsburg explained to me, collective bargaining is a fact of life at the university. In a given year, UIC negotiates as many as four contracts with one of more than 25 different unions. I figured that if a novice like me wanted to learn about unions and collective bargaining in higher education, Chicago wasn't a bad place to start.

Despite my unfamiliarity with unions, I knew one thing for certain: they were on the rise in higher education. According to the State of the Unions 2023 report, there was an uptick in organizing and strikes among higher education students and faculty during the pandemic, accelerating a five-decade growth trend.[4] Bloomberg Law's database of work stoppages shows that about 60 percent of the nearly 225,000 employees engaged in work stoppages in 2022 were educators, researchers, and other academic professionals.[5] Unions were increasingly prominent in shaping the higher education workplace and, as described in the introduction, the Four Rs of the Great Resignation, specifically resistance.

My trip to Chicago was eye-opening in several ways. On the one hand, it taught me that unions are about more than dues, picket lines, and bullhorns; they can be a catalyst for many of the organizational changes I am proposing in this book, such as career ladders, higher compensation, better leave policies, and support for mental health. On the other hand, hearing from university administrators persuaded me that while the relationship with unions was adversarial, it needn't be antagonistic, and institutions were not universally opposed to the goals of unions. But most of all, my conversations convinced me of the need for an additional set of changes to the cultures and structures of colleges and universities to achieve the goals of the Caring University—changes focused on buttressing worker rights and their voice in the workplace.

A Tool for Reimagining the Twenty-First-Century University

Aaron Krall was hired as a full-time lecturer of English at UIC in 2006 making $26,000. He was on a short-term contract, which was just one of several ways his job prevented him from making plans to stay at the university. In addition to the low pay that made it nearly impossible to live in Chicago, there was no career ladder or annual review policy for contingent faculty. Resources for professional development were scarce or, more frequently, nonexistent. And contingent faculty were not eligible to receive a computer or periodically upgrade it. UIC gave Krall a job, but it wasn't the kind of opportunity the university could boast about.

What has enabled Krall to continue teaching at UIC for 17 years is UIC United Faculty and the contracts it has secured through collective bargaining. Krall is now the president of the union, and he and the union's vice president, Therese Quinn, a professor of museum and exhibition studies, told me some of the union's biggest "wins" have been for contingent faculty. Successive rounds of contract negotiations raised the minimum salary for full-time contingent faculty to $37,500, then to $42,000,

$50,000, and most recently to $60,000. According to Krall, raising the minimum salary is partly designed to "stop the slide away from tenure and make it less economical or convenient to hire non-tenure-track faculty." Instructors and lecturers can now be promoted to the rank of senior instructor or lecturer—with a pay increase—based on their performance. Articles in the contract also stipulate processes for annual evaluations, disciplinary actions, and professional development.

The union transformed Krall's gig into a career. He was promoted to senior lecturer and has fewer worries about whether he will have a job from one year to the next. Thanks to the most recent negotiations, contingent faculty have annual contracts for the first three years of their appointment, followed by a three-year contract, then a five-year contract thereafter. Although this change does not entirely eliminate job precarity, multiyear contracts space out moments of vulnerability and—combined with clear disciplinary procedures—promote academic freedom. As Krall noted, it is impossible to enjoy academic freedom and participate in university life—like taking on the presidency of a union—when you are constantly under threat of not being renewed.

Not all unions in higher education feature a strong partnership between tenure-track and contingent faculty. In fact, contingent faculty often lead the charge for improved working conditions and plead with their tenure-track colleagues to join the cause.[6] And that was true at UIC for a time. Non-tenure-track faculty at UIC had attempted to organize as a union without success in the early 2000s. But then, the University of Illinois System announced across-the-board furloughs for all faculty in the wake of the Great Recession, and tenure-track faculty started taking the idea of a union more seriously.[7] By 2012, organizers submitted union authorization cards to be one bargaining unit representing all faculty.

Although the Illinois Supreme Court eventually ruled that tenure-track and contingent faculty had to bargain as separate units, the idea of a single union lives on.[8] The union's leadership consists of both tenure-track and contingent faculty. In the most recent round of bargaining, the union jointly negotiated two contracts, with equal representation from tenure-track and contingent faculty on the bargaining team. As

Krall explained about the union's united front, "From the very beginning, we went into it with the idea that the union could be a tool for reimagining what the twenty-first-century university is going to be like. If you're going to rely on so much non-tenure-track labor, what do those working conditions look like? How do you sustain a career as a non-tenure-track faculty member? What even is a career as a non-tenure-track faculty member?"

UIC United Faculty also has not focused solely on pay and job security. Quinn is particularly proud of the union's efforts aimed at "common good" bargaining, which aims to expand the scope of negotiations beyond wages and benefits by collaborating with other organizations around a set of shared demands that are beneficial to the wider community.[9] In the most recent contract negotiations, UIC United Faculty took up student concerns related to mental health, disability services, and gender-inclusive bathrooms. Although the university's labor relations team argued that student services do not belong in a faculty contract, the union asserted that faculty have increasingly been called on to support the well-being of students, which has implications for their workload and job experience. The union's common good demands were not fully met, but the university committed to investing $4.5 million over six years to enhance student mental health services.

One of UIC United Faculty's strategies has been to incorporate existing policies into the contract and push for more opportunities for *shared governance*—the structures and processes through which institutional governing boards, administrators, faculty, staff, and students jointly participate in planning, policies, and decisions.[10] This, too, has been a point of contention with the university's bargaining team, which argued that structures and processes for shared governance are already in UIC's statutes. But for the union, a contract puts relevant policies in a single, accessible, enforceable document that is regularly updated. Shared governance at UIC may be statutorily enshrined, Krall explained, but the faculty senate's role is "advisory all the way up." In a healthy organization, that advice is taken seriously, but it is not guaranteed. In the words of UIC United Faculty's website, the union "makes the promise of shared governance a reality by backing it with the power of collective bargaining."[11]

A contract by its very nature puts in writing a set of clear rights and responsibilities that apply to all parties. As Krall put it, "A union contract provides a structure where you can say, 'These are the rules we play by. Here's how you'll be evaluated. Here's when you'll be evaluated. If you cross some lines, here's how you'll be disciplined.' Everybody knows what the rules are and everybody is accountable to them." Clarity around policies and procedures isn't just beneficial for employees—it can be incredibly helpful for supervisors and leaders. Krall pointed out that without a detailed contract, department chairs can be thrust into decision-making situations without explicit rules, exposing them—and institutions—to legal risk. A contract allows institutions to hold faculty and administrators accountable to mutually agreed-on expectations.

As I inventoried the changes that collective bargaining produced at UIC, the vast majority of them seemed reasonable. In many ways, contingent faculty were asking for basic things that many higher education professionals already enjoy. And my conversation with GEO's copresidents, Marty Heath and Jennifer Vaccaro, likewise did not strike me as radical in terms of their description of the union's demands. They asked for pay raises and for the university to waive certain fees, especially considering record-high inflation. They proposed that teaching assistants be hired on nine-month appointments to cut down on late paychecks when people were rehired every semester. And they sought paid parental and bereavement leave. Vaccaro, a PhD student studying hyperbolic geometry (which she assured me is a real thing), explained that being part of a union hasn't indoctrinated her to a set of radical ideas; rather, it was trying to live on a graduate student stipend in Chicago that radicalized her.

Everyone I spoke with at UIC admitted that negotiations can be tense. Heath, a PhD student studying communication about disability, described moments of bewilderment during bargaining, such as when it was suggested that teaching assistants lacking reliable internet service could teach from their cars in a McDonald's parking lot. They often had to use personal experience to help the university's labor relations team understand certain positions. Although the relationship between unions and UIC administration is adversarial, it also was respectful. Ginsburg put it this way: "We spent nine months negotiating with faculty. At the end of the day, everyone's playing their role. It's not about you or me disliking each other. We're all people. We're all going to work together later."

However contentious negotiations might be, collective bargaining can engage employees in a meaningful process that gives them a seat at the table to co-construct their working conditions. That doesn't mean unions are necessary to address problems in the higher education workplace. But there is little doubt in my mind that unions have pushed UIC to enact organizational changes consistent with the Caring University—and to likely do so at a faster clip than if it was left to its own devices. Unions have generated conflict at UIC but also positive change—and the two are not entirely disconnected.

Not everyone is especially sanguine about the potential for unions and other forms of *collective action* (action taken by a group whose members share resources, knowledge, and interests to advance a common purpose) in higher education.[12] As a matter of fact, there is a consistent argument situating higher education's penchant for shared governance as an obstruction to transformation. As a result, there have been concerted efforts to undermine shared governance and therefore curtail employee rights, including their right to have a say in the workplace. In this chapter, I describe the forces driving these efforts, including some that originate outside academia and others that can be chalked up to institutional choices.

I argue that collective action reflects employees' desire to assert their rights and have a voice in the workplace. Anchored in concepts from workplace democracy and the vision platform of Higher Education Labor United, I describe three organization-level approaches to help higher education empower employees' rights and voice in the workplace. These approaches address employment security and improved working conditions for contingent faculty, collaborative shared governance, and support for workers' organizing efforts.

It is not coincidental that the Great Resignation happened during a period when many colleges and universities accelerated a trend of diminishing employee involvement in decision-making. What higher education workers want is to be meaningful participants in shaping institutions they care deeply about.

Forces Curtailing Employees' Rights and Voice

My first foray into shared governance was serving as a faculty senator for my department. I had only been an assistant professor for a few years and was testing the waters of university-level service. At the time, there wasn't any training or orientation for new senators—I simply showed up to the first meeting and pretended I understood Robert's Rules of Order. For most of that first term, I listened and voted, rarely speaking up.

But during one meeting late in the year, the chancellor gave a presentation on the institution's aspirations to be reclassified as a research university. His remarks directly implicated an academic program in my department and even connected to my research. When he opened the floor to questions, I raised my hand and asked a question reflecting concerns that my colleagues communicated in a department meeting. It was both exhilarating and terrifying at the same time—exhilarating because I was given the chance to directly speak with the chancellor, share my expertise, and represent the view of my colleagues, and terrifying because I was relatively new to the institution and early in my career. I half expected him to email me the next day and instruct me never to do that again.

But that's not what happened. It turned out that speaking up on behalf of my colleagues was exactly what the faculty senate was for. Over time, I became more comfortable sharing when I had something useful to add. Before long, I was on the curriculum committee, provost's advisory council, then the graduate council and senate budget committee. Through these experiences, I witnessed cross-departmental teams of colleagues discussing important issues and making updates to the faculty handbook, academic programs, and general education requirements. I experienced moments where faculty checked administrators and vice versa, pushing each side to clarify their positions and reach compromise. It was rarely a perfect system, but I came to appreciate how shared governance allowed the university to inclusively construct teams and create space for them to deliberate their way to solutions.

Higher education is one of the few workplaces in the United States where shared governance is practiced. This distinction is more often met with confusion than celebration, and there is no shortage of shared governance skeptics. One common critique is that shared governance is ineffective and actually an impediment to transformational change.[13] In his book on resistance to change in higher education, Brian Rosenberg, former president of Macalester College, argues that "like most systems of governance, shared governance within academia has strengths and weaknesses and is better suited to some situations than others."[14] He notes that colleges and universities are full of smart people equipped to solve big problems, transparency in decision-making is invaluable in times of crisis, and gathering input from many constituencies cuts down on errors. But he concludes that because shared governance is slow and too focused on consensus-building it is "far better at guarding against disruptive change than it is at enabling it."[15]

Evidence of how, precisely, shared governance affects organizational change is scarce, but that has not stopped detractors from characterizing it as symptomatic of higher education's aversion to change. This perception—that shared governance is a roadblock to transformation—is one of several forces that have caused or justified the diminution of employees' rights and voice in the workplace. Before the pandemic, scholars were writing about the "erosion" and "demise" of the faculty's voice in campus decision-making.[16] For example, Adrianna Kezar and colleagues contended that "in the last thirty years, most campuses have centralized decision-making among administrators and divested decision-making authority from faculty."[17] Higher education scholars Martin J. Finkelstein and colleagues argued that diminishing influence is one of ten trends responsible for "shunting" faculty into a new era.[18] This trend intensified during the pandemic, with one survey of nearly 600 faculty governing body leaders reporting that shared governance has been under "severe pressure."[19]

With its emphasis on inclusive committees, gathering input, asking questions, and revising assumptions, shared governance often gets sidelined in crises.[20] And the number and frequency of crises—from natural disasters to mass shootings, cyberattacks, and budget deficits—are increasing and happening all at once, creating more situations where leaders may feel justified in suspending shared governance. For example, the pandemic initially produced unexpected revenue losses and significant financial anxiety. During the early wave of campus closures, an *Inside Higher Ed* survey reported that 87 percent of college presidents were concerned about short-term financial challenges, and 89 percent were concerned about their institution's long-term financial outlook.[21] Writing on shared governance in this period of uncertainty, English professor Jolie A. Sheffer and colleagues observed, "To deal with budget shortfalls, some universities announced mass layoffs, reorganized units, and inaugurated faster decision-making processes—changes that dramatically reduced shared governance."[22]

A committee of the American Association of University Professors (AAUP) investigated the pandemic response of eight institutions, with a focus on their approaches to shared governance. The authors of the committee's report explained that the investigation was "prompted by opportunistic exploitation of catastrophic events."[23] The report details how some institutions under investigation suspended the faculty handbook, which, according to committee cochair Michael DeCesare, is "one of the most egregious violations of long-standing governance standards."[24] Several other institutions moved to fire tenured faculty without first declaring a financial exigency, which the AAUP defines as an "imminent financial crisis which threatens the survival of the institution as a whole."[25] Even in instances when colleges and universities declared financial exigency, the AAUP has found "abuses of academic governance in which administrations, in addition to terminating faculty appointments, eliminate academic programs, create new ones, or insist upon other academic restructuring to alleviate financial stress or to generate new sources of income."[26] In May 2021, six of the institutions under investigation were sanctioned by the AAUP for shared governance violations.[27]

In the intervening years, numerous institutions have faced budget crises, many of which are not the direct result of the pandemic but rather (in the words of Kezar and colleagues) "trends that broadly define our new reality of precarious work and its connection to unraveling the public good role of higher education."[28] In *The Gig Academy*, Kezar and her coauthors trace working relations and conditions in higher education to neoliberalism and its attendant effects on higher education—often described through the concept of academic capitalism. Acknowledging that "neoliberalism" is a fraught term because it has been used to describe just about everything, Kezar and colleagues see neoliberalism less as a "fixed order" and more as a "normative rationality that gradually reconfigures relationships between citizens, societies, states, and markets."[29] A defining feature of neoliberalism is that it prioritizes individual freedom and personal responsibility over shared welfare and shifts responsibility for the provision of basic needs and public goods from democratic institutions to private enterprises.

One result of neoliberalism in higher education is that public colleges and universities have been subjected to new forms of accountability; as a consequence, in many states, they receive less funding from the government on a per-student basis.[30] Competition for tuition-paying students and cost-cutting efforts intensified in due course. Higher education scholars Sheila Slaughter and Gary Rhoades developed the concept of academic capitalism to explain and describe these changes, with a particular focus on how the distribution of power within institutions has been altered. For example, they chart how academic capitalism extended "managerial control" in public institutions, granting administrators more authority to make decisions around institutional resources to pursue new revenue sources.[31] Although leaders did what they thought was best in the face of new financial realities, Slaughter and Rhoades argue that academic capitalism wasn't simply foisted on colleges and universities. As sociologists Laura T. Hamilton and Kelly Nielsen explained, many leaders embraced forms of "austerity administration" that lionized both enrollment growth and lower spending on labor, even when budgets were healthy.[32]

Robert A. Scott, president and professor emeritus of Adelphi College and Ramapo College of New Jersey, similarly points to the "increasingly corporate style of higher education" as a force compromising shared governance.[33] He gives particular attention to the fact that institutional governing boards and presidents are often specifically chosen and incentivized to focus on funding and fundraising; as a result, the institution "loses touch with the core functions of the institution and with faculty, students, and staff."[34] It is rarely the case that senior leaders are thought of or expected to serve as educators. Making matters worse, many of the groups whose members are asked to step into important governance roles are not properly trained for the task. "Few campuses," according to Scott, "devote resources to preparing faculty for governance or for leadership in faculty committees and senates."[35] Although some leaders argue that faculty are not stepping up and taking shared governance seriously, Scott argues the "fault lies with trustees and presidents who pay too little attention to this important dimension of university governance and leadership."[36]

Mixing academic capitalism with austerity administration leads to more higher education workers being hired as contingent staff. That is, they are hired as "freelancers" or "contractors" to complete a specific task but are not full-time employees and thus aren't granted the same rights and privileges as full-time employees of the organization. Full-time lecturers like Aaron Krall fall into this category, as do part-time adjuncts, whose numbers have steadily increased in higher education for the past 40 years. According to the AAUP, over two-thirds of all instructors in higher education were in contingent positions in 2021, up from 47 percent in 1987.[37] Today, fewer than one in four faculty members are in full-time tenured positions, down from 39 percent. Kezar and colleagues contend that the "decreased availability of permanent appointments altered the balance of power in university governance by leaving more decisions and processes to be managed by university administrators, reducing faculty autonomy."[38]

The "gig academy" is the term that Kezar and colleagues use to describe the "cluster of mutations that long-term restructuring toward cheap and disposable labor in higher education has wrought."[39] They argued that "this state of affairs ought not be perceived as normal, natural, or inevitable but as the product of institutional choices."[40] One dimension of the gig academy is fragmenting the workplace into "discrete blooms of subcontracted employees," which makes it harder for workers to organize or collaborate.[41] The gig academy relies on a stratified workforce consisting of managers and other employees who enjoy stable, well-compensated jobs while a much larger and interchangeable "reserve population" is funneled into short-term contracts, including growing numbers of postdoctoral and graduate student workers. Many workers in the gig academy aren't included in departmental decision-making and have little autonomy over their work, stripping them of the hallmarks of professionals in the workplace. A consequence of the gigification of the academy is a breakdown of community and increasingly strained relationships that lead to "declining satisfaction, morale and engagement, rising turnover and difficulty recruiting employees, and growing discrimination."[42]

The gig academy isn't just a threat to shared governance. It also compromises academic freedom—a concept that is frequently invoked by faculty and just as frequently misunderstood. *Academic freedom* does not grant faculty the right to say or do anything, no matter how objectionable. Rather, academic freedom is the ability to discuss topics that are relevant in the classroom and pursue and publish research without interference or censorship from campus leaders, boards, or policymakers. Academic freedom also grants faculty the ability to write and speak about matters of institutional governance without fear of discipline.[43] Courts have found the protection of academic freedom to be especially important on public campuses, which can be viewed as extensions of the government and, as such, cannot favor certain views while suppressing others. Academic freedom is often framed as an individual right, but it is upheld through the collective right of faculty to self-govern.[44] Academic freedom is protected by *tenure*, not because it prevents professors from being fired but, more importantly, because it sets clear parameters for faculty due process rights and continuing employment.

Attacks on tenure have not been limited to institutions facing a budget crisis. Wisconsin, Iowa, North Dakota, Florida, Texas, Georgia, and North Carolina have all seen bills in recent years championed by Republican lawmakers attempting to eliminate or constrain tenure.[45] Higher education scholar Barrett Taylor demonstrated how many states pursued a policy agenda of deinstitutionalization, depriving colleges and universities of material resources by cutting their funding but also undercutting their legitimacy—sowing mistrust, questioning expertise, and weakening independence. Efforts to erode trust "led to battles over control of the enterprise, with higher education's traditional mechanisms of shared governance under attack."[46] In response to these attacks, Taylor found many leaders have engaged in "partial defenses," such as emphasizing higher education's instrumental value as a contributor to economic development and centralizing administrative authority to position the organization to win competitions for students, funds, and status. These defenses have "perpetuated a cycle of wreckage by keeping individual colleges and universities afloat but leaving the deeper allegations . . . unanswered."[47]

According to William A. Herbert, executive director of the National Center for the Study of Collective Bargaining in Higher Education and the Professions, budget cuts, contingent appointments, the pandemic, and "a new variant of American anti-intellectualism" have swirled together to "create a ripe environment for the growth of union representation."[48] Between 2013 and 2019 alone, faculty represented by unions grew by 10 percent, with contingent faculty constituting three-quarters of the increase. Matt Johnson, a higher education scholar who served as president of Central Michigan University's union representing tenure-track faculty between 2020 and 2023, told me in an interview that "during COVID, [the union's] support was very, very high." Whereas typical meetings might see 25 percent of members attend, during the pandemic it was closer to 70 percent: "I had so many people share stories and thank us for the communication and putting their mind at ease. They've got kids running around, they're taking care of parents, dealing with all this kind of stuff. Just to know that somebody is out there trying to make some headway and trying to have our voice represented at these various committees that were really going fast offered a lot of solace for people." According to Johnson, it was also a time when they saw the most interest ever in unionization from entry-level and mid-level staff.

Autumn Kearney was an entry-level staff member who became involved in an organizing effort at the University of Michigan. Kearney, who is now a doctoral student, worked in admissions and learned about the union effort from a colleague. Part of her decision to get involved was the fact that the university's flexible work policy was vetted by the faculty governing body, not the staff who would be affected by it. "It created a very interesting power dynamic," she explained, "where they were like, *you* have to be here to serve students." Many of the staff she spoke with as part of the organizing effort pointed to instances when staff proposed ideas to improve working conditions and were shot down, only to see the idea implemented for faculty. Ultimately, Kearney started to see things more organizationally. "A lot of times, we're putting little Band-Aids on things. . . . But that's not sustainable. And so I'm trying to think about how we can . . . work together in a way that addresses the problem more collectively."

I have come to view unions, shared governance, academic freedom, and tenure as interdependent components of the higher education workplace designed to uphold employee rights and give them a voice. Just as the four components can reinforce one another, threats or attacks on one have ramifications for the others. While forces compromising shared governance were in play prior to 2020 (whether originating outside academia or initiated by institutions making values-driven choices that are subsequently cemented in policy or practice), the pandemic supercharged many of them. Staff and faculty alike felt their expertise and experiences weren't adequately considered when institutions responded to the pandemic.

For many higher education workers, the Great Resignation was a reaction to the forces undermining their rights and ability to have a voice in the workplace. The Caring University's answer to these cultural and structural problems is a more democratic higher education workplace.

Envisioning a More Democratic Higher Education Workplace

According to sociologist Barry Eidlin and labor expert Micah Uetricht, "A vast majority of Americans live a paradox: they check their deeply held democratic rights at the door every day when they show up for work."[49] Employers can limit what workers say, monitor their messages, and limit their bathroom breaks. They can hire, fire, and discipline workers largely at will. "To the extent that employers treat their workers well, it is entirely at their discretion, as revocable and subject to change without notice as a king's writ."[50] Yet there was a time when many policymakers and workers advocated for democratic rights and processes in the workplace. An early justification for collective bargaining—which was subsequently built in the National Labor Relations Act of 1935 and many state laws—was to establish the basis for "representative workplace democracy."[51]

The Center for Learning in Action at Williams College defines *workplace democracy* as the "application of democratic processes, such as voting, debate and participatory decision-making systems to the workplace."[52] Kezar and colleagues added due process and systems of appeal to the list of democratic processes, which they see as central to organized labor and collective bargaining.[53] Researchers have often conceptualized workplace democracy around the idea that an organization is analogous to a state: if we subscribe to the idea that citizens are granted some right to self-government or freely give their consent to being governed by someone else, why shouldn't workers similarly have the ability to participate—directly or indirectly—in decision-making that governs the workplace?[54] Often, workplace democracy combines a type of participatory management with forms of employee ownership, such as an employee stock ownership plan.[55]

The growth of unions in higher education is part of a trend to democratize the workplace. In the words of Kezar and colleagues, "collective action (through unions, alliances, and other collective efforts) is by far the most efficacious political tool that equity-oriented workers wield in pushing for greater workplace democracy."[56] Despite labor laws that impede unionization, there is evidence of a national resurgence of workers who, in the aftermath of the pandemic, want to have greater control and a voice in the workplace. The number of US workers in a union grew by 200,000 in 2022, and the National Labor Relations Board received 2,510 labor union petitions—a 53 percent increase over the previous year.[57] In 2020, an open letter on the need to democratize work was signed by more than 6,000 researchers from more than 700 universities and academic institutions around the world and subsequently published in 43 newspapers in 27 languages and 36 countries.[58]

Kezar and colleagues argued that higher education might "rediscover [collective action's] potency and utility" after decades of erosion, but they followed with a question: "With what vision and agenda?"[59] To answer this question, I took inspiration from the Higher Education Labor United (HELU) vision platform. HELU was formed during a 2021 summit of some 50 union groups (or "locals") working to develop a national labor strategy. It has since organized a second summit and formed a general assembly with delegates from each of the member organizations. The vision was developed as part of the first summit and has since been endorsed by over 130 locals representing 550,000 workers across 28 states.[60] Although the HELU vision platform includes multiple concrete commitments, I took note of several connected to shared governance, contingent employees, and working conditions.

Specifically, the vision platform calls for "collaborative shared governance" that includes the participation of "all categories of faculty and staff, student groups, and unions."[61] Another commitment focuses on improving working conditions for contingent faculty and staff through job security, pay equity, health care and retirement benefits, management of workload, collective bargaining, and shared governance. Lastly, the vision platform advocates for an end to precarious labor by increasing the density of full-time staff and increasing tenure density by moving contingent faculty into tenure-eligible positions.

There was a time when I would have viewed many of the items in this vision platform as too pie-in-the-sky and outside the norms of academia. Though it is true that the platform runs against prevailing trends, I see pieces of it coming to fruition in UIC United Faculty and GEO's contract negotiations. And I see the platform in a different light when I apply the lens of workplace democracy. Supporting the right of all workers to have fair, safe, and dignified workplaces feels more consistent with American democratic principles than giving ever more authority to a small number of managers.

Nevertheless, I recognize that for many leaders, all this talk of collective action and workplace democracy may be unfamiliar or uncomfortable—too close to labor activism. At the same time, I don't think one necessarily has to endorse the platform wholesale to learn from its message and initiate organizational change to support employee well-being. If those lessons are still a little unclear, I connect the dots below with three approaches to empowering employees' rights and voice in the workplace.

Approach 1: Caring Through Job Security and Improved Working Conditions for Contingent Faculty

In 2003, two of the AAUP's committees jointly produced the statement on "Contingent Appointments and the Academic Profession."[62] After 20 years, many of the statement's core claims about the treatment of contingent faculty remain true and the recommendations for addressing their poor working conditions continue to be relevant. These recommendations fall into seven categories, many of which directly target the shifts that gave rise to the gig academy. I want to highlight several of the recommendations that have not been addressed in previous chapters or are not discussed in subsequent approaches. The simple truth is that we often want faculty to be more engaged campus citizens, yet we don't grant most of them full citizenship rights. The Caring University is one where workers enjoy job security and fair employment processes.

First, the AAUP report argues against "segmenting" or "unbundling" faculty work. Kezar and colleagues explained that "the contemporary university has managed to break down complicated professional roles like those of academic faculty," which made it possible to casualize instructional labor.[63] According to the AAUP statement, deprofessionalization has the effect of threatening the quality of decision-making, academic freedom, and student learning. In response, AAUP argues that all faculty appointments, whether full-time or part-time, should be structured to recognize faculty work as an integrated whole. This means jobs should involve teaching, plus the ability to contribute to your discipline, remain current in the field through professional development, and participate in campus life so that all faculty members can lend their knowledge to important initiatives and decision-making.

Second, academic freedom requires that full-time appointments be protected by tenure, and there must be explicit pathways for high-performing, full-time contingent faculty to move into tenure-track positions. Part-time appointments can achieve a measure of academic freedom through longer contracts, earlier notice of reappointment, opportunities for advancement, peer review of performance, and due process. Although part-time faculty are not eligible for tenure, they can still be afforded due process protections, including written contracts that specify the terms of their appointment, written notice if their appointment is terminated during a contract period, a chance to appeal termination before a committee of peers, and the opportunity to state their case if they believe their academic freedom has been violated or they have been discriminated against. While this may read like a lengthy list, written notice and the ability to appeal decisions are standard due process rights built into our judicial system and other important academic processes like student conduct hearings. In essence, we already do this in higher education.

Third, the report does not advocate for an all-out end to all contingent faculty roles, but it does argue that the use of these positions should be reduced. There are situations where hiring someone on a part-time basis makes sense, such as to cover courses when someone goes on medical leave. But in practice today, institutions are employing contingent faculty far more routinely. Like HELU's vision platform, the report pushes for less reliance on contingent faculty—specifically, AAUP suggests no more than 15 percent of the total instruction within an institution and no more than 25 percent of instruction in each department. This threshold is not too high for business schools accredited through the Association to Advance Collegiate Schools of Business, which requires that at least 75 percent of instruction should come from "participation faculty" or those who are involved in activities central to the life of their school or academic program beyond teaching.[64]

In fact, the working conditions of contingent faculty have become a growing concern among accreditors in higher education, since evidence points to a relationship between the changing composition of faculty and student outcomes.[65] A 2014 report sponsored by the Council for Higher Education Accreditation noted that "faculty policies and practices have not been changed to ensure the growing segment of non-tenure-track faculty are properly supported and involved in activities that can help them foster optimal learning outcomes for students."[66] According to this report, contingent faculty often do not have access to onboarding, basic materials and supplies, office space, mentoring, sample materials or syllabi, or departmental learning outcomes. It is hard to believe that institutions have an avowed commitment to student success when these are the working conditions under which many of their faculty teach. One takeaway from the report was a clear sense that colleges and universities—in partnership with accreditors—should be doing more to support contingent faculty because doing so is integral to quality instruction.

Better support for contingent faculty isn't outside the realm of possibility. Jon Marcus wrote in *The Hechinger Report* about the counterexample provided by McGill University and other institutions in Canada.[67] There, contingent faculty are paid the equivalent of $7,000 per course—almost twice the average in the United States—and they have multiyear contracts, dedicated office space, and government-provided health insurance. They even receive an email address for nine months after a contract expires so that students can contact them for advice or recommendations. There are examples of better ways to support contingent faculty stateside, too. One comes from the University of Denver (DU), which won the 2021 Delphi Award, an annual award given by the Pullias Center for Higher Education at the University of Southern California and the American Association of Colleges and Universities to institutions in recognition of their work to transform support for contingent faculty.

In 2015, DU's board of trustees approved a new promotion and tenure document that created a new line and associated titles for full-time contingent faculty. In an effort to better recognize and value the work of these faculty, the new line was called Teaching and Professional Faculty (TPF) and included the titles of clinical, teaching, and research faculty, as well as librarians and professors of practice. As part of the change, over 200 full-time lecturers received renewable contracts, a pathway to promotion, and a defined role in shared governance. As a sign of their inclusion in shared governance, the president of the faculty senate has for many years been held by someone in a TPF position. Academic departments followed suit, creating more opportunities for TPF colleagues to be involved in decisions about hiring and evaluating faculty.[68]

Laura Sponsler was one of the first faculty hired into a TPF position, and she soon started asking questions: How does promotion in this new position work? What kind of documentation is necessary? She started working on these questions in her own college, but soon DU tapped her to be its first Resident-Scholar for TPF. Sponsler was tasked with educating the DU community about the realities of TPF and effective practices to support them. She conducted an audit of policies, procedures, and norms shaping the experiences of TPF, which culminated in a scorecard that the institution can use to self-assess its strengths and areas for improvement. The scorecard is based on higher education research showing the five elements of faculty work, including employment equity, collegiality, flexibility, professional growth, and autonomy and academic freedom. Sponsler has also been involved in beefing up onboarding and mentoring opportunities for TPF by establishing a learning community and yearly panels on pathways to promotion.

"I wrote those recommendations based on the five elements, and we've done every single one of them," Sponsler shared with pride. DU participates in an annual survey through the Collaborative on Academic Careers in Higher Education, and she was able to get the data disaggregated by tenure-track faculty and TPF. The plan is to create a data dashboard on faculty, creating more transparency around appointment types. DU has made huge strides, but Sponsler still sees areas for improvement: "We're in implementation; we haven't gotten to institutionalization yet. So I'm very transparent that this is a process." Sponsler has been thinking about ways to better support mid-career contingent faculty and pushing for them to be eligible for leadership roles. There are now several TPF in faculty director roles and fellowships. "There is a sense of university citizenship in a different way. Some faculty feel more connected to their discipline, but a lot of TPF feel very connected to the institution."

Deep change is possible when institutions empower the talent they have specifically recruited and hired to be full participants in organizational life. Yet too many employees remain second-class citizens, lacking the rights and resources to do their best work. They are too busy trying to survive and wondering if their contract will be renewed to invest in the workplace. It is a little like Americans who would very much like to vote but encounter all manner of obstacles preventing them from getting to the polls. The answer, in my view, is to improve democratic processes so that more people can meaningfully participate.

Approach 2: Caring Through Collaborative Shared Governance

Shared governance isn't just a quirk of higher education to be tolerated. When it is well designed and executed, shared governance is an invaluable asset for organizational change. It creates a set of structures and processes to facilitate sensemaking and organizational learning, allowing leaders and employees to debate, ask questions, and wrestle with the meaning of terms and data. Many of the changes that higher education badly needs, including those proposed in this book, are unlikely to materialize by administrative fiat—they will require the expertise and energy of workers. Leaders can try to squeeze those workers until they get on board, but I think a better approach is to enable collaborative shared governance.

In 2014, the State University of New York (SUNY) at Fredonia won the first-ever SUNY Shared Governance Award. I learned about the award and what precipitated it from a chapter that Fredonia's president at the time, Virginia Horvath, coauthored with the chairperson of the university senate, Rob Deemer.[69] In it, Horvath makes a compelling case for the power of shared governance: "I argue that more than ever, we need shared governance to have the best ideas driving decision-making, to ensure faculty and staff engagement for smooth implementation of any initiatives, and to promote and model civil democratic approaches to leadership."[70] This latter part is important to Horvath, who acknowledges that democratic processes can be messy, but she established as a core operating principle that "valuing shared governance means genuinely believing that what is created or determined collaboratively is better than what any individual might achieve."[71]

Horvath's list of basic ingredients for effective shared governance includes emphasizing collaboration from the start, setting a realistic timeline for change, providing multiple chances for input, and responding to employees' suggestions. According to Horvath, part of building an inclusive process is considering the perspective of opponents and bringing skeptics into the process at an early stage, because "skepticism is rooted in concerns the institution needs to address."[72] Deemer added a few important tactical considerations for shared governance to flourish, such as holding efficient meetings and completing projects, as faculty resistance often stems from the belief that they shouldn't bother because nothing gets done. But Horvath and Deemer also point to a set of deeper issues that require ongoing attention. One is that both leaders and faculty need to get beyond common defense routines. Sometimes leaders overreact to even healthy criticism or assume employees will say no to any proposal. Sometimes workers overreact to new initiatives or assume leaders will ignore questions and criticism. Although these scenarios are certainly possible, entering into shared governance as if positions are preordained isn't productive.

Shared governance is not something most leaders or employees innately know how to do—it has to be learned. To this end, Deemer emphasizes that the institution must commit to training leadership, faculty, and staff in *how* to practice shared governance. Additionally, staff and faculty need to know that participation in shared governance is valued by the institution. Ultimately, employees can't complain about a lack of respect for shared governance and then not show up. As Deemer put it, "Shared governance is not a luxury. It's the single most crucial aspect of an effective institution. Just as administrators and boards must not weaken or remove faculty roles in governance, faculty must not abdicate their role in governance responsibilities."[73] Horvath noted that she sets an early expectation with her direct reports that they must be fully engaged in shared governance. Deemer found that new leaders who came to SUNY Fredonia after having had negative experiences with shared governance in the past were "slowly but consistently won over by our culture of shared governance."[74]

I interviewed Horvath to talk through some of her thoughts on shared governance in more detail. She was quick to point out that shared governance requires considerable commitment. She and faculty and staff leaders spent years working on the university senate bylaws to ensure unambiguous policies and procedures. "We worked so hard on those bylaws," Horvath recalled. "And a lot of it was really sitting down and defining terms. What do we mean by shared governance? If you want people to have input, how do you create authentic opportunities for that?" If the rules of shared governance are not working, Horvath advises against trying to circumvent them. "See what you can do to work within the existing rules," she advises, "and then collaborate to change those rules if they need to be refined." But Horvath is also a realist in the sense that she understands shared governance does not always mean consensus or agreement. In her former role as vice president for academic affairs at SUNY Fredonia, Horvath had worked with the university senate budget committee to develop a plan they hoped they would never need to use: a process for evaluating academic programs should there need to be fewer of them. In her final years at Fredonia, the university faced enrollment and financial challenges, and Horvath used this governance-produced document to guide the process. But as pressures mounted, it fell to her to make difficult decisions, and people were angry.

Ultimately, Horvath and Deemer both emphasized the importance of trust. Referencing Fredonia's budget crisis, Horvath understood why people were upset—she wasn't happy about it, either. Although she could handle disagreement and conflict, she felt "shared governance is not going to work if I no longer have the trust of the faculty and staff." Deemer echoed this sentiment: "Strong collaboration cannot happen without trust on all sides." He elaborated that many of the stories about conflict with boards, administrators, faculty, and students often boil down to issues with trust: "Above all else, addressing this lack of trust and working together to eradicate it must be the most important aspects of building good shared governance."[75]

SUNY Fredonia has an active shared governance body, yet Deemer acknowledges that its role is ultimately advisory to the president. "That said, if a trusting and healthy collaboration can be fostered between governance and the president, the fact that the advisory relationship is in place rarely needs to be raised: both sides work to improve the institution with a shared sense of responsibility and ownership."[76] Collaborative shared governance therefore isn't so much about divvying up power and guarding territory as it is about mutual accountability. The power of shared governance lies in how it is practiced, and a growing consensus makes clear that it starts with trust and is sustained when everyone comes together in good faith to develop solutions as partners (Box 6.1 presents an example).

Approach 3: Caring Through Support for the Organizing Efforts of Workers

Whether it is written into the bylaws or a product of distrust, shared governance has limits. There are times when good ideas for change come from a university-wide subcommittee, but leadership fails to act on them. There are problems that a faculty senate may be disinclined to take up because they see it as outside their jurisdiction or interests. These scenarios make it possible for an issue like career advancement for contingent faculty to languish for years or for graduate assistants to be paid paltry wages in expensive places as living costs tick up. Institutions certainly have the authority to address these challenges, and yet they may pursue incentives that pull their attention elsewhere. Some higher education workers have turned to unions and collective bargaining to push for change. Unions aren't necessary to achieve the Caring University, but they are certainly compatible with it.

In the event that a group on campus pursues unionization or takes a strong position in collective bargaining, colleges and universities can choose how they respond. They could, for example, simply refuse to recognize a union, as Boston College did with its graduate students.[77] Or they could be like Northeastern University and hire a union-busting law firm and try to block full-time contingent faculty from unionizing based on the argument that they are "management."[78] Or they could follow Temple University's lead and stop paying or providing health care benefits to striking graduate students.[79] According to Maximillian Alvarez, a former associate editor of *The Chronicle of Higher Education*, "Too often, university administrators treat the right to organize as, at best, an annoying formality and, at worst, a problematic entitlement that they can choose not to honor—and, if they have the resources and disposition, must make it their mission to eliminate."[80]

But Michael Ginsburg, who has been working with unions at UIC for decades, suggests that university leaders take a different approach. "I don't think unions are something at all to be afraid of," he explained, "for institutions that don't have unions or only have a few. . . . It's something to understand; it's part of the current context of higher education." Instead of being antagonistic, he advised that leaders consider how to effectively work with unions and make sure they have an experienced, trusted professional who can negotiate. UIC only has one primary group of employees at this point that has not unionized. "They're getting very close to getting support from their members to create a union, and I've seen it coming. Why not that group as well? So, I've been preparing the leadership that it's something they're going to have to live with and manage going forward," he said.

Assuming unions are not, in fact, the bogeyman they are sometimes made out to be, the question becomes how to best support workers' organizing efforts. Ginsburg and his labor relations team have found through experience that it pays to be thoughtful about communications. Rather than using university web pages or press releases to hash out issues or advance arguments, Ginsburg says they try to stick to factual updates about the negotiation process. I came across an example of an institution whose communication around unionization was patently positive. After faculty voted to start a union chapter, Howard Community College issued a press release saying that it "congratulated prospective partner American Federation of Teachers." The press release explained the purposes and benefits of collective bargaining and declared, "The college is enthusiastic about the prospects of future collaboration and is excited to work in partnership with the faculty."[81] Although it is just a press release, it does set a cooperative tone, unlike other press releases that I have seen schools issue that were obviously antagonistic.

When the time comes to begin contract negotiations, Matt Johnson, the former president of the union at Central Michigan University, and Virginia Horvath, who spent her entire career at unionized campuses, both stressed the importance of relationships. "You need to have a working relationship first," Johnson told me. "One of the worst outcomes you can have is if the first time you see each other is across the formal bargaining table." He always made a point of talking with the university's head of labor relations, who he knows cares about the institution. "You're not friends, but you can also enjoy a collegial working relationship, even though at the heart of what you're doing is adversarial." Johnson also shared that a good negotiating principle is to not spring surprises on the other side. Horvath told a story about a contract negotiation at one institution where the two sides would meet at a group of three apartments—one for each side and one for joint meetings. "There were picnic tables outside. We agreed one day a week when we were there through lunch, we'd cook out and eat together," she said. "So, instead of hearing about how the faculty just don't want to change or all administrators care about is the bottom line, we'd get to know each other. We'd bring food and share it. And I think that helps a lot."

One of the surprising things I learned while researching this chapter was how unions and collective bargaining can be a vehicle for employee engagement. As is true with most group-based work, some people are more involved than others. Aaron Krall explained that nothing undercuts employee engagement more than having the effort go nowhere: "If you go and sit on committees and you feel like you're going to contribute to something that's going to happen at the policy level, and then upper administrators are like, 'Thank you for this report—now we're going to go do that other thing,' that disincentivizes participation." Krall pointed to a climate survey undertaken by faculty colleagues at UIC who "committed a lot of hours to putting together a survey, collecting data, analyzing the data. Then we got a new chancellor who canceled the committee. And then it's like, what's the point?" There is a different kind of stake when you are working with the union, Krall said. "At least there's the feeling that you might have some power to negotiate something that might happen."

Matt Johnson shared in our interview that administrators appreciate collective bargaining more than they might expect. "Anybody can form a committee and talk about issues," he said. "But having teeth embedded in platforms that get people at the table to talk about issues, to negotiate, and to agree on things, and then to have mechanisms in place when you don't agree . . . I think everybody believes that's a net positive." The contract at Johnson's institution is 112 pages. "The cost-of-living increase is half of a page. There's 111 other pages in there that talk about all these other important things. And I think those mechanisms really help make things go smoother," he said. Matthew Kinservik, vice provost for faculty affairs at the University of Delaware, confirmed this view: "I have learned to embrace the [collective bargaining agreement], not fear it. Instead of regarding it as the source of the dreaded grievance process, I have come to see it as an indispensable resource for administration, offering guidance for how to go about our business within the framework of shared governance."[82] He has even come to see that "conflict and resistance from a faculty union can be productive and salutary things."[83]

The sense I got was that, although the news only regularly covered strikes and walkouts, there are many contracts successfully negotiated with less fanfare. And Ginsburg knows that a negotiated contract is usually a "win" for the unions. "One of the things I have to do with leadership is explain that, ultimately, the union needs to be able to demonstrate a win to their members. We're never going to say, 'We won.' We don't win. For us," he said, "it's just about being happy to reach an agreement." At the same time, a union win is very often about better pay and working conditions for employees. Union wins at UIC have created jobs that the university can take some measure of pride in, which means workers are more inclined to stay and work hard for its benefit. Collective action to support employee well-being thus can truly be a win-win for both parties at the negotiating table.

Conclusion

As part of his regular column in *Inside Higher Ed*, Joshua Kim, director of online programs and strategy at Dartmouth College, outlined data

Box 6.1

Achieving More Collectively

The Case of the University of Minnesota

In 2023, the University of Minnesota (UMN) University Senate—comprising four constituent governing bodies representing students, faculty, professional and administrative employees, and civil service employees—unanimously passed a landmark resolution to support "a better U for employees." The Workforce Reinvestment Resolution came about through collaboration over shared concerns and collectively constructed priorities.

The resolution is structured around four core principles:

- **Principle 1: Provide livable, equitable, and competitive pay.** Prioritize increasing necessary resources in budgetary and strategic planning so that all employees receive a livable wage, employees with different identities who do similar work receive equitable pay, and employees receive pay that is competitive in appropriate labor markets.
- **Principle 2: Recruit, reward, and retain people.** Prioritize increasing necessary resources in budgetary and strategic planning for rewarding and recognizing work, imparting new value to the employment relationship, and boosting recruitment and retention in an increasingly talent-constrained environment.
- **Principle 3: Establish clear pathways for professional development and career advancement.** Develop career advancement opportunities for employees so that they can achieve their career goals, while taking into account that central university employees desire work that has an impact on the mission.
- **Principle 4: Foster a culture that promotes manageable workloads.** Invest in a culture that empowers people to prioritize work that is most impactful in fulfilling their roles and responsibilities, which will positively affect the university's ability to deliver on its mission and promote manageable workloads.

Part of what makes the Workforce Reinvestment Resolution unique is not just that it establishes a set of workplace principles for the university. It also spells out precisely where the UMN should invest to support the principles. Priorities include allocating a portion of annual salary increases as a flat-dollar cost-of-living adjustment for all employees and establishing a systemwide minimum per-credit-hour payment for courses for employees teaching on a per-credit-hour basis. The resolution calls for multiyear contracts for contingent faculty, paid family leave for graduate students, and making career ladders and advancement available to all employees. In short, it is the Caring University in the form of a senate resolution.

According to Colleen Flaherty Manchester, a professor in the School of Management and past chair of the senate executive committee, the seeds for

Box 6.1 (continued)

the resolution were planted in 2020, when leaders of the four senates started meeting regularly to discuss how to respond to constituents' concerns during the pandemic. The informal meetings, which began as simple check-ins, soon revealed common concerns. Through town halls, surveys, and informal luncheons, it became clear that there were systemic workplace problems that cut across units and colleges. They first considered having each senate write a separate resolution but worried it might make it possible for the university to favor certain groups or priorities over others. "We wanted a resolution to be multi-constituent," Mark Bee, the current chair and a professor of biology, explained to me. "The idea was that we could have a bigger impact together."

The resolution includes a set of requests, but it also acknowledges that not all of them can be addressed immediately. It recognizes that some priorities will have longer time horizons and require discussions about resources. Despite building in this flexibility, Manchester and Bee were adamant that their expectation is that UMN "goes big or goes home" in its response to the resolution. As Manchester said, "We're trying to be reasonable. But they can't just say things are off the table or we don't have the money." Bee agreed, saying what he wants to see from the resolution is that "the university legitimately recognizes there is a problem and commits itself to doing something about it." Bee pointed out that the university has a six-year capital plan that gets revised every year. "I've seen conversations among the board of regents about where trees are located. That's a lot of attention they're paying to an artistic rendering of a campus plan. We want them to pay attention to a human capital plan with that level of detail."

The group's early discussions received a significant boost from a somewhat unlikely source: the university's president at the time, Joan Gabel. According to Bee, "The president had a very strong and positive impact on the final form of the resolution. We met with her monthly and she came to our meetings. It was not an adversarial development. She was the source of the idea of organizing it around principles." The president made the case to other leaders that having a detailed list of priorities can be helpful for administrators. Shortly before the resolution was passed, it was announced that Gabel was leaving for another institution, sowing uncertainty about how a new president will respond.

Although it is a senate resolution that simply "requests" administrators act, the culture at UMN is one in which, at a minimum, a response is provided. To this end, the president charged the vice president for human resources and provost with forming a task force and generating a response. An early positive sign that university leaders are taking the resolution seriously is that they established an advisory group made up of people who helped to craft the resolution; they now sit in on the task force's meetings to provide context and explanations.

Although time will tell how UMN leaders respond, Bee and Manchester both signaled the upsides of working together across governing bodies and recognizing how working conditions and cultures are intertwined. "It ultimately comes back to mission," Bee said.

showing how public opinion of higher education has plummeted in a time of rising inequality and political polarization. He wondered if one reason for higher education's dimming appeal is that colleges and universities have themselves become sites of deep economic injustice. It is simply harder to buy the idea that institutions are devoted to lofty ideals when they are not paying people enough to afford rent or feed their families. Kim asks, "What if one of the core functions of the university was understood as creating and protecting secure middle-class jobs? Can't we have both student success and good jobs for everyone a school employs?"[84]

The institutions whose answer to these questions are yes—the ones that live in a world of both/and instead of either/or—won't just be better

Box 6.2

Chapter 6 Action Steps

- Avoid unnecessary segmentation or unbundling of jobs whose complexity calls for expertise and training. Dissembling jobs can facilitate casualization and impede collaboration and academic freedom.
- Protect full-time appointments with tenure and establish explicit pathways for high-performing full-time contingent faculty to move into tenure-track positions.
- Provide part-time faculty with due process rights, including written contracts, written notice of nonrenewal, and the opportunity to appeal decisions.
- Reduce reliance on contingent faculty.
- Combine rhetorical support for shared governance with actions to demonstrate its value to institutions, such as providing shared governance training, tamping down unproductive tropes and caricatures, and setting realistic timelines.
- Engender trust and mutual accountability through open communication, following through on commitments, and showing up for governance responsibilities.
- Tap into workers' interest in collective action to learn more about shared governance and unionization, including their historical roots and effective practices. Approach unionization with curiosity instead of fear.
- Support the organizing efforts of workers with thoughtful communications and building relationships with union leaders.
- Leverage the benefits of collective action's built-in mechanisms for employee engagement and accountability.
- Acknowledge positive institutional changes that come from collective action.

positioned to retain talent. They will be better equipped to navigate the public's waning confidence in higher education. At a time when social institutions central to democracy have come under attack, colleges and universities have often doubled down on competition, individualism, and dog-eat-dog survivalism. It does little to dispel the myth of higher education as a bastion for the elite when colleges and universities themselves appear to be exploitative employers. Many unions and shared governance bodies in higher education are pushing for an alternative vision of higher education premised on abundance, community, solidarity, and care.

College leaders should not just pay attention to employees' desire for a voice and the assertion of worker rights in the workplace because it will help address what led to the Great Resignation. They should empower collective action because it can be a powerful means of change and a way to model how higher education builds up both students and employees and leaves them better off. As Barrett Taylor noted, democracy isn't just about electing officials. "It is also the daily practice of relating to other citizens, of living full and fulfilling lives, of a robust civil society."[85] By creating a more democratic workplace through the steps outlined in Box 6.2, the Caring University fosters cultures and structures that support higher education's role as a social institution dedicated to human flourishing. That is a vision of the university that would get anyone's vote.

CHAPTER 7

Cultivating and Sustaining Caring Leaders

LAURA NELSON IS, in most respects, a typical higher education leader. As associate dean and director of academic affairs for the College of Veterinary Medicine at North Carolina State University (NCSU), she spends her days shepherding curricular change, monitoring degree requirements, managing accreditation paperwork, meeting with struggling students, and designing professional development programs. It's not the kind of stuff that earns many accolades, but as anyone who works in higher education can attest, it is what keeps the academic trains running.

But a couple things set Laura apart when it comes to higher education leadership. First, she did not come to leadership begrudgingly, by accident, or because she was seeking the spotlight. Rather, it was something she prepared for, found she was good at, and then actively sought out. Although she came to academia as a veterinary surgeon without leadership aspirations, Laura quickly took an interest in curriculum and was selected for a yearlong leadership development program for faculty who are interested in teaching. After adding a graduate certificate in teaching and learning, she started to see her career veering toward faculty development. Laura decided to apply for the associate dean role at NCSU when she realized there were relatively few people in veterinary colleges with her training and interests.

The second thing that makes Laura atypical, at least judged against what many faculty believe, is that she enjoys being an associate dean and has committed to staying in the role. Despite the challenges of moving to a new state and institution with her husband and three kids in tow, Laura told me, "It's been a very, very good experience. I'm really glad I did it." During her first five-year appointment, Laura navigated the pandemic, figuring out how to provide clinical instruction virtually. Since she still has things she wants to accomplish, Laura signed on for another five years. For many of us working in higher education, particularly through the Great Resignation, the idea of anyone staying in an administrative job for a decade is unfathomable.

Lastly, Laura differs from many higher education leaders in her sensitivity to the organizational determinants of employee well-being. Part of this sensitivity comes from personal experience. Laura called her three-year surgical residency an "exhaustion factory." People worked 14-hour days, then drank copiously to cope with the stress. By her second year, she was burned out and on antidepressants. Afterward, Laura was hired into a department with a very different workplace culture. Residents were nurtured instead of hazed, and her colleagues worked normal hours, had hobbies, and were healthier. For Laura, the stark contrast offered critical leadership lessons: "It was a phenomenally better environment to work and train in," she said. "That difference didn't just inform how I wanted to be an educator and how I thought about my life as a faculty member, but most importantly how I wanted to lead by example in how I trained residents."

Over the course of two interviews, I noticed that caring isn't a buzzword for Laura; it's integral to her leadership practice. For one thing, she prioritizes "lots and lots of listening, then taking steps to act on what I learned." Laura makes a habit of pausing before proposing any curricular changes to consider the structural implications, asking if they have the personnel and infrastructure to do it well. Her "theme," as she calls it, is to add resources whenever the school makes changes to people's job expectations. Laura explicitly includes staff in educator development initiatives, including access to completing certificate programs and travel to education conferences. When she sees good work, she lets the person—and their supervisor—know about it and how much it is appreciated. She models vulnerability while avoiding sliding into oversharing.

Part of Laura's rationale for caring leadership is biological: "In the veterinary context, you can't get performance out of an animal without considering how you take care of its physical and social needs." A dairy farmer would never think the way to produce more milk is to prod their herd all the time, yet many organizations think they can make employees do more by pushing them harder. Laura later shared (in a way that "does not involve cows") that her evolving leadership philosophy approximates a line she read in a journal article: "Leaders in higher education have a role to play in the living ecosystem of the socially constructed workplaces of faculty, staff and students."[1] According to Laura, if you want engaged employees, improved learning environments, and better science, "you have to fundamentally take care of people's needs."

There are more leaders like Laura out there—people who have prepared for leadership, are committed to building up institutions, and demonstrate care for the well-being of staff and faculty. But some of these leaders don't last long or give up on administration because of mistreatment, excessive workloads, and values-based conflict. Higher education needs to do a better job of supporting and sustaining the good leaders it already has. At the same time, institutions need *more* leaders like Laura who combine preparation, effectiveness, and care. There are people who have been thrust into leadership for which they are not prepared or well-suited and elevated for reasons unconnected to their people management skills. Higher education needs to take leadership preparation and development more seriously.

This chapter is about leadership problems in higher education, but I put a unique spin on the analysis. I argue that higher education is not on the whole populated by a bunch of narcissistic, avaricious administrators who have entered leadership for all the wrong reasons. Those people exist, just as they exist in other industries. But in higher education, they are outnumbered by people who came to leadership because they saw it as a space where they could meaningfully apply their talent and serve students, colleagues, and institutions. My goal is to show how caring leadership is often *constrained* by cultural and structural factors, including demanding expectations, inadequate training, toxic norms around who leaders are, and counterproductive perceptions of the value of administrative work.

Pulling off the organizational changes that underlie the Caring University requires cultivating a cadre of leaders who understand and work for the mutual vitality of institutions and employees. In the second half of the chapter, I describe what caring leadership looks like in higher education, emphasizing compassion, self-awareness, listening, intellectual humility, trust-building, vulnerability, critical hope, taking responsibility, and organizational thinking. I then propose multiple changes to the culture and structure of colleges and universities to support the emergence and retention of caring leaders, including rightsizing expectations and appreciating administrative work, improving leadership preparation and opportunities for renewal, and centering care in leadership selection and performance review.

The Great Resignation was made worse by the fact that conditions were poor for leaders to practice caring leadership. Reimagining the higher education workplace requires understanding and enriching the environment in which we cultivate and sustain caring leaders.

Leaders Are Human, Too

After the publication of a 2021 article I wrote about low morale among staff and faculty in higher education, I heard from a host of leaders who pointed out that conditions haven't exactly been rosy for them, either.[2] This was during the peak of pandemic-era crisis management in higher education, when one chancellor told me that "75 hours wasn't a busy week." Laura was one of the people who emailed me to share her experience as I started working on a follow-up article about the morale of leaders. "Personal burnout," she wrote, "and the sort of moral distress that comes from feeling as though you have no choice but to press forward . . . are topics of every candid conversation I've had with peers for over a year."

When we sat down for our interview, Laura explained that she and other associate deans of veterinary colleges met biweekly to share tips on how to teach future veterinarians online. Part of the meetings were recorded (so people could rewatch them) and the other part wasn't (so people could vent). "There came a point when the recording was turned off," she explained, "where it just became clear that absolutely everybody was really struggling." Laura and I had our own "camera off" moment just a few minutes later. She was describing caring for her school-age children, caring for overwhelmed faculty, and caring for anxious students. I asked her if we should worry that no one was caring for leaders like her. Pausing, Laura took a deep breath and conceded, "Yes."

An underlying premise of this chapter is that leaders are human, too. This seems like it should go without saying, but the truth is that many of us in higher education—and I am purposefully extending this chapter's audience beyond leaders—primarily see leaders when the recording is turned on. We see the "business" part but rarely see (and frankly don't ask about) the "feelings" part. We replace real people with the positions that they occupy, compartmentalizing the fact that we knew leaders as peers before they took on titles. It becomes easy to expect leaders will do whatever the job demands, irrespective of the hours or sacrifices. But before I am accused of selling a sob story, let me be clear that I hold leaders to high standards. This chapter isn't designed to persuade you that leaders deserve special treatment or sympathy. Very simply, I am suggesting that the well-being of our leaders matters, just as it matters for staff and faculty.

Colleges and universities should care about leaders because it is the right thing to do. But it is also the case that overlooking their well-being is bad for institutions. For one thing, it contributes to the "endless churn of administrators" that so thoroughly frustrates many employees.[3] At the presidential level, articles in the popular media speak of "surges," "waves," and "crushes" of departures—some the result of the "silver tsunami" of baby boomers retiring but others very clearly connected to burnout.[4] Surveys indicate that the average time that presidents and provosts stay in their roles has decreased to five and three years, respectively—not enough time to see initiatives through.[5] The 2023 American College President

Study found that over half of respondents planned to step down in the next five years.[6] Many campuses are in a liminal space of chronic interim leadership, where it is difficult to move new ideas forward because employees are waiting on permanent leaders. Leadership turnover puts organizations in a perpetual holding pattern.

It is also shortsighted not to care about leaders because we need compassionate, competent, and creative leaders to realize the Caring University. As I noted at the beginning of the book, organizational transformation depends on forward-thinking leaders, and the changes proposed in this book have little chance of materializing if we have ground down, pushed out, or dissuaded our brightest leaders. After writing about the importance of paying attention to the morale of leaders, I was surprised at how callous some of the responses were. It was as if we should simply surrender any consideration of someone's working conditions the minute they sign up for an administrative role or get paid a certain amount. A college or university that is oriented around employee well-being should not limit its care to certain levels of the organizational chart.

I readily acknowledge that instances of bad leadership grab headlines, especially situations involving ethical lapses, financial mismanagement, and sexual harassment. Similarly, there are individuals lacking the skills and disposition to lead that nevertheless find their way into supervisory roles or even the C-suite. Ample research shows that bad supervisors and managers can be costly for an organization and its employees, resulting in poor-performing teams, lower employee engagement, lower organizational commitment, and higher turnover intention.[7] The burnout, demoralization, and disengagement that precipitated the Great Resignation is undoubtedly tied to ineffective and uncaring leaders. Yet I have concluded that few of these problems arise from malicious individuals. Instead, they stem from organization-level cultures and structures that shape how leaders are prepared, selected, supported, and evaluated.

Beronda L. Montgomery, a biologist and the vice president of academic affairs at Grinnell College, helped me understand how leadership is shaped by an ecosystem. In her book *Lessons from Plants*, she writes: "For the most part, we begin from the expectation that the plant has the ability to grow and thrive. When the plant is not doing well, we ask questions about the health of the environment (does the plant have enough or too much light?) or about our own abilities as a caretaker (what am I doing wrong?). We do not immediately believe that the plant has deficits."[8]

When it comes to college and university leaders, the opposite tends to be true. Instead of questioning the "soil" the leader is "rooted in" or whether anyone is looking after the leader and helping prune their leaves and nurture their shoots, we often frame failings as individual deficits. This chapter encourages us to shift our focus to the health of the leadership ecosystem.

Inhospitable Terrain for Caring Leadership

One of the factors that prevents caring leaders from taking root and flourishing is the norm of mixing demanding expectations with low compassion. One of my interviewees, Vicki L. Baker, a department chair and higher education scholar who studies faculty careers, explained to me, "The pressures we put on leaders are just ratcheting up. We expect them to be on all the time, available all the time, and perfect all the time." Responsibilities for leadership positions have proliferated, rendering the jobs more complex. Completing lengthy task lists demands long workdays filled with back-to-back meetings, often punctuated with evening obligations. The CUPA-HR 2023 Higher Education Employee Retention Survey found that nearly double the percentage of supervisors versus nonsupervisors agree that they cannot complete their job tasks within normal full-time hours.[9]

Many staff and faculty have called on leaders to demonstrate compassionate leadership, but there is a legitimate question about whether employees are willing to reciprocate. In many cases, leaders are more likely to serve as a type of organizational lightning rod, absorbing all manner of critiques, anxieties, and frustrations. Laura Nelson told me that leaders experienced "real anger, real disagreements with students during the pandemic." Teresa Valerio Parrot, principal at TVP Communications, a communications strategy and services firm that works closely with senior leaders in higher education, noted in our interview that we often overlook the fact that presidents are stuck "between everybody on campus who is unhappy—because everybody's unhappy these days—and their board, which is also unhappy." Many people in higher education are disillusioned or angry, and that animus has a way of boiling up to leaders.

The type of persistent workplace stress that leads to burnout is common among leaders, but talking about how these positions damage mental health isn't. For example, Raynard S. Kington has characterized the job of president as "all-consuming, 24/7, and more personal" than other leadership positions he has occupied.[10] For Kington, the stress of being president caused him to have a panic attack, and it was years before he revealed this publicly. "Mental-health conditions remain extremely stigmatized in the management ranks," he explained. "Only a few college leaders have spoken openly about their mental health, and almost none have revealed serious mental-health problems on the job."[11] Part of the challenge is that asking for help, especially within small communities, can feel professionally risky, and senior leaders may struggle to find someone they can confide in. According to the 2023 American College President Study, over two-thirds of respondents struggled to find people who understand the experience of being president.[12]

It is hard for rank-and-file employees to understand the toll of leadership if leaders don't regularly interact with them. According to Valerio Parrot, "Senior leaders sometimes isolate themselves from their faculty, their staff, and their students," leaving them "out of touch with what these groups face on a day-to-day basis." The distance between senior leaders and employees not only contributes to loneliness but also means there aren't effective communication channels. As she went on to explain, "What is shared gets filtered through a 'game of telephone' up a hierarchy, so that by the time it gets to the senior leaders, they don't have a sense of the magnitude of the issue until it's in the student paper or in resignation notices."

Some staff and faculty are suspicious of senior leaders, questioning what motivates those in leadership positions, what they work on all day, and why there are so many of them. For Katharine Stewart, senior vice provost for faculty and academic affairs at NCSU, some of that suspicion is warranted. "I'm the first one to say that the kind of traditional suspicion that faculty have of administration is actually a healthy thing," she said. "It keeps everybody accountable to each other." Stewart believes that employees question why administrators are needed due to the fact that the work of some leaders often goes unseen. "I spend an enormous amount of my time on what could colloquially be called 'faculty behaving badly,'" she said, "but I can't talk about any of that to protect the people who are involved." In another part of her job—connected to academic policy—Stewart aspires for her work to go unnoticed by the faculty. "If we're doing it well, the faculty should be able to plausibly believe that fairies make the university-administered part of the promotion and tenure process happen." The goal isn't to obfuscate—it's to let faculty focus on what they were hired to do. "That comes from a position of respecting faculty work enough to do what many faculty say they want from administrators, which is largely to stay out of their way."

Many of the leaders I interviewed said they got into leadership because of the relationships and a genuine desire to serve. But lately, the relational side of leading has been harder to achieve. Although the days of social distancing are long gone, there are pockets of campus (especially academic departments) where people are less physically present; there are fewer opportunities for quick conversations to soften an email, generate buy-in for an idea, or rally colleagues for an impromptu lunch. According to Becky Corran, a former department chair at Doña Ana Community College in New Mexico, in the absence of those interactions, "the communication feels like it just becomes more task-y." At a time when new policies and protocols have multiplied, many leaders are in the unenviable position of having to act as compliance police. "Every week there's a new level of accountability," Corran said, "and that just takes away from the meaningful relationship-building type of management that I would like to do."

What Corran is describing is an additional set of challenges often ascribed to middle management. Mid-level leaders in both academic and student affairs are frequently responsible for implementing policies that they may not have crafted and have limited power to change. They are also a conduit for communication, relaying directives down the chain while also advocating upward, often acting as buffer in both directions. During the pandemic, Corran felt the "questions of middle management became less mundane and more life and death" as she communicated decisions to send faculty back into classrooms without sufficient policies to protect them. Although deans have far more power than chairs, they too often lead from the middle, with one scholar noting that "even in the best days, being an academic dean resembles living in a vise," where they are "squeezed from above and below as well as from inside and outside the university."[13] It is not always clear to mid-level leaders which constituents or interests they should prioritize, leading to role conflict and ambiguity.

There are a host of external demands on colleges and universities whose enactment falls on leaders, undercutting their ability to act on their values and lead with care. According to higher education leadership expert Joan Gallos, higher education leaders work within systems stretched to the limit; they are pushed to increase enrollments, reinvent academic programs, and enhance services and outcomes—all in the context of leadership instability: "You are the fifth dean in 7 years. In your first year on the job, you have already worked with two chancellors and two chief academic officers. . . . Do more with less is the campus mandate."[14] Marilee Bresciani Ludvik, a higher education scholar and leader, has stated that these accumulating demands are the reason leaders are unable to show compassion: "The pressure to mechanize, systematize, and decrease the cost of providing a higher education degree compounds the difficulty of treating each other with kindness and educating our students to do the same."[15] The machine organizations discussed in Chapter 3, with their heavy emphasis on efficiency, achievement, and getting ahead of the competition, consume much of the oxygen for caring leadership.

It doesn't help that many leaders step into roles with minimal formal preparation. There is a propensity to promote people into academic leadership roles because they were successful scholars. As Katharine Stewart at NCSU put it, "There's too much tendency to conflate markers of traditional faculty success with leadership ability." Frequent turnover has meant that some people are pushed into interim leadership roles that are meant to be temporary and therefore are not afforded much in the way of training or support. While reviewing research on the formal preparation of leaders, I came across studies that assessed the state of formal leadership training with descriptors like "minimal," "benign," "haphazard," and altogether "absent."[16] Although some institutions provide internal leadership development programs, many people with aspirations for leadership have to pay out-of-pocket for external learning opportunities. Those programs can be beneficial, but according to Erin Hennessy, executive vice president of TVP Communications, they often must quickly bring people up to speed. Some leadership development programs falter because they amount to what Beronda Montgomery called "imprinting"—that is, "patterning . . . individuals' behaviors after the norms of a recognized group."[17] We craft new leaders in the mold of old leaders who may not be what the present or future requires.

Administrative jobs aren't just taxing—they can often be thankless and unforgiving. We don't create much space for leaders to make mistakes, which reduces the likelihood that leaders are willing to be vulnerable and acknowledge their faults, which are key elements in humility. In *Generous Thinking: A Radical Approach to Saving the University*, Kathleen Fitzpatrick argued that academic culture has been defined by individualism and competition, where people are often rewarded solely for work that enables individual achievement or enhances institutional prestige. "Critical humility," writes Fitzpatrick, "is neither selected for nor encouraged in the academy," and the result is a zeal to prove one's worth and rightness by rejecting and shutting down alternative ideas.[18] Projecting confidence, having all of the answers, and offering critique "not in the spirit of generosity but rather as an attempt to create individual distinction" are celebrated.[19] Academic culture is too often much better at tearing people down than building them up.

These expectations infiltrate the standards by which we select and evaluate leaders. I coauthored a study where we asked search consultants at the top firms working in higher education to identify the factors that create inequities in presidential searches.[20] One of the study's themes is that search committees cling to traditional notions of "executive material." These vague concepts are often modeled after overly confident, extroverted, and charismatic leaders who can "command the room." It is no surprise that finding someone who fits these concepts frequently results in the selection of white men. One interview participant explained, "Presidential searches have a lot of trustees involved. . . . I cannot tell you how many times one of those outside people will make a pejorative comment about a woman or person of color during discussions of candidates: 'Oh, she doesn't look like she could go into a Fortune 500 CEO office and ask for $5 million.'" Leaders are usually evaluated on outcomes, what they achieve and produce, rather than how they learn from mistakes, treat their direct reports, and demonstrate effective people management. Boards sometimes feel their unique circumstances or challenges require immediate results, and so they are quick to fire and replace a leader who isn't producing the outcomes they value.

The leaders I have interviewed tend to talk about being exhausted, about sleepless nights, and about how being the messenger of difficult decisions takes a crushing toll on them. They questioned how sustainable it all was, and they marveled at how they were able to keep up the pace this long. These conditions have led to a dwindling crop of people willing and able to step into leadership. Inadequate preparation and support leaves new and veteran leaders vulnerable to job- or career-ending mistakes. The prerogatives of survival breed a type of hardness. Many leaders turn to distancing themselves from others and erecting defensive walls in an environment intolerant to weakness and impatient for the time it takes people to learn and change. Stewart has found that this terrain is especially inhospitable to compassionate, empathetic leaders who "are more likely to get burned out and crispy." They become, in the words of Gallos, "organizational toxin handlers," tending to others and absorbing the deep emotions of the workplace for the benefit of the organization.[21]

Just as a flower can sprout in the unlikeliest of places, it is not impossible for caring leaders to emerge in higher education's rocky and infertile soil. But there is a question of how long they can last or when they will get plucked by someone who recognizes their rarity. My research overwhelming indicates that staff, faculty, and leaders themselves are unhappy with the higher education leadership ecosystem and what it has wrought. Everyone seems to want *something* different without always being able to articulate what it is. So, I have gone back through my data and pulled additional research to pinpoint precisely what that something is so that we can better understand how to cultivate it.

What Is Caring Leadership in Higher Education?

"Caring" leadership doesn't get a lot of airtime in the higher education literature, but there has been research on adjacent concepts like compassion, trust, and vulnerability. I have cross-pollinated these studies with the examples and interviews that informed the organizational changes proposed in this book. For example, throughout the preceding chapters, there are leaders who paint a picture of what caring leadership looks like in practice. In addition, many of the people who reevaluated their jobs, sought reassignment, resorted to resistance, or resigned as part of the Great Resignation talked at some length during interviews about what they wanted from leaders—things that could have persuaded them to stay in a job or more fully engage in their work.

I have compiled a set of ten actions that characterize caring leadership, as shown in Box 7.1. This list is not meant to be exhaustive or definitive—if anything, it's a starting point. I have decided to focus on actions—what caring leaders actually do—to keep the discussion grounded in something concrete. Nevertheless, it is fair to say that most of these actions have corresponding affective dimensions regarding how leaders understand themselves and relate to others—caring leadership inherently involves flexing both interior and exterior muscles. Several of these actions overlap or are described in tandem in the research. Listening, for example, appears in discussions of several other actions. Instead of thinking of these actions as being different names for the same thing, I view them as being mutually reinforcing—performing one action can be beneficial for enacting others.

Compassion is a good place to start because it illustrates the conjunction of affect and action. Compassion is often viewed as an emotion, but researchers argue, it is a four-stage process that culminates in action.[22] The process begins with noticing others' suffering and making meaning of it, then progresses toward feeling empathic concern and acting to ameliorate the suffering. As Kathryn Waddington, a scholar studying

Box 7.1

Ten Actions of Caring Leaders

- **Compassion**: Noticing and addressing the working conditions and cultures that contribute to suffering within the workplace.
- **Self-Awareness**: Understanding your own emotions and the effect they have on colleagues while being honest with yourself and others about strengths and weaknesses.
- **Listening**: Actively engaging with another, suspending judgment, and being open to hearing what is said.
- **Intellectual Humility**: Being willing to change your views; being teachable, avoiding defensiveness, and recognizing the strengths of others.
- **Vulnerability**: Accepting the uncertainty, risk, and emotional exposure of authentically sharing feelings and experiences.
- **Trust-Building**: Showing up, being consistent, following through on promises, and telling the truth without sugarcoating reality.
- **Critical Hope**: Recognizing the complexity and messiness of problems while remaining optimistic about their resolution.
- **Responsibility-Taking**: Owning mistakes and imperfections as a means of repairing damaged relationships, modeling humility, and creating growth-oriented teams.
- **Equity-Mindedness**: Understanding higher education's past and present role in exclusion and stratification and applying a color-conscious lens to practices and policies.
- **Organizational Thinking**: Seeing the cultural and structural determinants of problems at the organizational level.

compassion in higher education, noted, "Compassion demands engagement in the suffering of others" and "holding space for pain."[23] Some suffering is inevitable and outside the control of leaders. But organizations also produce and even intensify suffering that could instead be prevented, diminished, or eliminated. Caring leaders are attuned to the inevitable suffering that comes with being human, but they are particularly motivated to notice and address working conditions and cultures that contribute to suffering within the workplace.

The Center for Creative Leadership explains that action to relieve suffering is what distinguishes compassion from empathy. The latter, they argue, can be helpful but often falls short because "simply feeling what someone else is feeling can be painful and not very productive."[24] Compassionate leadership begins with self-compassion, or being able to extend some grace to yourself and distinguish "small truths" (e.g., that presentation didn't go well) from "big lies" (e.g., I've lost the confidence of my team). The focus on self-compassion dovetails with another action that comprises caring leadership: emotional intelligence. A core component of emotional intelligence is *self-awareness* and self-management. Self-awareness is the ability to see yourself clearly—to understand your own emotions and the effect they have on colleagues. Self-awareness means being honest with yourself and others about strengths, weaknesses, needs, and ambitions. The next step is to translate the understanding gained from looking inward to action that benefits others.

The Center for Creative Leadership also lifts up expanding one's understanding of others through active *listening* as central to caring leadership.[25] Truth be told, listening is an action that comes up time and again in research on effective leadership, and interview participants frequently expressed a desire to be heard and for leaders to listen. Tony Belak and Kathryn Waddington noted that listening "requires active engagement with the other, the temporary suspension of judgment, and an openness to hearing whatever is said, whether pleasant, unpleasant, or benign."[26] Listening is also a fundamental action in Kathleen Fitzpatrick's conceptualization of generous thinking:

> What I'm hoping to develop, in myself most of all, is a generosity of mind, by which I mean to indicate an openness to possibility. That openness begins for me by trying to develop a listening presence in the world, which is to say a conversational disposition that is not merely waiting for my next opportunity to speak but instead genuinely focusing on what is being said to me, beginning from the assumption that in any given exchange I likely have less to teach than I have to learn.[27]

For Fitzpatrick, showing curiosity for others and genuinely listening to their experiences and ideas calls on and reinforces *intellectual humility*, creating "time and space to discover what we might learn if we are allowed to let go, just a tiny bit, of our investment in being right."[28] According to psychologist Mark R. Leary, intellectual humility means recognizing that your beliefs and ideas could be wrong specifically because you are aware that the evidence might be limited or you might not have the expertise to properly evaluate it.[29] Characteristics associated with intellectual humility include being willing to change your views, being teachable, avoiding defensiveness, and recognizing the strengths of other people. As management scholars Bradley P. Owens and David R. Hekman put it, "Humility captures how one views themselves in the world (more objectively), how they view others (more appreciatively), and how they receive new information or perspectives (more openly)."[30]

Admitting personal faults and limits is difficult for many leaders because, according to Brené Brown, we live in a culture defined by scarcity, shame, and fear. In this context, "we've confused *feelings* with *failing* and *emotions* with *liabilities*."[31] Caring leaders understand the need for *vulnerability*, which Brown defines as exposing yourself to "uncertainty, risk, and emotional exposure."[32] Vulnerability isn't the type of thing that you can do alone—leaders need some level of support, safety, and the suspension of judgment in order to open up and try new things. Perhaps one of the best examples of vulnerability in practice is when leaders ask for help. Vulnerability isn't unloading all your feelings and problems on others. Brown explains that appropriately sharing means having boundaries and "sharing our feelings and our experiences with people who have earned the right to hear them." But being vulnerable and open "is an integral part of the trust-building process."[33]

Trust-building is a cornerstone of caring leadership. In an organization, trust is a type of capital—just like financial or physical capital—that needs regular investment and stewardship. When leaders build trust capital, their constituents are more inclined to give them the benefit of the doubt and dial back skepticism. I interviewed several leaders about how they build trust, and none of them assumed they would be trusted simply because they stepped into leadership—they had to earn and keep trust.[34] Some leaders try to close the distance between themselves and employees by having frequent small group conversations with employees (other than their direct reports), showing up at events, and getting out of the boardroom as much as possible. For Patricia McGuire, president of Trinity Washington University, trust-building comes down to transparency and honesty: "You build a reservoir of trust over the years when [employees] realize you're being consistent, you're telling the truth, you're not sugarcoating reality, but you're also living up the value of taking care of people first."

The notion of not sugarcoating reality—of recognizing the messiness of problems while remaining optimistic about their resolution—underlies another action that makes up caring leadership: *critical hope*. Education scholar Kari Grain describes critical hope as not accepting "simple solutions" while pushing back "against the toxic positivity that sometimes accompanies feel-good narratives of hope."[35] She explains that critical hope means questioning the value of hope in every situation and bringing a "critical awareness of the problem (or many problems) at hand and the spark of spirit that . . . insists on hope."[36] The "critical" element of critical hope doesn't just imply importance or urgency—it also means having the courage to confront problems that arise from or lead to inequities. Caring leadership demands "an honest appraisal of the dark side of university life," as Marilee Bresciani Ludvik put it. Being able to say things are not okay is sometimes an essential first step in making them better.[37]

Given the complexity of problems and the desire to find solutions, leaders will inevitably make mistakes. Yet *taking responsibility* is not a routine leadership practice in higher education. Leaders are sometimes discouraged from owning mistakes and apologizing because institutions do not want to assume any legal risk or generate bad press.[38] Taking responsibility is nonetheless necessary to repair damaged relationships, and it models for others how to learn from errors, giving employees the freedom to similarly be "in process." It also legitimizes uncertainty, making it possible for organizations to experiment, embrace fluidity, and pursue small but continuous changes. Leaders who are willing to own their imperfections can create stronger, more resilient organizations. Accepting responsibility isn't just a matter of saying sorry—leaders have to fully understand how a decision or action fell short, then take proactive steps to prevent it from happening again and offer restitution. If a leader pledges to do better, they should share their progress and be held accountable.

Accountability is a key feature of equity-minded organizations and individuals (discussed in Chapter 5). Higher education scholar Estela Bensimon and colleagues explained that equity-minded individuals don't see inequities as naturally occurring phenomena but rather as a product of taken-for-granted practices and policies and inadequate institutional support—inequities are solvable problems of practice.[39] *Equity-mindedness* is the "mode of thinking exhibited by practitioners who are willing to assess their own racialized assumptions, to acknowledge their lack of knowledge in the history of race and racism, to take responsibility for the success of historically underserved and minoritized student groups, and to critically assess racialization in their own practices as educators and/or administrators"[40] Leaders who practice equity-mindedness notice patterns in outcomes by race, are aware that beliefs and practices assumed to be neutral can have outcomes that are racially disadvantageous, and understand that racism is not always overt.

In Chapter 1, I explained the need for *organizational thinking* to reimagine the higher education workplace. Organizational thinking means being able to see cultural and structural determinants of problems at the organizational level and even drawing on the wisdom of organizational theories to bring issues into focus. Beronda L. Montgomery refers to the type of leadership that pays close attention to the environment in which individuals work as "groundskeeping." As she explains, "Leaders functioning as groundskeepers . . . focus on whether the environmental landscape is conducive to supporting the development and advancement of individuals toward personally-defined goals."[41] Groundskeepers are more interested in getting to the root cause of issues than managing symptoms and understand the system well enough to apply solutions that are good for the broader ecosystem.

Caring leadership is not without costs. Feminist philosopher Nel Noddings distinguished "caring for" someone or something from "caring about" them. Whereas "caring about" is more diffuse and easier, "caring for" means relating with another person, being consistently present for them, and meeting their actual needs.[42] In this narrow sense, caring leadership adds an additional set of demands to already difficult jobs. Caring leaders can sometimes experience compassion fatigue, or the intense physical, emotional, and spiritual exhaustion that can derive from caregiving.[43] Caring leaders will grow weary and can lose the "spirit that insists on hope," necessitating opportunities to step away and renew their sense of purpose.[44] Fostering caring leadership also means understanding that leaders will sometimes get it wrong and need to make amends.

These ten actions describe what caring leaders do, but the next step in creating the Caring University is to scale up from the individual to the organization. This doesn't just mean amassing an aggregate of caring individuals; we also need to consider how care can be legitimated and nourished through values, practices, and routines.[45] How do we create organizational conditions for caring leadership and adjust the cultures and structures of colleges and universities accordingly? We can start by implementing three organization-level approaches that help institutions seed and nurture the next generation of caring leaders.

Approach 1: Caring Through Rightsizing Leadership Expectations and Appreciating Administrative Work

Higher education fails to attract and loses caring leaders in part because of unreasonable job demands combined with low regard for administrative work. As one department chair told me, she would need to work 80 hours a week to do the job well—so most weeks, she feels as if she's failing. Not every leadership job is overloaded with responsibilities, but my study of leaders over the last decade suggests that many universities place no boundaries on what they ask of people who step into these roles. During the pandemic, leaders were pulled into a nearly nonstop progression of meetings, and one leader intimated to me that it doesn't feel like their institution ever graduated from COVID "crisis mode." Competition and compliance have added tasks, yet institutions haven't added support staff or changed the nature of leadership jobs to account for these changes. Completing the job begins to eclipse how it gets done and at what cost.

In Chapter 3, I described how many higher education jobs are structured around ideal worker norms, where employees are expected to be constantly available, unfailingly loyal to the organization, and unencumbered by "personal burdens" that interrupt productivity.[46] The responsibilities of leadership jobs in higher education reflect ideal worker norms on steroids. In the same way that I proposed we needed to reset professional norms in higher education, we need to rightsize expectations of leaders. This means taking stock of their workload and making efforts to identify what is a priority and eliminate superfluous tasks. Some of the work that buries leaders originates from institutional choices—it comes from continuously adding initiatives without regard for the institution's capacity, haphazard responses to external pressures, and the competitive urge to push people harder. Tasks often trickle from the top down, accumulating on the desks of mid-level leaders. In other words, leaders—especially those at the top of the organization—sometimes create too much work for themselves and others. There is a special obligation for these leaders to monitor the relationship between goals and the labor required to complete them. The university is its people—you cannot advance one at the expense of the other.

Governing boards largely escaped scrutiny during the Great Resignation, but they play an important role in reimagining the higher education workplace, including through the expectations they establish for leaders. If a board's message to the president is to deliver on a long list of outcomes—grow enrollment, rise in the rankings, bring in more donations, elevate the institution's profile—that message gets pushed down to the cabinet, and the attendant pressures emanate throughout the organization. As Marilee Bresciani Ludvik explains: "Those working for the leader who needs to 'get it done' may suffer from pushing their minds and their bodies beyond exhaustion. With their own self-care in decline, they . . . become less responsible for their behavior and often, with or without awareness, they inflict harmful behaviors on others. And thus begins the vicious cycle of inhumane treatment."[47]

Alternatively, by attending to the well-being of leaders and managing expectations, boards can set a tone that reverberates across the organization. They can encourage leaders to take time off and build periods of respite into contracts. It is difficult to achieve the Caring University if the board is setting inhumane expectations for the institution and the people who lead it.

Underlying caring leadership are self-reflection, patient listening, and moments of calm to think about others and their experiences. Engaging in actions that demonstrate care is nearly impossible when your schedule is stacked with back-to-back meetings without a chance to come up for air. Steven Rogelberg, a professor of organizational science, found that employees are spending more time in total and more of their workdays in meetings, and this is particularly true for upper management.[48] The solution is not to get rid of meetings altogether but rather to fix dysfunctional meetings and (ideally) reduce the number and length of meetings that eat up one's time. Leaders can assess their own practices around meetings, including whether there is a compelling reason to meet, whether they are meeting for too long, and whether they have invited too many people. But colleges and universities can also establish meeting guidelines, such as helping to delineate times when meetings could be emails, limiting the practice of agenda-less standing meetings, and allowing leaders to protect a certain percentage of their week for non-meeting work.

As an example, Washington State University piloted a program to "reduce work-related fatigue and stress" principally by reducing meetings.[49] The program recommends that units across the university avoid standing meetings on Fridays and keep meetings to 45 minutes. The latter recommendation is designed to address "unrelenting virtual meetings." People often have to build in walking time when meetings happen in person.[50] With virtual meetings, people found they weren't getting a break between long stretches of meetings. In a press release for the pilot, the university's vice president for human resources explained that the goal was to encourage units to think a little more critically about their meeting practices, including the necessity of meeting, avoiding meetings around particularly stressful times and events, and avoiding messaging employees outside business hours or when they are on vacation. While the program is designed to benefit all employees, the data so far show that leaders in particular are spending too much time in meetings. Streamlining leadership's meeting schedules could potentially create more time and space in the workweek for them to engage in caring practices.

One by-product of reducing meetings is that it creates opportunities for leaders to step away from the boardroom and the same small group of people on their executive team and instead seek out situations where they can interact with a broader swath of employees. Many higher education workers know that a president, provost, and vice presidents are leading the institution—they just don't often see them outside the university magazines and social media posts. When Erin Hennessy was deputy chief of staff at Drew University, she would sit down with the person who oversaw the president's schedule and make sure the president was visibly present on campus, regularly interacting with staff and faculty. This was easier to accomplish at a small liberal arts college compared to a large research university, but Hennessy said it wasn't impossible. "It has to be strategic," she said. "And so, it isn't that I'm going to sit with every faculty member every year. But I'm going to pull a group of faculty in for breakfast at the beginning of the semester." At the end of the day, caring leadership is relational—leaders need to show up and be in a position to learn about the lives of the people they lead.

When I think about closing the distance between higher education leaders and employees, I am reminded of Mike Muñoz, the superintendent-president of Long Beach City College. My first introduction to Muñoz was a video of him in bright red sunglasses passing out paletas (a Mexican frozen treat) to students on the first day of class. Muñoz attributes his ability to connect with students and employees to his unwavering authenticity. He is very open about his own experiences as a first-generation, queer Latino who became a single father at age 20 and experienced homelessness and food insecurity en route to earning his bachelor's degree. Muñoz explained that he isn't broadcasting his past struggles; rather, he is disclosing pieces of his identity and lived experience as a way to relate with others on a human level and demonstrate compassion and empathy. Modeling authenticity is particularly important for Muñoz, who didn't see people like him stepping into presidencies and was afraid he would need to erase or hide aspects of himself to be taken seriously. He ultimately decided that becoming a president wasn't worth it if he couldn't be himself: "I'm going do this in my most authentic way," Muñoz explained, "and if it works great, we're all going to succeed, and I'm going to thrive." Judging by the joy he exhibits on the job, he was right.

Creating moments for leaders to authentically connect with employees can help staff and faculty better understand who leaders are, what motivates them, and the realities of administrative work. A persistent challenge for colleges and universities—one they share with many organizations—is an underappreciation for the importance of managerial competence. Higher education scholar Brendan Cantwell argued that "faculty cultures too often cultivate management ignorance,"[51] and they are fond of accusing colleagues who are interested in administration of "selling out" or crossing over to the "dark side." Writing in *Inside Higher Ed*, historian Elizabeth A. Lehfeldt argues that the faculty's low regard for administrative work "cheapens and degrades the good and honest work that is being done by hardworking, well-intentioned administrators" and exacerbates an "us versus them" mentality.[52] By undervaluing administrative work and positioning administrators as "different creatures who abandon any . . . previous faculty priorities and sensibilities," many potential leaders are discouraged from pursuing administrative roles while leaders are more likely to separate themselves.[53]

To cultivate and sustain caring leaders, staff and faculty need to be prepared to humanize higher education leadership. This means "creating safety for a leader to be able to be themselves and to relate and still be perceived as being a leader," said Valerio Parrot, adding, "I think there's probably times where leaders feel like they can't be themselves, and they can't open up and build those relationships, because that's not what's expected of them in the role."

Seeing leaders as humans also means improving how institutions show appreciation for good leadership. As was the case in Chapter 4, compensation is certainly part of it, but appreciation goes deeper than pay. As Katharine Stewart explained, "People often refer to these as thankless jobs, but that's a very good reason for someone to not want to do it. . . . I try to thank the administrators around me that I see doing good work because I know they're probably not hearing it very often." Colleges and universities depend on effective leaders to function, and better appreciating the value of administrative work can encourage employees with leadership potential to pursue these roles.

Approach 2: Caring Through Leadership Preparation and Opportunities for Renewal

Through her research and consulting, Vicki L. Baker has worked with all types of institutions, from research universities to community colleges. When it comes to leadership development, she told me, "There isn't any institution or institutional setting that's getting it fully right. I'm not taking a deficit mindset and suggesting they're all doing it wrong. There are just opportunities to be more intentional and strategic about investing in leadership development programs." Her observation speaks to the second organization-level approach that institutions need to embrace to create the organizational conditions for caring leadership. The Caring University doesn't leave good leadership up to chance—it proactively grows leaders and works to sustain them. (Box 7.2 presents an example.)

One recurring challenge that Baker sees is that institutions start leadership preparation too late. Many leadership development programs are designed for people who have ascended to specific titles associated with leadership, meaning people in those programs don't begin training for their role until they are already in it. Baker frequently encounters this problem with department chairs: "We don't do a good job preparing department chairs, and it's a critical role," she said. "The minute you put someone in that role and they're under-supported, they have zero interest in continuing beyond that." When institutions focus on leadership titles instead of actions, they overlook people who are leaders or have leadership potential but aren't a dean, director, or vice president. "If you're only going to invest in someone because they have a title," Baker explained, "you've already missed the mark in crafting and cultivating a leadership pipeline and pathway."

Baker has championed several ways that institutions can better prepare leaders and develop a leadership pipeline. One is to help high-potential people get plugged into leadership opportunities outside their particular silo. For example, institutions sometimes get stuck thinking that the leadership pathway for a student affairs professional is solely within student affairs. But there may be people with transferable leadership skills who would thrive in other parts of the organization. Leadership development requires investment—and not just in dedicated programs. Many employees are expected to layer leadership development on top of their existing responsibilities. The result is that leadership development programs get squeezed in where they can fit into the busy schedules of the participants. By contrast, Baker would like to see institutions integrate leadership preparation into jobs and free up time for participants to immerse themselves in an experience and get more out of it.

The lack of succession management in higher education is especially exasperating for Baker. When a leader steps down—which these days happens quite often—no one has been explicitly trained to take their place. As part of her fellowship with the American Council on Education, Baker is working with the provost of Hope College to create a department chair succession management and mentoring plan. In many ways, Baker is building from scratch because she is not aware of a program like this in existence. Rather than leaning on the traditional academic triumvirate of teaching, research, and service, Baker's program is based on what she calls the new triumvirate for chairs: leadership, management, and personnel development. She would like to see more people serve as assistant chairs or cochairs before stepping into the role so that they are able to sit in on meetings, see email exchanges, and understand what reports are required and when. "We have to identify people earlier in their careers and help them become long-term organizational contributors," Baker said. "Industry does this much better than we do—we don't really do it at all."

More professional development and leadership training isn't a panacea. Higher education scholar Crystal Chambers has explained that many Black women are pushed to upgrade their qualifications, gain new skills, take on additional service, and seek out multiple mentors. The problem isn't that they need more experience or mentoring. The concern is that they aren't granted the same opportunities to step into leadership roles. Researchers have found that women are frequently mentored but less likely to be promoted.[54] One reason is that they are not sponsored the same way men are. As higher education scholar Jorge

Burmicky explained, sponsorship involves a leader "advocating, recommending, and 'protecting' [a protégé] by drawing on their power, networks, and social capital."[55] What many women and leaders of color need is not necessarily another mentor or professional development opportunity but rather someone who is fighting for their advancement and bringing visibility to frequently overlooked strengths and experiences.

Because they are trying to get people quickly up to speed in roles they have already started, leadership development programs can tend to be overly tactical in telling people "here's what to do" to be effective. A critical question for leadership is consequently shortchanged: Why lead at all? Marjorie Hass, who served as president at two institutions for a total of 16 years before becoming president of the Council of Independent Colleges (CIC), explained that it is possible for high-achieving people to start marching down a path from professor to chair to dean to provost to president. Hass explained, "I do a lot of mentoring, particularly with women leaders . . . who've never had the opportunity to step back and say, 'Okay, if it was just up to me, where would I really be investing my time and energy? What is my why?' " CIC developed the Presidential Vocation and Institutional Mission program to guide leaders through a seminar-based "discernment process" to think through not only if they want to be a president but why and at what type of institution. Hass tries to underscore with her mentees that "it's not better to be a college president versus a long-serving senior faculty member. You haven't won anything by becoming president. Those are different paths to choose."

When she became the leader of CIC, Hass wanted to "think about something we could do . . . to intervene in a cycle where people were burning out or leaving the presidency before they were done with the leadership they could provide." The result was the Presidential Renewal program. Designed for presidents who have served for five years or more, this program helps them "sustain their leadership momentum with . . . attention to rest and recalibration." The program includes a four-day retreat during which participants "look at their life holistically and think about places where they feel supported, where they feel like they have good habits that are helping sustain them in this work, and where they recognize they need some other kinds of support services."[56] As part of a follow-up meeting, participants consider how they can translate their own renewal into practices that help others on their campuses. Although these programs exist outside of colleges and universities, the truth is that institutions often have to tap outside organizations for specialized professional development of those in high-ranking positions because institutions have few people who are experienced in those roles. There is value in facilitating participation in outside programs alongside in-house leadership development.

Although there are multiple programs designed to prepare leaders, few explicitly focus on helping existing leaders understand their purpose and attend to their mental health. According to Hass, "There's a certain sense that you've achieved a position that obviously has some prestige, some power and authority. Your life must be peachy keen and everything's rosy, and you don't even deserve to think about your own mental health, your own sustainability." This approach has noticeable consequences, including leaders struggling with mental health, higher turnover rates, and the cascading pressure of intense job demands. Cultivating caring leadership isn't just about identifying and training future leaders—it requires supporting the well-being of existing leaders through opportunities for renewal and consideration of their mental health.

Approach 3: Caring Through Leadership Selection and Performance Review

Search processes for leaders in higher education do not adequately consider someone's propensity for caring leadership. Instead, they focus on whether someone has the pedigree and experience to plausibly fulfill the responsibilities enumerated in book-length job descriptions and position profiles. The primary question asked of candidates is, "What have you previously accomplished, and can you do the same or better here?" as opposed to "What are your values, and how do you demonstrate them among the people you lead?" In some cases, institutions are seeking people who will be expected to be "fixers" or "problem-solvers," meaning they can hit the ground running and turn around a set of challenges they inherited from a predecessor. "They're looking for silver bullets," as Shawn Hartman, chief operating officer of Academic Search, told me.

There is nothing wrong with a search process that tries to determine if someone is qualified and has the skills to perform the job, but as Hartman explains, it reflects a type of myopathy common in leadership searches: "You need to have done something that sounds like this role, been at the same type of institution as the one conducting the search. You can't cross sectors." Checking boxes can crowd out efforts to understand if a leader has the wherewithal to notice others' experiences, understand their own emotions, be open to new ideas, and take responsibility for shortcomings. Admittedly, parsing these attributes as part of a search process is more difficult than identifying a required pedigree and having candidates rattle off accomplishments. Hartman pointed out that it is common for presidential position profiles to list a sense of humor as a desired trait. But how exactly do you do that during a Zoom interview, especially when the committee likely can't agree on what they find funny?

Still, Hartman sees ways that selection processes could be changed to yield more caring leaders. Instead of simply asking if candidates have experience with assessment or experience with enrollment management, he encourages more behavioral questions. For example, "Share with us the most challenging student experience you've had. How did you navigate it?" A big part of his role in assisting searches is taking time to develop questions that help committees get at skills and attributes underlying resume entries. Hartman has also found good leaders are much savvier about evaluating whether the institution is a place that will support them. "I think we have to acknowledge there is no perfect candidate," Hartman explained, "and the institution has to be prepared to support the individual's development." If you are bringing in someone with the expectation that they make a hard decision that has been put off for years, what are you doing to protect them? In some cases, Hartman sees value in hiring an interim leader to manage those difficult decisions so that a longer-term hire doesn't immediately step into a hornet's nest. Being thoughtful about transitions at all levels of the organization, including having a manual and standard operating procedures for every office, can help set up in-coming leaders for success.

In addition to integrating caring leadership into selection processes, the performance of leaders should be evaluated not just against progress on institutional outcomes but also how they treat direct reports, their success at building a functional team, and the extent to which they demonstrate actions associated with caring leadership. Too often leaders are lauded, promoted, and rewarded for donations, rankings, graduation rates, and construction projects without consideration for the well-being of employees whose labor was critical to accomplishing these goals. Put another way, "successful" leadership and caring leadership aren't necessarily one and the same. One of the actions that underlies caring leadership is that leaders take responsibility and hold themselves and others accountable to the people they lead, which means that processes for reviewing the performance of administrators should incorporate information or metrics related to the employee experience.

According to former provost and dean George Justice, "Nationally, there is no accepted process for conducting administrator reviews and no clearly articulated purposes, both of which are sorely needed."[57] In Justice's experience, practices vary and can be more inclined toward criticism than coaching. Connecting performance reviews to actions that demonstrate care should be an opportunity to help leaders grow and not a tool to push people out. To this end, Justice recommends that comments from employees should be placed within the context of what a leader was hired to do. Someone hired from outside the institution and tasked with addressing significant issues will not be universally popular, and it may take time for them to build trust. But leadership job descriptions should explicitly mention the qualities of caring leaders, and those ought to be front and center during performance reviews. Additionally, performance reviews should be pegged to specific duties and actions instead of relying too heavily on open-ended comments. Leaders should have a chance to review and discuss feedback on their performance and be afforded time to make improvements. There are caring ways of approaching leaders' performance reviews so that they don't inadvertently exacerbate the "churn" of administrators.

When higher education leaders need to work on specific skills or are struggling through context-dependent issues, coaching may be more

Box 7.2

Leading with Deep Care

The Case of Central Washington University

While collecting data for a project on presidential competencies, I met Jim Wohlpart, president of Central Washington University (CWU). He had volunteered to participate in a focus group and briefly mentioned having his senior staff participate in professional development on emotional intelligence. On a whim, I emailed and asked if he would be up for doing an interview. That conversation revealed Wohlpart's passion for leading with what he calls "deep care," and his actions at Central Washington exemplify caring leadership and many of the ideas in this book.

Wohlpart applied to only one presidential job—the one he now occupies at CWU. A year before launching the search, the board of trustees at CWU organized numerous listening sessions, which revealed a desire among students, employees, and other constituents for a different kind of leader. Wohlpart read through what the community wanted and saw alignment with his own values. Bringing those values forward in the institution's guiding documents became one of Wohlpart's early goals. The institution spent a full year developing a new vision—to be a "model learning community of equity and belonging"—and an accompanying mission. They spent a second year working on the values that would inform a new strategic plan so that the institution's vision, mission, values, and goals all fit together.

In his 2021 state of the university address, Wohlpart identified shared leadership and shared governance as foundational to drafting and operationalizing the new guiding documents. As he explained in our interview, "We have had many intentional conversations on what shared governance is here at CWU. We've done study groups around shared governance. And what I'm trying to help folks think about is how shared governance is extremely useful and needs to be honored in higher education, but it also has some rigid divisions of labor. If we can break some of those barriers down, we build trust and move toward shared leadership." He broadened the executive leadership team, then created a second group of administrators that is broader still, both of which he meets with regularly. Shared governance leaders from the faculty senate, faculty union, classified and exempt staff, and student government are invited to consequential conversations. "Leadership is layered and textured work," he explained. "It happens . . . from the executive leadership team down, but it also happens from the bottom up. Those two must meet each other on a regular basis to be able to have clarity of vision and purpose."

Another defining feature of Wohlpart's leadership is to embody an ethos of deep care. In his address on the state of the university, Wohlpart emphasized the importance of being able to hold multiple contradictory ideas at once. One is caring for individuals while also caring for the community. He has pushed

Box 7.2 (continued)

deans, in particular, to realize that what's best for the university as a whole might be giving up resources for another unit that needs them more. A second paradox, as Wohlpart put it, is that "when we care about someone, we're intent upon nurturing them, listening to them, and being empathetic to them. Deep care takes that a step forward and says . . . sometimes you have to give hard feedback or tell someone how they are showing up is not helpful." It is supporting people while holding them accountable. Wohlpart made it clear that this ethos doesn't mean much without action. "We have to change the structures, the systems, the policies. If we want to actually demonstrate care, it's not enough to talk about it." As a case in point, he brought in an expert who led the institution through an appreciative inquiry to create "new, more just and fair ways of evaluating faculty so that we can live into our vision."

Wohlpart has phrased these efforts as "working to create a whole person, human-centered university." A critical partner in this work, one that has previously been "demeaned and diminished," is human resources. In the past, human resources was very tactical and operations-oriented, focused on hiring procedures and administering benefits. "I've asked them to shift and be strategic and work on culture," he said. "How do we make sure that our employees have meaningful, purpose-filled work? How do we know that there is a leadership path for them, a professional development and growth path for them? How do we provide coaching, mentoring, and affinity groups so they have a sense of belonging?"

And then there was the emotional intelligence training that piqued my interest. Wohlpart relied on an expert from CWU's own business school to help guide his executive leadership team toward greater self-awareness and self-management. He also brought in an expert on leadership, courage, and vulnerability for a yearlong series of presentations and training on developing a learner mindset, psychological safety, and institutional thinking. Wohlpart warned participants, "This work will be hard. It will require us to become a learning organization, to investigate our patterns of thinking that invisibly guide so much of our daily operations—systems and structures that benefit the few, people like me, while excluding, disadvantaging, and even diminishing so many others."

The difficulty of translating deep care into action, according to Wohlpart, stems from the fact that "so many of us don't know how to do this. These are muscles that you have to practice over and over again, and you're going to fail and make mistakes." Moving from a "competitive, stab each other in the back siloed mentality" to a "whole person, human-centered university" isn't going to happen overnight. CWU now closely tracks climate surveys and markers of success, particularly retention of students of color and employees of color. And Wohlpart notes that not everyone is comfortable with "deep care," and a few leaders have left. Still, in two and a half years, Wohlpart believes that progress has been made, even if there is much more work ahead: "It takes time for culture to change."

helpful than leadership programs. Katharine Stewart, the senior vice provost for faculty academic affairs at NCSU, increasingly believes that institutions should provide or pay for leadership coaching for deans and department chairs during their first two years. As she explained, "If I'm doing a talk with [department] heads about how to manage a personnel issue, they'll all listen and say, 'Oh, this is very helpful information.' But when they encounter their first really nasty personnel issue, they are not going to be able to remember 75 percent of what I said." But if they have a coach—someone sufficiently removed from the department but with experience dealing with these issues—they can be a confidential sounding board, listen to a leader's fears and ideas, and offer advice. Although there is a benefit to having coaches outside the institution, Stewart offers to meet monthly with all new department heads. "They can come to my office and talk about whatever's on their mind, and they're not talking to their dean, and I'm not going to talk to their dean. . . . It is 100 percent designed to be a safety net for department heads as they get their heads around the job."

Conclusion

In January 2022, Eric Kelderman, a senior reporter at *The Chronicle of Higher Education*, wrote an article headlined "Who Wants to Be a College President?"[58] Two years later, Daniel W. Drezner, a professor of international politics, wrote an opinion essay for the same publication titled "You Could Not Pay Me Enough to Be a College President."[59] And that was a prevalent sentiment among the leaders I interviewed—the increasing compensation offered to leaders wasn't enough to cover the steep costs of leadership positions. Yet the strategy of many institutions seems to be throwing money at the problem, hoping that they can entice enough people to trade a few years of intense labor for an above-average paycheck. That strategy isn't working. You can pour water on a plant all day, but eventually its roots will rot. It's time to take a more balanced, ecological approach.

We need to repair the environment so that caring leaders emerge and flourish. We can and should continue to prepare people to step into

Box 7.3

Chapter 7 Actions Steps

- Set reasonable workload expectations for leaders, establishing priorities and reducing superfluous tasks.
- Consider an institution-wide policy designed to rein in the number and length of meetings, freeing up time for leaders to complete tasks, reflect, and interact with employees.
- Create ways of demonstrating appreciation for administrative work beyond additional compensation.
- Develop institution-wide leadership development programs that start earlier in an employee's career arc and are not solely for people who hold particular titles.
- Invest in coaching services or personnel for people in key leadership roles for their first two years on the job.
- Allow leaders to participate in renewal programs or temporarily step away from roles in order to restore their sense of purpose and attend to their mental health.
- Integrate the ten actions that define caring leadership into leadership selection and administrator performance review while making evaluation processes more caring.
- Specifically train leaders in actions that define caring leadership.

demanding leadership roles, but we also need to rethink the structure of the jobs and how we perceive administrative work. If we want humane leaders, we need to treat leaders as human. We should select leaders who demonstrate investment in caring leadership and evaluate their performance not only based on outcomes but also on how people were treated in achieving those outcomes. The organizational changes proposed in this book—including the three approaches outlined in this chapter—are possible in the absence of caring leaders, but the odds are drastically lower. Cultivating and sustaining caring leaders at every level of the organization through the steps described in Box 7.3 creates the best possible environment to germinate the Caring University.

CONCLUSION

First-Step Pathways to Change

THERE IS A DESIRE to think of the Great Resignation as a discrete event—something with a start and finish and a clean, measurable outcome. According to this view, the Great Resignation began unexpectedly in response to the mass transmission of COVID-19 and ended just as abruptly when popular media outlets stopped talking about it. The Great Resignation was about one thing—literal resignations—the bulk of which happened for a moment that is now thoroughly in the past. For those who subscribe to this line of thought, the most important thing to know about the Great Resignation is that it's over—time to move on and get back to normal.

As is so often the case, however, reality is more complicated. The Great Resignation was a spike in a trend line—the intensification of problems that predate the pandemic and continue to this day. As an umbrella concept, the Great Resignation describes not one outcome but multiple shifts in the workplace, each of them a signal from higher education employees to leaders. One of those signals is that staff and faculty are exhausted and dialing back their efforts in an act of self-preservation. Another is that employees are angry, joining together and standing up for better pay and policies. Yet another is that workers are fed up and voting with their feet, moving on in search of opportunities that better demonstrate care for their well-being. The signals add up to a big, blinking billboard that unmistakably says employees at colleges and universities across the country desperately want a reimagined workplace.

Leaders can respond to these signals in several ways. The traditional way has been to not respond at all, letting employees wither on the vine and walk away, then plugging replacements into unchanged jobs and organizations. More recently, the response has been a half-hearted attempt to attend to employee well-being through individualized solutions such as encouraging employees to set boundaries or download a meditation app. But after taking a walk or meditating, workers come back to the same excessive workloads, inflexible policies, and low compensation. The response that staff and faculty really want—the one they have been waiting for—recognizes that many workplace problems are baked into the organizational structures of colleges and universities. If leaders want to attract, grow, and retain talent, they need a response that truly sees the problems for what they are and where they originate.

The Caring University is a resource for crafting precisely that type of response. It offers possibilities for reimagining the higher education workplace through organization-level changes geared toward supporting employee well-being. In articulating a set of concrete approaches that draw on multidisciplinary research, 116 interviews, and three site visits, it tackles institutional choices that flow from and are reinforced by organizational norms and values—which then become embedded in organizational structures through policies and widely accepted practices that shape the everyday working conditions of employees. The solutions underpinning the Caring University are aimed specifically at organizational cultures and structures, supplanting self-care with *organizational care.*

The book describes 20 approaches in total to bring the Caring University to fruition, making it easy for even the most ambitious leaders to get overwhelmed. But the main message is that change is a journey, not a destination. All journeys offer important lessons and begin by taking first steps. Accordingly, I close the book with several lessons and first-step pathways for leaders to consider in collaboration with campus partners.

Lessons for Change

The Caring University isn't an official designation or honorific. Rather, it describes *collective*, *proactive*, *ongoing* work to enact *organizational changes* in support of employee well-being. I haven't yet encountered an institution that has mastered every organization-level change, but the preceding chapters share examples and case studies of units and institutions that are crafting, piloting, and implementing new ideas. The Caring University is not going to happen through a time-limited initiative, heroic leader, or crisis-provoked reaction. It is a collective project involving long-term planning and inclusive participation of everyone in the organization.

Just as important as what the Caring University entails is *how* colleges and universities engage in the journey. After all, we are not talking about easy change—we are talking about full-fledged institutional transformation. The Caring University calls for deep or "second-order" change, which higher education scholar Adriana Kezar defined as change that is "so substantial that it alters the operating systems, underlying values, and culture of an organization."[1] There isn't a magic formula or secret sauce for facilitating change that sinks deep into organizational values and practices. It's about doing the hard work of fostering new mindsets and campus routines.

The impetus for this book was mounting evidence that higher education staff and faculty were burned out from working cultures and conditions that undervalued their labor and compromised their mental and physical health. But its ultimate goal became offering an alternative vision of what the higher education workplace could be if you begin with the premise that all employees have talent, should be treated as whole people, and deserve to be cared for as essential contributors to organizational success. In conceptualizing that alternative vision, certain practices, ideas, and justifications related to care repeatedly emerged—not random dispersed stars but constellations imparting a message. I have translated that message in the form of lessons about why and how to undertake this work.

Lesson 1: Good Solutions Derive from a Good Understanding of the Problems

One of the threads connecting the examples and case studies in this book is that they started with an inquiry process. Once leaders or teams of employees noticed an issue, they undertook an investigation to learn more instead of assuming they knew its prevalence, causes, or effects. This manifested in surveys, focus groups, and one-on-one interviews, which allowed the individuals and units to figure out what to prioritize and what kind of program or initiative best addresses the problems that their colleagues experienced. Although the workplace problems chronicled in this book are common, they are not universal and can show up in different ways. This means that some of the approaches associated with the Caring University are not an ideal match for all units or institutions, and others may fall lower on the priority list. The lesson I take from this is that any effort to improve the higher education workplace needs to begin with an inquiry process to ensure solutions come from a deep understanding of the problems.

Lesson 2: Employee Well-Being and Student Success Are on the Same Team

For many colleges and universities, the last decade has been defined by a laser focus on student success, and institutions have now implemented widely accepted practices to support students, such as paying attention to transitions, belonging, and mental health. But overlooked in those efforts is the role of staff and faculty working conditions and cultures in achieving student outcomes. Supporting employee well-being begets more engaged employees committed to the mission and in a better position to teach, mentor, and advise students. The lesson I take from this is that investing in the well-being of workers is a research-based strategy to improve organizational performance, including efforts to better serve students.

Lesson 3: You Can Afford to Pursue the Caring University

One question that I regularly get from leaders when I present the ideas in this book is how to pay for changes at a time when many institutions are struggling with tight or diminishing resources. My glib answer is that we pay for the Caring University the same way we pay for everything in higher education: we value it, plan for it, and incrementally resource it. The question of how institutions can afford to support the well-being of employees glosses right over the first two items: valuing and planning. The institutions highlighted in this book are not swimming in resources, but their leaders identified what they valued and concluded that they could not afford to shortchange care. They developed a plan, and then as resources became available, they funded priorities in stages. The lesson I take from this is simple: pursuing the Caring University is a smart investment.

Lesson 4: Care Doesn't Imply a Lack of Structure or Accountability

Talk of care sometimes triggers a concern that we are coddling employees. What happened to putting in your time in a low-paying job and working hard to advance? Why can't we set high standards and expect workers to give their best? Aren't we going too far with special accommodations? While the preceding pages certainly challenge prevailing norms like the idea that sacrifice and suffering are just part of earning your keep in higher education, they do not advocate an absence of standards, accountability, or excellence. A key idea throughout the book is incorporating additional structure into the workplace by reducing ambiguity and clarifying policies. It is not just holding employees accountable but also envisioning a system of shared responsibility where leaders and institutions are accountable to their values and commitments. The higher education workplace of the past bred inequities through unclear accountability mandates and unfairly applied policies. The lesson I take from this is that the Caring University is all about better workplace policies and accountability as an organizational commitment.

Lesson 5: It All Comes Back to Trust

Sociologist Eric Klinenberg wrote an account of 2020 through the stories of seven New Yorkers.[2] Writing in the *New York Times* about what he learned from the people he interviewed, Klinenberg noted, "In the wake of COVID, all the larger institutions they had been taught to trust failed them. At the most precarious times in their lives, they found there was no system in place to help."[3] I heard similar sentiments in my interviews—staff and faculty felt abandoned and betrayed by institutions. So much of the Caring University is about restoring colleges and universities as institutions that employees can believe in again. Simply acknowledging the importance of employee well-being is part of the repair process. But trust is also a two-way street. Employees are more likely to trust when they are trusted. The Caring University trusts employees to know what conditions they need to be successful. It believes them when they say something in the organization isn't working or is causing preventable harm. It isn't going to treat them like they are crazy when they suggest their pay is inadequate. The lesson I take from this is that colleges and universities can start to embody institutions worthy of trust by taking their duty of care as employers seriously.

These lessons do not provide a recipe for guaranteed success, but they provide guideposts for a change journey and communicate helpful advice about why and how to pursue cultural and structural changes to the higher education workplace. Care begins with curiosity. Care can be mission-driven. Care doesn't have to break the bank. Care and accountability are partners. Care requires trust and can restore trust.

First-Step Pathways to Change

The Caring University proposes numerous possibilities, which means that leaders can customize a change process responsive to their organization's particular challenges and the context in which it operates. If designing a viable organizational change process were easy, we would likely see it happening more regularly, and fewer people complaining about higher education's inability to change.[4] The reality is that deep change can be incredibly hard, and as is true of all hard things, getting started is half the battle. Contained within the examples and case studies presented in this book are several potential pathways to help leaders take initial steps toward the Caring University.

Pathway 1: Start with a Sensemaking Exercise

One reason organizational change falters is that a change is announced before employees can make sense of it. They haven't been able to talk with colleagues from different units about how they understand an issue, what the change means for them, and their sense of purpose within the organization. Allowing time for employees to make sense of a situation before launching an initiative is time well spent. It helps to uncover the disparate understandings that people have and creates space for questions and skepticism. Amarillo College's data summit around student success (Chapter 2) is a good example of an early sensemaking exercise that allowed the organization to uncover mental models related to student success and present data to craft new mental models. I have also seen units and executive teams do similar exercises with "employee engagement" and "faculty success." In many cases, there are multiple understandings of organizational goals and how to best achieve them. Before you can begin a journey toward a shared vision, it helps to know where everyone is starting.

Pathway 2: Leverage the Strategic Plan

I didn't come into this project as an acolyte for strategic planning, but I started to notice in my research that many good things for employees were direct products of a strategic plan. There are institutions where the strategic plan isn't just a generic document created out of a sense of tradition; rather, it is a collectively produced set of goals that direct choices about resources. For example, the Employee Success Center was created at the University of Louisville because it was a specific goal in the strategic plan (Chapter 4). Intentionally integrating approaches discussed in this book into the strategic plan can be a way to jump-start (and fund) the change process. I have seen institutions use strategic plans to advance goals related to employee compensation, resources for parents, and professional development. I am under no illusions that profound organizational change runs through the strategic plan, but strategic planning presents an opportunity to help a unit or institution take those first steps toward transformation.

Pathway 3: Empower "Tempered Radicals"

Organizational scholar Debra Meyerson found that within most organizations are "cautious and committed catalysts . . . who slowly make difference."[5] She called these change agents "tempered radicals"—people who used their status as organizational insiders to both find success in their jobs while also "pushing and prodding the system through a variety of subtle processes," ultimately gaining the attention and support of others.[6] Tempered radicals amplify deviation, producing ripples that add up to significant organizational change. My research similarly revealed the power of change champions who, through their own small acts and little victories, are reinventing the higher education workplace.

The approaches that give rise to Caring University don't all have to come from flashy, top-down initiatives. Institutions can encourage change that bubbles up from the bottom or middle by empowering "tempered radicals" and the pockets of collective action they create. Yet it is difficult for these pockets to emerge and grow when units are chronically understaffed and employees hardly have time to eat lunch, let alone write a creative proposal. In keeping with the notion that workers have the best handle on the challenges they face and what they need to be successful, institutions can actively support staff and faculty who indicate a desire to devise and pilot small acts to improve policies and processes. This could take the form of small grants for teams or departments to implement a workplace change or reducing the normal responsibilities of people on a committee so that they can focus on developing and testing an idea (Chapter 2). Too often, good ideas aren't realized because they are left to a committee of people who don't have time for another committee. In some cases, empowering pockets of change means piloting a new policy or temporarily suspending an old policy. The goal is to give employees tools and resources to create novel approaches—and then committing to implementing effective practices and policies across the organization.

Pathway 4: Fix the Glaring Inequities

If a leader is on board with improving the higher education workplace and unsure where to start, addressing some of the long-standing, undeniable inequities is an option unlikely to ruffle many feathers. For example, if your institution has different parental or bereavement leave policies for different kinds of staff, graduate assistants, and faculty (Chapter 3), commit to improving the less generous policies so that all workers receive the best-available benefits. If lecturers receive less pay per course than other full-time faculty, bring their per-course pay up to parity (Chapter 6). If the pay of administrative assistants strikes you as wildly below what is asked of them (Chapter 1), start looking at policy and asking superiors where there is wiggle room to adjust it. Although addressing inequities may be just as hard as the other approaches, it is a reasonable place to start enacting change that can make a big difference for the most exploited employees in higher education.

Conclusion

In the four years that I have been researching the ideas that became this book, I have been privileged to meet scores of remarkable staff, faculty, graduate students, and leaders. Like countless employees in colleges and universities, they get up each morning and dedicate their talent to the project of higher education. Yet I am also reminded that several of them have persisted in higher education because of their sheer will. They fought to find a place in institutions that worked more diligently to push them out than honor their contributions and nourish their growth. But I also remember the many people who gave up on the possibility of a reimagined higher education workplace and (even before the Great Resignation) left in search of organizations that showed greater promise of caring about them.

As a result of my interviews and travel, one thing is crystal clear: change is possible. I have met so many people in so many places who want the Caring University, and quite a few are striving to make it happen, which tells me that this isn't a wild idea pulled from a utopian fantasy. While there are several very hard problems in higher education, reimagining the higher education workplace isn't one of them. Achieving the Caring University is about leaders deciding to steer colleges and universities down a new path. In many ways, this book is an attempt to tie together the ideas and initiatives I learned about that have promise but haven't yet been widely adopted. It is a humble effort at creating constellations out of the smattering of stars that first appear in the night sky—to help accelerate the diffusion of care as an organizing principle that applies to everyone in higher education, from custodians to presidents.

And it's about choosing right now to get started.

NOTES

Introduction. The Caring University

1. Dawn is a pseudonym. I used a pseudonym for interview participants who chose to be anonymous and whose stories are retold in some detail. For other interview participants who chose to be anonymous, I use general job titles. I use the real names and titles of prominent figures whose statements are public record and for interview participants who consented to have their name and title appear in the book. As I explain in the Note on Sources and Methods, all interview participants were able to review their quotations.

2. According to the National Center for Education Statistics, in fall 2020, the percentage of faculty at degree-granting postsecondary institutions who were at the associate professor or professor level and identified as American Indian/Alaska Native was less than one. In fact, it was small enough to be labeled with the symbol "#" instead of the fractional part.

3. Vizenor, *Survivance: Narratives of Native Presence*, 1.

4. Bichsel et al., "The CUPA-HR 2022 Higher Education Employee Retention Survey: Initial Results"; WittKiefer, "Chief Enrollment Management Officers in a Time of Change, Challenge and Opportunity"; National Association of Student Financial Aid Administrators, *Financial Aid Offices Face Intensifying Staffing Challenges amid Pandemic*; Anft, "The Staffing Crisis in Higher Ed: College Administrators' Views on Campus Employment."

5. McClure, "Higher Ed, We've Got a Morale Problem—and a Free T-Shirt Won't Fix It."

6. Selingo and Horn, "The Great Resignation in Higher Ed."

7. Bichsel et al., "CUPA-HR 2022 Higher Education Employee Retention Survey"; Bauman, "A Pandemic-Era Cut with a Hidden Price Tag"; Schuster and Finkelstein, *The American Faculty*; McClure, "Your Pay Is Terrible? You're Not Alone."

8. NASPA: Student Affairs Administrators in Higher Education, "The Compass Report: Charting the Future of Student Affairs"; Walton, "Right Now, Your Best Employees Are Eyeing the Exits."

9. Hawes and Reynolds, "Radical Retention: How Higher Education Can Rise to the Challenges of the Great Resignation and Beyond"; McClure, "Higher Ed Is a Land of Dead-End Jobs."

10. Anft, "The Staffing Crisis in Higher Ed."

11. Fitzpatrick, *Generous Thinking: A Radical Approach to Saving the University.*

12. Kezar, *How Colleges Change*, 85.

13. US Surgeon General, *Framework for Workplace Mental Health and Well-Being*, 6.

14. Fitzpatrick, *Generous Thinking*.

15. For more information about the data informing this book, please see the Note on Sources and Methods.

16. Lewis and Heckman, "Talent Management: A Critical Review"; Garcia-Perez et al., *Critical Capabilities and Competencies for Knowledge Organizations*.

17. Tugend, "On the Verge of Burnout: COVID-19's Impact on Faculty Well-Being and Career Plans"; Marken and Agrawal, "K-12 Workers Have Highest Burnout Rate in U.S."

18. McClure, "Burnout Is Coming to Campus. Are College Leaders Ready?"

19. Ellerbeck, "The Great Resignation Is Not Over: A Fifth of Workers Plan to Quit in 2022."

20. Nightingale and Nightingale, *Unmanageable: Leadership Lessons from an Impossible Year*, 9.

21. Bishundat, Velazquez Phillip, and Gore, "Cultivating Critical Hope: The Too Often Forgotten Dimension of Critical Leadership Development."

22. Thompson, "Three Myths of the Great Resignation."

23. National Center for Health Statistics, "Nearly One in Five American Adults Who Have Had COVID-19 Still Have 'Long COVID.'"

24. Faria-e-Casto, "The COVID Retirement Boom."

25. US Bureau of Labor Statistics, "6.2 Million Unable to Work Because Employer Closed or Lost Business Due to the Pandemic."

26. Tucker, "Men Have Now Recouped Their Pandemic-Related Labor Force Losses While Women Lag Behind."

27. DePillis, "U.S. Survey Shows an Uptick in Job Openings, and Not in Layoffs."

28. Iacurci, "Workers Still Quitting at High Rates—and Getting a Big Bump in Pay."

29. Bichsel et al., "CUPA-HR 2022 Higher Education Employee Retention Survey."

30. Anft, "The Staffing Crisis in Higher Ed."

31. National Association of Student Financial Aid Administrators, *Financial Aid Offices Face Intensifying Staffing Challenges amid Pandemic*.

32. Hersey, *Rest Is Resistance: A Manifesto*.

33. Bauman, "Higher Ed's Work Force Has Returned to Its Pre-Pandemic Size."

34. WittKiefer, "Chief Enrollment Management Officers in a Time of Change, Challenge and Opportunity"; SimpsonScarborough, "A Question of Value: The Higher Ed Marcom Professional Development and Salary Study"; Bichsel et al., "CUPA-HR 2022 Higher Education Employee Retention Survey."

35. Maslach and Leiter, "How to Measure Burnout Accurately and Ethically."

36. World Health Organization, "Burnout an 'Occupational Phenomenon': International Classification of Diseases."

37. Pope-Ruark, *Unraveling Faculty Burnout: Pathways to Reckoning and Renewal*.

38. Wigert and Agrawal, "Employee Burnout, Part 1: The 5 Main Causes."

39. Nagoski and Nagoski, *Burnout: The Secret to Unlocking the Stress Cycle*, 9.

40. Malesic, *The End of Burnout: Why Work Drains Us and How to Build Better Lives*, 62.

41. Malesic, *The End of Burnout*, 55.

42. Malesic, 77.

43. Afrahi et al., "Work Disengagement."

44. Kahn, "Psychological Conditions of Personal Engagement and Disengagement at Work."

45. Santoro, "Good Teaching in Difficult Times: Demoralization in the Pursuit of Good Work," 3.

46. Santoro, "Good Teaching in Difficult Times," 2.

47. Sugrue, "Understanding the Effect of Moral Transgressions in the Helping Professions," 17.

48. Sugrue, "Understanding the Effect of Moral Transgressions in the Helping Professions," 20.

49. Kendrick, "The Low Morale Experience of Academic Librarians."

50. Nyunt, Pridgen, and Thomas, "Disrupting Student Affairs Staff Departure."

Chapter 1. Organizational Problems of the Higher Education Workplace

1. Williams, "'It's Just My Face'"; Breeden, "Our Presence Is Resistance."

2. Gonzales, Kanhai, and Hall, "Reimagining Organizational Theory for the Critical Study of Higher Education," 507.

3. Kezar, *Understanding and Facilitating Change in the 21st Century: Recent Research and Conceptualizations.*

4. Kezar, *How Colleges Change: Understanding, Leading, and Enacting Change*, 86.

5. Williams, "'It's Just My Face,'" 1.

6. Kezar, DePaola, and Scott, *The Gig Academy*; Sallee, *Creating Sustainable Careers in Student Affairs: What Ideal Worker Norms Get Wrong and How to Make It Right*; Schuster and Finkelstein, *The American Faculty*; Griffin, "Institutional Barriers, Strategies, and Benefits to Increasing the Representation of Women and Men of Color in the Professoriate"; Reyes, *Academic Outsider.*

7. Peterson, "The Study of Colleges and Universities as Organizations."

8. Labaree, *A Perfect Mess.*

9. Ray, "A Theory of Racialized Organizations."

10. Meyer and Rowan, "Institutionalized Organizations."

11. McClure and Titus, "Spending Up the Ranks?"; O'Meara, "Striving for What?"

12. DiMaggio and Powell, "The Iron Cage Revisited."

13. Bastedo, "Organizing Higher Education: A Manifesto."

14. Birnbaum, *How Colleges Work: The Cybernetics of Academic Organization and Leadership.*

15. Birnbaum, "The Life Cycle of Academic Management Fads."

16. Peters, "Bureaucracy and Bureaucratic Effectiveness."

17. Birnbaum, *How Colleges Work: The Cybernetics of Academic Organization and Leadership.*

18. Peters, "Bureaucracy and Bureaucratic Effectiveness."

19. Kezar, *How Colleges Change.*

20. Harris et al., *Academic Leadership and Governance of Higher Education.*

21. Birnbaum, "The Life Cycle of Academic Management Fads."

22. Kezar, *How Colleges Change*; Harris et al., *Academic Leadership and Governance of Higher Education*.

23. Harris et al., *Academic Leadership and Governance of Higher Education*.

24. Kezar, *How Colleges Change*.

25. Kezar, DePaola, and Scott, *The Gig Academy*.

26. Kezar, DePaola, and Scott.

27. Harper, "COVID-19 and the Racial Equity Implications of Reopening College and University Campuses."

28. Harris et al., *Academic Leadership and Governance of Higher Education*.

29. Birnbaum, *How Colleges Work*.

30. Birnbaum, 4.

31. Birnbaum.

32. Kaplin and Lee, *The Law of Higher Education, 5th Edition: Student Version*.

33. Lane, "The Spider Web of Oversight," 632.

34. McClure, "Higher Ed Is a Land of Dead-End Jobs."

35. Martin, "Stop Whining About Lack of Career Opportunities."

36. Gagliardi, *How Colleges Use Data*.

37. Slaughter and Rhoades, *Academic Capitalism and the New Economy*.

38. McClure, "Building the Innovative and Entrepreneurial University."

39. Mollencamp, "Higher Ed Is Investing in Student Success Tech."

40. Schuster and Finkelstein, *The American Faculty*.

41. Kezar, DePaola, and Scott, *The Gig Academy*.

42. Marshall et al., "Attrition from Student Affairs."

43. Magolda, *The Lives of Campus Custodians*, 145.

44. Hamilton and Nielsen, *Broke: The Racial Consequences of Underfunding Public Universities*.

45. Hamilton and Nielsen, *Broke*, 6.

46. Hamilton and Nielsen, 96.

47. Hamilton and Nielsen, 97.

48. Hamilton and Nielsen, 120.

49. Hamilton and Nielsen, 140.

50. Greene, "Diversity University."

51. Zambrana, *Toxic Ivory Towers: The Consequences of Work Stress on Underrepresented Minority Faculty*.

52. Labaree, *A Perfect Mess*.

53. Griffin, "Institutional Barriers, Strategies, and Benefits to Increasing the Representation of Women and Men of Color in the Professoriate."

54. Gagliardi et al., *American College President Study 2017*.

55. Ardoin, "The Classed Construct of Student Affairs Work," 218.

56. Quaye et al., " "Why Can't I Just Chill?" 609.

57. Rankin et al., "2010 State of Higher Education for LGBT People."

58. Pryor and Hoffman, " 'It Feels like Diversity as Usual.' "

59. Acker, "Inequality Regimes," 441.

60. Acker, 443.

61. Ray, "A Theory of Racialized Organizations," 36.

62. McCambly and Colyvas, "Institutionalizing Inequity Anew: Grantmaking and Racialized Postsecondary Organizations"; Nguemeni Tiako, South, and Ray, "Medical Schools as Racialized Organizations"; Liera and Hernandez, "Color-Evasive Racism in the Final Stage of Faculty Searches."

63. Eckel and Kezar, "Key Strategies for Making New Institutional Sense."

64. Kezar, *How Colleges Change.*

65. Kezar.

66. Kezar, 87.

67. Tierney, *The Impact of Culture on Organizational Decision-Making: Theory and Practice in Higher Education*, 25.

68. Foster Wallace, *This Is Water: Some Thoughts, Delivered on a Significant Occasion, about Living a Compassionate Life.*

Chapter 2. Making the Employee Experience a Strategic Priority

1. Schmalz and Mangan, "Food, Child Care, Rent."

2. Aspen Institute, "Aspen Prize for Community College Excellence."

3. Goldrick-Rab and Cady, "Supporting Community College Completion with a Culture of Caring: A Case Study of Amarillo College," 1.

4. Amarillo College, "Culture of Caring Poverty Summit Handbook," 2.

5. Amarillo College, 4.

6. Bustamante, "Budget Cuts and Buyouts Save $3.6 Million in President's Plan."

7. Document in author's possession.

8. Hinton, *A Practical Guide to Strategic Planning in Higher Education.*

9. Morphew and Hartley, "Mission Statements."

10. Society for College and University Planning, "Integrated Planning Glossary."

11. Apple, Inc., "Careers at Apple."

12. Wegmans, "About Us."

13. Starbucks, "Culture and Values."

14. Ingram and Choi, "What Does Your Company Really Stand For?" 40.

15. Wyatt, "Concepts, Ideas, Visions: Thematic Characteristics of Strategic Plans Among Elite, International Universities."

16. Hinton, *A Practical Guide to Strategic Planning in Higher Education.*

17. Burke et al., "Predictive Analysis of Student Data: A Focus on Engagement and Behavior"; Wong, "Higher Education Turns to Data Analytics to Bolster Student Success."

18. SHRM, "Managing Employee Surveys," para. 3.

19. Selingo and Horn, "The Great Resignation in Higher Ed."

20. National Center for Education Statistics, "National Study of Postsecondary Faculty (NSOPF): Overview."

21. Townsend and Rosser, "Workload Issues and Measures of Faculty Productivity."

22. Ziker, "The Long, Lonely Job of Homo Academicus."

23. O'Meara, Kuvaeva, and Nyunt, "Constrained Choices."

24. Culpepper et al., "The Terrapin Time Initiative."

25. Brayboy, "The Implementation of Diversity in Predominantly White Colleges and Universities," 75.

26. O'Meara et al., "Faculty Work Activity Dashboards."

27. American Association of University Professors, "Background Facts on Contingent Faculty Positions."

28. Kezar, DePaola, and Scott, *The Gig Academy.*

29. Marshall et al., "Attrition from Student Affairs."

30. Walton, "Right Now, Your Best Employees Are Eyeing the Exits"; Sallee, *Creating Sustainable Careers in Student Affairs: What Ideal Worker Norms Get Wrong and How to Make It Right.*

31. NASPA: Student Affairs Administrators in Higher Education, "The Compass Report: Charting the Future of Student Affairs."

32. Harper, "COVID-19 and the Racial Equity Implications of Reopening College and University Campuses."

33. Cho and Brassfield, "An Afterthought."

34. Lawler, *Reinventing Talent Management: Principles and Practices for the New World of Work*, ix.

35. Berger and Berger, *The Talent Management Handbook.*

36. Berger and Berger, 3–4.

37. Lawler, *Reinventing Talent Management.*

38. Gallup, "Employee Experience."

39. University of California, "Integrated Talent Management."

40. Weick, Sutcliffe, and Obstfeld, "Organizing and the Process of Sensemaking," 409.

41. Weick, Sutcliffe, and Obstfeld, 409.

42. Weick, Sutcliffe, and Obstfeld, 409.

43. Association of Community College Trustees, "Part 2: Meet Maria, Amarillo College's Most Promising Student."

44. Robert and Reinitz, *2023 EDUCAUSE Horizon Action Plan: Data Governance.*

45. Robert and Reinitz.

46. Robert and Reinitz; Reinitz, "The Impact of Analytics on the Higher Education Workforce."

47. O'Meara et al., "Faculty Work Activity Dashboards."

48. O'Meara et al., "Faculty Work Activity Dashboards," 35.

Chapter 3. Creating Working Cultures and Conditions for Real (Not Ideal) Workers

1. Adams, Hazelwood, and Hayden, "Student Affairs Case Management: Merging Social Work Theory with Student Affairs Practice."

2. Acker, "Hierarchies, Jobs, Bodies: A Theory of Gendered Organizations," 149.

3. Laloux, *Reinventing Organizations.*

4. Thomason and Williams, "What Will Work-Life Balance Look Like After the Pandemic?"; Boland et al., "Reimagining the Office and Work Life After COVID-19"; Guzman, "Pursuing Work-Life Balance in a Post-Pandemic World."

5. Davies and Frink, "The Origins of the Ideal Worker."

6. Wade, "The 8-Hour Workday Is a Counterproductive Lie."

7. University of Maryland Special Collections, "Labor, Recreation, and Rest: The Movement for the Eight-Hour Day."

8. Davies and Frink, "Origins of the Ideal Worker."

9. Davies and Frink, 23.

10. Davies and Frink.

11. Davies and Frink.

12. Acker, "Hierarchies, Jobs, Bodies."

13. Davies and Frink, "Origins of the Ideal Worker"; Zhavoronkova, Khattar, and Brady, "Occupational Segregation in America." There's an entire Twitter hashtag documenting famous men in academia and literature thanking their wives for typing, transcribing, proofreading, and coauthoring manuscripts; see Mazanec, "#ThanksForTyping Spotlights Unnamed Women in Literary Acknowledgments."

14. Kwolek-Folland, *Engendering Business*, 67.

15. Davies and Frink, "Origins of the Ideal Worker," 27.

16. Davies and Frink, 20.

17. J. C. Williams, "Deconstructing Gender."

18. Arenofsky, *Work-Life Balance*; Raja and Stein, "Work-Life Balance."

19. Davies and Frink, "Origins of the Ideal Worker," 33.

20. Gardner, "Fitting the Mold of Graduate School"; Sallee, "Performing Masculinity"; Perez, "Problematizing Socialization in Student Affairs Graduate Training."

21. Gardner, "Fitting the Mold of Graduate School"; Perez, "Problematizing Socialization in Student Affairs Graduate Training"; Sallee, "Performing Masculinity."

22. Perez, "Problematizing Socialization in Student Affairs Graduate Training," 99.

23. Perez, 99.

24. Perez, 107.

25. Perez, 104.

26. B. M. Williams, "It's Just My Face," 69.

27. Gardner, "Fitting the Mold of Graduate School."

28. Morgan, "Higher Ed Job Descriptions Can't Compete. Here's How to Fix Them."

29. McClure, "Having Trouble Hiring at Your College?"

30. Laloux, *Reinventing Organizations*, 143.

31. I am using the term "disabilities" to include both visible disabilities and nonvisible or less-visible disabilities, including mental health issues, learning conditions, and forms of neurodivergence. According to the Association on Higher Education and Disability (AHEAD), there are two common ways to convey disability as part of one's identity: person-first language and identity-first language. Person-first language distances the individual from the disability (i.e., she is a woman with a disability). This language is often taught as most appropriate in professional settings or when the speaker or author doesn't know an individual's preference. AHEAD uses identity-first language, which claims disability as a central part of one's identity and uses direct language (i.e., I'm autistic). In this chapter, I generally follow AHEAD's practice and use identity-first language; see Association on Higher Education and Disability, "AHEAD Statement on Language."

32. Newport and Wilke, "Desire for Children Still Norm in US."

33. Ward and Wolf-Wendel, *Academic Motherhood: How Faculty Manage Work and Family*; Ollilainen, "Ideal Bodies at Work." Though much of the research I found focuses on mothers, I am using the broader term "caregiver" to account for the fact that people are caring for more than just children—and in many cases, caring for family members beyond children receives even less support.

34. Ollilainen, "Ideal Bodies at Work," 961.

35. Ollilainen, 962.

36. Ogden, "Working Mothers Face a 'Wall' of Bias—but There Are Ways to Push Back."

37. Olabisi, "The Pregnancy Drop."

38. Ward and Wolf-Wendel, *Academic Motherhood: How Faculty Manage Work and Family*, 30.

39. Docka-Filipek et al., "'Professor Moms' and 'Hidden Service' in Pandemic Times."

40. Guth, "Parental Leave Data of America's Research Universities"; Zahneis, "What Higher Ed's Paid Parental-Leave Policies Look Like."

41. FMLA provides up to 12 workweeks of unpaid, job-protected leave for specified family and medical reasons. See National Partnership for Women and Families, "Key Facts."

42. Center on Early Childhood, "Overdue: A New Child Care System That Supports Children, Families, and Providers."

43. Winston, "'My Body Is a Clock,'" para. 9.

44. Winston, para. 9.

45. Okoro et al., "Prevalence of Disabilities and Health Care Access by Disability Status and Type Among Adults—United States, 2016."

46. Humphreys et al., "'To Prove I'm Not Incapable, I Overcompensate': Disability, Ideal Workers, the Academy," 14.

47. Andrzejewski, "Academics Don't Talk About Our Mental Illnesses. We Should," para. 3.

48. Evans et al., *Disability in Higher Education*, 208.

49. Olkin, "Academic Leaders with Disabilities: How Do We Know If We Are Winning When No One Is Keeping Score?" 203.

50. Evans et al., *Disability in Higher Education*.

51. Stewart and Collins, "Constructing Disability: Case Studies of Graduate Students and New Professionals with Disabilities in Student Affairs."

52. Bloch, *Passion and Paranoia*, 2.

53. Bloch, 2.

54. Stewart, "Hard Grief for Hard Love: Writing Through Doctoral Studies and the Loss of My Mother," 32.

55. Shelton and Sieben, *Narratives of Hope and Grief in Higher Education*, 2.

56. Gilbert et al., "The C.A.R.E. Model of Employee Bereavement Support."

57. Mallick, "It's Time to Rethink Corporate Bereavement Policies."

58. Vickers, "A Guide to Grief in Public Administration."

59. Laloux, *Reinventing Organizations*, 28.

60. Laloux, 143.

61. Laloux, 143.

62. Laloux, 4.

63. Laloux, 45.

64. B. M. Williams, "It's Just My Face."

65. Perez, "Problematizing Socialization in Student Affairs Graduate Training," 110.

66. Perez, "Problematizing Socialization," 111.

67. Perez, 111.

68. Detert, "Quiet Quitting and the Great Resignation Have a Common Cause—Dissatisfied Workers Feel They Can't Speak Up in the Workplace."

69. Edmondson, *The Fearless Organization.*

70. Edmondson, xvi.

71. National Partnership for Women and Families, "Key Facts."

72. Fuesting and Schmidt, "Benefits in Higher Education Annual Report: Key Findings and Comprehensive Tables on Healthcare, Wellness, Paid Time Off, Tuition, and Retirement Benefits for the 2020–21 Academic Year."

73. UNICEF, "Family-Friendly Policies: Redesigning the Workplace of the Future."

74. Reichlin Cruse et al., "Evaluating the Role of Campus Child Care in Student Parent Success: Challenges and Opportunities for Rigorous Study."

75. Option B, "Be an Agent for Change: An HR Leader's Guide to Expanding Bereavement and Compassionate Leave," 5.

76. Option B, "Be an Agent for Change," 6.

77. US Office of Personnel Management, "Federal Employee Assistance Programs," para. 1.

78. Brooks and Ling, "'Are We Doing Enough': An Evaluation of the Utilization of Employee Assistance Programs to Support the Mental Health Needs of Employees During the COVID-19 Pandemic."

79. Centre for Excellence in Universal Design, "About Universal Design," para. 1.

80. Hicks, "The Dignity-Centered Organization."

81. Warzel and Petersen, *Out of Office: The Problem and Bigger Promise of Working from Home*, 63.

82. Warzel and Petersen, *Out of Office*, 63.

83. Evans et al., *Disability in Higher Education.*

84. Evans et al.

85. PricewaterhouseCoopers, "Productivity Has Risen with Remote/Hybrid Working, but Worker Trust May Pose a Larger Challenge"; Yoe, "Hybrid Work Seems to Be Working Out Just Fine"; Wigert and White, "The Advantages and Challenges of Hybrid Work."

86. McClure, "The Future of Work Is Flexible. Will Higher Ed Stay Stuck in the Past?"

87. Rutgers University defines a compressed workweek as a schedule that allows an employee to maintain a full-time schedule, but work hours are performed over less than five days per week or ten days per pay period. Flex workday refers to a work schedule

that provides for nonwork periods in a workday and extends the amount of the workday while working the same number of hours in the day—for example, a schedule of work time from 9:00 a.m. to 12:00 pm, with a three-hour nonwork period, followed by work time from 3:00 p.m. to 7:30 p.m. Hybrid is a work arrangement where an employee is both regularly scheduled to work at an assigned university work location for a minimum number of days during a workweek and at an alternate work location for the remaining scheduled workdays in a workweek.

88. Brown, "Why We'll Never Be the Same Again (and Why It's Time to Talk About It)."

89. Warzel and Petersen, *Out of Office: The Problem and Bigger Promise of Working from Home.*

90. Warzel and Petersen, *Out of Office*, 45.

91. Warzel and Petersen, 52.

92. Warzel and Petersen, 45.

93. Gaston Gayles, "Humanizing Higher Education: A Path Forward in Uncertain Times," 554.

94. Gaston Gayles, 555.

Chapter 4. Committing to Professional Growth and Fair Compensation

1. University of Louisville, "Compensation and Total Rewards Study—Human Resources."

2. Yetter, "U of L Scandals Under James Ramsey: A Timeline."

3. University of Louisville, "Strategic Plan 2019–2022."

4. "U of L Compensation Study Thread Discussion."

5. Campus Pride, "Campus Pride Index—University of Louisville."

6. Finkelstein, Conley, and Schuster, *The Faculty Factor: Reassessing the American Academy in a Turbulent Era.*

7. Kezar, DePaola, and Scott, *The Gig Academy.*

8. Hawes and Reynolds, "Radical Retention: How Higher Education Can Rise to the Challenges of the Great Resignation and Beyond."

9. Collins-Brown, Cruz, and Torosyan, "The 2016 POD Network Membership Survey: Past, Present, and Future."

10. Wright, *Centers for Teaching and Learning: The New Landscape in Higher Education.*

11. Azubuike et al., "COACHE Summary Tables 2019: Selected Dimensions of the Faculty Workplace Experience."

12. NASPA: Student Affairs Administrators in Higher Education, "The Compass Report: Charting the Future of Student Affairs."

13. National Education Association, "NEA Education Support Professional Earnings Report."

14. Kezar, DePaola, and Scott, *The Gig Academy*; Donadel, "Strikes and Unions."

15. College and University Professional Association for Human Resources, "Simple Metrics."

16. College and University Professional Association for Human Resources, "4 Considerations for Using Salary Data to Inform Compensation Decisions on Campus."

17. American Association of University Professors, "Background Facts on Contingent Faculty Positions."

18. American Federation of Teachers, *An Army of Temps: AFT 2020 Adjunct Faculty Quality of Work/Life Report.*

19. Kezar, DePaola, and Scott, *The Gig Academy.*

20. Colby, "Part-Time Faculty Benefits."

21. Kezar, DePaola, and Scott, *The Gig Academy*, 46.

22. College and University Professional Association for Human Resources, "Workforce Pay Increases."

23. Finkelstein, Conley, and Schuster, *The Faculty Factor: Reassessing the American Academy in a Turbulent Era*, 327.

24. American Association of University Professors, "The Annual Report on the Economic Status of the Profession, 2021–22."

25. Coca et al., "Basic Needs Insecurity in the Higher Education Instructional Workforce."

26. Graduate Assistants United at the University of Florida, "UF Graduate Assistant Stipend Survey Report."

27. O'Meara, "Half-Way Out," 292.

28. Terpstra and Honoree, "Faculty Perceptions of Problems with Merit Pay Plans in Institutions of Higher Education."

29. HigherEdJobs, "2019–20 CUPA-HR Salary Data."

30. Finkelstein, Conley, and Schuster, *The Faculty Factor*, 328.

31. Finkelstein, Conley, and Schuster.

32. Bichsel and McChesney, "The Gender Pay Gap and the Representation of Women in Higher Education Administrative Positions."

33. Fuesting, "Higher Ed Administrators: Trends in Diversity and Pay Equity from 2002 to 2022."

34. Colby and Fowler, "Data Snapshot: IPEDS Data on Full-Time Women Faculty and Faculty of Color."

35. Clery, "Higher Education Faculty Salary Analysis: 2021–22."

36. Li and Koedel, "Representation and Salary Gaps by Race-Ethnicity and Gender at Selective Public Universities."

37. Bichsel and McChesney, "The Gender Pay Gap and the Representation of Women."

38. Finkelstein, Conley, and Schuster, *The Faculty Factor.*

39. Kezar, DePaola, and Scott, *The Gig Academy*, 40.

40. Kezar, DePaola, and Scott.

41. Bauman, "A Pandemic-Era Cut with a Hidden Price Tag."

42. Robbins, "Why Employees Need Both Recognition and Appreciation."

43. College and University Professional Association for Human Resources, "The Top Predictor of Higher Ed Employee Retention May Surprise You."

44. Kegan and Laskow Lahey, *An Everyone Culture: Becoming a Deliberately Developmental Organization*, 87.

45. Kegan and Laskow Lahey, *An Everyone Culture*, 88.

46. Kegan and Laskow Lahey, 96.

47. Schwartz, "Create a Growth Culture, Not a Performance-Obsessed One," para. 1.

48. Schwartz, para. 3.

49. Gonzalez, "Using the Right Rewards Program to Help Your Talent Management Program Fuel Transformation."

50. Chapman and White, *The 5 Languages of Appreciation in the Workplace: Empowering Organizations by Encouraging People.*

51. Robbins, "Why Employees Need Both Recognition and Appreciation," para. 5.

52. Chapman and White, *The 5 Languages of Appreciation in the Workplace.*

53. Wright, *Centers for Teaching and Learning: The New Landscape in Higher Education.*

54. POD Network and American Council on Education, "A Center for Teaching and Learning Matrix."

55. Collins-Brown, Cruz, and Torosyan, "The 2016 POD Network Membership Survey: Past, Present, and Future."

56. Wright, *Centers for Teaching and Learning.*

57. Gonzalez, "Using the Right Rewards Program."

58. McFeely and Wigert, "This Fixable Problem Costs US Businesses $1 Trillion."

59. Terpstra and Honoree, "Faculty Perceptions of Problems with Merit Pay Plans."

60. Corrigan, "LinkedIn's First CHRO," para. 5.

Chapter 5. Pursuing Cultural and Structural Change for Equity and Belonging

1. U.S. Citizenship and Immigration Services, "Frequently Asked Questions: What Is Deferred Action for Childhood Arrivals?"

2. I use the term "minoritized" instead of "minority" in this chapter as a way of acknowledging that underrepresentation is socially constructed. According to higher education scholar Shaun Harper, "Persons are not born into a minority status, nor are they minoritized in every social context (e.g., their families, racially homogenous friendship groups, or places of worship). Instead, they are rendered minorities in particular situations and institutional environments that sustain an overrepresentation of whiteness" (Harper, "Race Without Racism: How Higher Education Researchers Minimize Racist Institutional Norms," p. 9).

3. Yale University, "STARS."

4. I refer to a collection of narratives, stories, and firsthand accounts several times throughout the chapter. Rather than cite them each time, I am listing here the sources that I consulted containing these narratives. This is not an exhaustive list, and not all stories are collected in memoirs or edited volumes. Reyes, *Academic Outsider*; Minthorn, Nelson, and Shotton, *Indigenous Motherhood in the Academy*; Beemyn, *Trans People in Higher Education*; Gutierrez y Muhs et al., *Presumed Incompetent: The Intersection of Race and Class for Women in Academia*; Phelps-Ward and Kim, *The*

Power of Names in Identity and Oppression; Bonner et al., *Black Faculty in the Academy*; Vance and Harrison, *Disabled Faculty and Staff: Intersecting Identities in Higher Education*; Ardoin and Martinez, *Straddling Class in the Academy.*

5. Kezar et al., *Shared Equity Leadership: Making Equity Everyone's Work*; González Stokas, *Reparative Universities: Why Diversity Alone Won't Solve Racism in Higher Education*; Griffin, "Institutional Barriers, Strategies, and Benefits to Increasing the Representation of Women and Men of Color in the Professoriate."

6. Turner, González, and Wood, "Faculty of Color in Academe"; Griffin, "Institutional Barriers, Strategies, and Benefits"; Zambrana, *Toxic Ivory Towers: The Consequences of Work Stress on Underrepresented Minority Faculty.*

7. According to sociologists Eduardo Bonilla-Silva and Crystal E. Peoples, "Most colleges in the United States are HWCUs (historically white colleges and universities) with a history, demography, curriculum, climate, and a set of symbols and traditions that embody and reproduce whiteness and white supremacy. This organizational reality explains why 'isolated' racist incidents happen again and again in institutions that claim to be race neutral" (Bonilla-Silva and Peoples, "Historically White Colleges and Universities: The Unbearable Whiteness of (Most) Colleges and Universities in America," p. 1491).

8. McGhee, *The Sum of Us: What Racism Costs Everyone and How We Can Prosper Together.*

9. National Museum of African American History and Culture, "Social Identities and Systems of Oppression."

10. National Equity Project, "Lens of Systemic Oppression."

11. Crenshaw, *On Intersectionality: Essential Writings*; Hill Collins and Bilge, *Intersectionality*; Center for Intersectional Justice, "What Is Intersectionality."

12. Betts, "Living in the Margins of the Academy," 57.

13. Padilla, "Ethnic Minority Scholars, Research, and Mentoring."

14. Reyes, *Academic Outsider*, 10.

15. Reyes, 42.

16. Reyes, 41.

17. Reyes, 104.

18. Reyes, 104.

19. Ahmed, *On Being Included: Racism and Diversity in Institutional Life*, 25.

20. Ahmed, *On Being Included*, 28.

21. Ahmed, 52.

22. Ahmed, 71.

23. González Stokas, *Reparative Universities: Why Diversity Alone Won't Solve Racism in Higher Education*, 28.

24. González Stokas, *Reparative Universities*, 28.

25. Foste and Tevis, "Critical Whiteness Praxis in Higher Education," 6.

26. Ozias and Pasque, "Toward Definitions of Whiteness and Critical Whiteness Studies," 24.

27. Ray, "A Theory of Racialized Organizations."

28. Nyunt, Pridgen, and Thomas, "Disrupting Student Affairs Staff Departure."

29. ACPA Presidential Task Force, *Report on 21st Century Employment in Higher Education*, 9.

30. Liera and Desir, "Taking Equity-Mindedness to the Next Level: The Equity-Minded Organization," 2.

31. Liera and Desir, "Taking Equity-Mindedness to the Next Level," 2.

32. Liera and Desir, 3.

33. Liera, "Lead the Change Series Q&A with Román Liera."

34. Griffin, "Institutional Barriers, Strategies, and Benefits," 313.

35. Gasman and Perdomo, "Achieving Equity: A Toolkit for Racially Inclusive Faculty Hiring."

36. Liera and Hernandez, "Color-Evasive Racism in the Final Stage of Faculty Searches."

37. Hall, "Centering Joy and Community for the Wellbeing of Black Faculty," 76.

38. Okello, "Epistemic Asphyxiation," 116.

39. Okello, 121.

40. O'Meara and Templeton, *Equity-Minded Reform of Faculty Evaluation: A Call to Action.*

41. O'Meara and Templeton, 6.

42. O'Meara et al., *Translating Equity-Minded Principles into Faculty Evaluation Reform.*

43. O'Meara et al., *Translating Equity-Minded Principles*, 14.

44. Quaye et al., " "Why Can't I Just Chill?"

45. B. M. Williams, "For Colored Girls Fighting to Survive When a Presidential Title Isn't Enough."

46. B. M. Williams, "For Colored Girls Fighting to Survive," para. 10.

47. González Stokas, *Reparative Universities*, 104.

48. González Stokas, 107.

49. González Stokas, 125.

50. González Stokas, 125.

51. González Stokas, 210.

52. González Stokas, 106.

53. González Stokas, 204.

54. Kezar, "Higher Education DEI Efforts Are in Trouble. Here's How We Change That," para. 5.

55. Kezar et al., *Shared Equity Leadership*, vii.

56. Kezar et al., "Culture Change Requires Personal and Organizational Changes," 40.

57. Kezar et al., *Shared Equity Leadership*, 6.

58. Kezar et al., 3.

59. Fulton, "Everyone's Work."

60. Holcombe et al., *Organizing Shared Equity Leadership: Four Approaches to Structuring the Work*, 16.

61. Fulton, "Everyone's Work," para. 9.

Chapter 6. Empowering Employees' Rights and Voice

1. Okai, Aguilar, and Schottel, "The Development of the UIC Neighborhood"; Loerzel, "Displaced."

2. Open House Chicago, "UIC University Hall."

3. AFL-CIO, "Collective Bargaining."

4. Milkman and van der Naald, "The State of the Unions 2023: A Profile of Organized Labor in New York City, New York State, and the United States."

5. Wallender, "Starbucks, Education Strikes Fuel 17-Year High in Work Stoppages."

6. Petit, "The New Tenured Radicals."

7. Dettro, "Furloughs, Hiring Freeze in Store for All U of I Campuses."

8. Jaschik, "Court Rejects Faculty Union."

9. Rutgers School of Management and Labor Relations, "Examples of Bargaining for the Common Good Demands."

10. State University of New York, "Campus Governance Leaders Toolkit: What Is Shared Governance?"

11. UICUF, "UIC United Faculty Commitments."

12. Root Cause, "Collective Action Framework."

13. Eckel, "The Role of Shared Governance in Institutional Hard Decisions."

14. Rosenberg, *"Whatever It Is, I'm Against It": Resistance to Change in Higher Education*, 99.

15. Rosenberg, *"Whatever It Is, I'm Against It,"* 99.

16. Kezar, DePaola, and Scott, *The Gig Academy*; Finkelstein, Conley, and Schuster, *The Faculty Factor: Reassessing the American Academy in a Turbulent Era*; Berube et al., "COVID-19 and Academic Governance."

17. Kezar, DePaola, and Scott, *The Gig Academy*, 86.

18. Finkelstein, Conley, and Schuster, *The Faculty Factor*, 11.

19. Tiede, "Survey Data on the Impact of the Pandemic on Shared Governance," para. 11.

20. Deemer and Horvath, "Shared Governance—From Both Sides of the Fence."

21. Inside Higher Ed, "Responding to the COVID-19 Crisis: A Survey of College and University Presidents."

22. Sheffer et al., "Pieces of the Puzzle," para. 1.

23. Berube et al., "COVID-19 and Academic Governance," 2.

24. Zahneis, "Shared Governance Was Eroding Before Covid-19. Now It's a Landslide, AAUP Report Says," para. 12.

25. American Association of University Professors, "Financial Exigency, Academic Governance, and Related Matters," para. 13.

26. American Association of University Professors, "Financial Exigency," para. 5.

27. Sheffer et al., "Pieces of the Puzzle."

28. Kezar, DePaola, and Scott, *The Gig Academy*, 13.

29. Kezar, DePaola, and Scott, 14.

30. Kunkle and Laderman, "State Higher Education Finance: FY 2022."

31. Slaughter and Rhoades, *Academic Capitalism and the New Economy: Markets, State, and Higher Education.*

32. Hamilton and Nielsen, *Broke: The Racial Consequences of Underfunding Public Universities.*

33. R. A. Scott, "Leadership Threats to Shared Governance in Higher Education," 2.

34. R. A. Scott, "Leadership Threats to Shared Governance," 3.

35. R. A. Scott, 4.

36. R. A. Scott, 4.

37. American Association of University Professors, "Data Snapshot."

38. Kezar, DePaola, and Scott, *The Gig Academy*, 15.

39. Kezar, DePaola, and Scott, 20.

40. Kezar, DePaola, and Scott, 20.

41. Kezar, DePaola, and Scott, 21.

42. Kezar, DePaola, and Scott, 86.

43. AAUP, "FAQs on Academic Freedom."

44. J. W. Scott, *Knowledge, Power, and Academic Freedom.*

45. Bauer-Wolf, "Anti-Tenure Bills Stall in State Legislatures."

46. Taylor, *Wrecked: Deinstitutionalization and Partial Defenses in State Higher Education Policy*, 13.

47. Taylor, *Wrecked*, 18.

48. Herbert, "A New Morning in Higher Education Collective Bargaining, 2013–2019," 114.

49. Eidlin and Uetricht, "The Problem of Workplace Democracy," 70.

50. Eidlin and Uetricht, 70.

51. Herbert, "A New Morning in Higher Education Collective Bargaining, 2013–2019," 115.

52. Center for Learning in Action, "What Is Workplace Democracy?" para. 1.

53. Kezar, DePaola, and Scott, *The Gig Academy.*

54. Frega, "Employee Involvement and Workplace Democracy."

55. Center for Learning in Action, "What Is Workplace Democracy?"

56. Kezar, DePaola, and Scott, *The Gig Academy*, 152.

57. National Labor Relations Board, "Election Petitions Up 53%, Board Continues to Reduce Case Processing Time in FY22"; Economic Policy Institute, "Unionization Increased by 200,000 in 2022."

58. #DemocratizingWork, "Work: Democratize, Decommodify, Remediate." A global initiative, #DemocratizingWork lists signees and organizational endorsements on its website.

59. Kezar, DePaola, and Scott, *The Gig Academy*, 152.

60. Higher Education Labor United, "About."

61. Higher Education Labor United, "Vision Platform," 2.

62. American Association of University Professors, "Contingent Appointments and the Academic Profession."

63. Kezar, DePaola, and Scott, *The Gig Academy*, 23.

64. Kezar, Maxey, and Eaton, "An Examination of the Changing Faculty."

65. Kezar, DePaola, and Scott, *The Gig Academy.*

66. Kezar, Maxey, and Eaton, "An Examination of the Changing Faculty," 9.

67. Marcus, "Canada Treats Adjunct Faculty Better than the US—and It Pays Off."

68. Harper and Kezar, "Institutionalizing a Culture of Respect for Teaching and Professional Faculty at the University of Denver."

69. Deemer and Horvath, "Shared Governance—From Both Sides of the Fence."

70. Deemer and Horvath, "Shared Governance," 23.

71. Deemer and Horvath, 25.

72. Deemer and Horvath, 26.

73. Deemer and Horvath, 30.

74. Deemer and Horvath, 30.

75. Deemer and Horvath, 31.

76. Deemer and Horvath, 35.

77. Anderson, "Boston College Grad Student Workers to Rally for Rights, Protections."

78. Thys, "Northeastern Faculty Members Withdraw Union Petition."

79. Bowman, "Temple University Cuts Tuition and Health Benefits for Striking Graduate Students."

80. Alvarez, "Stonewalled, Disrespected, and Dismissed," para. 2.

81. Howard Community College, "Howard Community College Congratulates Prospective Partner American Federation of Teachers," para. 2.

82. Kinservik, "Case Study: University of Delaware," 231.

83. Kinservik, 232.

84. Kim, "David Leonhardt's New Book, a Call to Celebrate Every University Employee," para. 10.

85. Taylor, *Wrecked*, 16.

Chapter 7. Cultivating and Sustaining Caring Leaders

1. Cherkowski et al., "Conceptualising Leadership and Emotions in Higher Education: Wellbeing as Wholeness," 166.

2. McClure, "Why We Should Care About College Leaders' Morale, Too."

3. Lehfeldt, "The Endless Churn of Administrators Leaves Faculty Feeling Dizzy."

4. McLean, "Why Are HBCU Presidential Departures Surging?"; Pollard and Lorin, "Crush of College Leaders Retiring at Once Spurs Search Challenge"; Lemons, "Another Wave of Presidential Departures?"

5. Kline, "Survey Results: Short Tenure for Higher Ed's Top Leaders."

6. Melidona et al., *The American College President Study: 2023 Edition.*

7. Fukui, Wu, and Salyers, "Impact of Supervisory Support on Turnover Intention"; Hussain et al., "Examining the Impact of Abusive Supervision on Employees' Psychological Wellbeing and Turnover Intention"; Wolor et al., "Impact of Toxic Leadership on Employee Performance."

8. Montgomery, *Lessons from Plants*, 146.

9. Bichsel et al., "The CUPA-HR 2023 Higher Education Employee Retention Survey."

10. Kington, "Presidents Don't Talk About Their Panic Attacks," para. 3.

11. Kington, para. 5.

12. Melidona et al., *The American College President Study.*

13. Gallos, "The Dean's Squeeze," 174.

14. Gallos, "Learning from the Toxic Trenches," 4.

15. Bresciani Ludvik, "Learning About Consequences, Community, Creativity and Courage," 156.

16. Favero, "Disciplinary Variation in Preparation for the Academic Dean Role"; McDade, *Leadership in Higher Education*; Dill, "The Deanship: An Unstable Craft"; Wolverton et al., "Stress in Academic Leadership: US and Australian Department Chairs/Heads."

17. Montgomery, "Academic Leadership: Gatekeeping or Groundskeeping?" 3.

18. Fitzpatrick, *Generous Thinking: A Radical Approach to Saving the University*, 40.

19. Fitzpatrick, *Generous Thinking*, 41.

20. Burmicky et al., *Equity-Minded Principles for Presidential Searches in Higher Education.*

21. Gallos, "Learning from the Toxic Trenches."

22. Bresciani Ludvik, "Learning About Consequences, Community, Creativity and Courage"; Kanov et al., "Compassion in Organizational Life."

23. Waddington, "Introduction: Why Compassion? Why Now?" 13; Belak and Waddington, "What Constitutes a Compassionate University?" 171.

24. Center for Creative Leadership, "Moving Towards (Better) Leadership: Resources for Leading with Compassion, Wellbeing and Belonging," 7.

25. Center for Creative Leadership, "Moving Towards (Better) Leadership."

26. Belak and Waddington, "What Constitutes a Compassionate University?" 173.

27. Fitzpatrick, *Generous Thinking*, 34.

28. Fitzpatrick, 41.

29. Leary, "The Psychology of Intellectual Humility."

30. Owens and Hekman, "How Does Leader Humility Influence Team Performance?" 1089.

31. Brown, *Daring Greatly: How the Courage to Be Vulnerable Transforms the Way We Live, Love, Parent, and Lead*, 35.

32. Brown, *Daring Greatly*, 34.

33. Brown, 45.

34. McClure, "College Leaders Make Mistakes. Here's Why They Should Apologize for Them."

35. Grain, *Critical Hope: How to Grapple with Complexity, Lead with Purpose, and Cultivate Transformative Social Change*, 21.

36. Grain, *Critical Hope*, 22.

37. Bresciani Ludvik, "Learning about Consequences, Community, Creativity and Courage," 61.

38. McClure, "College Leaders Make Mistakes."

39. Bensimon, Dowd, and Witham, "Five Principles for Enacting Equity by Design."

40. McNair, Bensimon, and Malcom-Piqueux, *From Equity Talk to Equity Walk: Expanding Practitioner Knowledge for Racial Justice in Higher Education*, 20.

41. Montgomery, "Academic Leadership," 4.

42. Noddings, *Caring: A Relational Approach to Ethics and Moral Education, Updated.*

43. Figley and Roop, *Compassion Fatigue in the Animal-Care Community.*

44. Grain, *Critical Hope*, 21.

45. Kanov et al., "Compassion in Organizational Life."

46. Sallee, *Creating Sustainable Careers in Student Affairs: What Ideal Worker Norms Get Wrong and How to Make It Right.*

47. Bresciani Ludvik, "Learning About Consequences, Community, Creativity and Courage," 157.

48. Rogelberg, *The Surprising Science of Meetings: How You Can Lead Your Team to Peak Performance.*

49. Wolcott, "No Standing Meetings on Fridays," para. 1.

50. Wolcott, para. 7.

51. Cantwell, "The Left's Contradictory Goals for Higher Ed," para. 25.

52. Lehfeldt, "Stop Calling It the Dark Side," para. 4.

53. Lehfeldt, para. 10.

54. Ibarra, Carter, and Silva, "Why Men Still Get More Promotions than Women."

55. Burmicky, "Advancing Presidential Careers," 3.

56. Council of Independent Colleges, "Presidential Renewal Program," para. 4.

57. Justice, "How to Improve the Administrator-Review Process," para. 5.

58. Kelderman, "Who Wants to Be a College President?"

59. Drezner, "You Could Not Pay Me Enough to Be a College President."

Conclusion. First-Step Pathways to Change

1. Kezar, *How Colleges Change*, 85.

2. Klinenberg, *2020: One City, Seven People, and the Year Everything Changed.*

3. Klinenberg, "We Were Wrong About What Happened to America in 2020," para. 14.

4. Zemsky, *Checklist for Change: Making Higher Education a Sustainable Enterprise*; Rosenberg, "*Whatever It Is, I'm Against It.*"

5. Meyerson, "The Tempered Radicals," 16.

6. Meyerson, 16.

REFERENCES

Acker, Joan. “Hierarchies, Jobs, Bodies: A Theory of Gendered Organizations.” *Gender & Society* 4, no. 2 (June 1990): 139–58. https://doi.org/10.1177/089124390004002002.

Acker, Joan. “Inequality Regimes: Gender, Class, and Race in Organizations.” *Gender & Society* 20, no. 4 (August 2006): 441–64. https://doi.org/10.1177/0891243206289499.

ACPA Presidential Task Force. *Report on 21st Century Employment in Higher Education.* Washington, DC: ACPA, College Student Educators International, 2022.

Adams, Sharika D., Sherry Hazelwood, and Bruce Hayden. “Student Affairs Case Management: Merging Social Work Theory with Student Affairs Practice.” *Journal of Student Affairs Research and Practice* 51, no. 4 (2014): 446–58.

AFL-CIO. “Collective Bargaining.” Accessed December 9, 2023. https://aflcio.org/what-unions-do/empower-workers/collective-bargaining.

Afrahi, Bahare, John Blenkinsopp, Juan Carlos Fernandez de Arroyabe, and Mohammed Shamsul Karim. “Work Disengagement: A Review of the Literature.” *Human Resource Management Review* 32, no. 2 (June 2022): 100822. https://doi.org/10.1016/j.hrmr.2021.100822.

Ahmed, Sara. *On Being Included: Racism and Diversity in Institutional Life.* Durham, NC: Duke University Press, 2012. https://www.dukeupress.edu/on-being-included.

Alvarez, Maximillian. “Stonewalled, Disrespected, and Dismissed: At Many Universities, Organized Labor Is Treated with Contempt.” *The Chronicle of Higher Education*, March 17, 2023. https://www.chronicle.com/article/stonewalled-disrespected-and-dismissed.

Amarillo College. “Culture of Caring Poverty Summit Handbook,” 2019. https://www.actx.edu/president/filecabinet/222.

American Association of University Professors. “The Annual Report on the Economic Status of the Profession, 2021–22.” Washington, DC: AAUP, June 21, 2022. https://www.aaup.org/report/annual-report-economic-status-profession-2021-22.

American Association of University Professors. “Background Facts on Contingent Faculty Positions,” July 14, 2006. https://www.aaup.org/issues/contingency/background-facts.

American Association of University Professors. “Contingent Appointments and the Academic Profession.” American Association of University Professors, 2003. https://www.aaup.org/report/contingent-appointments-and-academic-profession.

American Association of University Professors. “Data Snapshot: Tenure and Contingency in US Higher Education,” March 16, 2023. https://www.aaup.org/article/data-snapshot-tenure-and-contingency-us-higher-education.

American Association of University Professors. "FAQs on Academic Freedom," June 15, 2023. https://www.aaup.org/programs/academic-freedom/faqs-academic-freedom.
American Association of University Professors. "Financial Exigency, Academic Governance, and Related Matters," April 28, 2004. https://www.aaup.org/report/financial-exigency-academic-governance-and-related-matters.
American Federation of Teachers. *An Army of Temps: AFT 2020 Adjunct Faculty Quality of Work/Life Report.* Washington, DC: American Federation of Teachers, 2020.
Anderson, Karen. "Boston College Grad Student Workers to Rally for Rights, Protections." WCVB, March 10, 2020. https://www.wcvb.com/article/boston-college-graduate-student-workers-to-rally-for-rights-protections-threatening-strike/31301055.
Andrzejewski, Alicia. "Academics Don't Talk About Our Mental Illnesses. We Should." *The Chronicle of Higher Education*, July 5, 2023. https://www.chronicle.com/article/academics-dont-talk-about-our-mental-illnesses-we-should.
Anft, Michael. "The Staffing Crisis in Higher Ed: College Administrators' Views on Campus Employment." Research Brief. *The Chronicle of Higher Education*, 2022. https://connect.chronicle.com/rs/931-EKA-218/images/RoadAhead_Huron_ResearchBrief.pdf.
Apple, Inc. "Careers at Apple: Read Our People's Shared Values Stories." Accessed August 14, 2023. https://www.apple.com/careers/us/shared-values.html.
Ardoin, Sonja. "The Classed Construct of Student Affairs Work." In *Creating Sustainable Careers in Student Affairs: What Ideal Worker Norms Get Wrong and How to Make It Right*, edited by Margaret W. Sallee, 218–38. Sterling, VA: Stylus, 2021.
Ardoin, Sonja, and becky martinez, eds. *Straddling Class in the Academy: 26 Stories of Students, Administrators, and Faculty from Poor and Working-Class Backgrounds and Their Compelling Lessons for Higher Education Policy and Practice.* Sterling, VA: Stylus, 2019.
Arenofsky, Janice. *Work-Life Balance.* Santa Barbara, CA: Greenwood, 2017.
Aspen Institute. "Aspen Prize for Community College Excellence." The Aspen Institute College Excellence Program, April 17, 2023. https://highered.aspeninstitute.org/aspen-prize/.
Association of Community College Trustees. "Part 2: Meet Maria, Amarillo College's Most Promising Student." *In the Know with ACCT*, January 14, 2020. https://intheknowwithacct.podbean.com/e/part-2-meet-maria-amarillo-colleges-most-promising-student/.
Association on Higher Education and Disability. "AHEAD Statement on Language," 2019. https://www.ahead.org/professional-resources/accommodations/statement-on-language.
Azubuike, N. O., R. T. Benson, A. Kumar, and Mathews, K. "COACHE Summary Tables 2019: Selected Dimensions of the Faculty Workplace Experience," 2019. https://coache.gse.harvard.edu/publications/coache-summary-tables-2019-selected-dimensions-faculty-workplace-experience.
Bastedo, Michael N. "Organizing Higher Education: A Manifesto." In *The Organization of Higher Education: Managing Colleges for a New Era*, edited by Michael N. Bastedo,

3–17. Baltimore: Johns Hopkins University Press, 2012. https://doi.org/10.56021/9781421404479.

Bauer-Wolf, Jeremy. "Anti-Tenure Bills Stall in State Legislatures." *Higher Ed Dive*, June 2, 2023. https://www.highereddive.com/news/anti-tenure-bills-state-legislatures/651859/.

Bauman, Dan. "Higher Ed's Work Force Has Returned to Its Pre-Pandemic Size." *The Chronicle of Higher Education*, October 11, 2022. https://www.chronicle.com/article/higher-eds-work-force-has-returned-to-its-pre-pandemic-size.

Bauman, Dan. "A Pandemic-Era Cut with a Hidden Price Tag." *The Chronicle of Higher Education*, October 4, 2022. https://www.chronicle.com/article/a-pandemic-era-cut-with-a-hidden-price-tag.

Beemyn, Genny, ed. *Trans People in Higher Education*. Albany, NY: SUNY Press, 2019. https://sunypress.edu/Books/T/Trans-People-in-Higher-Education.

Belak, Tony, and Kathryn Waddington. "What Constitutes a Compassionate University?" In *Towards the Compassionate University*, edited by Kathryn Waddington, 170–90. New York: Routledge, 2021.

Bensimon, Estela M., Alicia C. Dowd, and Keith Witham. "Five Principles for Enacting Equity by Design." *Diversity & Democracy* 19, no. 1 (2016): 8–11.

Berger, Lance A., and Dorothy R. Berger, eds. *The Talent Management Handbook*. 3rd ed. Columbus, OH: McGraw-Hill, 2018.

Berube, Michael, Michael Decesare, Ruben J. Garcia, Pippa Holloway, Susan Jarosi, and Henry Reichman. "COVID-19 and Academic Governance." American Association of University Professors, May 24, 2021. https://www.aaup.org/report/covid-19-and-academic-governance.

Betts, Katherine H. "Living in the Margins of the Academy." In *Disabled Faculty and Staff: Intersecting Identities in Higher Education*, edited by Mary Lee Vance and Elizabeth G. Harrison, 57–62. Vol. 2. Huntersville, NC: Association on Higher Education and Disability, 2023.

Bichsel, Jacqueline, Melissa Fuesting, Jennifer Schneider, and Diana Tubbs. "The CUPA-HR 2022 Higher Education Employee Retention Survey: Initial Results." College and University Professional Association for Human Resources, July 2022. https://www.cupahr.org/surveys/research-briefs/higher-ed-employee-retention-survey-findings-july-2022/.

Bichsel, Jacqueline, Melissa Fuesting, Diana Tubbs, and Jennifer Schneider. "The CUPA-HR 2023 Higher Education Employee Retention Survey." College and University Professional Association for Human Resources, September 2023. https://www.cupahr.org/surveys/research-briefs/higher-ed-employee-retention-survey-findings-september-2023/.

Bichsel, Jacqueline, and Jasper McChesney. "The Gender Pay Gap and the Representation of Women in Higher Education Administrative Positions." College and University Professional Association for Human Resources, February 2017. https://www.cupahr.org/surveys/research-briefs/2017-gender-pay-gap-and-representation-of-women-in-higher-education-administrative-positions/.

Birnbaum, Robert. *How Colleges Work: The Cybernetics of Academic Organization and Leadership*. San Francisco: Jossey-Bass, 1988.

Birnbaum, Robert. "The Life Cycle of Academic Management Fads." *Journal of Higher Education* 71, no. 1 (2000): 1–16. https://doi.org/10.2307/2649279.

Bishundat, Devita, Daviree Velazquez Phillip, and Gore. "Cultivating Critical Hope: The Too Often Forgotten Dimension of Critical Leadership Development." *New Directions for Student Leadership* 159 (2018): 91–102.

Bloch, Charlotte. *Passion and Paranoia: Emotions and the Culture of Emotion in Academia*. New York: Routledge, 2016.

Boland, Brodie, Aaron De Smet, Rob Palter, and Aditya Sanghvi. "Reimagining the Office and Work Life After COVID-19." *McKinsey & Co* (blog), June 8, 2020. https://www.mckinsey.com/capabilities/people-and-organizational-performance/our-insights/reimagining-the-office-and-work-life-after-covid-19.

Bonilla-Silva, Eduardo, and Crystal E. Peoples. "Historically White Colleges and Universities: The Unbearable Whiteness of (Most) Colleges and Universities in America." *American Behavioral Scientist* 66, no. 11 (2022): 1490–1504. https://doi-org.liblink.uncw.edu/10.1177/00027642211066047.

Bonner, Fred A., II, Aretha Faye Marbley, Frank Tuitt, Petra A. Robinson, Rosa M. Banda, and Robin L. Hughes, eds. *Black Faculty in the Academy: Narratives for Negotiating Identity and Achieving Career Success*. New York: Routledge, 2014. https://doi.org/10.4324/9781315852164.

Bowman, Emma. "Temple University Cuts Tuition and Health Benefits for Striking Graduate Students." NPR, February 10, 2023. https://www.npr.org/2023/02/10/1155762537/temple-university-grad-strike.

Brayboy, Bryan M. J. "The Implementation of Diversity in Predominantly White Colleges and Universities." *Journal of Black Studies* 34, no. 1 (September 2003): 72–86. https://doi.org/10.1177/0021934703253679.

Breeden, Roshaunda L. "Our Presence Is Resistance: Stories of Black Women in Senior-Level Student Affairs Positions at Predominantly White Institutions." *Journal of Women and Gender in Higher Education* 14, no. 2 (May 2021): 166–86. https://doi.org/10.1080/26379112.2021.1948860.

Bresciani Ludvik, Marilee. "Learning About Consequences, Community, Creativity and Courage: Cultivating Compassion in Higher Education Leadership." In *The Pedagogy of Compassion at the Heart of Higher Education*, edited by Paul Gibbs, 155–72. Cham, Switzerland: Springer, 2017. https://doi.org/10.1007/978-3-319-57783-8_11.

Brooks, C. Darren, and Jeff Ling. "'Are We Doing Enough': An Evaluation of the Utilization of Employee Assistance Programs to Support the Mental Health Needs of Employees During the COVID-19 Pandemic." *Journal of Insurance Regulation* 39, no. 8 (2020): 1–34.

Brown, Brené. *Daring Greatly: How the Courage to Be Vulnerable Transforms the Way We Live, Love, Parent, and Lead*. New York: Gotham Books, 2012.

Brown, Brené. "Why We'll Never Be the Same Again (and Why It's Time to Talk About It)." Accessed February 6, 2024. https://brenebrown.com/podcast/why-well-never-be-the-same-again-and-why-its-time-to-talk-about-it/.

Burke, Michelle, Amelia Parnell, Alexis Wesaw, and Kevin Kruger. "Predictive Analysis of Student Data: A Focus on Engagement and Behavior." National Association of

Student Personnel Administrators, 2017. https://www.naspa.org/report/predictive-analysis-of-student-data-a-focus-on-engagement-and-behavior.

Burmicky, Jorge. "Advancing Presidential Careers: Operationalizing Sponsorship in Higher Education." *Journal of Higher Education* (January 2024): 1–31. https://doi.org/10.1080/00221546.2024.2301916.

Burmicky, Jorge, Kevin R. McClure, Jordan Gonzales, and Cameron J. McCoy. *Equity-Minded Principles for Presidential Searches in Higher Education*. Washington, DC: American Council on Education, 2023. https://www.acenet.edu/Documents/Equity-Minded-Presidential-Searches.pdf.

Bustamante, Alma. "Budget Cuts and Buyouts Save $3.6 Million in President's Plan." *The Ranger*, February 11, 2016. https://acranger.com/2016/02/11/budget-cuts-and-buyouts-save-3-6-million-in-presidents-plan/.

Campus Pride. "Campus Pride Index—University of Louisville." Tumblr. Accessed September 20, 2023. https://www.campusprideindex.org/campuses/details/492?campus=university-of-louisville%5D.

Cannon, Loren. "The Nontenured Faculty Perspective." In *Straddling Class in the Academy: 26 Stories of Students, Administrators, and Faculty from Poor and Working-Class Backgrounds and Their Compelling Lessons for Higher Education Policy and Practice*, edited by Sonja Ardoin and becky martinez, 112–28. New York: Routledge, 2019.

Cantwell, Brendan. "The Left's Contradictory Goals for Higher Ed." *The Chronicle of Higher Education*, January 24, 2024. https://www.chronicle.com/article/the-lefts-contradictory-goals-for-higher-ed.

Center for Creative Leadership. "Moving Towards (Better) Leadership: Resources for Leading with Compassion, Wellbeing and Belonging," May 2, 2023. https://www.ccl.org/articles/white-papers/towards-better-leadership-resources-for-compassion-wellbeing-belonging/#download.

Center for Intersectional Justice. "What Is Intersectionality." Accessed November 6, 2024. https://sharing4good.org/article/what-intersectionality-center-intersectional-justice.

Center for Learning in Action. "What Is Workplace Democracy?" Accessed December 12, 2023. https://learning-in-action.williams.edu/breaking-the-mold/what-is-workplace-democracy/.

Center on Early Childhood. "Overdue: A New Child Care System That Supports Children, Families, and Providers." Stanford University, December 2022. https://rapidsurveyproject.com/our-research/overdue-new-child-care-system-that-supports-children-families-providers.

Centre for Excellence in Universal Design. "About Universal Design." Accessed July 2, 2024. https://universaldesign.ie/about-universal-design.

Chapman, Gary, and Paul White. *The 5 Languages of Appreciation in the Workplace: Empowering Organizations by Encouraging People*. Woodmere, NY: Northfield Publishing, 2012.

Cherkowski, Sabre, Benjamin Kutsyuruba, Keith Walker, and Megan Crawford. "Conceptualising Leadership and Emotions in Higher Education: Wellbeing as

Wholeness." *Journal of Educational Administration and History* 53, no. 2 (2020): 158–71. https://doi.org/10.1080/00220620.2020.1828315.

Cho, Katherine S., and Lauren Brassfield. "An Afterthought: Staff of Color and Campus Wellness Within Higher Education Responses to COVID-19." *American Behavioral Scientist*, August 23, 2022. https://doi.org/10.1177/00027642221118254.

Clery, Sue. "Faculty Salaries, 2021–22." In *Collateral Damage: Effects of the Pandemic on Academe, Continued*. Washington, DC: National Education Association, 2023. https://www.nea.org/sites/default/files/2022-03/NEA%20HE%20Salary%20Report%202022_0.pdf.

Coca, Vanessa, Gregory Kienzl, Sara Goldrick-Rab, and Brianna Richardson. "Basic Needs Insecurity in the Higher Education Instructional Workforce." The Hope Center for College, Community, and Justice, November 2020. https://www.luminafoundation.org/wp-content/uploads/2020/12/basic-needs-insecurity-in-the-higher-education-instructional-workforce.pdf.

Colby, Glenn. "Part-Time Faculty Benefits." *AAUP Data* (blog), July 8, 2022. https://data.aaup.org/pt-faculty-benefits/.

Colby, Glenn, and Chelsea Fowler. "Data Snapshot: IPEDS Data on Full-Time Women Faculty and Faculty of Color." American Association of University Professors, 2020. https://www.aaup.org/sites/default/files/Dec-2020_Data_Snapshot_Women_and_Faculty_of_Color.pdf.

College and University Professional Association for Human Resources. "4 Considerations for Using Salary Data to Inform Compensation Decisions on Campus." *CUPA-HR* (blog), November 15, 2022. https://www.cupahr.org/blog/4-considerations-for-using-salary-data-to-inform-compensation-decisions-on-campus/.

College and University Professional Association for Human Resources. "Simple Metrics: How to Use Compa-Ratios to Guide Compensation Decisions." *CUPA-HR* (blog), October 23, 2023. https://www.cupahr.org/blog/simple-metrics-how-to-use-compa-ratios-to-guide-compensation-decisions/.

College and University Professional Association for Human Resource. "The Top Predictor of Higher Ed Employee Retention May Surprise You." *CUPA-HR* (blog), September 12, 2023. https://www.cupahr.org/blog/the-top-predictor-of-higher-ed-employee-retention-may-surprise-you-2023-09-12/.

College and University Professional Association for Human Resources. "Workforce Pay Increases." *CUPA-HR* (blog). Accessed October 4, 2024. https://www.cupahr.org/surveys/workforce-data/workforce-pay-increases/.

Collins-Brown, Eli, Laura Cruz, and Roben Torosyan. "The 2016 POD Network Membership Survey: Past, Present, and Future." POD Network, 2016. https://podnetwork.org/content/uploads/2016podmembershipreportprintnomarks.pdf.

Corrigan, John. "LinkedIn's First CHRO: 'Supply of Qualified Talent Isn't Going to Increase,'" June 30, 2022. https://www.hcamag.com/us/specialization/learning-development/linkedins-first-chro-supply-of-qualified-talent-isnt-going-to-increase/411439.

Council of Independent Colleges. "Presidential Renewal Program." Accessed January 28, 2024. https://cic.edu/opportunity/presidential-renewal-program/.

Crenshaw, Kimberle. *On Intersectionality: Essential Writings*. New York: New Press, 2017. https://scholarship.law.columbia.edu/books/255/.

Culpepper, Dawn, Sarah Kilmer, O'Meara KerryAnn, Misra Joya, and Audrey J. Jaeger. "The Terrapin Time Initiative: A Workshop to Enhance Alignment Between Faculty Work Priorities and Time-Use." *Innovative Higher Education* 45, no. 2 (April 2020): 165–79. https://doi.org/10.1007/s10755-019-09490-w.

Davies, Andrea Rees, and Brenda D. Frink. "The Origins of the Ideal Worker: The Separation of Work and Home in the United States from the Market Revolution to 1950." *Work and Occupations* 41, no. 1 (February 2014): 18–39. https://doi.org/10.1177/0730888413515893.

Deemer, Rob, and Virginia Horvath. "Shared Governance—From Both Sides of the Fence." In *Shared Governance in Higher Education*, vol. 2: *New Paradigms, Evolving Perspectives*, edited by Sharon F. Cramer, 21–36. Albany, NY: SUNY Press, 2017.

DeMichiel, Antonia. "A Double-Sided Coin: Tokenization as a New Professional." In *Disabled Faculty and Staff: Intersecting Identities in Higher Education*, vol. 2, edited by Mary Lee Vance and Elizabeth G. Harrison, 63–66. Huntersville, NC: Association on Higher Education and Disability, 2023.

#DemocratizingWork. "Work: Democratize, Decommodify, Remediate." Accessed December 12, 2023. https://democratizingwork.org.

DePillis, Lydia. "US Survey Shows an Uptick in Job Openings, and Not in Layoffs." *New York Times*, February 1, 2023. https://www.nytimes.com/2023/02/01/business/economy/labor-jolts-report-layoffs.html.

Detert, James. "Quiet Quitting and the Great Resignation Have a Common Cause—Dissatisfied Workers Feel They Can't Speak up in the Workplace." *The Conversation*, October 11, 2022. http://theconversation.com/quiet-quitting-and-the-great-resignation-have-a-common-cause-dissatisfied-workers-feel-they-cant-speak-up-in-the-workplace-190390.

Dettro, Chris. "Furloughs, Hiring Freeze in Store for All U of I Campuses." *The State Journal-Register*, January 4, 2010. https://www.sj-r.com/story/news/education/2010/01/05/furloughs-hiring-freeze-in-store/41757960007/.

Dill, William R. "The Deanship: An Unstable Craft." In *The Dilemma of the Deanship*, edited by D. E. Griffiths and D. J. McCarty, 261–84. Danville, IL: Interstate Printers and Publishers, 1980.

DiMaggio, Paul J., and Walter W. Powell. "The Iron Cage Revisited: Institutional Isomorphism and Collective Rationality in Organizational Fields." *American Sociological Review* 48, no. 2 (1983): 147–60. https://doi.org/10.2307/2095101.

Docka-Filipek, Danielle, Crissa Draper, Janice Snow, and Lindsey B. Stone. "'Professor Moms' and 'Hidden Service' in Pandemic Times: Students Report Women Faculty More Supportive and Accommodating amid US COVID Crisis Onset." *Innovative Higher Education*, April 24, 2023, 1–25. https://doi.org/10.1007/s10755-023-09652-x.

Donadel, Alcino. "Strikes and Unions: Graduate Students Marshal Their Forces Nationwide." *University Business* (blog), February 10, 2023. https://universitybusiness.com/strikes-and-unions-graduate-students-marshal-their-forces-nationwide/.

Drezner, Daniel W. "You Could Not Pay Me Enough to Be a College President." *The Chronicle of Higher Education*, December 14, 2023. https://www.chronicle.com/article/you-could-not-pay-me-enough-to-be-a-college-president.

Eckel, Peter D. "The Role of Shared Governance in Institutional Hard Decisions: Enabler or Antagonist?" *Review of Higher Education* 24, no. 1 (2000): 15–39.

Eckel, Peter D., and Adrianna Kezar. "Key Strategies for Making New Institutional Sense: Ingredients to Higher Education Transformation." *Higher Education Policy* 16, no. 1 (March 2003): 39–53. https://doi.org/10.1057/palgrave.hep.8300001.

Economic Policy Institute. "Unionization Increased by 200,000 in 2022: Tens of Millions More Wanted to Join a Union, but Couldn't." Accessed December 12, 2023. https://www.epi.org/press/unionization-increased-by-200000-in-2022-tens-of-millions-more-wanted-to-join-a-union-but-couldnt/.

Edmondson, Amy C. *The Fearless Organization: Creating Psychological Safety in the Workplace for Learning, Innovation, and Growth*. New York: Wiley, 2018.

Eidlin, Barry, and Micah Uetricht. "The Problem of Workplace Democracy." *New Labor Forum* 27, no. 1 (2018): 70–79.

Ellerbeck, Stefan. "The Great Resignation Is Not Over: A Fifth of Workers Plan to Quit in 2022." World Economic Forum, June 24, 2022. https://www.weforum.org/agenda/2022/06/the-great-resignation-is-not-over/.

Evans, Nancy J., Ellen M. Broido, Kirsten R. Brown, and Autumn K. Wilke. *Disability in Higher Education: A Social Justice Approach*. New York: Wiley, 2017.

Faria-e-Casto, Miguel. "The COVID Retirement Boom." Federal Reserve Bank of St. Louis, *Economic Synopses* 25 (2021). https://research.stlouisfed.org/publications/economic-synopses/2021/10/15/the-covid-retirement-boom.

Favero, Marietta. "Disciplinary Variation in Preparation for the Academic Dean Role." *Higher Education Research and Development* 25, no. 3 (August 2006): 277–92.

Figley, Charles R., and Robert G. Roop. *Compassion Fatigue in the Animal-Care Community*. Washington, DC: Humane Society Press, 2006.

Finkelstein, Martin J., Valerie Martin Conley, and Jack H. Schuster. *The Faculty Factor: Reassessing the American Academy in a Turbulent Era*. Baltimore: Johns Hopkins University Press, 2016.

Fitzpatrick, Kathleen. *Generous Thinking: A Radical Approach to Saving the University*. Baltimore: Johns Hopkins University Press, 2019.

Foste, Zak, and Tenisha L. Tevis. "On the Enormity of Whiteness in Higher Education." In *Critical Whiteness Praxis in Higher Education: Considerations for the Pursuit of Racial Justice on Campus*, 1–18. New York: Routledge, 2022.

Foster Wallace, David. *This Is Water: Some Thoughts, Delivered on a Significant Occasion, about Living a Compassionate Life*. New York: Hachette Book Group, 2017.

Frega, Roberto. "Employee Involvement and Workplace Democracy." *Business Ethics Quarterly* 31, no. 3 (July 2021): 360–85. https://doi.org/10.1017/beq.2020.30.

Fuesting, Melissa. "Higher Ed Administrators: Trends in Diversity and Pay Equity from 2002 to 2022." College and University Professional Association for Human Resources, November 2023. https://www.cupahr.org/surveys/research-briefs/higher-ed-administrators-trends-in-diversity-pay-equity-november-2023/.

Fuesting, Melissa, and Anthony Schmidt. "Benefits in Higher Education Annual Report: Key Findings and Comprehensive Tables on Healthcare, Wellness, Paid Time Off, Tuition, and Retirement Benefits for the 2020–21 Academic Year." College and University Professional Association for Human Resources, June 2021. https://eric.ed.gov/?id=ED616016.

Fujiwara, Lynn. "Racial Harm in a Predominantly White 'Liberal' University: An Institutional Autoethnography of White Fragility." In *Presumed Incompetent II: Race, Class, Power, and Resistance of Women in Academia*, edited by Yolanda Flores Niemann, Gabriella Gutierrez y Muhs, and Carmen G. Gonzalez, 107–117. Louisville, CO: Utah State University Press, 2020.

Fukui, Sadaaki, Wei Wu, and Michelle P. Salyers. "Impact of Supervisory Support on Turnover Intention: The Mediating Role of Burnout and Job Satisfaction in a Longitudinal Study." *Administration and Policy in Mental Health and Mental Health Services Research* 46, no. 4 (July 2019): 488–97. https://doi.org/10.1007/s10488-019-00927-0.

Fulton, Amy. "Everyone's Work." *Inside Higher Ed*, April 27, 2023. https://www.insidehighered.com/opinion/career-advice/diversity/2023/04/27/everyones-work.

Gagliardi, Jonathan S. *How Colleges Use Data*. Baltimore: Johns Hopkins University Press, 2022.

Gagliardi, Jonathan S., Lorelle L. Espinosa, Jonathan M. Turk, and Morgan Taylor. *American College President Study 2017*. Washington, DC: American Council on Education, 2017.

Gallos, Joan V. "The Dean's Squeeze: The Myths and Realities of Academic Leadership in the Middle." *Academy of Management Learning & Education* 1, no. 2 (December 2002): 174–84. https://doi.org/10.5465/amle.2002.8509367.

Gallos, Joan V. "Learning from the Toxic Trenches: The Winding Road to Healthier Organizations—and to Healthy Everyday Leaders." *Journal of Management Inquiry* 17, no. 4 (December 2008): 354–67. https://doi.org/10.1177/1056492608320580.

Gallup. "Employee Experience." Accessed July 2, 2024. https://www.gallup.com/workplace/242252/employee-experience.aspx.

García Peña, Lorgia. *Community as Rebellion: A Syllabus for Surviving Academe as a Woman of Color*. Chicago: Haymarket Books, 2022.

Garcia-Perez, Alexeis, Juan Gabriel Cegarra-Navarro, Denise Bedford, Margo Thomas, and Susan Wakabayashi. *Critical Capabilities and Competencies for Knowledge Organizations*. Leeds, UK: Emerald Publishing, 2019.

Gardner, Susan K. "Fitting the Mold of Graduate School: A Qualitative Study of Socialization in Doctoral Education." *Innovative Higher Education* 33, no. 2 (August 2008): 125–38. https://doi.org/10.1007/s10755-008-9068-x.

Gasman, Marybeth, and Rebecca Perdomo. "Achieving Equity: A Toolkit for Racially Inclusive Faculty Hiring." Rutgers University–New Brunswick, Samuel DeWitt Proctor Institute for Leadership, Equity, and Justice, February 2024.

Gaston Gayles, Joy. "Humanizing Higher Education: A Path Forward in Uncertain Times." *Review of Higher Education* 46, no. 4 (2023): 547–67.

Gilbert, Stephanie, Jane Mullen, E. Kevin Kelloway, Jennifer Dimoff, Michael Teed, and Taegen McPhee. "The C.A.R.E. Model of Employee Bereavement Support." *Journal*

of Occupational Health Psychology 26, no. 5 (2021): 405–20. https://doi.org/10.1037/ocp0000287.
Goldrick-Rab, Sara, and Clare Cady. "Supporting Community College Completion with a Culture of Caring: A Case Study of Amarillo College." The Hope Center for College, Community, and Justice, June 2018.
Gonzales, Leslie D., Dana Kanhai, and Kayon Hall. "Reimagining Organizational Theory for the Critical Study of Higher Education." In *Higher Education: Handbook of Theory and Research*, edited by Michael B. Paulsen, 505–59. Cham, Switzerland: Springer, 2018. https://doi.org/10.1007/978-3-319-72490-4_11.
Gonzalez, Juan Pablo. "Using the Right Rewards Program to Help Your Talent Management Program Fuel Transformation." In *The Talent Management Handbook: Making Culture a Competitive Advantage by Acquiring, Identifying, Developing, and Promoting the Best People*. 3rd ed. Columbus, OH: McGraw-Hill, 2018.
González Stokas, Ariana. *Reparative Universities: Why Diversity Alone Won't Solve Racism in Higher Education*. Baltimore: Johns Hopkins University Press, 2023.
Graduate Assistants United at the University of Florida. "UF Graduate Assistant Stipend Survey Report," Fall 2021. https://www.ufgau.org/blog/stipend-survey-results-report.
Grain, Kari. *Critical Hope: How to Grapple with Complexity, Lead with Purpose, and Cultivate Transformative Social Change*. New York: Penguin Random House, 2022.
Graves, Kei. "Typing My Way out of the Cisheteronormative Closet at a Community College." In *Trans People in Higher Education*, edited by Genny Beemyn, 69–78. Albany, NY: SUNY Press, 2019.
Greene, Jay P. "Diversity University: DEI Bloat in the Academy." Washington, DC: The Heritage Foundation, 2021. https://www.heritage.org/education/report/diversity-university-dei-bloat-the-academy.
Griffin, Kimberly A. "Institutional Barriers, Strategies, and Benefits to Increasing the Representation of Women and Men of Color in the Professoriate." In *Higher Education: Handbook of Theory and Research*, edited by Laura W. Perna, 277–349. Cham, Switzerland: Springer, 2020. https://doi.org/10.1007/978-3-030-31365-4_4.
Guth, Claire B. "Parental Leave Data of America's Research Universities." *LaborED* (blog). Accessed August 11, 2023. https://laboredlab.com/data/.
Gutierrez y Muhs, Gabriella, Yolanda Flores Niemann, Carmen G. Gonzalez, and Angela P. Harris, eds. *Presumed Incompetent: The Intersection of Race and Class for Women in Academia*. Louisville, CO: Utah State University Press, 2012.
Guzman, Karen. "Pursuing Work-Life Balance in a Post-Pandemic World." *Pursuing Work-Life Balance in a Post-Pandemic World* (blog), February 17, 2023. https://som.yale.edu/story/2023/pursuing-work-life-balance-post-pandemic-world.
Hall, Candace N. "Centering Joy and Community for the Wellbeing of Black Faculty." *Journal of Faculty Development* 37, no. 1 (January 2023): 76–79.
Hamilton, Laura T., and Kelly Nielsen. *Broke: The Racial Consequences of Underfunding Public Universities*. Chicago: University of Chicago Press, 2021.
Harper, Jordan, and Adrianna Kezar. "Institutionalizing a Culture of Respect for Teaching and Professional Faculty at the University of Denver." Delphi Project

Database. Pulias Center for Higher Education, University of Southern California, 2021.
Harper, Shaun R. "COVID-19 and the Racial Equity Implications of Reopening College and University Campuses." *American Journal of Education* 127, no. 1 (November 2020): 153–62. https://doi.org/10.1086/711095.
Harper, Shaun R. "Race Without Racism: How Higher Education Researchers Minimize Racist Institutional Norms." *The Review of Higher Education* 36, no. 1 (2012): 9–29. https://dx.doi.org/10.1353/rhe.2012.0047.
Harris, James T., Jason E. Lane, Jeffrey C. Sun, and Gail F. Baker. *Academic Leadership and Governance of Higher Education*. Sterling, VA: Stylus, 2022.
Hawes, Carrie, and Samara Reynolds. "Radical Retention: How Higher Education Can Rise to the Challenges of the Great Resignation and Beyond." *National Association of Colleges and Employers* (blog), August 1, 2022. https://www.naceweb.org/career-development/best-practices/radical-retention-how-higher-education-can-rise-to-the-challenges-of-the-great-resignation-and-beyond/.
Herbert, William A. "A New Morning in Higher Education Collective Bargaining, 2013–2019." In *Collective Bargaining in Higher Education: Best Practices for Promoting Collaboration, Equity, and Measurable Outcomes*, edited by J. D. Julius, 113–36. New York: Routledge, 2021.
Hersey, Tricia. *Rest Is Resistance: A Manifesto*. New York: Little Brown Spark, 2022.
Hicks, Donna. *Leading with Dignity: How to Create a Culture That Brings Out the Best in People*. New Haven, CT: Yale University Press, 2022.
HigherEdJobs. "2019–20 CUPA-HR Salary Data." Accessed September 20, 2023. https://www.higheredjobs.com/salary/.
Higher Education Labor United. "About." Accessed December 12, 2023. https://higheredlaborunited.org/about/.
Higher Education Labor United. "Vision Platform," September 2021. https://higheredlaborunited.org/media/2021/09/HELU-Platform.pdf.
Hill Collins, Patricia, and Sirma Bilge. *Intersectionality*. London: Polity, 2016.
Hinton, Karen E. *A Practical Guide to Strategic Planning in Higher Education*. Ann Arbor, MI: Society for College and University Planning, 2012.
Holcombe, Elizabeth, Adrianna Kezar, Jude Paul Matias Dizon, Darsella Vigil, and Natsumi Ueda. *Organizing Shared Equity Leadership: Four Approaches to Structuring the Work*. Washington, DC: American Council on Education, 2022. https://pullias.usc.edu/download/organizing-shared-equity-leadership-four-approaches-to-structuring-the-work/.
Howard Community College. "Howard Community College Congratulates Prospective Partner American Federation of Teachers." Accessed December 12, 2023. https://www.howardcc.edu/about-us/news--press/news/howard-community-college--congratulates-prospective-partner--american-federation-of-teachers-/.
Humphreys, Elizabeth, Jess Rodgers, Nicole L. Asquith, Sally A. Yaghi, Ashleigh Foulstone, Ryan Thorneycroft, and Peta S. Cook. "'To Prove I'm Not Incapable, I Overcompensate': Disability, Ideal Workers, the Academy." *Economic and Labour Relations Review* 33, no. 4 (2022): 698–714. https://doi.org/10.1177/10353046221125642.

Hussain, Kanwal, Zuhair Abbas, Saba Gulzar, Abdul Bashiru Jibril, and Altaf Hussain. "Examining the Impact of Abusive Supervision on Employees' Psychological Wellbeing and Turnover Intention: The Mediating Role of Intrinsic Motivation." *Cogent Business & Management* 7, no. 1 (January 2020). https://doi.org/10.1080/23311975.2020.1818998.

Iacurci, Greg. "Workers Still Quitting at High Rates—and Getting a Big Bump in Pay." *CNBC*, January 4, 2023. https://www.cnbc.com/2023/01/04/workers-still-quitting-at-high-rates-and-getting-a-big-bump-in-pay.html.

Ibarra, Herminia, Nancy M. Carter, and Christine Silva. "Why Men Still Get More Promotions than Women." *Harvard Business Review*, September 1, 2010. https://hbr.org/2010/09/why-men-still-get-more-promotions-than-women.

Ingram, Paul, and Yoonjin Choi. "What Does Your Company Really Stand For?" *Harvard Business Review*, November 1, 2022. https://hbr.org/2022/11/what-does-your-company-really-stand-for.

Inside Higher Ed. "Responding to the COVID-19 Crisis: A Survey of College and University Presidents." *Inside Higher Ed and Hanover Research*, March 2020. https://www.insidehighered.com/sites/default/files/media/IHE_COVID-19_SurveyofPresidents_20200327.pdf.

Jaschik, Scott. "Court Rejects Faculty Union." *Inside Higher Ed*, March 22, 2012. https://www.insidehighered.com/news/2012/03/23/appeals-court-rejects-faculty-union-u-illinois-chicago.

Johnson, Timothy. "A Personal Exploration of Involvement: A Black Male's Experience at a PWI and an HBCU." Master's Thesis, University of North Carolina Wilmington, 2016.

Justice, George. "How to Improve the Administrator-Review Process." *The Chronicle of Higher Education*, November 1, 2021. https://www.chronicle.com/article/how-to-improve-the-administrator-review-process.

Kahn, William A. "Psychological Conditions of Personal Engagement and Disengagement at Work." *Academy of Management Journal* 33, no. 4 (December 1990): 692–724. https://doi.org/10.5465/256287.

Kanov, Jason M., Sally Maitlis, Monica C. Worline, Jane E. Dutton, Peter J. Frost, and Jacoba M. Lilius. "Compassion in Organizational Life." *American Behavioral Scientist* 47, no. 6 (February 2004): 808–27. https://doi.org/10.1177/0002764203260211.

Kaplin, William A., and Barbara A. Lee. *The Law of Higher Education, 5th Edition: Student Version*. New York: Wiley, 2014.

Kegan, Robert, and Lisa Laskow Lahey. *An Everyone Culture: Becoming a Deliberately Developmental Organization*. Cambridge, MA: Harvard Business Review, 2016.

Kelderman, Eric. "Who Wants to Be a College President?" *The Chronicle of Higher Education*, January 3, 2022. https://www.chronicle.com/article/who-wants-to-be-a-college-president.

Kendrick, Kaetrena Davis. "The Low Morale Experience of Academic Librarians: A Phenomenological Study." *Journal of Library Administration* 57, no. 8 (November 2017): 846–78. https://doi.org/10.1080/01930826.2017.1368325.

Kezar, Adrianna. "Higher Education DEI Efforts Are in Trouble. Here's How We Change That." *Diverse Issues in Higher Education*, March 14, 2023. https://www.diverseeducation.com/opinion/article/15352470/higher-education-dei-efforts-are-in-trouble-heres-how-we-change-that.

Kezar, Adrianna. *How Colleges Change: Understanding, Leading, and Enacting Change.* New York: Routledge, 2018.

Kezar, Adrianna. *Understanding and Facilitating Change in the 21st Century: Recent Research and Conceptualizations.* Vol. 28. ASHE-ERIC Higher Education Report 4. San Francisco: Jossey-Bass, 2001.

Kezar, Adrianna, Tom DePaola, and Daniel T. Scott. *The Gig Academy: Mapping Labor in the Neoliberal University.* Baltimore: Johns Hopkins University Press, 2019. https://doi.org/10.1353/book.68032.

Kezar, Adrianna, Elizabeth Holcombe, Jordan Harper, and Natsumi Ueda. "Culture Change Requires Personal and Organizational Changes: Lessons from the Shared Equity Leadership Model." *Change: The Magazine of Higher Learning* 55, no. 1 (January 2023): 39–46. https://doi.org/10.1080/00091383.2023.2151806.

Kezar, Adrianna, Elizabeth Holcombe, Darsella Vigil, and Jude Paul Matias Dizon. *Shared Equity Leadership: Making Equity Everyone's Work.* Washington, DC: American Council on Education, 2021. https://www.acenet.edu/Documents/Shared-Equity-Leadership-Work.pdf.

Kezar, Adrianna, Daniel Maxey, and Judith Eaton. "An Examination of the Changing Faculty: Ensuring Institutional Quality and Achieving Desired Student Learning Outcomes." Council for Higher Education Accreditation and the Delphi Project on the Changing Faculty for Student Success, January 2014. https://pullias.usc.edu/download/an-examination-of-the-changing-faculty-ensuring-institutional-quality-and-achieving-desired-student-learning-outcomes/.

Kim, Joshua. "David Leonhardt's New Book, a Call to Celebrate Every University Employee." *Inside Higher Ed*, December 11, 2023. https://www.insidehighered.com/opinion/blogs/learning-innovation/2023/12/11/david-leonhardts-book-call-celebrate-every-university.

Kingston, Raynard S. "Presidents Don't Talk About Their Panic Attacks." *The Chronicle of Higher Education*, December 4, 2023. https://www.chronicle.com/article/presidents-dont-talk-about-their-panic-attacks.

Kinservik, Matthew J. "Case Study: University of Delaware." In *Collective Bargaining in Higher Education*, edited by Daniel J. Julius, 231–43. New York: Routledge, 2021.

Kline, Missy. "Survey Results: Short Tenure for Higher Ed's Top Leaders." *CUPA-HR* (blog). Accessed January 26, 2024. https://www.cupahr.org/blog/survey-results-administrators/.

Klinenberg, Eric. *2020: One City, Seven People, and the Year Everything Changed.* New York: Penguin Random House, 2024.

Klinenberg, Eric. "We Were Wrong About What Happened to America in 2020." *New York Times*, January 31, 2024. https://www.nytimes.com/2024/01/31/opinion/covid-2020-recovery-society.html.

Kunkle, Kelsey, and Sophia Laderman. "State Higher Education Finance: FY 2022." State Higher Education Executive Officers Association, 2023.

Kwolek-Folland, Angel. *Engendering Business*. Baltimore: Johns Hopkins University Press, 1994. https://doi.org/10.56021/9780801848605.

Labaree, David F. *A Perfect Mess: The Unlikely Ascendancy of American Higher Education*. Chicago: University of Chicago Press, 2019.

Laloux, Frederic. *Reinventing Organizations: A Guide to Creating Organizations Inspired by the Next Stage of Human Consciousness*. Brussels: Nelson Parker, 2014.

Lane, Jason E. "The Spider Web of Oversight: An Analysis of External Oversight of Higher Education." *Journal of Higher Education* 78, no. 6 (November 2007): 615–45.

Lawler, Edward E., III. *Reinventing Talent Management: Principles and Practices for the New World of Work*. Oakland, CA: Berrett-Koehler, 2017.

Leary, Mark R. "The Psychology of Intellectual Humility." John Templeton Foundation, September 2018. https://www.templeton.org/wp-content/uploads/2020/08/JTF_Intellectual_Humility_final.pdf.

Lehfeldt, Elizabeth A. "The Endless Churn of Administrators Leaves Faculty Feeling Dizzy." *Times Higher Education*, April 30, 2023. https://www.timeshighereducation.com/blog/endless-churn-administrators-leaves-faculty-feeling-dizzy.

Lehfeldt, Elizabeth A. "Stop Calling It the Dark Side." *Inside Higher Ed*, June 13, 2017. https://www.insidehighered.com/advice/2017/06/14/closing-divide-between-faculty-and-administrators-essay.

Lemons, L. Jay. "Another Wave of Presidential Departures?" *Inside Higher Ed*, March 9, 2021. https://www.insidehighered.com/views/2021/03/10/more-presidents-may-be-leaving-will-their-colleges-be-ready-it-opinion.

Lewis, Robert E., and Robert J. Heckman. "Talent Management: A Critical Review." *Human Resource Management Review* 16, no. 2 (June 2006): 139–54. https://doi.org/10.1016/j.hrmr.2006.03.001.

Li, Diyi, and Cory Koedel. "Representation and Salary Gaps by Race-Ethnicity and Gender at Selective Public Universities." *Educational Researcher* 46, no. 7 (October 2017): 343–54. https://doi.org/10.3102/0013189X17726535.

Liera, Román. "Lead the Change Series Q&A with Román Liera." *AERA Educational Change Special Interest Group*, no. 146 (2023): 1–7.

Liera, Román, and Steve Desir. "Taking Equity-Mindedness to the Next Level: The Equity-Minded Organization." *Frontiers in Education* 8 (July 2023). https://doi.org/10.3389/feduc.2023.1199174.

Liera, Román, and Theresa E. Hernandez. "Color-Evasive Racism in the Final Stage of Faculty Searches." *Review of Higher Education* 45, no. 2 (2021): 181–209.

Loerzel, Robert. "Displaced: When the Eisenhower Expressway Moved In, Who Was Forced Out?" Accessed December 8, 2023. https://interactive.wbez.org/curiouscity/eisenhower/.

Magolda, Peter. *The Lives of Campus Custodians*. Sterling, VA: Stylus, 2016.

Malesic, Jonathan. *The End of Burnout: Why Work Drains Us and How to Build Better Lives*. Los Angeles: University of California Press, 2022.

Mallick, Mita. "It's Time to Rethink Corporate Bereavement Policies." *Harvard Business Review*, October 5, 2020. https://hbr.org/2020/10/its-time-to-rethink-corporate-bereavement-policies.

Marcus, Jon. "Canada Treats Adjunct Faculty Better than the US—and It Pays Off for Students." *The Hechinger Report*, October 28, 2023. https://hechingerreport.org/canada-treats-its-adjunct-professors-better-than-the-us-does-and-it-pays-off-for-students/.

Marken, Stephanie, and Sangeeta Agrawal. "K-12 Workers Have Highest Burnout Rate in US," Gallup, June 13, 2022. https://news.gallup.com/poll/393500/workers-highest-burnout-rate.aspx.

Marshall, Sarah M., Megan Moore Gardner, Carole Hughes, and Ute Lowery. "Attrition from Student Affairs: Perspectives from Those Who Exited the Profession." *Journal of Student Affairs Research and Practice* 53, no. 2 (April 2016): 146–59. https://doi.org/10.1080/19496591.2016.1147359.

Martin, Mike. "Stop Whining About Lack of Career Opportunities." *The Chronicle of Higher Education*, January 5, 2023. https://www.chronicle.com/blogs/letters/stop-whining-about-lack-of-career-opportunities.

Maslach, Christina, and Michael P. Leiter. "How to Measure Burnout Accurately and Ethically." *Harvard Business Review*, March 19, 2021. https://hbr.org/2021/03/how-to-measure-burnout-accurately-and-ethically.

Mazanec, Cecilia. "#ThanksForTyping Spotlights Unnamed Women in Literary Acknowledgments." NPR, March 30, 2017. https://www.npr.org/2017/03/30/521931310/-thanksfortyping-spotlights-unnamed-women-in-literary-acknowledgements.

McCambly, Heather, and Jeannette A. Colyvas. "Institutionalizing Inequity Anew: Grantmaking and Racialized Postsecondary Organizations." *Review of Higher Education* 46, no. 1 (2022): 67–107.

McClure, Kevin R. "Building the Innovative and Entrepreneurial University: An Institutional Case Study of Administrative Academic Capitalism." *Journal of Higher Education* 87, no. 4 (July 2016): 516–43. https://doi.org/10.1080/00221546.2016.11777412.

McClure, Kevin R. "Burnout Is Coming to Campus. Are College Leaders Ready?" *EdSurge*, August 14, 2020. https://www.edsurge.com/news/2020-08-14-burnout-is-coming-to-campus-are-college-leaders-ready.

McClure, Kevin R. "College Leaders Make Mistakes. Here's Why They Should Apologize for Them." *EdSurge*, November 16, 2022. https://www.edsurge.com/news/2020-11-16-college-leaders-make-mistakes-here-s-why-they-should-apologize-for-them.

McClure, Kevin R. "The Future of Work Is Flexible. Will Higher Ed Stay Stuck in the Past?" *EdSurge*, May 2, 2022. https://www.edsurge.com/news/2022-05-02-the-future-of-work-is-flexible-will-higher-ed-stay-stuck-in-the-past.

McClure, Kevin R. "Having Trouble Hiring at Your College? Try Improving the Jobs." *EdSurge*, August 11, 2022. https://www.edsurge.com/news/2022-08-11-having-trouble-hiring-at-your-college-try-improving-the-jobs.

McClure, Kevin R. "Higher Ed Is a Land of Dead-End Jobs." *The Chronicle of Higher Education*, December 2, 2022. https://www.chronicle.com/article/higher-ed-is-a-land-of-dead-end-jobs.

McClure, Kevin R. "Higher Ed, We've Got a Morale Problem—and a Free T-Shirt Won't Fix It." *EdSurge*, September 27, 2021. https://www.edsurge.com/news/2021-09-27-higher-ed-we-ve-got-a-morale-problem-and-a-free-t-shirt-won-t-fix-it.

McClure, Kevin R. "Why We Should Care About College Leaders' Morale, Too." *EdSurge*, December 1, 2021. https://www.edsurge.com/news/2021-12-01-why-we-should-care-about-college-leaders-morale-too.

McClure, Kevin R. "Your Pay Is Terrible? You're Not Alone." *The Chronicle of Higher Education*, March 21, 2024. https://www.chronicle.com/article/your-pay-is-terrible-youre-not-alone.

McClure, Kevin R., and Marvin A. Titus. "Spending Up the Ranks? The Relationship Between Striving for Prestige and Administrative Expenditures at US Public Research Universities." *Journal of Higher Education* 89, no. 6 (November 2018): 961–87. https://doi.org/10.1080/00221546.2018.1449079.

McDade, Sharon A. *Leadership in Higher Education*. Washington, DC: ERIC Clearinghouse on Higher Education, 1988.

McFeely, Shane, and Ben Wigert. "This Fixable Problem Costs US Businesses $1 Trillion." Gallup, March 13, 2019. https://www.gallup.com/workplace/247391/fixable-problem-costs-businesses-trillion.aspx.

McGhee, Heather. *The Sum of Us: What Racism Costs Everyone and How We Can Prosper Together*. New York: Penguin Random House, 2021.

McKay, Dwanna L. "Mvskoke Eckvlke (Muscogee Motherhood) in Academic Spaces." In *Indigenous Motherhood in the Academy*, edited by Robin Starr Minthorn, Christine A. Nelson, and Heather J. Shotton, 83–91. New Brunswick, NJ: Rutgers University Press.

McLean, Danielle. "Why Are HBCU Presidential Departures Surging?" *Higher Ed Dive*, July 24, 2023. https://www.highereddive.com/news/hbcu-presidential-turnover-departures-higher-ed/688665/.

McNair, Tia Brown, Estela M. Bensimon, and Lindsay Malcom-Piqueux. *From Equity Talk to Equity Walk: Expanding Practitioner Knowledge for Racial Justice in Higher Education*. New York: Wiley, 2020.

Melidona, Danielle, Benjamin G. Cecil, Alexander Cassell, and Hollie Chessman. *The American College President Study: 2023 Edition*. Washington, DC: American Council on Education, 2023.

Meyer, John W., and Brian Rowan. "Institutionalized Organizations: Formal Structure as Myth and Ceremony." *American Journal of Sociology* 83, no. 2 (1977): 340–63. https://www.ccsa.ufpb.br/gets/contents/documentos/meyer_rowan_teoria_institucional.pdf.

Meyerson, Debra E. "The Tempered Radicals." *Stanford Social Innovation Review*, Fall 2004. https://ssir.org/pdf/2004FA_feature_meyerson.pdf.

Milkman, Ruth, and Joseph van der Naald. "The State of the Unions 2023: A Profile of Organized Labor in New York City, New York State, and the United States." CUNY School of Labor and Urban Studies, August 31, 2023. https://academicworks.cuny.edu/cgi/viewcontent.cgi?article=1020&context=slu_pubs.

Minthorn, Robin Zape-tah-hol-ah, Christine A. Nelson, and Heather J. Shotton, eds. *Indigenous Motherhood in the Academy.* New Brunswick, NJ: Rutgers University Press, 2022.

Mollencamp, Daniel. "Higher Ed Is Investing in Student Success Tech: Is It a 'New Golden Age' or Just Vague Talk?" *EdSurge*, June 21, 2022. https://www.edsurge.com/news/2022-06-21-higher-ed-is-investing-in-student-success-tech-is-it-a-new-golden-age-or-just-vague-talk.

Montgomery, Beronda L. "Academic Leadership: Gatekeeping or Groundskeeping?" *Journal of Values-Based Leadership* 13, no. 2 (July 2020). https://doi.org/10.22543/0733.132.1316.

Montgomery, Beronda L. *Lessons from Plants.* Cambridge, MA: Harvard University Press, 2021.

Morgan, Brynna. "Higher Ed Job Descriptions Can't Compete. Here's How to Fix Them." *EAB* (blog), December 1, 2022. https://eab.com/insights/blogs/business-affairs/higher-ed-job-descriptions-cant-compete/.

Morphew, Christopher C., and Matthew Hartley. "Mission Statements: A Thematic Analysis of Rhetoric Across Institutional Type." *Journal of Higher Education* 77, no. 3 (2006): 456–71. https://doi.org/10.1353/jhe.2006.0025.

Nagoski, Emily, and Amelia Nagoski. *Burnout: The Secret to Unlocking the Stress Cycle.* New York: Random House, 2020.

Name, Susie E. "Making Visible the Dead Bodies in the Room: Women of Color/QPOC in Academic." In *Presumed Incompetent II: Race, Class, Power, and Resistance of Women in Academia*, edited by Yolanda Flores Niemann, Gabriella Gutierrez y Muhs, and Carmen G. Gonzalez, 168–76. Louisville, CO: Utah State University Press, 2020.

NASPA: Student Affairs Administrators in Higher Education. "The Compass Report: Charting the Future of Student Affairs." NASPA, March 2022. https://naspa.org/about/future-of-student-affairs-report/the-compass-report-charting-the-future-of-student-affairs.

National Association of Student Financial Aid Administrators. *Financial Aid Offices Face Intensifying Staffing Challenges amid Pandemic.* Washington, DC: NASFAA, 2022. https://www.nasfaa.org/uploads/documents/Financial_Aid_Offices_Face_Intensifying_Staffing_Challenges_Amid_Pandemic.pdf.

National Center for Education Statistics. "National Study of Postsecondary Faculty (NSOPF): Overview." Accessed August 14, 2023. https://nces.ed.gov/surveys/nsopf/.

National Center for Health Statistics. "Nearly One in Five American Adults Who Have Had COVID-19 Still Have 'Long COVID.'" Centers for Disease Control and Prevention, June 22, 2022. https://www.cdc.gov/nchs/pressroom/nchs_press_releases/2022/20220622.htm.

National Education Association. "NEA Education Support Professional Earnings Report," April 2023. https://www.nea.org/sites/default/files/2023-04/nea-esp-earnings-report-2023.pdf.

National Equity Project. "Lens of Systemic Oppression." Accessed October 26, 2023. https://www.nationalequityproject.org/frameworks/lens-of-systemic-oppression.

National Labor Relations Board. "Election Petitions Up 53%, Board Continues to Reduce Case Processing Time in FY22." Accessed December 12, 2023. https://www.nlrb.gov/news-outreach/news-story/election-petitions-up-53-board-continues-to-reduce-case-processing-time-in.

National Museum of African American History and Culture. "Social Identities and Systems of Oppression." Accessed October 24, 2023. https://nmaahc.si.edu/learn/talking-about-race/topics/social-identities-and-systems-oppression.

National Partnership for Women and Families. "Key Facts: The Family and Medical Leave Act," February 2023. https://nationalpartnership.org/report/fmla-key-facts/.

Newport, Frank, and Joy Wilke. "Desire for Children Still Norm in US." Gallup, September 25, 2013. https://news.gallup.com/poll/164618/desire-children-norm.aspx.

Nguemeni Tiako, Max Jordan, Eugenia C. South, and Victor Ray. "Medical Schools as Racialized Organizations: A Primer." *Annals of Internal Medicine* 174, no. 8 (August 2021): 1143–44. https://doi.org/10.7326/M21-0369.

Nightingale, Johnathan, and Melissa Nightingale. *Unmanageable: Leadership Lessons from an Impossible Year.* Toronto: Raw Signal Press, 2021.

Noddings, Nel. *Caring: A Relational Approach to Ethics and Moral Education, Updated.* 2nd ed. Berkeley: University of California Press, 2013.

Nyunt, Gudrun, Rachel Pridgen, and Isaiah Thomas. "Disrupting Student Affairs Staff Departure: Examining Needed Changes to the Field of Student Affairs to Attract and Retain a Diverse Workforce." *Journal of College Student Development* 65, no. 2 (2024): 183–200.

Ogden, Lesley Evans. "Working Mothers Face a 'Wall' of Bias—but There Are Ways to Push Back." *Science*, April 10, 2019. https://www.science.org/content/article/working-mothers-face-wall-bias-there-are-ways-push-back.

Okai, Kenneth, Dulce Aguilar, and Tyler Schottel. "The Development of the UIC Neighborhood." ArcGIS StoryMaps, November 29, 2022. https://storymaps.arcgis.com/stories/285a297c8b974eba8e463e4a19ab88c9.

Okello, Wilson Kwamogi. "Epistemic Asphyxiation: Whiteness, Academic Publishing, and the Suffocation of Black Knowledge Production." In *Critical Whiteness Praxis in Higher Education*, edited By Zak Foste and Tenisha L. Tevis, 115–34. Oxfordshire: Taylor and Francis, 2022.

Okoro, Catherine A., NaTasha D. Hollis, Alissa C. Cyrus, and Shannon Griffin-Blake. "Prevalence of Disabilities and Health Care Access by Disability Status and Type Among Adults—United States, 2016." *MMWR. Morbidity and Mortality Weekly Report* 67 (2018). https://doi.org/10.15585/mmwr.mm6732a3.

Okun, Tema. "White Supremacy Culture." 1999. https://www.whitesupremacyculture.info/uploads/4/3/5/7/43579015/okun_-_white_sup_culture_2020.pdf.

Olabisi, Ronke M. "The Pregnancy Drop: How Teaching Evaluations Penalize Pregnant Faculty." *Humanities and Social Sciences Communications* 8, no. 1 (October 2021): 1–10. https://doi.org/10.1057/s41599-021-00926-3.

Olkin, Rhoda. "Academic Leaders with Disabilities: How Do We Know If We Are Winning When No One Is Keeping Score?" In *Women as Leaders in Education:*

Succeeding Despite Inequity, Discrimination, and Other Challenges, edited by Jennifer L. Martin, 201–17. Santa Barbara, CA: ABC-CLIO, 2011.

Ollilainen, Marjukka. "Ideal Bodies at Work: Faculty Mothers and Pregnancy in Academia." *Gender and Education* 32, no. 7 (October 2020): 961–76. https://doi.org/10.1080/09540253.2019.1632808.

O'Meara, KerryAnn. "Half-Way Out: How Requiring Outside Offers to Raise Salaries Influences Faculty Retention and Organizational Commitment." *Research in Higher Education* 56, no. 3 (2015): 279–98.

O'Meara, KerryAnn. "Striving for What? Exploring the Pursuit of Prestige." In *Higher Education: Handbook of Theory and Research*, edited by John C. Smart, 121–79. Amsterdam: Springer Netherlands, 2007. https://doi.org/10.1007/978-1-4020-5666-6_3.

O'Meara, KerryAnn, Elizabeth Beise, Dawn Culpepper, Joya Misra, and Audrey Jaeger. "Faculty Work Activity Dashboards: A Strategy to Increase Transparency." *Change: The Magazine of Higher Learning* 52, no. 3 (May 2020): 34–42. https://doi.org/10.1080/00091383.2020.1745579.

O'Meara, KerryAnn, Alexandra Kuvaeva, and Gudrun Nyunt. "Constrained Choices: A View of Campus Service Inequality from Annual Faculty Reports." *Journal of Higher Education* 88, no. 5 (September 2017): 672–700. https://doi.org/10.1080/00221546.2016.1257312.

O'Meara, KerryAnn, and Lindsey Templeton. *Equity-Minded Reform of Faculty Evaluation: A Call to Action*. Washington, DC: American Council on Education, 2022. https://www.acenet.edu/Documents/Equity-Minded-Faculty-Evaluation-Principles.pdf.

O'Meara, KerryAnn, Lindsey Templeton, Dawn Culpepper, and Damani White-Lewis. *Translating Equity-Minded Principles into Faculty Evaluation Reform*. Washington, DC: American Council on Education, 2022. https://www.acenet.edu/Documents/Equity-Minded-Faculty-Evaluation-Reform.pdf.

Open House Chicago. "UIC University Hall." Accessed December 8, 2023. https://openhousechicago.org/sites/site/uic-university-hall.

Option B. "Be an Agent for Change: An HR Leader's Guide to Expanding Bereavement and Compassionate Leave." Accessed November 16, 2023. https://39729081.fs1.hubspotusercontent-na1.net/hubfs/39729081/Hosted%20PDFs/OB—Grief%20Awareness%20Day%20Resources—HR%20Leaders.pdf https://optionb.org/bereavement-at-work.

Owens, Bradley P., and David R. Hekman. "How Does Leader Humility Influence Team Performance? Exploring the Mechanisms of Contagion and Collective Promotion Focus." *Academy of Management Journal* 59, no. 3 (2016): 1088–1111. https://www.jstor.org/stable/24758253.

Ozias, Moira L., and Penny Pasque. "Toward Definitions of Whiteness and Critical Whiteness Studies: Disruption and Response-Ability." In *Critical Whiteness Praxis in Higher Education*, edited By Zak Foste and Tenisha L. Tevis, 21–47. New York: Routledge, 2022.

Padilla, Amado M. "Ethnic Minority Scholars, Research, and Mentoring: Current and Future Issues." *Educational Researcher* 23, no. 4 (1994): 24–27. https://doi.org/10.2307/1176259.

Pena, Maria. "Regarded as Such? Who Says So?" In *Disabled Faculty and Staff: Intersecting Identities in Higher Education*, vol. 2, edited by Mary Lee Vance and Elizabeth G. Harrison, 15–20. Huntersville, NC: Association on Higher Education and Disability, 2023.

Perez, Rosemary J. "Problematizing Socialization in Student Affairs Graduate Training." In *Creating Sustainable Careers in Student Affairs: What Ideal Worker Norms Get Wrong and How to Make It Right*, edited by Margaret W. Sallee, 97–118. Sterling, VA: Stylus, 2021.

Peters, B. Guy. "Bureaucracy and Bureaucratic Effectiveness." In *The SAGE Handbook of Political Science*, edited by Dirk Berg-Schlosser, Bertrand Badie, and Leonardo Morlino, 953–69. London: SAGE, 2020.

Peterson, Marvin W. "The Study of Colleges and Universities as Organizations." In *Sociology of Higher Education: Contributions and Their Contexts*, edited by Patricia J. Gumport, 147–86. Baltimore: Johns Hopkins University Press, 2007.

Petit, Emma. "The New Tenured Radicals." *The Chronicle of Higher Education*, April 23, 2020. https://www.chronicle.com/article/the-new-tenured-radicals/.

Phelps-Ward, Robin, and Wonjae Phillip Kim, eds. *The Power of Names in Identity and Oppression: Narratives for Equity in Higher Education and Student Affairs*. New York: Routledge, 2023.

POD Network, and American Council on Education. "A Center for Teaching and Learning Matrix." Professional and Organizational Development (POD) Network, 2018. https://podnetwork.org/resources/center-for-teaching-and-learning-matrix/.

Pollard, Amelia, and Janet Lorin. "Colleges Vie for New Bosses as Harvard, MIT Lead Retirement Wave." Bloomberg, August 18, 2022. https://www.bloomberg.com/news/articles/2022-08-18/crush-of-college-leaders-retiring-at-once-spurs-search-challenge.

Pope-Ruark, Rebecca. *Unraveling Faculty Burnout: Pathways to Reckoning and Renewal*. Baltimore: Johns Hopkins University Press, 2022.

PricewaterhouseCoopers. "Productivity Has Risen with Remote/Hybrid Working, but Worker Trust May Pose a Larger Challenge," November 18, 2021. https://www.pwc.com/gx/en/news-room/press-releases/2021/pwc-future-of-work-survey-2021.html.

Pryor, Jonathan T., and Garrett D. Hoffman. "'It Feels like Diversity as Usual': Navigating Institutional Politics as LGBTQ+ Professionals." *Journal of Student Affairs Research and Practice* 58, no. 1 (January 2021): 94–109. https://doi.org/10.1080/19496591.2020.1740717.

Quaye, Stephen John, Shamika N. Karikari, Kiaya Demere Carter, Wilson Kwamogi Okello, and Courtney Allen. "'Why Can't I Just Chill?': The Visceral Nature of Racial Battle Fatigue." *Journal of College Student Development* 61, no. 5 (2020): 609–23. https://doi.org/10.1353/csd.2020.0058.

Raja, Siva, and Sharon L. Stein. "Work-Life Balance: History, Costs, and Budgeting for Balance." *Clinics in Colon and Rectal Surgery* 27, no. 2 (June 2014): 71–74. https://doi.org/10.1055/s-0034-1376172.

Rankin, Sue, Warren Blumenfeld, Genevieve N. Weber, and Frazer, Somjen. "2010 State of Higher Education for LGBT People." National College Climate Survey, Campus Pride, 2010.

Ray, Victor. "A Theory of Racialized Organizations." *American Sociological Review* 84, no. 1 (2019): 26–53. https://journals.sagepub.com/doi/10.1177/0003122418822335.

Reichlin Cruse, Lindsey, Lashawn Richburg-Hayes, Amanda Hare, and Susana Contreras-Mendez. "Evaluating the Role of Campus Child Care in Student Parent Success: Challenges and Opportunities for Rigorous Study." Institute for Women's Policy Research, October 2021. https://eric.ed.gov/?id=ED617783.

Reinitz, Betsy. "The Impact of Analytics on the Higher Education Workforce," *EDUCAUSE Review*, August 21, 2019. https://er.educause.edu/blogs/2019/8/the-impact-of-analytics-on-the-higher-education-workforce.

Reyes, Victoria. *Academic Outsider: Stories of Exclusion and Hope*. Palo Alto, CA: Stanford University Press, 2022.

Robbins, Mike. "Why Employees Need Both Recognition and Appreciation." *Harvard Business Review*, November 12, 2019. https://hbr.org/2019/11/why-employees-need-both-recognition-and-appreciation.

Robert, Jenay, and Betsy Reinitz. *2023 EDUCAUSE Horizon Action Plan: Data Governance*. Boulder, CO: EDUCAUSE, 2023. https://library.educause.edu/-/media/files/library/2023/3/2023horizonapdatagovernance.pdf?la=en&hash=FA306932947338DB9353D05A48369FFBB6A9C653.

Rogelberg, Steven G. *The Surprising Science of Meetings: How You Can Lead Your Team to Peak Performance*. Oxford: Oxford University Press, 2019.

Root Cause. "Collective Action Framework." Accessed December 9, 2023. https://rootcause.org/method/collective-action-framework/.

Rosenberg, Brian. *"Whatever It Is, I'm Against It": Resistance to Change in Higher Education*. Cambridge, MA: Harvard Education Press, 2023.

Rutgers School of Management and Labor Relations. "Examples of Bargaining for the Common Good Demands." Accessed December 9, 2023. https://smlr.rutgers.edu/faculty-research-engagement/center-innovation-worker-organization-ciwo/bargaining-common-good.

Sallee, Margaret W., ed. *Creating Sustainable Careers in Student Affairs: What Ideal Worker Norms Get Wrong and How to Make It Right*. Sterling, VA: Stylus, 2021.

Sallee, Margaret W. "Performing Masculinity: Considering Gender in Doctoral Student Socialization." *Journal of Higher Education* 82, no. 2 (2011): 187–216. https://doi.org/10.1353/jhe.2011.0007.

Santoro, Doris A. "Good Teaching in Difficult Times: Demoralization in the Pursuit of Good Work." *American Journal of Education* 118, no. 1 (2011): 1–23. https://www.jstor.org/stable/10.1086/662010.

Schmalz, Julia, and Katherine Mangan. "Food, Child Care, Rent: This College Goes the Extra Mile to Serve Low-Income Students." *The Chronicle of Higher Education*, April 3, 2019. https://www.chronicle.com/article/a-culture-of-caring.

Schuster, Jack H., and Martin J. Finkelstein. *The American Faculty: The Restructuring of Academic Work and Careers*. Baltimore: Johns Hopkins University Press, 2008.

Schwartz, Tony. "Create a Growth Culture, Not a Performance-Obsessed One." *Harvard Business Review*, March 7, 2018. https://hbr.org/2018/03/create-a-growth-culture-not-a-performance-obsessed-one.

Scott, Joan Wallach. *Knowledge, Power, and Academic Freedom*. New York: Columbia University Press, 2019.

Scott, Robert A. "Leadership Threats to Shared Governance in Higher Education." *Journal of Academic Freedom* 11 (2020): 1–17. https://www.aaup.org/JAF11/leadership-threats-shared-governance-higher-education.

Selingo, Jeff, and Michael Horn. "The Great Resignation in Higher Ed," *Future U*, February 6, 2023. https://www.futureupodcast.com/episodes/the-great-resignation/.

Sheffer, Jolie A., Lisa K. Hanasono, Charles Kanwischer, W. John Koolage, Mary-Jon Ludy, Laura Landry-Meyer, Ekaterina I. Noyes, M. Elise Radina, and Jerry Schnepp. "Pieces of the Puzzle." *Liberal Education*, Winter 2022. https://www.aacu.org/liberaleducation/articles/pieces-of-the-puzzle.

Shelton, Stephanie Anne, and Nicole Sieben, eds. *Narratives of Hope and Grief in Higher Education*. Cham, Switzerland: Springer, 2020. https://doi.org/10.1007/978-3-030-42556-2.

SHRM. "Managing Employee Surveys." Society for Human Resource Management, March 30, 2023. https://www.shrm.org/resourcesandtools/tools-and-samples/toolkits/pages/managingemployeesurveys.aspx.

SimpsonScarborough. "A Question of Value: The Higher Ed Marcom Professional Development and Salary Study," 2022. https://info.simpsonscarborough.com/salary-study-2022.

Slaughter, Sheila, and Gary Rhoades. *Academic Capitalism and the New Economy: Markets, State, and Higher Education*. Baltimore: Johns Hopkins University Press, 2004.

Society for College and University Planning. "Integrated Planning Glossary," 2019. https://www.scup.org/resource/integrated-planning-glossary/.

Starbucks. "Culture and Values: Starbucks Coffee Company." Accessed August 14, 2023. https://www.starbucks.com/careers/working-at-starbucks/culture-and-values.

State University of New York. "Campus Governance Leaders Toolkit: What Is Shared Governance?" Accessed December 9, 2023. https://www.suny.edu/about/shared-governance/sunyvoices/cgl-toolkit/shared-governance/.

Stewart, D-L, and Kathy Collins. "Constructing Disability: Case Studies of Graduate Students and New Professionals with Disabilities in Student Affairs." *College Student Affairs Journal* 32, no. 1 (Spring 2014): 19–33. https://www.proquest.com/docview/1611000699?sourcetype=Scholarly%20Journals.

Stewart, Terah J. "Hard Grief for Hard Love: Writing Through Doctoral Studies and the Loss of My Mother." In *Narratives of Hope and Grief in Higher Education*, edited by Stephanie Anne Shelton and Nicole Sieben Springer, 27–37. London: Palgrave Macmillan, 2020.

Sugrue, Erin. "Understanding the Effect of Moral Transgressions in the Helping Professions: In Search of Conceptual Clarity." *Social Service Review* 93, no. 1 (March 2019): 4–25. https://doi.org/10.1086/701838.

Taylor, Barrett J. *Wrecked: Deinstitutionalization and Partial Defenses in State Higher Education Policy*. New Brunswick, NJ: Rutgers University Press, 2022.

Terpstra, David E., and Andre L Honoree. "Faculty Perceptions of Problems with Merit Pay Plans in Institutions of Higher Education." *Journal of Business and Management* 14, no. 1 (2008): 43–59. https://jbm.johogo.com/pdf/volume/1401/JBM-1401-03-full.pdf.

Thomason, Bobbi, and Heather Williams. "What Will Work-Life Balance Look Like After the Pandemic?" *Harvard Business Review*, April 16, 2020. https://hbr.org/2020/04/what-will-work-life-balance-look-like-after-the-pandemic.

Thompson, Derek. "Three Myths of the Great Resignation." *The Atlantic*, December 8, 2021. https://www.theatlantic.com/ideas/archive/2021/12/great-resignation-myths-quitting-jobs/620927/.

Thys, Fred. "Northeastern Faculty Members Withdraw Union Petition," WBUR, November 15, 2018. https://www.wbur.org/news/2018/11/14/northeastern-university-faculty-union-filing.

Tiede, Hans-Jeorge. "Survey Data on the Impact of the Pandemic on Shared Governance." American Association of University Professors, May 24, 2021. https://www.aaup.org/report/survey-data-impact-pandemic-shared-governance.

Tierney, William G. *The Impact of Culture on Organizational Decision-Making: Theory and Practice in Higher Education*. Sterling, VA: Stylus, 2008.

Townsend, Barbara K., and Vicki J. Rosser. "Workload Issues and Measures of Faculty Productivity." *Thought & Action: The NEA Higher Education Journal* (Fall 2007): 7–20. https://eric.ed.gov/?id=EJ1070674.

Tucker, Jasmine. "Men Have Now Recouped Their Pandemic-Related Labor Force Losses While Women Lag Behind." National Women's Law Center, February 2022. https://nwlc.org/wp-content/uploads/2022/02/January-Jobs-Day-updated.pdf.

Tugend, Alina. "On the Verge of Burnout: COVID-19's Impact on Faculty Well-Being and Career Plans." Research Brief. *The Chronicle of Higher Education*, 2020. https://connect.chronicle.com/rs/931-EKA-218/images/Covid%26FacultyCareerPaths_Fidelity_ResearchBrief_v3%20%281%29.pdf.

Turner, Caroline, Juan González, and J. Luke Wood. "Faculty of Color in Academe: What 20 Years of Literature Tells Us." *Journal of Diversity in Higher Education* 1, no. 3 (September 2008): 139–68. https://doi.org/10.1037/a0012837.

UICUF. "UIC United Faculty Commitments." Accessed December 9, 2023. https://uicunitedfaculty.org/.

UNICEF. "Family-Friendly Policies: Redesigning the Workplace of the Future." Policy Brief, July 2019. https://www.unicef.org/documents/family-friendly-policies-redesigning-workplace-future.

University of California. "Integrated Talent Management." Accessed June 12, 2023. https://ucnet.universityofcalifornia.edu/working-at-uc/your-career/talent-management/index.html.

University of Louisville. "Compensation and Total Rewards Study—Human Resources." Accessed September 20, 2023. https://louisville.edu/hr/compensation/compensation-and-total-rewards-study.

University of Louisville. "Strategic Plan 2019–2022." Accessed September 20, 2023. https://louisville.edu/strategic-plan/strategic-plan-2019-2022.
University of Maryland Special Collections. "Labor, Recreation, and Rest: The Movement for the Eight-Hour Day." University Libraries. Accessed July 29, 2023. https://exhibitions.lib.umd.edu/unions/labor/eight-hour-day.
"U of L Compensation Study Thread Discussion." Reddit. *R/Louisville*, July 12, 2023. www.reddit.com/r/Louisville/comments/14xx7cb/u_of_l_compensation_study_thread_discussion/.
US Bureau of Labor Statistics. "6.2 Million Unable to Work Because Employer Closed or Lost Business due to the Pandemic." *TED: The Economics Daily*, July 8, 2021.
US Citizenship and Immigration Services. "Frequently Asked Questions: What Is Deferred Action for Childhood Arrivals?" November 13, 2023. https://www.uscis.gov/humanitarian/consideration-of-deferred-action-for-childhood-arrivals-daca/frequently-asked-questions.
US Office of Personnel Management. "Federal Employee Assistance Programs." Accessed August 11, 2023. https://www.opm.gov/policy-data-oversight/worklife/employee-assistance-programs/.
US Surgeon General. *Framework for Workplace Mental Health and Well-Being*. Washington, DC: Office of the US Surgeon General, 2022. https://www.hhs.gov/surgeongeneral/priorities/workplace-well-being/index.html.
Vance, Mary Lee, and Elizabeth G. Harrison, eds. *Disabled Faculty and Staff: Intersecting Identities in Higher Education*. Vol. 2. Huntersville, NC: Association on Higher Education and Disability, 2023.
Vickers, Margaret H. "A Guide to Grief in Public Administration." *Administrative Theory & Praxis* 28, no. 2 (July 2006): 245–61. https://doi.org/10.1080/10841806.2006.11029533.
Vizenor, Gerald, ed. *Survivance: Narratives of Native Presence*. Lincoln: University of Nebraska Press, 2008.
Võ, Linda Trinh. "Navigating the Academic Terrain: The Racial and Gender Politics of Elusive Belonging." In *Presumed Incompetent: The Intersection of Race and Class for Women in Academia*, edited by Gabriella Gutierrez y Muhs, Yolanda Flores Niemann, Carmen G. Gonzalez, and Angela P. Harris, 93–112. Louisville, CO: Utah State University Press, 2012.
Waddington, Kathryn. "Introduction: Why Compassion? Why Now?" In *Towards the Compassionate University*, edited by Kathryn Waddington, 5–22. New York: Routledge, 2021.
Wade, Lizzie. "The 8-Hour Workday Is a Counterproductive Lie." *Wired*, November 21, 2019. https://www.wired.com/story/eight-hour-workday-is-a-lie/.
Wallender, Andrew. "Starbucks, Education Strikes Fuel 17-Year High in Work Stoppages." Bloomberg Law, January 10, 2023. https://news.bloomberglaw.com/daily-labor-report/starbucks-education-strikes-fuel-17-year-high-in-work-stoppages.
Walton, Marci. "Right Now, Your Best Employees Are Eyeing the Exits." *The Chronicle of Higher Education*, February 16, 2022. https://www.chronicle.com/article/how-to-keep-your-staff-from-leaving.

Ward, Kelly, and Lisa Wolf-Wendel. *Academic Motherhood: How Faculty Manage Work and Family.* New Brunswick, NJ: Rutgers University Press, 2012.
Warzel, Charlie, and Anne Helen Petersen. *Out of Office: The Problem and Bigger Promise of Working from Home.* New York: Knopf, 2021.
Wegmans. "About Us." Accessed August 14, 2023. https://www.wegmans.com/about-us/.
Weick, Karl E., Kathleen M. Sutcliffe, and David Obstfeld. "Organizing and the Process of Sensemaking." *Organization Science* 16, no. 4 (August 2005): 409–21. https://doi.org/10.1287/orsc.1050.0133.
Wigert, Ben, and Sangeeta Agrawal. "Employee Burnout, Part 1: The 5 Main Causes." Gallup, July 12, 2018. https://www.gallup.com/workplace/237059/employee-burnout-part-main-causes.aspx.
Wigert, Ben, and Jessica White. "The Advantages and Challenges of Hybrid Work." Gallup, September 14, 2022. https://www.gallup.com/workplace/398135/advantages-challenges-hybrid-work.aspx.
Williams, Brittany M. "For Colored Girls Fighting to Survive When a Presidential Title Isn't Enough." *Medium* (blog), September 30, 2023. https://drbritwilliams.medium.com/for-colored-girls-fighting-to-survive-when-a-presidential-title-isnt-enough-b9f11f5d69e0.
Williams, Brittany M. "'It's Just My Face': Workplace Policing of Black Professional Women in Higher Education." *Journal of Women and Gender in Higher Education* 16, no. 2 (April 2023): 67–89. https://doi.org/10.1080/26379112.2023.2172730.
Williams, Joan C. "Deconstructing Gender." *Michigan Law Review* 87, no. 4 (1989): 797–845. https://doi.org/10.2307/1289293.
Winston, Sara J. "'My Body Is a Clock': The Private Life of Chronic Care." *New York Times*, June 29, 2023. https://www.nytimes.com/2023/06/29/opinion/photography-multiple-sclerosis-chronic-care.html.
WittKiefer. "Chief Enrollment Management Officers in a Time of Change, Challenge and Opportunity," December 2, 2022. https://www.wittkieffer.com/thought-leadership/chief-enrollment-management-officers-in-a-time-of-change-challenge-and-opportunity/.
Wolcott, R. J. "No Standing Meetings on Fridays." *WSU Insider* (blog), February 1, 2022. https://news.wsu.edu/news/2022/02/01/no-standing-meetings-on-fridays/.
Wolor, Christian Wiradendi, Ardiansyah Ardiansyah, Rofi Rofaida, Ahmad Nurkhin, and Mahmoud Ali Rababah. "Impact of Toxic Leadership on Employee Performance." *Health Psychology Research* 10, no. 4 (2022): 57551. https://doi.org/10.52965/001c.57551.
Wolverton, Mimi, Walter H. Gmelch, Marvin L. Wolverton, and James C. Sarros. "Stress in Academic Leadership: US and Australian Department Chairs/Heads." *Review of Higher Education* 22, no. 2 (1999): 165–85. https://eric.ed.gov/?id=EJ579945.
Wong, Wylie. "Higher Education Turns to Data Analytics to Bolster Student Success." *EdTech Magazine.* Accessed May 20, 2023. https://edtechmagazine.com/higher/article/2021/10/higher-education-turns-data-analytics-bolster-student-success.
World Health Organization. "Burnout an 'Occupational Phenomenon': International Classification of Diseases," May 28, 2019. https://www.who.int/news/item/28-05-2019-burn-out-an-occupational-phenomenon-international-classification-of-diseases.

Wright, Mary C. *Centers for Teaching and Learning: The New Landscape in Higher Education*. Baltimore: Johns Hopkins University Press, 2023.

Wyatt, Thomas. "Concepts, Ideas, Visions: Thematic Characteristics of Strategic Plans among Elite, International Universities." PhD diss., University of Georgia, 2011. https://esploro.libs.uga.edu/esploro/outputs/doctoral/Concepts-ideas-visions-thematic-characteristics-of/9949334944702959.

Yale University. "STARS." Science and Quantitative Reasoning Education, 2023. https://science.yalecollege.yale.edu/stem-fellowships/funding-stem-opportunities-yale/stars.

Yetter, Deborah. "U of L Scandals Under James Ramsey: A Timeline." *Courier Journal*, June 17, 2016. https://www.courier-journal.com/story/news/politics/2016/06/17/u-l-scandals-under-james-ramsey-timeline/86035838/.

Yi, Varaxy, L. J. Thaviseth, and V. S. Na. "Voicing Names, Naming Voices: (Re) Clamation by Southeast Asian American Women in Higher Education." In *The Power of Names in Identity and Oppression: Narratives for Equity in Higher Education and Student Affairs*, edited by Robin Phelps Ward and Wonjae Phillip Kim, 141–53. New York: Routledge.

Yoe, Jonathan. "Hybrid Work Seems to Be Working Out Just Fine." Bureau of Labor Statistics, May 2023. https://www.bls.gov/opub/mlr/2023/beyond-bls/hybrid-work-seems-to-be-working-out-just-fine.htm.

Young, Jemimah L., and Dorothy E. Hines. "Promotion While Pregnant and Black." In *Presumed Incompetent II: Race, Class, Power, and Resistance of Women in Academia*, edited by Yolanda Flores Niemann, Gabriella Gutierrez y Muhs, and Carmen G. Gonzalez, 73–82. Louisville, CO: Utah State University Press, 2020.

Zahneis, Megan. "Shared Governance Was Eroding Before Covid-19. Now It's a Landslide, AAUP Report Says." *The Chronicle of Higher Education*, May 26, 2021. https://www.chronicle.com/article/shared-governance-was-eroding-before-covid-19-now-its-a-landslide-aaup-report-says.

Zahneis, Megan. "What Higher Ed's Paid Parental-Leave Policies Look Like." *The Chronicle of Higher Education*, March 28, 2023. https://www.chronicle.com/article/what-higher-eds-paid-parental-leave-policies-look-like.

Zambrana, Ruth Enid. *Toxic Ivory Towers: The Consequences of Work Stress on Underrepresented Minority Faculty*. New Brunswick, NJ: Rutgers University Press, 2018.

Zemsky, Robert. *Checklist for Change: Making Higher Education a Sustainable Enterprise*. New Brunswick, NJ: Rutgers University Press, 2013.

Zhavoronkova, Marina, Rose Khattar, and Matthew Brady. "Occupational Segregation in America." Center for American Progress, March 29, 2022. https://www.americanprogress.org/article/occupational-segregation-in-america/.

Ziker, John. "The Long, Lonely Job of Homo Academicus." Boise State University, *The Blue Review*, March 31, 2014. https://www.boisestate.edu/bluereview/faculty-time-allocation/.

INDEX

Box text is indicated by *b*.

academic capitalism, 45–46, 215
academic freedom, 208, 217, 222–23
Academic Outsider (Reyes), 179
academic publishing and white epistemologies, 192–93
Acker, Joan, 50, 97, 100
ACPA-College Student Educators International, 186
Alvarez, Maximillian, 230–31
Amarillo College (AC), 57–64; "Culture of Caring," 57–58; organizational learning, 61–63; sensemaking, 80–81, 276; values alignment, 61–62; "whole student" approach, 58; workload and staffing, 87
Andrzejewski, Alicia, 107
Ardoin, Sonja, 49
Arton, Joseph, 156–57, 162
Aspen Prize for Community College Excellence, 57
attachment by employees, 43
austerity, cultural logics of, 48
austerity administration, 215–16
authenticity, 258–59

Baker, Vicki L., 242–43, 260–61
Bastedo, Michael, 39
Bauman, Dan, 20, 150
Bee, Mark, 234*b*
Belak, Tony, 251
Bendapudi, Neeli, 131–32
Benson, Todd, 70
betrayal, 19–20
Bevin, Matt, 131
Bichsel, Jackie, 71–72
Birnbaum, Robert, 42–43
Bloch, Charlotte, 108–9
Boston College, 229
Brassfield, Lauren, 76
Brayboy, Bryan, 74–75
Brown, Brené, 252
budget crises, erosion of shared governance, 214
Buford, Brian, 130, 134–38, 167
bureaucracies, 39–40; dual power structure, 40–41
Burmicky, Jorge, 261–62
burnout: defined, 22–24; leadership stress and, 241, 243–47; pandemic effect, 23*b*; spike in, 12

Cadigan, Steve, 166
Campus Pride Index, 134
Cannon, Loren, 182*b*
Can't Even (Peterson), 24
Cantwell, Brendan, 259
Cardinal Leadership Institute (UofL), 137, 160–61
career ladders: and career pathways, 154–57, 167; for faculty and staff, 138–40; University Advising Center (University of South Carolina), 155–56
Career Navigation Center (UVa), 157
caregiving, 104–6
caregiving responsibilities, 115–16
caring leadership, 238–60; appreciating administrative work, 269*b*; caring for/about, 254–55; caring leadership training, 269*b*; coaching services, 269*b*; compassion, 249–51; constraints on, 240; critical hope, 250*b*, 253; deep care, 266*b*–67*b*; described, 238–39; emotional intelligence training, 267*b*; equity-mindedness, 250*b*, 254 (*see also* equity-minded organizations); integrate

caring leadership (*continued*)
action steps, 269*b*; intellectual humility, 250*b*, 251–52; leadership development, 269*b*; leadership preparation, 259; listening, 249, 251; meeting practices, 269*b*; organizational conditions, 255–70; organizational thinking, 250*b*; renewal opportunities, 262–63, 269*b*; responsibility-taking, 250*b*, 253–54; self-awareness, 250*b*, 251; trust-building, 250*b*, 252–53; vulnerability, 250*b*, 252; workload expectation, 269*b*
Caring University: collectivism, 5–6; defined, 8; employee well-being, 7; ongoing, 6; organizational changes, 6–7; proactivity, 6
Center for Creative Leadership, 250–51
centers for faculty development and teaching, 159–60, 167
Central Washington University (CWU), 266*b*
Chambers, Crystal, 261
Cho, Katherine, 76
Choi, Yoonjin, 15, 66–67
Científico Latino, 173
Clemo, Lorrie, 125*b*–26*b*
cluster hiring, 191, 203
coaching, Career Navigation Center (UVa), 156–57
Colby, Glen, 145
Collaborative on Academic Careers in Higher Education (2019), 144
Collaborative on Academic Careers in Higher Education (COACHE), 69, 225
collective action, 211, 235*b*
collective bargaining, 205–36; "common good" bargaining, 209–10; contingent faculty, 207–9; and cooperation, 229–32; defined, 205–6; and employee engagement, 231; and graduate employees, 210–11; Howard Community College, 230; and shared governance, 209; UIC, 206, 208–9; University of Minnesota, 233*b*–34*b*
Collins, Kathy, 108
Community as Rebellion (Peña), 178*b*
compassion, 249
compensation, 144–50, 161–66; annual cost-of-living adjustments, 162, 167; caring through salary increases and pay equity, 161–66; challenges in increasing, 147–48; contingent faculty, 145–46; decreasing benefits, 149–50; equity-based pay increases, 147–48, 167; executive compensation, 149, 163–64, 164*b*, 167; gender and racial pay gaps, 149; merit pay, 147–48, 165; and morale, 163*b*–64*b*; pay disparities, 148–49; RIT, 165–66; stagnation of, 146, 161–62; Trinity Washington University, 163*b*–64b; UMass Amherst, 165
complexity, 27
contingent faculty: challenges, 75, 143; collective bargaining, 207–11; growth of, 145–46; higher education accreditation and, 223–24; improved working conditions, 222–24; McGill University, 224; protection of, 207–11, 235*b*; and shared governance, 41–42, 216 (*see also* "gig academy"); University of Denver (DU), 224–25
corporate values, 66
Corran, Becky, 245–46
Cottom, Tressie McMillan, 5–6
cultivating and sustaining caring leaders, 29
cultural and structural change for equity and belonging, 28
"cultural taxation," 177, 179
CUNY, 170
CUPA-HR, 72, 146, 243

data gathering: action steps, 91; beyond surveys, 87; climate surveys, 69–70, 231; collection, analysis, and action, 71; data governance plan, 82, 85; dialogue, 70; engagement surveys, 69–70; enhanced data practices, 82–85; exit interviews/surveys, 71; limited, 68; managing data, 84; surveys, 69–70; workload surveys, 74–75
Davies, Andrea Rees, 98–101
DeCesare, Michael, 214
Deemer, Rob, 226–29
deep care, 266*b*
deep change, 6–7; and contingent faculty, 225–26; organizational learning, 59

Deferred Action for Childhood Arrivals (DACA), 170
DEI: IUPUI, 201*b*–2b; in promotion and tenure policies, 201*b*–2b; and shared equity leadership, 198–99; siloed from campus culture, 198. *See also* equity-minded organizations; equity-minded principles (O'Meara & Templeton); marginalized employees
deliberately developmental employers (DDOs), 151–53; stretch experiences, 151, 156–57, 160
deliberatively developmental organizations, 138
DeMichiel, Antonia, 117–19, 178*b*
demoralization, 22–23, 23*b*, 25–26
deprofessionalization, 41–42, 222–23, 235*b*
Desir, Steve, 175, 186–87. *See also* equity-minded organizations
Detert, Jim, 113
Dickson, Thomas, 121
Diede, Martha Kalnin, 143–44
Disabled Faculty and Staff (Pena), 183*b*
discrimination, abuse, and inequitable access, 179; narratives of, 180*b*
discrimination and inequality: climate and other cultural barriers, 49; compositional diversity, 48–49; inequality regimes, 50; organizational, 49–50; racialized organizations, 50. *See also* marginalized employees
disengagement, 22–23, 23*b*, 24
Donahue, Kari, 131–32
Drezner, Daniel W., 268
D'Youville University, 125*b*–26*b*

Eckel, Peter, 52
Edmondson, Amy, 114
effective communication, 155
Eidlin, Barry, 219
emotions, culture of, 108–9
employee dissatisfaction, 150
the employee experience: defined, 78; missing from guiding documents, 65; neglect of, 45–46; and organizational performance, 64
employee rights, erosion of, shared governance and, 213–14
employees of color, 49
employees with disabilities, 106–8
employee well-being: including leaders, 241–42; organizational determinants of, 238; as strategic priority, 67. *See also* Amarillo College (AC)
empowering employees' rights and voice, 29
End of Burnout, The (Malesic), 22–23; "epistemic asphyxiation," 192
Epps, JoAnne, 196
equity and belonging commitments, 174
equity-minded competencies, 191
equity-mindedness, 28
equity-minded organizations: accountability and developing a "theoretical practice," 195–98, 253–54; creating, 186–88; defined, 187; equitable hiring processes and outcomes, 189–91; hiring and retention, 189–91; Liera & Desir on, 186–88; shared principles, 198–203; valuing the expertise and labor of marginalized employees, 192–95, 203
equity-minded principles (O'Meara & Templeton): accountability, 194; agency and representation, 194; clarity, 194; consistency, 194; context, 194; credit, 194; flexibility, 194; transparency, 194
Evans, Nancy J., 107, 119
evolutionary organizations, 97, 111–12, 113
expertise and recognition, 41
exploitative environments, 55

faculty development, 143–44
faculty diversity: data collection, 69; language issues, 69
faculty senate, 212–13
faculty work activity dashboard, 87
fair compensation, 28, 130
Federation of Organized Trades and Labor Unions, 98
Fernandez, Robert W., 169
Finkelstein, Martin J., 146, 149, 213
Fitzpatrick, Kathleen, 247, 251
flexibility in the workplace, 128*b*; IUPUI, 201*b*–2*b*; Rutgers University, 121–23; University of Iowa, 121
Forster, Julie M., 141
Foste, Zak, 185

Four Rs, The, 18*b*; reassignment, 17–18, 19; reevaluation, 17–18; resignation, 17–18, 20–21; resistance, 17–18, 20
Freudenberger, Herbert, 23
Frink, Brenda, 98–101
Fulton, Amy, 199–200

Gabel, Joan, 234*b*
Gallos, Joan, 246, 248
García Peña, Lorgia, 178*b*
Gardner, Susan K., 103
Garvey, Jason C., 82–83
Gaston Gayles, Joy, 127, 128
gendered separation of work and home, 98
generous thinking, 251
Generous Thinking (Fitzpatrick), 247
Gibau, Gina Sanchez, 201*b*–2b
"gig academy:" and academic freedom, 217; and shared governance, 216–17
Gig Academy, The (Kezar), 214–15
Ginsburg, Michael, 203, 210–11, 230, 232
Goldman, Olivia, 173
Gonzales, Leslie, 35, 193–95
Gonzalez, Ángel, 197
Gonzalez, Juan Pablo, 152, 162
González Stokas, Ariana, 185, 196–97
governing boards, 256
Grain, Kari, 253
Granger, Benjamin, 84
Great Resignation, 3–4, 18*b*; leadership response to, 271; as multiple shifts, 270; and organizational care, 271; quitting and resignations, 16–17; reduction of workforce, 16; reimagining the workplace after, 15. *See also* burnout; demoralization; disengagement; Four Rs, The
grieving and bereavement, 109–10
Griffin, Kimberly, 189–90
Gross, Liz, 70
guardrails, 123–27, 128*b*
guiding documents: action steps, 91; mission statements, 65–66; neglect of employee experience, 65; values statements, 66
Guth, Claire B., 106

Hall, Candace, 191
Hamilton, Laura T., 47–48, 215
Harper, Shaun, 42
Hartman, Shawn, 263–64
Harvey Mudd College, 88*b*–89*b*
Hass, Marjorie, 262
Hawes, Carrie, 141
H. Betts, Katherine, 177
Heath, Marty, 210
Hechinger Report, The, 224
Heimbrock, Sydney, 84
Hekman, David R., 252
Hennessy, Erin, 247, 258
Hernandez, Theresa E., 190–91
Hersey, Tricia, 17
hidden curriculum, 37
hierarchy, 41; and information dissemination, 53
Higher Education Labor United (HELU), 221
Hines, Dorothy E., 180*b*
hiring and retention, 189–91, 197–98, 203
Hoffman, Garrett D., 49
Horvath, Virginia, 226–29, 231
Howard Community College, 230
Humphreys, Elizabeth, 107
Hunt, Jaime, 142
hypervigilance, isolation, alienation, and, 178*b*

ideal worker norms, 97–110; in administration, 255; disembodiment, 100; gender segregation and, 100; in higher education, 101–10; pregnancy and parenting, 105–6; professionalism, 99–100; and professional masking, 104–6, 108; racial segregation and, 100
Indiana University-Purdue University Indianapolis, 201*b*–2*b*
Indigenous Motherhood in the Academy (McKay), 180*b*
indigenous scholars, 1–2
inequity, 34
information-sharing and communication, 53, 61–62
Ingram, Paul, 66–67
institutional barriers, 3
institutionalizing DEI, 184–86
Institutional Model of Faculty Diversity, 189–90, 203

Integrated Postsecondary Education Data System (IPEDS), 72
intersectionality, 177

Johnson, Matt, 218, 231, 232
Johnson, Timothy, 182*b*
Jones, Wil, Jr., 122–23
Justice, George, 265

Kearney, Autumn, 218–19
Kegan, Robert, 138, 151. *See also* deliberately developmental employers (DDOs)
Kelderman, Eric, 268
Kendrick, Kaetrena Davis, 25
Kezar, Adrianna: academic deprofessionalization, 41–42; benefit reduction, 149; complexity, 27; culture and organizational change, 36; *The Gig Academy* (Kezar), 214–15; loss of faculty voice, 213; organizational justice, 53; organizational learning, 53; precarity, 214–16; second-order change, 6–7, 272; sensemaking, 51; shared equity leadership, 198–99; state legislatures targeting campus-based DEI, 198; on workplace democracy, 220–21
Kim, Joshua, 232, 235–36
Kington, Raynard S., 244
Kinservik, Matthew, 232
Klinenberg, Eric, 274
Krall, Aaron, 207–10, 231
Kwolek-Folland, Angel, 100

labor. *See* the employee experience
labor movement in higher education, 20
Lahey, Lisa Laskow, 138, 151. *See also* deliberately developmental employers (DDOs)
Laloux, Frederic, 97, 104, 110–12, 113, 127. *See also* evolutionary organizations
Lawler, Edward E., 76
leadership: caring leadership (*see* caring leadership); defined, 5; expectations and evaluations, 247–48; isolation, 244–45; mental health, 244; turnover and burnout, 241–42, 245–46
leadership, caring. *See* caring leadership
leadership development, 137, 199–200, 216, 237; department chairs, 260–61; lack of, 246; late preparation, 260; leadership coaching, 268; leadership pipeline and pathway, 260–61; organization-level cultures and structures, 242; racial and gender inequities, 261–62; succession management, 261
leadership ecosystem: appreciating administrative work, 259; compassion, 243–44; importance of, 242–43; institutional appreciation for good leadership, 259; leadership selection, 263–64; organizational conditions, 255–64; performance review, 265; rightsizing leadership expectations, 255–58
Leary, Mark R., 251–52
leave policies, 114–16, 128*b*
Lehfeldt, Elizabeth A., 259
Lessons from Plants (Montgomery), 242–43
LGBTQ+ employees, 49
Liera, Román, 175, 186–87, 190–91. *See also* equity-minded organizations
listening: continuous listening, 83; leadership skill, 114, 153, 176, 238, 249, 251; and organizational change, 53
Lowery-Hart, Russell, 59, 60–61, 80
Ludvik, Marilee Bresciani, 246, 256

machine organizations, 110–11, 246
Magolda, Peter, 47
Manchester, Colleen Flaherty, 233*b*–34*b*
Marcus, Jon, 224
marginalization in higher education workforce, 174
marginalized employees, 175–95; discrimination, abuse, and inequitable access, 180*b*; faculty evaluation policies, 194–95; isolation alienation and hypervigilance, 181, 182*b*; stress, mental health, and physical consequences, 181–84, 183*b*; structural and systemic, 175–77; tokenization, hypervisibility, and invisibility, 177–79, 178*b*
Maslach, Christina, 22–23
Mathews, Kiernan, 69
McDaniels, Laura, 134
McGill University, 224
McGuire, Patricia, 163*b*–64*b*, 252–53
McKay, Dwanna L., 180*b*

meeting practices, 257–58
mentoring, 171, 172
Meyerson, Debra, 277
Mishra, Kimberly, 116–17
mission statements, 65–66
Montgomery, Beronda L., 242, 247, 254
morale, and compensation, 163*b*–64*b*
Moss, Michael, 68
Muñoz, Mike, 258

Nagoski, Emily and Amelia, 22
National Science Foundation ADVANCE Institutional Transformation grant, 165–66
Nelson, Laura, 237–38
neoliberalism, 47, 215
Nesselbush, Danielle, 126*b*
new initiatives audits, action steps, 91
New Leadership Academy (U of Utah), 199–200
Nielsen, Kelly, 47, 215
Noddings, Nel, 254
non-faculty employees, 72
North Carolina State University (NCSU), 237–38
Northeastern University, 229

Okello, Wilson, 192, 195–96, 197
Okun, Tema, 186
Olabisi, Ronke M., 105
Olkin, Rhoda, 107–8
Ollilainen, Marjukka, 105
O'Meara, KerryAnn, 74, 87, 147
Opperman, Mary, 70
opportunity blocks, 31–34
Option B, 116
organizational change: Amarillo College (AC), 57–63; better workplace policies and accountability, 274; change management, 54; cultural theories of change, 54–55; deep change, 51–53, 52*b*; equity-mindedness pathway, 278; ethical concerns, 53; inquiry processes, 273; leadership, 242; organizational justice, 53; organizational learning, 52*b*; sensemaking, 51–52; sensemaking pathway, 276; is a smart investment, 274; strategic planning pathway, 276–77; student success *plus* employee well-being, 273; in support of employee well-being, 272; "tempered radicals" pathway, 277–78; trust, 274
organizational characteristics, 39–43
organizational complexity, 35, 39–43, 44*b*
organizational culture, 53–54; of fear, 110–11; of trust and abundance, 111. *See also* Tierney, William
organizational development, 5
organizational learning: Amarillo College (AC), 61–62; deep change, 59; organizational change, 52*b*
organizational problems, structure and culture, 31–56
organizational thinking, 254
Owen, Robert, 98
Owens, Bradley P., 252

Palucki Blake, Laura, 88*b*–89*b*
pandemic effects: author's story, 10–13; Great Resignation as, 15, 21–22; listening, 70; making sense of, 23*b*; reduction of workforce, 16; on staff of color, 76; unions and strikes, 218; on working cultures and conditions, 94–96; workload, 75–76; on workload and staffing, 47
Parrot, Teresa Valerio, 243–44
Pasque, Penny, 185
Pena, Maria, 183*b*
people management skills, 84
Perez, Rosemary J., 102, 113
Perry, David, 117
"Personal Exploration of Involvement, A" (Johnson), 182*b*
Petersen, Anne Helen, 124, 127
Pipelines and Pathways Working Group (UVa), 156
Pope-Ruark, Rebecca, 22
Power of Names in Identity and Oppression, The (Thaviseth), 178*b*
preexisting stressors, 22
Presidential Renewal program (CIC), 262–63
Presidential Vocation and Institutional Mission program (CIC), 262
Presumed Incompetent: Fujiwara, Lynn, 183*b*; Nam, Susie E., 183*b*; Võ, Linda Trinh, 182*b*

Presumed Incompetent II (Young & Hines), 178*b*
prioritizing the employee experience, 27, 57–70, 92
professional growth and development: Cardinal Leadership Institute (UofL), 137, 160–61; career ladders, 138–41, 154–57; coaching, 157–59, 167; commitments to sustaining, 159; developing in-house resources, 157–61; Employee Success Center, UofL, 160; equity of access, 167; for faculty, 139–40; Office for Faculty Advancement (Duke), 157–59; out-of-pocket, 142–43; outsourcing, 142; for staff, 140
professionalism, 99–100; resetting norms, 112–13, 128*b*; white supremacist notions of, 103
Pryor, Jonathan T., 49
psychological safety, 113–14, 128*b*
Pullias Center for Higher Education (USC), 224

Quinn, Therese, 207–9

"racial battle fatigue," 196
racialized organizations, 50, 186–87
racial social structure, 37–38
racial stratification, 42
racism, 76
"radical retention" in higher education, 141
Ramsey, James, 131
Ray, Victor, 37–38, 50, 186–87
recognition and appreciation ecosystem, 136–37, 150, 153, 167
Reinitz, Betsy, 82
Reinventing Organizations (Laloux), 104
Reinventing Talent Management (Lawler), 76; reparations, 196–97
Reparative Universities (González Stokas), 196
resistance, 92; unions and strikes, 206–7
responsibility-taking, 250*b*, 253
Reyes, Victoria, 179, 181
Reynolds, Samara, 141
Rhoades, Gary, 45, 215
Rivinius, Jessica, 154–55
Robbins, Mike, 153
Rochester Institute of Technology, 165–66
Rogelberg, Steven, 257
Rosenberg, Brian, 213
Rosser, Vicki, 73
Ryan, James, 156

Sandberg, Sheryl, 116
Schatzel, Kim, 133
Schwartz, Tony, 152
scientific management, 99
Scott, MacKenzie, 63
Scott, Robert A., 215–16
sensemaking, 51–53, 80, 113, 226, 276
shared equity leadership: distributed responsibility, 200, 203; Kezar on, 198–99; New Leadership Academy (U of Utah), 199–200; redefining leadership, 199
shared governance: AAUP report, 213–14; and the Caring University, 29; collaborative shared governance, 226–29; and collective bargaining, 209; and economic justice, 232, 235–36; and erosion of employee rights, 213–14; HELU vision for, 221; obstruction to transformation, 211, 213; SUNY at Fredonia, 226–29; value demonstrations, 235*b*
Sheffer, Jolie A., 214
Shelton, Stephanie Anne, 109
Shuck, Brad, 24–25, 70
Sieben, Nicole, 109
siloing, 42, 62, 72
Simon, Anne, 171
Slaughter, Sheila, 45, 215
socialization, 102–3; and professionalism, 102–3; white male norms of, 103
socialization (professional), 102–3
Society for College and University Planning, 68
Sponsler, Laura, 225
staff of color, hidden service agendas, 75, 76
staff workload: hourly, 75; salaried, 75
STARS, 172
Stewart, D-L, 108
Stewart, Katharine, 244–45, 246, 248, 259, 268
Stewart, Terah J., 108–9
Straddling Class in the Academy (Cannon), 182*b*

strategic plan document: neglect of employee experience, 67; U of L, 131–32
succession planning, 77
Sugrue, Erin, 25
SUNY at Fredonia, 226–29
survivance, 2
systems of oppression, 185. *See also* whiteness

talent, 67
talent management, 76
Talent Management Handbook (Gonzalez), 152
talent management strategy, 152; action steps, 91; described, 77–78; language, symbols, and values, 79–82 (*see also* sensemaking); University of California (UC) model, 78, *79*
Taylor, Barrett, 217–18, 236
Templeton, Lindsey, 193–95
Temple University, 229
tenure, attacks on, 217–18
Tevis, Tenisha L., 185
Thaviseth, Latana Jennifer, 178*b*
32-Hour Workweek, The, 125*b*–26*b*
Thompson, Derek, 16, 17
Tierney, William, 54–55
tokenization, hypervisibility, and invisibility, discrimination, 179
total rewards, 152–53
Townsend, Barbara, 73
Trans People in Higher Education (Graves), 178*b*
trust and mutual accountability, 235*b*
turnover and retention, costs of, 162

Uetricht, Micah, 219
UMass Amherst, 165
undocumented students, 169–70
unions and strikes, 218, 220. *See also* collective bargaining
universal design, 117–20, 128*b*
University Advising Center (University of South Carolina), 155–56
University of Denver (DU), 224
University of Illinois Chicago (UIC), 203, 206, 208–9, 231
University of Louisville (UofL): becoming a deliberately developmental employer, 166; Cardinal Leadership Institute, 137, 160–61; compensation study, 131–32; Employee Success Center, 130–31, 134–38, 153, 160, 166–67, 276–77; scandals and challenges, 130–35; strategic planning, 131–32
University of Minnesota, 233*b*–34*b*
University of Utah, 199–200

Vaccaro, Jennifer, 210
values alignment, 67
values statements, 66
Veneruso, Samantha Streamer, 139–40
Võ, Linda Trinh, 182*b*

Waddington, Kathryn, 249–50, 251
Wallace, David Foster, 55
Ward, Kelly, 105–6
Warzel, Charlie, 124, 127
Weick, Karl, 79
well-being, staff and faculty, 65–67. *See also* the employee experience
West, Meagan, 134
whiteness: in academic publishing, 192–93; as a system of oppression, 185; white supremacy culture, 103, 185–86
white supremacy culture: and professionalism, 103; systematic and structural, 185–86
Whitlock, Diane, 134
"Who Wants to Be a College President?" (Kelderman), 268
Williams, Brittany M., 37, 103, 196
Williams, Joan, 100
Wilson, Brooke, 109–10
Winston, Sarah J., 106–7
Wisdom, Maria LaMonaca, 157–59
Wohlpart, Jim, 266*b*
Wolf-Wendel, Lisa, 105–6
working cultures and conditions, 92–112; creating guardrails, 97; expanding options for hybrid and remote work, 97; improving supports for caregivers, 97; and real workers, 27; for real workers, 97; relationship with Great Resignation, 97; resetting professional norms, 97;

unrealistic standards, 94–95. *See also* ideal worker norms
work-life balance: as a gendered expression, 101; history of term, 98; suburbanization and, 100
workload and staffing: action steps, 91; administrative negligence toward, 73; assessing and evaluating, 86, 88*b*–89*b*; measuring, 74; negative growth, 46–48; new initiatives audits, 85–86; products vs. load, 74; risks of overload, 90; standards, 90
workplace challenges: non-pandemic related, 4; pandemic related, 3–4
workplace culture survey, Miami University, 154–55
workplace democracy, 219–22; defined, 220
workplace well-being: action steps, 128*b*; caregiving responsibilities, 115–16; committing to growth & compensation, 7–9; cultivating caring leaders, 7–9; empowering rights & voice, 7–9; flexibility, 119–23, 128*b*; guardrails, 123–27, 128*b*; humanizing policies & practices, 7–9; leave policies, 114–16, 128*b*; prioritizing employees' experience, 7–9; realizing equity & belonging, 7–9; resetting professional norms, 112–14, 128*b*; Rutgers University, 121–23; universal design, 117–20, 128*b*; University of Iowa, 121; University of Washington, 114–17
Wright, Mary C., 160

"You Could Not Pay Me Enough to Be a College President" (Drezner), 268
Young, Jemimah Li, 180*b*

Ziker, John, 74